Open Jerusalem

Edited by

Vincent Lemire (*Gustave Eiffel University; Centre de recherche français in Jerusalem*)
Angelos Dalachanis (*French National Center for Scientific Research, Institute of Early Modern and Modern History*)

VOLUME 3

C000088279

The titles published in this series are listed at *brill.com/opje*

Imaging and Imagining Palestine

Contents

Foreword

Salim Tamari

The contributions of this volume are framed by the overlooked context of the British Mandate, providing a significant overview of photography and the social histories of the period. They cover a wide range of themes based on a re-reading of social history through several archival collections (American Colony, École Biblique, National Geographic), institutional records of service (mission schools, orphanages, monasteries and charities), family albums (Jawhariyya, Luci, Mushabek), portrait photography (Ra'ad, Whiting, Scholten), urban-scapes and aerial photography (Scholten, Bavarian State Archive, Australian War Memorial).

Added to the rich archival material, is the consideration of how we read and restitute images and their histories. This includes debates on methodologies for decolonising and indigenising photography as well as re-examining and 're-narrating' photographs that have not been published.

Reading social history through photography has been a crucial antidote to the absence and loss of Palestinian material patrimony through wars and conquests. Alongside professional photographers, family albums constituted the portable artifacts of memory that is used today to reconstruct the daily life of bourgeois quotidian.

Among the case studies in this volume dealing with archival fonds and conceptual approaches to photography, it celebrates, and in one case, resurrects from oblivion, the work of four outstanding photographers of Palestine. Lars Larsson, John D. Whiting, Frank Scholten and Khalīl Ra'ad. Both Whiting and Larsson were pioneering photographers associated with the American Colony, and both traversed the Ottoman and Mandate periods.

The leading figure in their photography was Lars (Lewis) Larsson, head of the photographic department in the American Colony and, later, the Swedish consul in Jerusalem. Larsson was the author of the iconic picture of the surrender of Jerusalem by Mayor Ḥusayn Hashim al-Ḥusaynī in the hills of Sheikh Bader on 9th December, 1917 which was reproduced all over the world signalling the fall of Ottoman rule, and the capture of Palestine by the British.

Biblification of these photographic collections is a major theme that is examined by a number of contributors. One of the richest of those compendiums is undoubtedly that of the École Biblique in Jerusalem, whose main focus has been the documentation of archaeological excavations and sites in the late 19th century and Mandate period.

FIGURE 0.1   *The Surrender of Jerusalem*, 1917. Lars (Lewis) Larsson
IMAGE FROM THE WASIF JAWHARRIYYA ALBUM. COURTESY OF THE
INSTITUTE FOR PALESTINE STUDIES

The launching of the Scholten collection from Leiden has been an opportune
moment to examine the ethnographic work of the great Dutch photographer
Frank Scholten. Less than one-tenth of that collection has been published in
his seminal study of Jaffa life in the 1920s – a work which is imbued with haunt-
ing and lyrical imageries.[1]

Scholten appears to have been forgotten, while his work, subsumed under
the rubric of biblification of the Levantine landscape, was eclipsed by an ava-
lanche of 'Holy Land photographic albums'. In a genre that we might call a
deconstructive biblification, Scholten's uniqueness is derived from his exceptional ability to combine landscape photography with intimate vignettes of
urban life showing the varied communitarian makeup of Palestinian society
that permeate his oeuvre. Scholten's intimacy with his subjects is visible in
much of his portraiture: leisurely groups frolicking in the sands of Nabī Rūbīn,
seasonal celebrations of religious holidays, men and women of all walks in
life in the marketplace. The ribboned girl holding an Easter egg is an iconic
Scholtian image – a subject which reassesses his work within the context of
biblification with which he was long associated and pigeonholed.

In analysing local photography in Palestine, the case of Khalīl Ra'ad shows a
duality can be seen in his substantial involvement in the military photography

---

1   Frank Scholten and George Robinson, *Palestine Illustrated. Including references to passages
    illustrated in the Bible, the Talmud and the Koran* (London: Longmands & Co, 1931).

FIGURE 0.2 *Ribboned Girl with Easter Egg*; Frank Scholten, Jaffa 1921–23
IMAGE COURTESY OF NINO & UBL

of WWI when he served as a publicist for the Ottoman war effort,[2] as well as his immersion in Biblical theme photography during the Mandate period. This duality perhaps best embodies the contradictions of modernity and biblification in the photography of Palestine during the shift from Ottoman to British rule.

The albums of Wasif Jawhariyya likewise show him as a participant and observer of performative theatre (the shadow play – karagoz – and its earlier more primitive manifestations in *sunduq al 'ajab* – the wondrous 'magic box'). His photographic collection preserves and immortalises a world that is no longer with us.

Jawhariyya's use of the photographic images to illustrate the transformation of the cityscape and to ceremonial processions (Nabī Mūsā, Sittuna Maryam, the Saturday of Light Easter parade) – all of which transcended their original religious content into public syncretic celebrations, capturing the impacts of political developments in Palestine.[3]

---

2 Salim Tamari, "The War Photography of Khalil Raad: Ottoman Modernity and the Biblical Gaze," *Jerusalem Quarterly* 52 (2013): 25–37.

3 This is the topic of a collective project on Palestinian family albums that is undertaken by three participants in the Leiden conference, but which will appear in a separate volume. Issam Nassar, Stephen Sheehi and Salim Tamari, *Camera Palestina: Photography and Displaced Histories of Palestine* (Berkeley: University of California Press, forthcoming).

Acknowledgments

This volume is one of the results of a Dutch Research Council (NWO) research project (Dec. 2017–Dec. 2022) *CrossRoads: European Cultural diplomacy and Arab Christians in Palestine (1920–1950). A connected History.*

We would like to thank the NWO for financing this research project, as well as the Netherlands Institute for the Near East (NINO) for its support of the international workshop where the papers of this book were first presented and discussed, for the opening of the Frank Scholten photographic collection and its support for the various steps towards an exhibition and a catalogue. Our sincere gratitude goes to Vincent Lemire and Angelos Dalachanis, the series editors, for their enthusiasm and support to welcome a volume on photography from the very beginning and to the *Open Jerusalem* Team.

We are grateful to many colleagues in Leiden, Jerusalem, Paris, London, New York, Beirut and elsewhere who, through their contributions to the conference, the workshops and through extended email conversations helped us to flesh out our questions and approaches. We would like to thank some of our partners for their support and their scholar in residence programs we greatly benefited from in our way to this volume (Ecole française de Rome, Ecole biblique et archéologique de Jérusalem, Al Ma'mal Foundation Jerusalem and the Australian Archaeological Institute in Athens). There are also a number of archives who have been very supportive of this project (the American Colony Archive Jerusalem, the Leiden University special collections, the National Geographic Society archive, the Palestine Museum Digital archive and the Palestine Exploration Fund).

We would also like to thank Sarah Irving for her invaluable work and brain storming during her postdoctoral research at Leiden University and our constant rich exchanges since, Salim Tamari for our many discussions, his insightful comments during the workshop and his foreword, Heleen Murre-van den Berg for paving the way of *CrossRoads* during and after the *Arabic and its Alternatives* project (2012–2017), Lara van der Hammen for her constant and efficient support to the *CrossRoads* team, Carolien van Zoest for helping to facilitate and coordinate NINO's support and Rachel Lev for her precious help with captions for articles related to the American Colony. We would also like to thank the *Rijksmuseum Oudheden* (RMO) for hosting sections of the workshop and the exhibition *Frank Scholten: Archaeology and Tourism in the 'Holy Land'* (May to October 2020).

Finally, we thank the colleagues who contributed to this volume in particular, those who published, and those who for various reasons could not write but contributed to our discussions.

Figures

Notes on Contributors

Nadi Abusaada

Nadi Abusaada is a Ph.D. Candidate in Architecture at the University of Cambridge. He is a Cambridge Trust scholar and a member of the Centre for Urban Conflicts Research. His Ph.D. research focuses on urban transformation in modern Palestine (1880–1940), particularly the rise of municipalities and architectural changes in this period. More broadly, he is interested in the relationship between the built environment and sociopolitical dynamics in cities. Nadi is currently the Co-Editor in Chief for the 2019/20 issue of *Scroope: The Cambridge Architectural Journal*. Nadi holds an M.Phil. in Architecture and Urban Studies from the University of Cambridge and an H.B.A. in Architecture from the University of Toronto.

Özge Calafato

Özge Calafato is a cultural studies scholar focusing on the relationship between vernacular photography, gender, memory and cultural identity. In 2020, she completed her PhD dissertation on photographic representations of the Turkish middle classes from the 1920s to the 1930s at the Amsterdam School for Cultural Analysis, the University of Amsterdam. From 2014 to 2020 she was the Assistant Director for the Akkasah Center for Photography at NYU Abu Dhabi, home to an archive of the photographic heritage of the Middle East and North Africa. She has a Bachelor's Degree in Political Science and International Relations from Boğaziçi University in Istanbul, and a Master's Degree in Journalism from the University of Westminster in London.

Abigail Jacobson

Abigail Jacobson is a historian working on social and urban history of late Ottoman and Mandatory Palestine and the Eastern Mediterranean. Her main research interest is the history of ethnically and nationally mixed spaces and communities, especially during times of war and conflict. Her first book is entitled *From Empire to Empire: Jerusalem between Ottoman and British Rule* (Syracuse University Press, 2011). Her second book, *Oriental Neighbors: Middle Eastern Jews and Arabs in Mandatory Palestine* (Brandeis/New England University Press, 2016), is co-authored with Dr. Moshe Naor. The book won the Yonatan Shapira award for the best book in Israel studies for 2017, as well as the best book award from the Center for the Relations of Muslims, Jews and Christians at the Open University in Israel (2017).

Yazan Kopty

Yazan Kopty is a writer, researcher, and oral historian. His work centres around the acts of listening and narrating, focusing especially on memory as resistance and community-sourced histories. He is a National Geographic Explorer and lead investigator of *Imagining the Holy*, a research project that seeks to examine and connect thousands of images of historic Palestine from the National Geographic Society archive with Palestinian community elders, cultural heritage experts, and field researchers to add new layers of indigenous knowledge and narrative to the images. He previously established and headed the oral history and intangible cultural heritage programs at Qatar Museums. His forthcoming debut novel is inspired by oral histories he conducted with his grandparents and his family archive of films, photographs, and documents.

Rachel Lev

Rachel Lev heads the American Colony Archive Collections in Jerusalem. She gained experience both as a curator and an exhibition designer starting as a junior curator in the fields of Prints and Drawings and Photography and later as an exhibition designer where she created many temporary and permanent displays. She established and heads the American Colony Archive Collections in Jerusalem and consults with researchers and curators with regard to primary sources essential to the collection. Rachel's interest lies in the relationship between perception and presentation of content in space; and the relation between dominant and alternative narratives in art and photography, specifically in the work of the American Colony Photo-Dept. photographers (1896–1934).

Issam Nassar

Issam Nassar is an historian of photography and the Middle East at Illinois State University. Nassar taught at the University of California at Berkeley in 2006; Bradley University in 2003–2006 and al-Quds University in 1998–2003. He is associate editor of *Jerusalem Quarterly* (Arabic: *Hawliyat al-Quds*) and author of a number of books and articles, among them: *Different Snapshots: The History of Early Local Photography in Palestine, European Portrayals of Jerusalem: Religious Fascinations and Colonialist Imaginations*, Lewiston, NY: The Edwin Mellen Press, 2006. *Gardens of Sand*, edited with Clark Worswick and Patricia Almarcegui, TrunerPhoto Middle East, October 2010. *I Would Have Smiled: Photographing the Palestinian Refugee Experience*, co-edited with Rasha Salti (Jerusalem: Institute for Palestine Studies, 2009).

Norig Neveu

Norig Neveu is a research fellow at the French National Center for Scientific Research (CNRS) based in IREMAM (Aix-en-Provence, France). As a specialist of Modern history, she has been conducting research for the last ten years in the Middle East, especially in Jordan and Palestine. Her present research focuses on sacred topographies, religious politics and authorities in Jordan, Palestine and Iraq between the 19th and 21st centuries. Thanks to this long-term approach she observes the evolution of tribal and kinship networks and the reconfiguration of the sources of religious authorities in the region. She has published several articles on local pilgrimages, sacred topographies, religious tourism and its impact on local societies. Since 2017, she is one of the coordinators of the MisSMO research program about Christian missions in the Middle East since the late 19th century (https://missmo.hypotheses.org/).

Inger Marie Okkenhaug

Inger Marie Okkenhaug (Ph.D. University of Bergen 1999) is a Professor of History at Volda University College, Norway. From 2000–2009, Okkenhaug was a researcher at the University of Bergen. In addition to a number of published chapters and articles, she is the author of *"The Quality of Heroic Living, of High Endeavour and Adventure." Anglican Mission, Women and Education in Palestine, 1888–1948* (Brill, 2002) and the co-editor of *Gender, Religion and Change in the Middle East: Two Hundred Years of History* (Berg, 2005); *Interpreting Welfare and Relief in the Middle East* (Brill, 2008); *Protestant Mission and Local Encounters in the Nineteenth and Twentieth Centuries* (Brill, 2011); *Transnational and Historical Perspectives on Global Health, Welfare and Humanitarianism* (Portal Books, 2013). Among her most recent publications is "Religion, Relief, and Humanitarian Work among Armenian Women Refugees in Mandatory Syria, 1927–1934", *Scandinavian Journal of History* 40/3, 2015; "Scandinavian Missionaries in Palestine: The Swedish Jerusalem Society, Medical Mission and Education in Jerusalem and Bethlehem, 1900–1948", *Tracing the Jerusalem Code: Christian Cultures in Scandinavia*, 3., ed. Ragnhild J. Zorgati, (forthcoming) and "Orphans, Refugees and Relief in the Armenian Republic, 1922–1925", *Aid to Armenia*, eds. Joanne Laycock and Francesca Piana (forthcoming). Okkenhaug's latest book, *En norsk filantrop. Bodil Biørn og armenerne, 1905–1934* (2016) deals with Norwegian mission and humanitarian work among the Armenians in the years from 1905 to 1940. Okkenhaug is also a co-producer of a documentary film *War, Women and Welfare in Jerusalem*, 2009, financed by the Norwegian Research Council.

Karène Sanchez Summerer

Karène Sanchez Summerer is Associate Professor at Leiden University. She is the PI of the research project (2018–2022), *'CrossRoads- A connected history between Europeans' cultural diplomacy and Arab Christians in Mandate Palestine, 1918–1948'* (project funded by the Dutch Research Council NWO, https://crossroadsproject.net). She is the co-editor of the series *Languages and Culture in History* with Prof. Em. W. Frijhoff, Amsterdam University Press. Since 2017, she is one of the coordinators of the MisSMO research program about Christian missions in the Middle East since the late 19th century.

Last publications: she co-edited with Sary Zananiri (eds.), *European Cultural Diplomacy and Arab Christians in Palestine, 1918–1948. Between Contention and Connection* (Palgrave MacMillan, 2020); with Inger Marie Okkenhaug (eds.), Brill LSIS series 11, *Mission and Humanitarianism in the Middle East, 1860–1950- Ideologies Rhetoric and Practices*, 2020; with Philippe Bourmaud (eds.), *Missions/Powers/Arabization*, Special issue *Social Sciences and Missions*, Brill, 32/3–4, 2019; with Heleen Murre-van den Berg, and T. Baarda (eds.), *Arabic and its alternatives: Religious minorities and their languages in the emerging nation states of the Middle East (1920–1950)*, Brill series *Christians and Jews in Muslim Societies* 5.

Rona Sela

Rona Sela is a curator and researcher of visual history and art. Her research focuses on the visual historiography of the Palestinian-Israeli conflict, the history of Palestinian photography and colonial Zionist/Israeli photography, colonial Zionist/Israeli archives, archives under occupation, seizure and looting of Palestinian archives and their subjugation to repressive colonial mechanisms, visual representation of conflict, war, occupation, exile, immigration, and human rights violations, and on constructing alternative postcolonial mechanisms and archives. She has also conducted research on the development of alternative contemporary visual practices connected to civil society that seek to replace the old Israeli gatekeepers. She has published many books, catalogues, and articles on these topics and curated numerous exhibitions. Her first film is entitled *Looted and Hidden – Palestinian Archives in Israel* (2017, film-essay).

Stephen Sheehi

Stephen Sheehi is the Sultan Qaboos bin Said Chair of Middle East Studies. He holds a joint appointment as Professor of Arabic Studies in the Department of Modern Languages and Literatures and the Program of Asian and Middle Eastern Studies. Prof. Sheehi's work meets at the intersection of cultural, visual, art, and social history of the modern Arab world, starting with the late Ottoman Empire and the Arab Renaissance (*al-nahdah al-'arabiyah*). His scholarly interests include photography theory, psychoanalysis, post-colonial theory, Palestine, and Islamophobia.

Salim Tamari

Salim Tamari is Professor of Sociology (Emeritus), Birzeit University; Research Associate, Institute for Palestine Studies; Editor, *The Jerusalem Quarterly*. Recent Publications: *Mountain Against the Sea: A Conflicted Modernity* (UCP, 2008); with Issam Nassar, *The Storyteller of Jerusalem: The Life and Times of Wasif Jawhariyyeh* (Olive Branch Press, 2013); *Year of the Locust: Erasure of the Ottoman Era in Palestine*; The *Great War and the Remaking of Palestine* (UC Press, 2018); with Munir Fakhr Ed Din, *Landed Property and Public Endowments in Jerusalem* (Mu'assasat al-Dirāsāt al-Filasṭīnīyah, 2018). *Camera Palestina: Photography and Displaced Histories of Palestine* (UC Press, forthcoming).

Aude Aylin de Tapia

Aude Aylin de Tapia is a historian, currently Postdoctoral Fellow at Aix Marseille University and Lecturer at the University of Strasbourg (France). Her research interest focuses on history and anthropology of Christian communities and interreligious relations in the Ottoman Empire and Republic of Turkey. She works on this topic by using various kinds of written, oral, iconographic, and audiovisual sources. In 2018, she has co-organized the symposium "The First Century of Photography: Photography as History/ Historicizing Photography in (Post)-Ottoman Territories (1839–1939)" in Istanbul, Turkey.

Sary Zananiri

Sary Zananiri is an artist and cultural historian. He completed a PhD in Fine Arts at Monash University in 2014. He co-edited *European Cultural Diplomacy and Arab Christians in Palestine, 1918–1948. Between Contention and Connection* (Palgrave MacMillan, 2020) with Karène Sanchez Summerer, and exhibits and curates widely, most recently *Frank Scholten: Archaeology and Tourism in the 'Holy Land'* at the Rijksmuseum Oudheden (May–October 2020). He produced a short documentary with Maartje Alders *Frank Scholten Photographing Palestine*. He recently received a research grant from the Palestine Museum for the project 'Orthodox Aesthetics: Christianity, Solidarity and the Secularisation of Palestinian Religious Art'. He is also producing a digital humanities project *Mapping the Mandate: Frank Scholten in the 'Holy Lands'*. Sary is currently a Postdoctoral Researcher on the NWO funded project *CrossRoads: European Cultural Diplomacy and Arab Christians in Palestine, 1918–1948* and the Netherlands Institute for the Near East at Leiden University.

Notes on Transliteration

In the volume we have opted for different transcription standards, with Arabic and Ottoman Turkish according to IJMES *International Journal of Middle East Studies* table; Armenian and Hebrew are in an anglicised transcription.

For personal and place names, full transcriptions as well as simplified and/ or anglicised forms have been allowed, depending on the sources and general familiarity with one or another transcription.

CHAPTER 1

Imaging and Imagining Palestine: An Introduction

Sary Zananiri

The British Mandate period in Palestine was a tumultuous time, one that began with the cessation of more than four centuries of Ottoman rule and culminated in the *Nakba* with the creation of the State of Israel. In this respect, we might view it as a period of significant transition, transformation and, ultimately, displacement and dislocation. From a cultural and social perspective, the Mandate period saw the continuation of the modernisation project begun under the Ottomans. This process is entangled and evident in photographic perspectives, which during this time was also marked by significant shifts and developments in technology that enabled new modes of photography, in turn impacting the imaging and imagining of Palestine.

The first photograph of Palestine was taken in Jerusalem in 1839, the same year in which the process was invented, making it one of the first places in the world to be imaged using the new process.[1] In the years to follow, photographs of Palestine formed the basis of photobooks and postcards. By the early twentieth century, non-professional photographers began to take similar photographs, as well.

This volume attempts to create a first overview of photography during the British Mandate, bringing together scholars and experts from disciplines ranging from history to cultural studies to architectural theorists, archivists and creative practitioners. It intentionally focuses on the interactions of photographic production and its effects within indigenous Palestinian communities rather than Jewish and Zionist photography of the Yishuv, which although inflected across this volume, is well documented and researched.[2]

In light of this, defining what constitutes Palestinian photography is a controversial topic. Here Issam Nassar offers a useful framework for defining 'local photography', that is predicated upon questions of photographic production and consumption.

---

1   Issam Nassar, "Early local photography in Jerusalem," *History of Photography* 27, no. 4 (2003): 322.
2   See for instance, Vivienne Silver-Brody, *Documentors of the Dream: Pioneer Jewish Photographers in the Land of Israel 1890–1933* (Lincoln, Nebr.: University of Nebraska Press, 1999).

© SARY ZANANIRI, 2021 | DOI:10.1163/9789004437944_002

[L]ocal photography would be any photography that represented social life in Palestine as opposed to the depictions of biblical landscapes, on the one hand, and Zionist photography, which tended to focus almost exclusively on the Jewish settlement project in Palestine, on the other.[3]

Underscoring Nassar's argument here is an understanding that analysis of photography should be intersected with questions of indigeneity, processes of identity formation that shifted radically from the late Ottoman period to the British Mandate, and the effects of migration and mobility both within the Ottoman Empire (during and after its demise), and from elsewhere.

1   Towards an Understanding of Indigenous Photography in Palestine

The term 'Indigenous Lens' was discussed and problematised at length by Ritter and Schweiwiller in *The Indigenous Lens? Early Photography in the Near and Middle East*. Notwithstanding their broader geographical focus, and their focus on photographic histories of the nineteenth century, their definition of an indigenous lens 'serves as a metaphor for local and vernacular photographic practices, visual traditions, actors, uses, and contexts of photography, or in other words, for an alternative view of photo history in the region'.[4] Such designations, of course, overlap and intersect with Nassar's ideas of local photography, but a category of indigenous photography might also give us an understanding of the specificities of local modes of production, consumption and circulation of photography.

Earlier in the Ottoman period, there is the notable example of Menden John Diness. A Jewish immigrant who arrived in 1849, Diness who hailed from Odessa, presents a particularly curious case. He converted to Protestantism amongst much scandal in Jerusalem's international milieu before later emigrating to the US.[5] His story speaks to transnational and transcommunal political affinities present in Ottoman Palestine as well as the boundaries of communal

---

3   Issam Nassar, "Familial Snapshots Representing Palestine in the Work of the First Local Photographers," *History and Memory* 18, no. 2 (2006): 144.

4   Markus Ritter and Staci G. Schweiwiller, eds., *The Indigenous Lens? Early Photography in the Near and Middle East*, 8. *Studies in Theory and History of Photography* (Berlin/Boston: De Gruyter, 2017): 12.

5   Dror Wahrman, "Developing a Photographic Milieu: Mendel John Diness and The Beginning of Photography in Jerusalem," in *Capturing the Holy Land: M.J. Diness and the Beginnings of Photography in Jerusalem*, edited by Dror Wahrman, Carney E. S. Gavin, Nitza Rosovsky (Cambridge MA: Harvard University Press, 1993), 8–35.

porosity – and indeed the results of their transgression – that would later shape the politicised context of the British Mandate.

In the years before and after Palestine was shifting from Ottoman rule to British Mandate, a number of Jewish, and generally Zionist, art photographers such as Yaacov Ben-Dov, Zvi Oron-Orushkes and Ya'acov Ben Kaltor, to name but a few, migrated to Palestine and came to prominence as photographers under British rule.[6] Alongside these are slightly later examples of photojournalists that visited or migrated to Palestine against the backdrop of European antisemitism in the 1930s like Tim Gidal, Felix H. Man, Kurt Hübschmann, Otto Umbehr, Robert Capa, show the interesting parallels of Zionist transnational mobility of the medium[7] to the contributions in this volume in which Christianity is predominantly implicated.

Tsadok Bassan is a salient example of Jewish photography in Palestine with which to consider assertions of local and indigenous photography. As a member of the Old Yishuv, born in Jerusalem to a third-generation family in Palestine,[8] he seems exceptional in the categorisation of localness in comparison to other Jewish photographers of the period, though, at the same time, is clearly not indigenous. More research is needed to understand the significance of his practice and his exploration of Old Yishuv communal life, although the assertion he was 'the first Jerusalem photographer'[9] does actively negate other practices, such as those of early Armenian contributions or Arab figures like Khalīl Ra'ad who predate or were contemporaneous to him. Bassan tests the ways in which we might delineate the ascription of indigeneity, but also underscores the complexities, importance and limitations of considering the indigenous lens, particularly given the fraught, contemporary context in which nationalist ideologies colour our understanding of photography in retrospect. For a well-known early Zionist example, we could look to the Russian immigrant Yeshayahu Rafflovich, who was active as a photographer from the

---

6   A useful and extensive of biographical list of local photographers is compiled by Shimon Lev and Hamutal Wachtel in the catalogue accompanying the exhibition *The Camera Man: Women and Men Photograph Jerusalem 1900–1950* (Jerusalem: Tower of David Museum, 2016), 140–126.

7   Rebekka Grossmann, "Image Transfer and Visual Friction: Staging Palestine in the National Socialist Spectacle," *The Leo Baeck Institute Yearbook* 64, no. 1 (2019): 22–23.

8   Sue Serkes, "For a photogenic Jerusalem, a look at how locals first captured their city," *Times of Israel* 26th May, 2016. https://www.timesofisrael.com/for-photogenic-jerusalem-a-look-at-how-locals-first-captured-their-city/#gs.g99sd4.

9   See for instance the exhibition curated by Guy Raz, *Tsadok Bassan – Orphan Girls* at Jerusalem Artists House, 24th September–13th November, 2005. https://www.art.org.il/?exhibitions=tsadok-bassan-orphan-girls&lang=en.

1890s[10] and more closely typifies patterns of Jewish photographic production in Palestine.

There is currently no evidence of indigenous Jewish-Arab photographic practices, paralleling those of Christian and Muslim Arabs or the ancient and longstanding Armenian community of Palestine prior to its significant expansion resulting from the genocide and World War I.[11] It is clear, however, that indigenous Jewish communities were, along with many others, photographic subjects for both local and visiting photographers alike, often within the Biblical rubrics outlined below.

The establishment of Jewish-run commercial studios during the Mandate period, such as Palphot, an enterprise that is still active in the 'Holy Land' souvenir market today,[12] also underscores Jewish participation in the lucrative market for biblical souvenirs. However, Palphot's co-founder Tova Dorfzaun's problematic assertion that 'when we came here, I had to admit I had doubts about succeeding – because there was so little here to photograph',[13] displays just one aspect of the conceptual complexities involved in widening the scope of this volume further.

Early photography in Palestine was indeed marked significantly by mobility, from European photographers, both Jewish and Christian, who travelled to the region, as well as internal mobility within the Ottoman Empire. Such internal Ottoman mobility, by the time of the British Mandate and the creation of the new nation-states that exist today, viewed from a current perspective gives an appearance of internationalism to contemporary understandings of national origin. Khalīl Raʿad, born in present day Lebanon, or the works of Armenians like Issay Garabedian or Garabed Krikorian, both born in present day Turkey, are poignant examples. However, Ottoman mobility needs to be viewed within the broader context of Ottoman communalism, the spread of communities and the networks, both local and regional, that enabled them. Notwithstanding the complex context of the shift from Ottoman subjecthood to the new nationalist identifications that were cemented by the borders

10   Yeshayahu Nir, *The Bible and the Image: The History of Photography in the Holy Land 1839–1899* (Philadelphia: Philadelphia University Press, 1986), 248.

11   Raymond Kevorkian, "From a monastery to a neighbourhood: Orphans and Armenian refugees in the Armenian quarter of Jerusalem (1916–1926), reflexions towards an Armenian museum in Jerusalem", in Special issue 'Eastern Christianity in Syria and Palestine and European cultural diplomacy (1860–1948). A connected history', ed. by Karène Sanchez Summerer and Konstantinos Papastathis, *Contemporary Levant*, 6: 1 (2021).

12   Tim Semmerling, *Israeli and Palestinian postcards: Presentations of national self* (Austin, TX: University of Texas Press, 2004), 13.

13   Ibid 14.

imposed by the Franco-British authored Sykes-Picot agreement during the World War I, a significant indigenous photographic milieu came to prominence by the time of the British Mandate. This includes the brothers Najīb and Jamāl Albīnā, Ḥannā Ṣāfiyya and the Ḥanāniyya brothers (whose studio would later be bought by Kahvedjian) in Jerusalem, Dāwūd Sabūnjī and ʿĪsā Sawabīnī (whose Jewish apprentice, Rachmann, would go on to practice in Tel Aviv)[14] in Jaffa, Zakariyyā Abū Fahīla in Bethlehem and, of course, Karīma ʿAbūd who is recognised as the first female professional photographer in the region[15] to name but a handful. This underscores the significant research yet to be undertaken on photography in Palestine.

2 Modern Images and Biblical Imaginings

In the last two decades research on photography in and of Palestine specifically, and the Arab World in general, has grown considerably.[16] Significantly

---

14   Nassar, *Familial Snapshots*, 146.

15   Issam Nassar, 'Early Local Photography in Palestine: The Legacy of Karimeh Abbud', *Jerusalem Quarterly* 46 (2011).

16   For instance, Issam Nassar, Patricia Almarcegui, and Clark Worswick, *Gardens of sand: Commercial photography in the Middle East, 1859–1905* (Madrid: Turner; 2010); Issam Nassar, *Photographing Jerusalem: the Image of the City in Nineteenth Century Photography* (Boulder: East European Monographs, 1997); Mitri Raheb, Ahmad Mrowat, and Issam Nassar, *Karīmah ʿAbbūd: rāʾidat al-taṣwīr al-niswī fī Filasṭīn, 1893–1940* (Bethlehem: Diyar Press, 2011); Noorderlicht Foundation and Wim Melis, eds, *Nazar: Photographs from the Arab world* (New York: Aperture, 2004); Hanna Safieh, *A Man and his Camera: Hanna Safieh: Photographs of Palestine, 1927–1967* (Jerusalem: 1999); Issam Nassar, *European Portrayals of Jerusalem religious fascinations and colonialist imaginations* (Lewiston: Edwin Mellen Press, 2006); Stephen Sheehi, *The Arab Imago: A Social History of Portrait Photography, 1860–1910* (Princeton: Princeton University Press, 2016); Markus Ritter, Staci Gem Scheiwiller, eds., *The Indigenous Lens?: Early Photography in the Near and Middle East* (Berlin: de Gruyter, 2018); Stephen Sheehi, "The Nahda after-image: or all photography expresses social relations," *Third Text: Critical Perspectives on Contemporary Art and Criticism* 26, no. 117 (2012): 401–414; Gil Pasternak, *The Handbook of Photography Studies* (London: Bloomsbury Visual Arts, 2020); Elias Sanbar and Salim Tamari, *Jérusalem et la Palestine: le fonds photographique de l'École Biblique de Jérusalem* (Paris: Hazan, 2013); Rona Sela, *Ḥalil Raʿad, tatslumim 1891–1948* (Tel Aviv: Muzeʾon Naḥum Gutman, 2010); Ariella Azoulay, *From Palestine to Israel: A Photographic Record of Destruction and State Formation, 1947–1950* (London: Pluto, 2011); Elias Sanbar, *The Palestinians: Photographs of a Land and Its People from 1839 to the Present Day* (New Haven: Yale University Press, 2015); Ali Behdad and Luke Gartlan, eds., *Photography's Orientalism New Essays on Colonial Representation* (Los Angeles: Getty Research Institute, 2013); Ali Behdad, "Orientalism and the Politics of Photographic Representation", *The Trans-Asia Photography Review* 10, no. 2 (2020); Ali Behdad, "Mediated Visions: Early Photography of the Middle East and

however, there is much yet to be said and to be researched as this volume attests, making clear the archival gaps in the field. As photography outside Europe and North America is relegated to regionalised and, implicitly, inferior quality,[17] one of the most pressing issues in the research of photography in Palestine is, indeed, the question of how the photographic process – one of the technological fruits of modernity – bestows or denies that modernity.

The transformations of the late Ottoman period were many. Modernity was more than just technological or bureaucratic innovation, though these were formative at a macro level. It was also a lived experience that 'colonized local politics, cultural practices, and everyday life by bringing into the discussion a consequence of modernity: modernity draws and redraws boundaries of class, and, critically, the ideas, institutions, and politics associated with modernity have given rise to a uniquely modern middle class'.[18]

The ways in which modernity and religious narrative collide in the case of the photography of Palestine gives us a particular avenue for understanding different aspects of social history, especially given its prevalence by the time of the British Mandate. Photographs produced in Palestine by indigenous Palestinians and non-Palestinians alike had a significant audience in the West as the many publications from the German Georg Landauer's *Palästine: 300 Bilder* (1925) in the early the British Mandate period to the Australian war photographer Frank Hurley's *The Holy City* (1949) just after its disastrous end.[19]

'Holy Land' photography the nineteenth century would develop into a lucrative market, with many Europeans, and later North Americans, Australians and New Zealanders, travelling the region to produce photographs, postcards, travel books and atlases. The reading of the Palestinian landscape through Biblical narrative was commonplace, eschewing the modern in favour of the putatively ancient. Such photographs sit within the rubric of what Nassar describes as

Orientalist Network", *History of Photography* (2017): 362–375; Ali Behdad, "Orientalism and the history of photography in the Middle East": 82–93 in *Inspired by the East*, eds. William Greenwood and Lucien De Guise (London, British Museum Press, 2020); Lorenzo Kamel, *Imperial Perceptions of Palestine: British Influence and Power in Late Ottoman Times* (London: I.B. Tauris, 2016); Amanda Burritt, *Visualising Britain's Holy Land in the Nineteenth Century* (Cham: Palgrave MacMillan, 2020) have all written about photography and visual culture in Palestine specifically or the region at large.

17   Issam Nassar, "Bearers of Memory: Photo Albums as Sources of Historical Study in Palestine", chapter 5 in this volume.

18   Keith Watenpaugh, *Being Modern in the Middle East Revolution, Nationalism, Colonialism, and the Arab Middle Class* (Princeton: Princeton University Press, 2006), 8.

19   See for instance Nur Masalha, *The Palestine Nakba: Decolonising History, Narrating the Subaltern and Reclaiming Memory* (London: Zed Books, 2012) and Ilan Pappe, *The Ethnic Cleansing of Palestine* (Oxford: Oneworld, 2015).

biblification, that is, the reading of Palestine through Biblical narrative, effectively projecting the land and its people backwards into an ancient past, while also excising the modern from the photographic frame.[20]

Perhaps unsurprisingly, technological developments also had significant impacts on photography, its production, distribution and circulation. The daguerreotype, developed by Louis-Jacques-Mandé Daguerre in 1839 would give way to Frederick Scott Archer's wet-plate collodion method, which became the standard by late 1850s. Professional studio and landscape photography reached a peak in the 1860s and 1870s.[21] The introduction of Box Brownie camera in 1900 sparked a significant technological shift, enabling portable equipment and quick exposures times[22] and the global economic boom in period after World War I, further democratised the medium,[23] coinciding with the beginning of the British Mandate in Palestine.

From the context of an earlier photographic market addressing pilgrims and 'arm-chair' tourists at home in the West,[24] local photographic studios would emerge in Palestine from the late nineteenth century onwards.[25] The Armenian community was instrumental in the growth of indigenous photographic studios, with the medium introduced locally by the Armenian Patriarch Issay

---

20 Issam Nasser, "Biblification in the Service of Colonialism: Jerusalem in Nineteenth-century Photography," *Third Text* 20, no. 374 (2006): 317–326.

21 Zeynep Çelik and Edhem Eldem, eds., *Camera Ottomana: Photography and Modernity in the Ottoman Empire, 1840–1914* (Istanbul: Koç University Press, 2015).

22 Brian Coe and Paul Gates, *The Snapshot Photograph: The rise of Popular Photography 1888–1939* (London: Ash & Grant, 1977): 22.

23 Ibid 36.

24 Randy Innes, "Jerusalem Revisited: On Auguste Salzmann's Photo-Topography," *Religion and the Arts* 15, no. 3 (2011): 306–337; Emmie Donadio, "Seeing is believing: Auguste Salzmann and the photographic representation of Jerusalem," in *Jerusalem idea and reality*, eds. Tamar Mayer and Suleiman Mourad (Milton Park, Abingdon, Oxon; New York: Routledge, 2008), 140–154; Abigail Solomon-Godeau, "A Photographer in Jerusalem, 1855: Auguste Salzmann and His Times," *October* 18 (1981): 91–107; Douglas M. Haller, *In Arab Lands: The Bonfils collection of the University of Pennsylvania Museum* (Cairo: The American University in Cairo Press, 2000), 11–27; Keri Berg, "The imperialist lens: Du Camp, Salzmann and Early French photography," *Early Popular Visual Culture* 6, 1 (2007): 1–17; Francis Frith, Julia van Haaften, and J.E. Manchip White, *Egypt and the Holy Land in historic photographs* (New York/London: Dover Publications; Constable, 1980), 77; Douglas Nickel, *Francis Frith in Egypt and Palestine: A Victorian Photographer Abroad* (Princeton: Princeton University Press, 2004).

25 This includes the studio of Garabed Krikorian, Khalīl Raʿad, ʿĪsā Sawabīnī, Karīma ʿAbūd and Dāwūd Sabūnjī to name a handful.

Garabedian to train young Armenians[26] through the Armenian Patriarchate[27] quickly giving rise to both Armenian and Arab commercial photographic studios in Palestine.[28]

This underscores several questions fundamental to this volume. Firstly, it highlights the role of the market for photography. That is to say consumers had a strong role in dictating photographic production, whether it was biblified material for the Western market or the commissioning of photography either for personal portraits,[29] use in scholarship,[30] or indeed even by the state.[31] Added to these categories, with the increasing accessibility of the medium, was the growth of amateur photography amongst the middle and upper classes globally, but also, and pertinent to the context of Palestine, amongst soldiers.[32]

Secondly, and related to questions of cultural consumption and production, are the class connotations of photography. While photographic images were becoming increasingly commonplace and accessible, particularly with the invention of the cheap and portable cameras for non-professional use, the medium still required a certain financial investment, skewing access to photographic production by class.

Third, is the role of Christianity. While photography was far from being the sole purview of Christian communities[33] – either Palestinian or globally – the influence of Christianity in photography of Palestine was great. On the one hand, biblified photography was lucrative and greatly in demand in

26   Badr El-Hage, "Khalil Raad – Jerusalem Photographer", *Jerusalem Quarterly* 11–12 (2001): 34.

27   George Hintlian is quoted on the subject in Yeshayahu Nir, *The Bible and the Image: The History of Photography in The Holy Land, 1839–1899* (Philadelphia: University of Pennsylvania Press, 2017), 121.

28   Salim Tamari, *The Great War and the Remaking of Palestine* (Berkeley: University of California Press, 2017), chapter 8; Nir, *The Bible and the Image: The History of Photography in The Holy Land, 1839–1899*, 235.

29   See for instance Issam Nassar, "Early Local Photography in Palestine: The Legacy of Karimeh Abbud", *Jerusalem Quarterly* 46 (2011): 23–31.

30   For instance, collections related to archaeology such as photographic archives at the Dominican École biblique et archéologique française de Jérusalem or the London-based Palestine Exploration Fund.

31   See for instance Salim Tamari, "The War Photography of Khalil Raad: Ottoman Modernity and the Biblical Gaze," *Jerusalem Quarterly* 52 (2013): 25–37.

32   Coe and Gates, *The Snapshot Photograph*, 30–35.

33   All we need to do is to look to the example of Muhammad Sadiq Bey's photography of Mecca and Medina in 1861, to see the swift adoption of photography outside of the Christian dominated photographic milieu in Palestine. Stephen Sheehi, *The Arab Imago: A Social History of Portrait Photography 186–1910* (New Jersey: Princeton University Press: 2016): 1.

FIGURE 1.1   *Jerusalem from the Mount of Olives*, 14th December 1917. Captain Arthur Rhodes,
             The New Zealand Canterbury Rifles
             IMAGE COURTESY OF THE PALESTINE EXPLORATION FUND

the western market. On the other, the role of indigenous Christians – both
Arab and Armenian – was significant, particularly around the establishment of photographic studios and the commercial practice of photography
in Palestine. This reflects the historical diversity and cosmopolitan nature of
urban dwellers, a result of the Ottoman policy of higher taxation on minorities, making urban livelihoods increasingly more tenable through the period
of Ottoman rule.[34] This had significant impacts on Palestinian social structure
by the British Mandate period.[35]

   This process of biblification created a contradiction. Photography was a
modern medium that enabled the production and reproduction of images.
It has continued, since 1839, to be the object of constant technological
development. However, market dictates of the plural subject matter of the
medium – which in the case of Palestine cut across popular, scholarly and state
sponsored imaging – delineated and delimited the bestowal of modernity,

---

34   The impacts of Ottoman taxation regimes in the 17th Century and their aftereffects are
     dealt with at length in Felicita Tramontana, "The Poll Tax and the Decline of the Christian
     Presence in the Palestinian Countryside in the 17th Century," *Journal of the Economic
     and Social History of the Orient* 56, nos. 4–5 (2013): 631–652. During the British Mandate
     period, the specific focus of minorities by agents of Western cultural diplomacy further
     cemented opportunities for Christian Palestinians and the class status they had develop.
     See, for example, Karène Sanchez Summerer and Sary Zananiri, eds., *European Cultural
     Diplomacy and Arab Christians in British Mandate Palestine, 1918–1948. Between Contention
     and Connection* (London: Palgrave McMillan, 2020).
35   See for instance Sherene Seikaly, *Men of Capital: Scarcity and Economy in Mandate
     Palestine* (Palo Alto, CA: Stanford University Press, 2015) or Watenpaugh, *Being Modern in
     the Middle East.*

projecting the image back into the imagined ancient past. By the time of the British Mandate, imaging conventions established during the nineteenth century still held significant sway, despite both the significantly increased accessibility to the medium and its increasingly plural modes of operation. The range of photographs from the British Mandate period show this plurality morphing in different ways: scholarly uses in fields like archaeology or anthropology; commercial portraits, production of souvenirs and travelogues; the documentation of current affairs and social events; humanitarian imaging that marked the plight of orphans and refugees during the turbulent years of the First World War and its aftermath; or information-gathering in the course of urban renewal and, indeed, even espionage. That is to say, many of these photographs actively produced or ruminated upon historical, or quasi-historical, narratives, projecting multiple points of view in which religious narrative is often embedded, sometimes in the subtlest of ways.

3   Biblification and Orientalism: Towards an Understanding
       of Legibility in Photography

Embedded within the tumultuous context of the multifarious medium of photography is an interplay between biblification, Orientalism and modernity. While biblification made legible the landscapes and people of the 'Holy Land' through a process of reading via Biblical interpretation,[36] Orientalism operated through an inverse procedure. As Edward Said notes in the opening to his seminal work of the same name 'Orientalism is a style of thought based upon an ontological and epistemological distinction made between "the Orient" and (most of the time) "the Occident".[37]

In this regard, we can see the interactions of biblification and Orientalism in photography – and elsewhere – as affecting a process of delimiting and accessioning both the landscapes and people of Palestine into the western Biblical imaginary, whether through scholarly or more popular modes of the medium. While biblification made familiar the foreign other, Orientalism actively marked the delimitation of otherness. The net result of these twin processes is the demarcation of a mode of 'civility'. This civility implicitly attempts to

---

36   For a longer discussion on Biblical readings of Palestine in imagery, see Sary Zananiri, "From Still to Moving Image: the Shifting Representation of Jerusalem and Palestinians in the Western Biblical Imaginary", *Jerusalem Quarterly* 67 (2016): 64–81.

37   Edward Said, *Orientalism* (New York: Vintage Books, 1979), 2.

assume the neutral positioning of a western Biblical imaginary that is rooted in the lived experience of modern western bourgeoisie. That is to say, a recouping of the ancient spiritual roots of Western Christianity set against the wild and untameable otherness of an implicitly Islamic 'Orient'.

Implicit, and perhaps complicit, in this twin process is the role of modernity. The assumptions of progress, objectivity and the scientific neutrality of modern methodologies (and the subsequent Occidental attitudes to civil questions of education, health, welfare and the built environment that it entails), produced a thoroughly partial and subjective point of perspective from which biblification and Orientalism, as imaging systems, are constructed. This parallels the broader social and cultural contexts that are explored in a number of the contributions included in this volume.

Within the often transnational histories of imaging Palestine, we find a complex confluence of actors involved in photographic production, photographic subjects, circulation networks and audiences. These also need to be read within the context of Palestinian class structures, in which middle-class urban Palestinians, participated. It is worth noting the over-representation of Christians in this middle-class,[38] particularly in cities like Jerusalem, with its significant photographic market.

This matrix of class dynamics and transnationalism produces particularised perspectives. With few exceptions, Western photographers tended to focus on biblified production, often rural communities cast as heirs of an ancient Biblical past, holy sites and Biblical archetypes for circulation in the West. Meanwhile, local photographers variously addressed similar international markets, but also worked on commission for local middle-class populations, institutions and the state(s). This dynamic produced skewed visions of Palestine and its social histories during the Mandate that cut across class divides.[39] Figures such as rural *fallāḥīn* (villagers or peasants) or Bedouins, along with other indigenous curiosities for the Western market like the Samaritans or the Domari (often described as *Nawar* in Arabic or 'Gypsies' in English), for instance, may have heavily populated ethnographic elements the Biblical lens as photographic subjects, but sustained examples of photographic production from

---

38   See for instance Salim Tamari, *Mountain against Sea. Essays on Palestinian Society and Culture* (Berkeley: University of California Press, 2008).

39   Jewish communities in Palestine can be seen as operating across a similar binary between ancient biblical actors and modern subjects, but embedded within Zionist ideology, and its reception particularly in Europe, was the fundamentally modern nature of the Zionist project. Rebekka Grossmann deals with this tension at length in "Negotiating Presences: Palestine and the Weimar German Gaze," *Jewish Social Studies* 23, no.2 (2018): 137–172.

within such communities are rare to come by, if they exist at all, and present very significant gaps in current historiography, let alone attempts to decolonise the photography of Palestine.

The absent-present qualities of such communities underscore the relationship of photographer to camera, and camera to subject, hinting at the extent of archival silences in textual material into which photography may give us some insight. Several chapters in this volume address the silent role of such relations in Palestine and further afield, with workers, peasants, Samaritans, Bedouins and Domari who are often well recorded in photography, but only minimally discussed, and generally not by name in corresponding textual records, while middle class actors, regardless of their ethnic, religious or national backgrounds are much better represented.

In one of the discussions during the conference[40] that led to this publication, Stephen Sheehi described the relationship between biblification and modernity as a mode of *Biblical Moderne*, a useful tool for thinking through the paradoxical push-pull temporality of photography in Palestine. At one and the same moment a product of modernity, but also constantly recalling, if not actively imposing, the Biblical past.

This certainly raises questions about the configuration of biblification, Orientalism and modernity and the ways in which the putative ancient past is remediated to the understanding and aestheticisation of the more recent past on which this volume is focused. The attempts to reconcile the Biblical and the scientific that the Biblical Moderne entails can be seen as an attempt to reconcile the spiritual and the temporal. It could, indeed, be argued that organisations such as the Pro-Jerusalem Society, under the auspices of Charles Ashbee, went so far as to *actualise* the Biblical Moderne in stone and mortar[41] with the urban planning policies that they developed in Jerusalem as a consequence of the British occupation of Palestine.

In curating this volume, a diversity of material was sought to reflect the breadth of different photographic archives. The various chapters engage with archives from the scholarly to those which were commercial in nature and, of course, archives of home photography that developed significantly during the course of the Mandate. In dealing with such a plethora of material, this volume

---

40   *Imaging and Imagining: Photography and Social History in British Mandate Palestine* was held at Leiden University, 16–18 October 2019 and convened by the editors as part of NWO (the Dutch Research Council) VIDI project *CrossRoads: European Cultural Diplomacy and Arab Christians. A Connected History (1920–1950)*.

41   The impacts of the Pro-Jerusalem Society are dealt with at length in Rana Barakat, "Urban Planning, Colonialism and the Pro-Jerusalem Society", *Jerusalem Quarterly* 65 (2016), 22–34.

considers the ways in which different modes of photography shed light on social histories. Likewise, this volume intentionally addresses these different modes through an interdisciplinary framework, bringing a diversity of expertise necessary to approach the already diverse archival context.

The title *Imaging and Imagining Palestine* attempts to deal with the often-fraught contradictions of photography in Palestine. The ambiguous nature of photography, which purports to be a process of 'documentation', shapes, frames and narrates Palestine across a plethora of fields, as the following chapters make clear.

4   Approaching Photography in Palestine

This volume is divided into three sections. The first deals with specific archives containing photography in Palestine, the second with individual photographers and the third with conceptual approaches to photography. This taxonomy neatly divides the chapters by their approaches. But, beyond these broad ways of engaging with the subject, the interdisciplinary nature of the contributions and contributors addresses a number of different themes in terms of subject matter.

Often, the modern social apparatus that is tethered to photography ultimately relies on Biblical tropes developed in the nineteenth century. One particular poignant example is humanitarian photography, as explored by Abigail Jacobson. As Jacobson shows, the sponsorship of orphans in the American Colony's Christian Herald Orphanage was the practice of a modern institution with a transnational remit. But, it was fundamentally linked to American philanthropy centred on Protestant Christian networks, with photographic materials using Orientalist tropes to garner donations to charities. Even though the material she discusses effectively deals with the impacts of modernity, in this case the aftereffects of the First World War with its social and cultural ramifications, Christian narratives are fundamental to the questions of charity with which she deals, effectively purveying new modes of biblification, through auspices of the charitable.

The photographs of Inger Marie Okkenhaug's chapter shows the role of Swedish aesthetics in mediating a position between the Arab communities that sat within the remit of the Swedish School, funders in Sweden and the American Colony. The images hint at the social dynamics where the increasingly Palestinian teaching staff intermingled with an ordered Swedish world. Okkenhaug's chapter gives us a sense of the ways in which cultural affiliation and cultural diplomacy interacted within the visuality of the Swedish School.

Karène Sanchez Summerer and Norig Neveu's chapter also deals with transnational connections, in the form of the École biblique et archéologique française de Jérusalem (EBAF), a photographic collection that drew from a number of Catholic missionary institutions in Palestine. They deal with the diverse nature of Catholic imaging of Palestine from more scholarly archaeological and anthropological photographs to more personal collections that indicate the changing relationships between the missionaries and their congregants and were used for reporting either to national or religious authorities. The chapter traces the diversity of photographic material produced by EBAF, and other associated Catholic agencies, tracing how photographic production shifted over the course of the Mandate.

Issam Nassar's chapter is the only one which deals overtly with non-professional photography. Nassar looks at three family albums as an archival source, analysing the ways in which each are narrated. The albums of Wasif Jawharriya, Julia Luci and George Mushabak each narrate a particular perspective on the British Mandate period, giving us a comparative set of micro-histories. The nature of such albums, designed for private uses and circulations, focuses more on life events than nationalist politics of the day. In conceiving of the importance of such photography, Nassar points to their use in understanding the quotidian middle-class urban life.

Rona Sela considers similar remediations of Palestine from an indigenous lens with the works of Khalīl Raʿad, particularly in relationship to his archaeological photography. Sela argues that Raʿad's engagement with New Testament narrative and archaeology provides an insight into nationalist reconfigurations of biblification and that, as an Arab Christian, his work engages carefully with the colonialist overtones of archaeology and biblified cultural material through the photographic market itself.

Rachel Lev also deals with a singular photographer, John D. Whiting from the American Colony in Jerusalem. Lev's chapter cross-references the Palestinian born Whiting's photographic albums with his travel diaries. In linking the two sources, Lev traces a plural photographic practice looking at the ways in which Whiting negotiated a position between his upbringing in Jerusalem and his American identity. Delving into Whiting's broad corpus, she considers his role in producing publications about Palestine, brokering collections of cultural materials for travellers, facilitating tours and even intelligence gathering, all of which underscore his position as a mediator between Palestine and world beyond, particularly the USA.

This transnational connection can also be seen elsewhere. The Frank Scholten Collection, in particular, gives us a sense of the complexities of transnational connection. The intention behind the production of Scholten's large corpus was fundamentally vested in the Biblical, but he also undermined typical readings by going into great detail around the ethnic, confessional and class dynamics of his subjects. His taxonomic methodology, which borrowed from disciplines as diverse as theology, art history and sexology, cut across confessional divides whilst also reifying communal description, a significant example, indeed, of the collision of religious and scholarly narrative that the Biblical Moderne entails.

Yazan Kopty looks at single collection, the National Geographic Society's accumulation of photographic images of Palestine and how we might re-interpret the collection through a contemporary lens. Kopty's chapter deals with an institutional acquisition of photographs from multiple sources and poses multiple questions that problematise the photographic gaze, proposing to recoup readings and re-articulations of such biblified photographic material. Given the historical entwinement of colonialism and photography in the imaging of Palestine, Kopty proposes an *indigenisation* of the archive through his project *Imagining the Holy*, positioning this as an alternative framework within contemporary calls for decolonisation. Such a project is particularly useful in reinstating the social histories of such archives through community sourced accounts, bringing to bear the elision of personal histories through contemporary technologies.

Likewise, Stephen Sheehi's contribution proposes a conceptual method for re-envisioning photography in Palestine. Sheehi's methodology provocatively invites us to radically rethink the truth-value of photographs and their role in (re)constructing social history. He questions attempts to seek the 'truth value' of photography, seeking to clarify a methodology of decolonisation as distinct from a project that seeks to recover lost histories. Sheehi proposes a 'seizure of the means of knowledge production', complicating such a call further with the problem of class, as fundamental to understanding the implications of photography. The chapter underscores the amount of work yet to be done, both in dealing with unpublished archives, but more importantly in reconceptualising the field of photography in Palestine in its entirety.

Focusing on the impacts of aerial photography, Nadi Abusaada considers the weight brought to bear by a pairing of dual forces: the technological development of the medium and the impacts of Biblical and Orientalist images of Palestine in shaping attitudes to the built environment and the urban modernisation project itself. In doing so, Abusaada considers the romanticisation of architectural heritage, but also the ways in which such heritage was radically altered and reshaped in the light of colonial modernity. Like Frank Scholten, his paper exemplifies ideas of the *Biblical Moderne* in producing the British colonial landscape of the Mandate era.

5   Framing Photography and Social History

Photographs of the Mandate era continue to circulate through many networks, often acquiring new meanings in their remediation. What is clear across all contributions to this volume is that photography is a medium that was designed to be reproduced and circulated, and that this has particular significance in the case of Palestine.

Imaging and Imagining Palestine re-examines the possibilities of recouping aspects of the past through the study of photography. It considers the state and institution building so fundamental to the British Mandate period, as well as their significant undoing by its close, grappling with networks implicitly embedded in such enterprises. It also attempts to contextualise them within a broader transnational narrative that better explains the complex social milieu in Mandate Palestine.

This edited volume thus asks crucial questions. What can photographs tell us of the British Mandate as a site of connection and interconnection? How has the meaning of photographs taken in the period shifted since their initial production? Do they indeed present possibilities for recouping the past? What information does the analysis of photography, both as a record itself and in its the afterlife of circulation, yield for the research of social histories?

If we are to take photography – a significant marker of cultural production – as an index of the complex social histories involved in networks of production, consumption and distribution, then perhaps a Cultural Studies approach to cultural diplomacy, like that of David Clark, might represent a useful model for framing the social, cultural and political importance of photography. He defines four actors in his approach to meaning-making in cultural diplomacy: policy makers, agents (both institutional and individual) who implement cultural diplomacy, cultural practitioners and cultural consumers.[42] In thinking about the process of meaning-making, those actors who are producing photographs are equally engaged as those who are consuming photographic production. He stipulates that:

> Cultural consumption is, firstly, a complex process of meaning-making, in which the boundary between cultural 'producers' and 'consumers' is blurred; and, secondly, that in the realm of culture both production and consumption are intrinsically bound up with the articulation and negotiation of identity in a social context.[43]

---

42   David Clarke, "Theorising the role of cultural products in cultural diplomacy from a cultural studies perspective," *International Journal of Cultural Policy* 22, no. 2 (2016): 154.

43   Ibid., 153.

The actors considered in this volume are involved in production ranging from commercial photographers to recorders of humanitarian crises, archaeologists and ethnographers, indigenous and foreign alike, with these categories often overlapping, let alone the plethora of cultural consumers. We might look to Abusaada's chapter to see the direct intersections of policy-making and photography in the shaping urban life. But for most chapters, a convoluted matrix of agents, practitioners and consumers dictate the ways in which the market – and implicitly Christianity – shaped the photography of the Mandate period.

The implications of meaning-making for Palestinian social and cultural histories is significant in thinking through the context of photography. It upends straightforward readings of photographic production, but also beckons further analysis of such complex networks.[44] The cultural consumers involved in the process of meaning-making are as varied as the agents and practitioners involved in its production and, given our chronological distance from the period, are also an unstable and changing demographic. They might include pilgrims, tourists, scholars, governmental agents, donors, private networks of friends and acquaintances and of course those for whom Palestine had religious resonances.

6   Photographic Instability: Old Photographs and New Meanings

Part of the problem in imaging Palestine is that so much weight is brought to bear on an image. Images, and photography in particular, have become part of both the contestation and substantiation of political narrative. In the highly politicised terrain of Palestine, photographs have come to be regarded as 'modes of proof' about a historical past. The impact of lineages of imaging systems before, during and since the British Mandate has had consistent effects on the ways in which we might think about the medium and the state of perpetual cultural, social and political turbulence since. This political turbulence makes for an increased instability of the photographic document, particularly in retrospect.

A poignant example of this instability of the photographic document is exemplified by the series of photographic exhibitions curated by Ali Kazak, the former Director of the PLO Information Office, in Australia. The first

---

44   We might look to further complications of these networks as does Behdad in regards to the Orientalist networks of photography in the nineteenth century. See Ali Behdad, "Mediated Visions: Early Photography of the Middle East and Orientalist Network," *History of Photography: Special Issue: Photography and Networks*, guest eds. Owen Clayton and Jim Cheshire, 41, no. 4 (2017): 362–375.

exhibition was held in Storey Hall, at the Royal Melbourne Institute for Technology in 1979. While many of the photographs dealt with contemporary political issues – sometimes in brutally graphic ways – a significant section of the exhibition was dedicated to the use of historical imagery, particularly biblified and Orientalist representations of Palestine, both as prints and photographs. Kazak asserts that such material was useful in proving the existence of the Palestinian people in the political context of 1970s and 80s Australia. Arguably, it also points the shifting self-perception of Palestinians, in line with the reimagining of the Palestinian *falaheen* as a symbol of Marxist resistance so prevalent in the period, which had an overlap with the class-skewed images produced by Orientalist and biblified imaging. In this way, the use of popular Western historical imagery became a means to subvert political discourse, effectively challenging their representational limitations, and perhaps the intention of the original works, in a period before digital technologies enabled easy access to and circulation of images.

The enormous shifts in digital technological developments have enabled photographs to circulate in ways that were unthinkable in the periods when the original photographs were originally produced. Facebook groups such as Mona Halaby's *British Mandate Jerusalemites Photo Library* use such means to attempt to recoup the past through period-specific photographic materials drawn from institutional and family archives alike, in this case providing a public platform with over 20,000 followers.[45] Such platforms are knowledge-sharing devices with a public interface, but have their effects on the process of meaning-making, generating new meanings in the ways in which they (re-)instate Palestinian narrative. Notwithstanding the reliance on materials available from the period (and the social biases inherent to such material), through Halaby's carefully researched textual annotations, as well as those sourced from her interlocutors and followers, photographic materials are animated and activated in ways that traditional archives are not, making it a community locus as well as a page of much research interest for those in the field.

On an institutional level, the Palestine Museum initiated a digitisation project aimed at documenting and preserving family albums in 2015.[46] The ongoing family album project operated under the slogan 'Your memories, your pictures,

---

45   See British Mandate Jerusalemites Photo Library, https://www.facebook.com/BMJeru salemitesPhotoLib/, accessed 3rd May, 2021.

46   The fruits of this and other digitisation initiatives by the Palestine Museum can be viewed through their online portal https://palarchive.org.

FIGURE 1.2 A reproduction from Ali Kazak's exhibitions on Palestine, 1979. Mostly likely
reproduced from Captain Charles Wilson's *Picturesque Palestine* (1891)
IMAGE COURTESY OF ALI KAZAK

our heritage'.[47] The instatement of the national *through* the social underscores the cultural importance associated with the documentation of daily life in what had typically been the preserve of the private sphere. The archive, which spans a considerably larger period than just the British Mandate, shows the development of intimate familial portraiture and, from a social and techno-logical perspective, the ways in which family snapshot photography evolved over time, making it important not just as a project for Palestinian history, but indeed a chronological study of the medium itself.

The Palestine Museum's digitisation presents a very different strategy to Kazak's earlier Australian exhibitions. While both insist on photography and image production practices as important modes of disseminating Palestinian narrative, a shift in focus from Western cultural production to a focus on domestic photographic practices emphasises the significant growth in interest of indigenous voice, in this case through the accumulation of micro histories rooted in the family album.

The need for a comprehensive overview of Palestinian photography dur-ing the British Mandate is all the more urgent with the growth of online archives, image repositories and digital humanities methodologies. With the digitisation of photographic collections, images are more available than ever before. The need to research and contextualise such material is all the more important to understand the shortcomings of photography and the pho-tographic archive as well as what they explicate that other primary sources of historical study do not.

It is also clear that the photographic archives to which we refer are also prone to their own biases, by virtue of the market, questions of the socio-economic status of producers, and the rubrics of Christianity, both in the production and marketing of photography in and from Palestine. This underscores the signifi-cant amount of work that still needs to be undertaken. Much work has looked at biblification with respect to Western collections and such materials have already been analysed as products of colonial claim,[48] effectively underscoring cultural entwinement with political policy.

With the implications of biblification, Christian narratives create a multi-farious series of interactions that intersect with class. While on the one hand the representation of Palestine and Palestinians in both photography and scholarship led to significant erasures, it is also evident that class formation

---

47   'The Palestine Museum's Family Album Project: The Intimate Side of Life in Palestine' press release from the Palestine Museum 13th May 2015, reproduced by *Jadaliyya*, accessed 27th October 2020 https://www.jadaliyya.com/Details/32080.

48   Nassar, "'Biblification' in the Service of Colonialism", 317–326.

FIGURE 1.3 *Hanna Bastoli and family members on her engagement day*, 1924. (Hanna Bastoli, George Ayyoub and her mother-in-law, Hilwa Al-Douiri). From Maha as-Saqqa's photo album, *0027.01.0054*
IMAGE COURTESY OF THE PALESTINE MUSEUM AND MAHA AS-SAQQA

FIGURE 1.4 *Bassam Shakaa as a child*, 1933. From the Bassām ash-Shakʻaʼs photo album,
          0050.01.0386
          IMAGE COURTESY OF THE PALESTINE MUSEUM AND ASH-SHAKAA FAMILY

FIGURE 1.5   *A family trip with friends*, c.1940–45. Ghassan Abdullah Collection, *0156.01.0068*
IMAGE COURTESY OF THE PALESTINE MUSEUM AND THE ABDULLAH FAMILY

and modernity played a significant role in the selective highlighting of certain Palestinian groups over others. Internal Palestinian dynamics of class formation also point toward mercantile Palestinian complicity in the photographic erasure of Palestinian modernity, through the proffering of biblified materials to the Western photographic market. This is an irony given that this was precisely the same class most actively involved in the documentation of Palestinian modernity through carte de visites and other forms of photography in the nineteenth and early twentieth century[49] or through vernacular photography in the interwar period. As Sheehi reminds us in his chapter, 'the decolonisation of photography is not magical undoing ... an ahistorical process or a reading through nationalist frameworks that sees indigenous photography as 'speaking back' to power ... [the] decolonisation of photography should not seek an 'epistemic reconstruction' ... awaking dormant histories are not the same as hoping to resurrect arcane or dead practices, fetishising them as authentic culture'.

A Palestinian deployment of Biblical narrative in the case of photographers like Khalīl Raʿad, can also be viewed as an intervention into biblification as an imaging system when read within the category of agents in Clark's cultural studies approach to meaning-making in cultural diplomacy. Raʿad used the international interest in the biblified photography of Palestine as a platform for proffering an indigenous vision that counters the colonial lens. Arguably, the photographs from the Armenian General Benevolent Union in the epilogue, that will be included as part of the collections in the new Armenian Museum in Jerusalem, also implicitly deployed the Biblical in requests for humanitarian donations from the West. In considering Palestinian agency, it does raise important questions about how biblification and its transmission between Palestinians and Europeans functioned. A partial answer can be found in question of class dynamics and the urban-rural divide in Palestinian society.

This volume synthesises both social history and photography, attempting to garner an overview of the British Mandate. But also, this volume shows us the limitations of photography as a study for social history, particularly in relation to questions of class, confession and colonialism, let alone questions of gender and sexuality. Given this, we proffer this volume as a gesture towards mapping the plurality of photography, its circulations and its conceptualisation, both during the Mandate period and in retrospect since.

---

49   See Stephen Sheehi's chapter, "The Carte de Visite: The Sociability of New Men and Women," in his book *The Arab Imago: A Social History of Portrait Photography 1860–1910* (Princeton: Princeton University Press, 2016), 53–74.

Bibliography

Azoulay, Ariella. *From Palestine to Israel a photographic record of destruction and state formation, 1947–1950*. London: Pluto, 2011.

Behdad, Ali and Gartlan, Luke, eds. *Photography's Orientalism new essays on colonial representation*. Los Angeles: Getty Research Institute, 2013.

Behdad, Ali. "Mediated Visions: Early Photography of the Middle East and Orientalist Network." *History of Photography:* Special Issue 'Photography and Networks', guest editors Owen Clayton and Jim Cheshire 41, no. 4 (2017): 362–375.

Behdad, Ali. *Orientalism and the Politics of Photographic Representation*. Ann Arbor, MI: Michigan Publishing, University of Michigan Library.

Behdad, Ali. "Orientalism and the History of Photography in the Middle East". In *Inspired by the East*, edited by William Greenwood and Lucien De Guise, 82–93. London, British Museum Press, 2020.

Berg, Keri. "The imperialist lens: Du Camp, Salzmann and early French photography." *Early Popular Visual Culture* 6, 1 (2007): 1–17.

British Mandate Jerusalemites Photo Library. https://www.facebook.com/BMJeru salemitesPhotoLib/.

Burritt, Amanda. *Visualising Britain's Holy Land in the Nineteenth Century*. Switzerland: Palgrave Macmillan, 2020.

Capturing the Holy Land: M.J. Diness and the Beginnings of Photography in Jerusalem. Cambridge MA: Harvard University Press, 1993.

Clarke, David. "Theorising the role of cultural products in cultural diplomacy from a cultural studies perspective." *International Journal of Cultural Policy* 22, no. 2 (2016): 147–163.

Çelik, Zeynep and Edhem Eldem, eds. *Camera Ottomana: Photography and Modernity in the Ottoman Empire, 1840–1914*. Istanbul: Koç University Press, 2015.

Coe, Brian. and Gates, Paul. *The snapshot photograph: The rise of popular photography, 1888–1939*. London: Ash and Grant, 1977.

Donadio, Emmie. "Seeing is believing: Auguste Salzmann and the photographic representation of Jerusalem." In *Jerusalem Idea and Reality*, edited by Tamar Mayer and Suleiman Mourad, 140–154. Milton Park, Abingdon, Oxon; New York: Routledge, 2008.

El-Hage, Badr. "Khalil Raad – Jerusalem Photographer", *Jerusalem Quarterly* 11–12 (2001): 34–39.

Frith, Francis, van Haaften, Julia, and Manchip White, J.E. *Egypt and the Holy Land in Historic Photographs*. New York/London: Dover Publications; Constable, 1980.

Grossmann, Rebekka. "Negotiating Presences: Palestine and the Weimar German Gaze." *Jewish Social Studies* 23, no. 2 (2018): 137–172.

Grossmann, Rebekka. "Image Transfer and Visual Friction: Staging Palestine in the National Socialist Spectacle." *The Leo Baeck Institute Yearbook* 64, no, 1 (2019): 19–45.

Haller, Douglas, M. *In Arab lands: The Bonfils collection of the University of Pennsylvania Museum*. Cairo: The American University in Cairo Press, 2000.

Innes, R. "Jerusalem Revisited: On Auguste Salzmann's Photo-Topography." *Religion and the Arts* 15, no. 3 (2011): 306–337.

Kamel, Lorenzo. *Imperial Perceptions of Palestine: British Influence and Power in Late Ottoman Times*. London: I.B. Tauris, 2016.

Kevorkian, Raymond. "From a monastery to a neighbourhood: Orphans and Armenian refugees in the Armenian quarter of Jerusalem (1916–1926), reflexions towards an Armenian museum in Jerusalem." In Special issue 'Eastern Christianity in Syria and Palestine and European cultural diplomacy (1860–1948). A connected history', guest editors Karène Sanchez Summerer and Konstantinos Papastathis, *Contemporary Levant*, 6: 1 (2021).

Lev, Shimon. and Wachtel, Hamutal. Catalogue accompanying the exhibition *The Camera Man: Women and Men Photograph Jerusalem 1900–1950*. Jerusalem: Tower of David Museum, 2016.

Masalha, Nur. *The Palestine Nakba: Decolonising History, Narrating the Subaltern and Reclaiming Memory*. London: Zed Books, 2012.

Nassar, Işsam. *Photographing Jerusalem: the image of the city in nineteenth century photography*. Boulder: East European Monographs, 1997.

Nassar, Issam. "Early local photography in Jerusalem." *History of Photography* 27, 4 (2003): 320–332.

Nassar, Issam. *European portrayals of Jerusalem religious fascinations and colonialist imaginations*. Lewiston: Edwin Mellen Press, 2006.

Nassar, Issam, "Familial Snapshots Representing Palestine in the Work of the First Local Photographers." *History and Memory* 18, no. 2 (2006): 139–155.

Nasser, Issam. "'Biblification' in the Service of Colonialism: Jerusalem in Nineteenth-century Photography." *Third Text* 20, issue 374 (2006): 317–326.

Nassar, Issam, Patricia Almarcegui, and Clark Worswick eds. *Gardens of sand: commercial photography in the Middle East 1859–1905*. Madrid: Turner, 2010.

Nickel, Douglas. *Francis Frith in Egypt and Palestine: A Victorian photographer abroad*. Princeton: Princeton University Press, 2004.

Nir, Yeshayahu. *The Bible and the Image: The History of Photography in The Holy Land, 1839–1899*. Philadelphia: University of Pennsylvania Press, 2017.

Noorderlicht (Foundation) and Melis, Wim. *Nazar: photographs from the Arab world*. New York: Aperture 2004.

Palestine Museum "The Palestine Museum's Family Album Project: The Intimate Side of Life in Palestine" Press release, 13th May 2015, reproduced by Jadaliyya, https://www.jadaliyya.com/Details/32080.

Pappe, Ilan. *The Ethnic Cleansing of Palestine*. Oxford: Oneworld, 2015.

Pasternak, Gil. *The Handbook of Photography Studies*. London: Bloomsbury Visual Arts, 2020.

Raheb, Mitri., Mrowat, Aḥmad., and Nassar, Issam. *Karīmah ʿAbbūd: rāʾidat al-taṣwīr al-niswī fī Filasṭīn, 1893–1940*. Bethlehem: Diyar Press, 2011.

Ritter, Markus and Schweiwiller, Staci, eds., *The Indigenous Lens? Early Photography in the Near and Middle East*, 8. *Studies in Theory and History of Photography*. Berlin/ Boston: De Gruyter, 2017 http://search.ebscohost.com/login.aspx?direct=true&scope =site&db=nlebk&db=nlabk&AN=1684601.

Safieh, Hanna. 1999. *A man and his camera: Hanna Safieh: photographs of Palestine, 1927–1967*. Jerusalem: Raffi Safieh.

Said, Edward. *Orientalism*. New York: Vintage Books, 1979.

Sanbar, Elias and Tamari, Salim. *Jérusalem et la Palestine: le fonds photographique de l'École Biblique de Jérusalem*. Paris: Hazan, 2013.

Sanbar, Elias. *The Palestinians: Photographs of a Land and its People from 1839 to the Present day*. New Haven: Yale University Press, 2015.

Sanchez Summerer, Karène and Zananiri, Sary, eds. *European Cultural Diplomacy and Arab Christians in British Mandate Palestine, 1918–1948. Between Contention and Connection*. London: Palgrave McMillan, 2020.

Seikaly, Sherene. *Men of Capital: Scarcity and Economy in Mandate Palestine*. Palo Alto, CA: Stanford University Press, 2015.

Sela, Rona. *Ḥalil Raʾad, tatslumim 1891–1948*. Tel Aviv: Muzeʾon Naḥum Guṭman, 2010.

Semmerling, Tim. *Israeli and Palestinian postcards: Presentations of national self*. Austin, TX: University of Texas Press, 2004.

Serkes, Sue. "For a photogenic Jerusalem, a look at how locals first captured their city," *Times of Israel* 26th May, 2016. https://www.timesofisrael.com/for-photogenic -jerusalem-a-look-at-how-locals-first-captured-their-city/#gs.g99sd4.

Sheehi, Stephen. 2012. "The Nahḍa after-image: or all photography expresses social relations". *Third Text: Critical Perspectives on Contemporary Art and Criticism*. 26 (117): 401–414.

Sheehi, Stephen. *The Arab Imago: A Social History of Portrait Photography 1860–1910*. Princeton: Princeton University Press, 2016.

Silver-Brody, Vivienne. *Documentors of the Dream: Pioneer Jewish Photographers in the Land of Israel 1890–1933*. Lincoln, Nebr.: University of Nebraska Press, 1999.

Solomon-Godeau, Abigail. "A Photographer in Jerusalem, 1855: Auguste Salzmann and His Times." *October* 18 (1981): 91–107.

Tamari, Salim. *Mountain against Sea. Essays on Palestinian Society and Culture*. Berkeley: University of California Press, 2008.

Tamari, Salim. "The War Photography of Khalil Raad: Ottoman Modernity and the Biblical Gaze." *Jerusalem Quarterly* 52 (2013): 25–37.

Tamari, Salim. *The Great War and the Remaking of Palestine.* Berkeley: University of California Press, 2017.

Tramontana, Felicita. "The Poll Tax and the Decline of the Christian Presence in the Palestinian Countryside in the 17th Century." *Journal of the Economic and Social History of the Orient* 56, nos. 4–5 (2013): 631–652.

Watenpaugh, Keith. *Being Modern in the Middle East Revolution, Nationalism, Colonialism, and the Arab Middle Class.* Princeton: Princeton University Press, 2006.

Zananiri, Sary. "From Still to Moving Image: the Shifting Representation of Jerusalem and Palestinians in the Western Biblical Imaginary", *Jerusalem Quarterly* 67 (2016): 64–81.

PART 1

In and out of the Archives: Photographic Collections and the Historical Case Studies

..

'Little Orphans of Jerusalem': The American Colony's Christian Herald Orphanage in Photographs and Negatives

Abigail Jacobson

Marie Aboud, eight, is a little maid of the Greek Orthodox Church. Her father, George Aboud, is paralyzed from shell-shock, and her mother, Wardy/Wandy, is dead. Marie's family came from the mountains of Ajalon in northeastern Palestine. Some Moslems wanted to take Marie from her helpless father by force, which meant to make her somebody's concubine. To avoid this he sent her to Jerusalem to a distant relative of her mother's. This person is very poor and unable to feed her own family of three children. Marie is stunted and thin, but bright and lovable. (Fig. 2.1)[1]

⁙

This brief description of little Marie is one of 33 descriptions of girls, aged 3–15, that appear in the Record Book of girls who received support through the American Colony Christian Herald Orphanage in Jerusalem (1918 to 1923, estimated dates). The pages of the Record Book are organised uniformly, give a sense of a catalogue or an index of the orphans and already hints to the power dynamics involved in this institution, as discussed below. On the right-hand corner is the girl's portrait photograph with a brief biographic outline including her name, religion, family history if known, place of residence before joining the Orphanage and a description of her character. In some cases, such

---

1 Bertha Spafford Vester and Christian Herald Orphanage, *Record Book listing girls receiving support through the Christian Herald Orphanage, as supervised by the American Colony.* Library of Congress, American Colony Collection, Manuscript/Mixed Material. https://www.loc.gov/item/mamcol.092/, 5. (Hereafter: Record Book). The Record Book and the Album are both preserved by the Library of Congress as part of the American Colony Collection. The American Colony Archive in Jerusalem holds the negatives of the photographs, as well as vast collections on the different activities and endeavours of the American Colony.

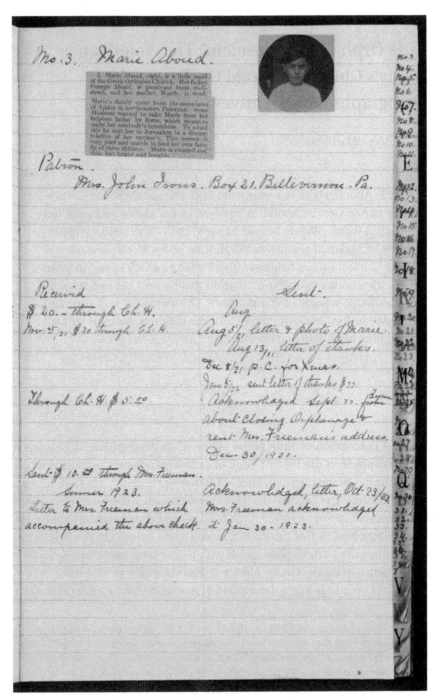

FIGURE 2.1   'No. 3: Marie Aboud'. Part of Christian Herald Orphanage
Record Book, 5.
IMAGE COURTESY OF THE AMERICAN COLONY ARCHIVE

as in the case of 10 years old Salfeetie, listed as number 17 in the Book, this description also includes the destiny that awaited the girl had she not been sent to the Orphanage, again suggesting the close link between the moral mission and institutional power: '[t]here was nothing for such a child but to roam the streets and learn all kinds of wickedness, had not the Orphanage opened its loving gates'.[2]

The Record Book with the girls' biographical descriptions joins another visual source that can teach us something about this institution: an annotated Photographic Album dedicated to the Christian Herald Orphanage, documenting life in the Orphanage. The Album consists of photographic prints, featuring trips and excursions held by the Orphanage, daily life and activities of the girls and staff, celebrations and, again, individual photographic portraits of the girls.[3] The Record Book and Photograph Album of the Orphanage offer us an opportunity to bring back to life this somewhat forgotten venture, one of a number of orphanages and welfare institutions in post-World War I Jerusalem (and Palestine). These records enable us to ask many questions, both about the history of the Orphanage and the girls who stayed there, but also about photography as site of investigation and documentation. Specifically, this chapter will critically address the connections between the medium of photography and the acts of humanitarianism, as playing out in the case of the Orphanage.

As suggested by Issam Nassar, photographs should be regarded as visual documents which cannot be separated from the historical context and circumstances in which they were produced.[4] This chapter, then, aims at uncovering the history of the Orphanage within the overall activities organised by the American Colony, as well as the social life of the images included in these albums.[5] What is the main narrative that the Album and Book wish to portray and to whom? What can they teach us about the institution, the people behind the camera and their intended audience? Was there any significance in the way the albums were organised, the taxonomy of the images and the staging of the girls in the photographs? Who was excluded from the albums? And how is the Orphanage connected to its surrounded socio-political and urban

2 Ibid., 21.
3 Unknown, American Colony in Jerusalem, and Christian Herald Orphanage. Photograph Album, Christian Herald Orphanage. Palestine, 1919. Unpublished Album, Library of Congress, American Colony Collection Photograph. https://www.loc.gov/item/mamcol.091/. (Hereafter: Album).
4 Issam Nassar, *Photographing Jerusalem: The Image of the City in Nineteenth Century Photography* (Boulder: East European Monographs, 1997), 24–26.
5 Stephen Sheehi, *The Arab Imago: A Social History of Portrait Photography, 1860–1910* (Princeton: Princeton University Press, 2016), 55.

context of post-World War I Jerusalem, the early years of British colonial rule and to the grand project of humanitarian aid and relief efforts during this period?

1   Establishing the Context: The American Colony in Jerusalem

The American Colony Christian Herald Orphanage in Jerusalem opened in 1918 and closed in 1922 or 1923. The Orphanage, as its name indicates, was operated by the American Colony in Jerusalem, in conjunction with the *Christian Herald* newspaper, which was in charge of the financial support and the contributions for the Orphanage.[6] The nature of cooperation between the New York-based newspaper, which used photographs in order to promote humanitarian aid projects around the world, and the American Colony in Jerusalem will be discussed below. In order to fully contextualise the activities and nature of the Orphanage, then, it is essential to first understand its host institution, the American Colony in Jerusalem.

Established in 1881 by a group of 17 Americans from Chicago and 2 British citizens, the American Colony was led by Horatio Gates Spafford and Anna T. Spafford. Driven by Evangelical Protestant motivations and explaining their pilgrimage from Chicago to the Holy Land in spiritual and messianic terms, the founding group was joined in 1896 by a group of 77 Swedes and Swedish-Americans and 28 Anglo-Americans, who were influenced by the ideas and charisma of Anna Spafford as the Colony's leader. By 1900 the Colony consisted of around 150 people, mostly Swedes and Americans, as well as others coming from Britain, Canada, Denmark, India and Lebanon, among other places.[7]

During its almost 70 years of existence, the American Colony was a prominent religious, creative, educational and commercial institution in Jerusalem. It developed business enterprises, ran philanthropic and humanitarian projects (the Christian Herald Orphanage being one of them) and developed a commercial photography department, a guest house and a store. It became

---

6   In her memoir, Bertha Spafford Vester, the daughter of the founders of the American Colony and one of its leading figures, mentions that it was Major Theodore Waters, the assistant editor of the *Christian Herald* and a major in the Red Cross, who first suggested that the newspaper would offer support for the work done by the American Colony in Jerusalem. Bertha Spafford Vester, *Our Jerusalem: An American Family in the Holy Land 1881–1949* (Jerusalem: Ariel Publishing House, 1992), 297.

7   Ruth Kark, "Post Civil War American Communes: A Millenarian Utopian Commune Linking Chicago and Nôs, Sweden to Jerusalem," *Communal Societies* 15 (1995): 75–114.

a meeting place and a centre for tourists, explorers, ethnographers, diplomats, political leaders, religious figures, artists and scholars.

Unlike the *Christian Herald* newspaper, which, as will be discussed below, held missionary aspirations and used the language of the mission as part of the act of contributing money to the Orphanage, the American Colony was not a missionary institution. As such, one way of understanding its activities and existence is to place it within the context of nineteenth-century American Evangelical Protestantism and American religious communes, which were often utopian and premillennialist in nature.[8] Within the context of American Studies, another perspective is that offered by Milette Shamir, who argues that the American Colony is an example of a wider cultural desire within American national discourse and analyses the connection between the 'motherly' character of the Colony, as manifested also in its charity work, and the Protestant American imaginary of the Holy Land.[9]

The American Colony was known for its matriarchal nature, under the dominant leadership of the founding 'mother' Anna Spafford and, later, her daughter Bertha Spafford Vester. Bertha, who became the leader of the Colony after the passing of Anna in 1923, was one of the second generation of Colony members who assumed leadership roles in the early 1900's.[10] Bertha was a prominent figure in running the Orphanage as well as the liaison between the donors and the Orphanage. She is featured in some of the photographs of the Orphanage, together with several teachers who were members of the Colony, mainly Ruth Whiting and Hulda Larsson Beaumont. Other members of the American Colony featured in the Orphanage's photographs were Ernest Forrest Beaumont, Hulda's husband, who was the Colony's dentist and a self-taught artist, draftsman, surveyor, city engineer and archaeologist.[11] In addition to Colony members, other teachers were employed at the Orphanage, such as a certain Milly Jacobs who appears several times in the Orphanage's records.

The charity work carried out by the Colony members is central for understanding its unique position in the city and the region as a whole, as well as in

---

8   Yaakov Ariel and Ruth Kark, "Messianism, Holiness, Charisma and Community: The American-Swedish Colony in Jerusalem, 1881–1933," *Church History* 65 (1996): 641–658.

9   Milette Shamir, "'Our Jerusalem': Americans in the Holy Land and Protestant Narratives of National Entitlement," *American Quarterly* 55, no. 1 (2003): 29–60.

10   For some of the main account of the American Colony see Helga Dudman and Ruth Kark, *The American Colony: Scenes from a Jerusalem Saga* (Jerusalem: Carta, 1998); Jane Fletcher Geniesse, *American Priestess: The Extraordinary Story of Anna Spafford and the American Colony in Jerusalem* (New York: Nan A. Talese, 2008); Odd Karsten Tveit, *Anna's House: A Story from Stavanger to Jerusalem* (Oslo: Cappelen, 2000).

11   Jack Green, "From Chicago to Jerusalem (and Back Again): The Untold Story of E.F. Beaumont," *The Oriental Institute News and Notes* 227 (2015): 15–19.

the context of the Orphanage. Different projects began in the Colony's early years and were especially important during the crisis of World War I and its aftermath. Aiming to extend support to women and children in need, the Colony established medical clinics, soup kitchens, schools and workshops to support girls and women, as well as a hospital. The Christian Herald Orphanage, then, was one aid project among several organised by the American Colony. These projects started during World War I, continued throughout the British Mandate in Palestine with one, the Spafford Children Centre, that continues to operate since 1925 to the present day. Most of these institutions served all those in need, regardless of ethnic and national background and, as mentioned above, had no missionary aspirations. The Christian Herald Orphanage, discussed here, is unique in this sense.

Another major enterprise carried out by the American Colony which is relevant for discussion of the Orphanage is the American Colony Photo Department (ACPD). The ACPD's photographers documented landscape, people and all major events of the time, creating one of the largest visual archives of Middle East history. Established in 1898, the ACPD operated until 1930 under the leadership of Swedish Lewis Larsson, together with Olof, Lars and Nils Lind, Jamil and Najib Albina, Eric and Edith Matson and John D. Whiting. As demonstrated also by Rachel Lev's contribution to this volume, the work of the Photo Department included thematic photographic albums, panoramic photographs, aerial photography, motion pictures, postcards, souvenirs, glass-lantern slides and travel albums. The photographers guided tourists, archaeologists, ethnographers, fellow photographers, scholars, pilgrims and explorers through Palestine and the region and served as interpreters of the region's history, culture, geography and current realities.[12] Even though there is no clear indication that the ACPD's photographers were responsible for the Orphanage's Photograph Album, the fact that the original negatives of this

---

12   On the work of the American Colony Photography Department see, for example: Barbara Bair, "The American Colony Photography Department: Western Consumption and "Insider" Commercial Photography," *Jerusalem Quarterly* 44 (2010): 28–38; Rachel Lev, "Visionaries and Creators: Members and Creative Ventures of the American Colony in Jerusalem, 1881–1948" (Exhibition Catalogue) (Jerusalem: American Colony Archive Collection, 2014); Dov Gavish, "The American Colony and its Photographers," in *Zev Vilnay's Jubilee Volume: Essays on the History, Archaeology, and Lore of the Holy Land, Presented to Zev Vilnay*, ed. Ely Schiller (Jerusalem: Ariel Publishing House, 1987) (in Hebrew). To use Michèle Hannoosh's suggestion, it is important to understand the ACPD's photographic experience, both within the local and regional context of the Levant. See Michèle Hannoosh, "Practices of Photography: Circulation and Mobility in the Nineteenth-Century Mediterranean," *History of Photography* 40: 1 (2016): 3–27.

Album are kept at the American Colony Archive Collection suggests that this is indeed the case. As such, this Album joins other visual records of the ACPD and should be analysed keeping this context in mind. It is this Album and the narrative that it entails to which we now turn.

2   Narrating the Orphanage: The Photograph Album

The black leather-bound Photograph Album featuring the Christian Herald Orphanage comprises 97 black-and-white photographic prints, of which 46 are individual portrait photographs of the Orphanage girls. Most of the photographs are titled in black ink handwriting below the photographs including the Orphanage girls' names below their individual portraits. The Orphanage Record Book is organised alphabetically and lists the girls with clippings of their portrait and biographical notes at the top of each entry.

The visual narration of the Album comprises three parts. The first, from pages 1 to 17, features high quality black-and-white and sepia photographs, presenting daily life in the Orphanage. Most of the first part consists of two photographs per page, organised one below the other. Pages 13 to 17 consist of between one and five photographs per page. The second part spans pages 18 to 23. It features individual portraits of the Orphanage girls. An assembly of 13 loose photographs (not pasted in) constitute the third part of the Album. These photographs were scanned by the Library of Congress and appear on their website as complementary visual narration of the first part, featuring mainly snapshots of events, picnics, trips, birthdays, play time and holidays where girls and staff are shown together. Captions of these photographs are handwritten in pencil on the back of the photograph. It may well be that the visual editing of the third part was completed after the Album was already arranged.

The Album narrates the Orphanage's daily life, including outdoor activities and trips, indoor activities, events and celebrations. They are mostly group photographs. The first page presents the location and the main actors, opening with two photographs, organised vertically: the top one is entitled 'Christian Herald Orphanage Conducted by the American Colony' showing the front façade of the Orphanage building. Below it is a photograph entitled 'Playground of the Orphanage', showing girls playing in front of the Orphanage building. In both pictures the building and playground are isolated from their surrounding environment, without any clear indication of their exact location (Fig. 2.2). The next page (page 2) displays two group photographs, one above the other: 'Sir Arthur [Chief Administrator in Palestine] and Lady Money during a visit

FIGURE 2.2 'Christian Herald Orphanage Conducted by the American Colony' and
'Playground of the Orphanage'. Part of the Christian Herald Orphanage
Photograph Album, 1.
IMAGES COURTESY OF THE AMERICAN COLONY ARCHIVE

FIGURE 2.3   'Sir Arthur and Lady Money during a visit to the Orphanage' and 'Untitled'. Part of
the Christian Herald Orphanage Photograph Album, 2.
IMAGE COURTESY OF THE AMERICAN COLONY ARCHIVE

to the Orphanage' is displayed at top and, at the bottom, a group photograph of the girls and their teachers from the American Colony in Jerusalem (among them Bertha Vester and Ruth Whiting are seen standing on the left next to the girls), in a beautiful garden at the entrance to the building. In the far distant upper middle right of the photograph one can see the Augusta Victoria Stiftung (Foundation) with its tower, located on the north-east side of Mount of Olives. (Fig. 2.3). Already, by examining these two first pages, one can capture two very different photographic languages: a snapshot of playful girls, running barefoot and swinging on the swing set, versus a well-staged scene in which the girls are well-dressed, all wearing white cottons dresses and facing the camera. These two photographic languages of the Album, the seemingly un-staged scenes versus the staged ones, will reappear in different sections throughout the Album, conveying both a joyful, free ambience as well as a disciplined one. Both of them portray a rather distanced, not personal, image of the girls.[13]

As we continue turning the pages of the Album, we uncover parts of the daily routine of the girls. For example, photographs on page 4 consist of interior scenes of classrooms, the top one (captioned, 'One of the classes. Milly Jacob teacher') showing girls sitting in front of writing desks and a small bell placed on the teacher's desk. The lower photograph is titled 'Kindergarten', where ten girls are sitting around a large wooden table, with a convertible blackboard at the background with the letters A and O written on it, suggesting that the girls are learning the alphabet (Fig. 2.4). The photograph on page 5, captioned 'Recess', features another scene from the school-life of the Orphanage: the girls are sitting barefoot on the floor, facing the camera, seemingly playing, some holding dolls and toys. Photographs on page 6, 'Sewing Class with Ruth Whiting as the teacher' (top image) and another where the girls are 'Learning how to mend and Darn', (bottom image) take place outdoors; later we witness a gardening lesson in a blooming garden, where the girls seem very busy and happy.

The girls are also documented on laundry day and are seen hanging the laundry in front of the building. A cooking class is then featured, followed by three pictures of them in the dining room. What is interesting about the meal pictures is the way the table is set: each girl has a plate and cup, maybe with a spoon, with a glass of water. In the middle of the tables stand small vases with flowers, possibly wild flowers picked in the garden or on one of the excursions (which are featured later in the Album). The last photograph of this series – 'daily routine' – shows the girls washing the dishes.[14] Some of these images are

---

13   Photograph Album, 1–2.
14   Photograph Album, 3–12.

FIGURE 2.4   'One of the Classes' and 'Kindergarten'. Part of the Christian Herald Orphanage
Photograph Album, 4.
IMAGE COURTESY OF THE AMERICAN COLONY ARCHIVE

similar to those mentioned by Okkenhaug in her paper on the Swedish School in Jerusalem. As can be seen, both institutions highlighted the domestic training of the girls and their outdoors activities in their photographs as part of their fundraising efforts.

This part seems to take the viewer of the Album through the very daily routine and the main components of the education that is provided by the Orphanage, namely both in-class learning and more practical training aspect of the girls' education: cooking, sewing and darning. This fits nicely into the discourse of scientific domesticity that dominated women's education during the early twentieth century, which viewed women's role as primarily located in the domestic sphere. The tasks that the girls learn also had moral dimensions to them. Laundry, for example, may have reflected the spiritual, as well as physical virtue of cleanliness.[15]

The photographs in the third part of the Album feature mostly outdoor activities, such as excursions taking place in 1920–1921, mainly to Ein Karem (and a few to Hebron), where we see the girls play, swing and enjoy picnics. Interestingly, there are no photographs of the girls traveling to any of the religious sites, which are located very close geographically to the Orphanage. Judging from the images, the excursions were only for the purpose of fun and play. Other photographs of this section show the girls playing with snowballs in front of the Orphanage building in the winter of 1920. One of the interesting photographs in this part shows three horse-wagons on their way to 'Ain Karim,' (Ein Karem). The first wagon covers most of the photographic space, thus constituting the central image: it is packed with some 30 cheerful girls looking at the camera. The second wagon appears to be the teachers' carriage and the third is outside the photographic frame. The girls on the wagon seem playful and excited and the two horsemen seem pleased as well. It seems that

---

15   See Beth Baron, *The Women's Awakening in Egypt: Culture, Society, and the Press* (New Haven: Yale University Press, 1994), 155–158; Ela Greenberg, *Preparing the Mothers of Tomorrow: Education and Islam in Mandate Palestine* (Austin: University of Texas Press, 2010), mainly 134–167; Omnia Shakry, "Schooling Mothers and Structured Play: Child Rearing in Turn-of-the-Century Egypt," in *Remaking Women: Feminism and Modernity in the Middle East*, ed. Lila Abu-Lughod (Cairo: AUC Press, 1998), 126–170. On girls' education and domesticity within the context of Quaker missionary education in Palestine see Enaya Hammad Othman, *Negotiating Palestinian Womanhood: Encounters between Palestinian Women and American Missionaries, 1880s–1940's* (Lanham: Lexington Books, 2016). On the symbolism of girls' domestic tasks in a different context see Linda Mahood and Barbara Littlewood, "The "Vicious" Girl and the "Street-Corner" Boy: Sexuality and the Gendered Delinquent in the Scottish Child-Saving Movement, 1850–1940," *Journal of the History of Sexuality* 4:4 (1994): 560–564.

one of the girls is holding the horse whip (Fig. 2.5).[16] This image alludes to the social connections and hierarchy between the girls and their teachers. The excursions and outdoor play were important in perceptions of hygiene and schooling – claiming that children (and adults) needed sunlight, fresh air and movement in order for them to become healthy and strong, and to overcome the poor physical condition of many children, especially underscored in the context of the Orphanage.[17]

The Album also features various celebrations held at the Orphanage. There are two identical photographs taken during Christmas 1919, on page 3 and towards the end of the Album on page 32. The latter's quality is much better as the photograph is very sharp.[18] The picture shows the girls, dressed nicely and wearing shoes (some other pictures show many of them barefoot), one of them, possibly a Muslim girl, with a headscarf, with their teachers (Ruth Whiting being one of them) and possibly again General Arthur Money at the back, standing in front of a large, well-decorated Christmas Tree. The photograph is taken in a well-decorated room with large curtains. One of the striking features of this photograph is the fact that each of the girls is holding what seems to be a Christmas present: mostly, they hold dolls, though the one standing in the middle of the front row, who looks like a boy and wears trousers, is holding a wooden carriage. Other than one of the girls, who is smiling and seems to be leaning towards one of the teachers, all the girls and teachers seem to be very serious (Fig. 2.6).[19] With the presents and the tree, this photograph alludes to a family-like Christmas atmosphere, which may send a message to the donors abroad, hinting at the way the girls are treated in the Orphanage. Other celebrations that we see in the Album are a birthday party held outdoors, with a table again decorated with flowers[20] and another lunch party which is described as 'Easter lunch for Mohammadan girls'.[21] Both the Christmas and Easter photographs are odd, considering the fact that many of the girls in

---

16   Photograph Album, 28.
17   On the connection between hygiene, physical education and nationalism in the process
      of Muslim girls' education in mandatory Palestine see Greenberg, *Preparing the Mothers*,
      138–150. On hygiene education and the process of nation-building within the Jewish com-
      munity see Dafna Hirsch, *Banu Lekan Lehavi et haMa'arav: Hanchalat Higiena uBniyat
      Tarbut Bahevra Hayehudit Bitkufat Hamnadat* (Sede Boqer: The Ben Gurion Research
      Institute, 2014) (in Hebrew). On domestic management and its influence on men and
      women in Mandatory Palestine see Sherene Seikaly, *Men of Capital: Scarcity and Economy
      in Mandate Palestine* (Stanford: Stanford University Press, 2016), mainly 53–76.
18   Photograph Album, 3, 32.
19   Photograph Album, 32.
20   Photograph Album, 40.
21   Photograph Album, 48–49.

FIGURE 2.5 'Untitled'. Part of the Christian Herald Orphanage Photograph Album, 28.
IMAGE COURTESY OF THE AMERICAN COLONY ARCHIVE

FIGURE 2.6 'Christmas 1918, C.H. Orphanage'. Part of the Christian Herald Orphanage
Photograph Album, 32.
IMAGE COURTESY OF THE AMERICAN COLONY ARCHIVE

the Orphanage were Muslim. This raises some questions regarding what may be the missionary agenda of the Orphanage and the possible connection between the project of proselytisation and humanitarian aid, as will be discussed below.

Another set of interesting photographs appear on page 11 and 50 of the Album. The photographs show a commencement ceremony in an outdoor setting (as the caption of one of them indicates), where guests are seen seated under a large tent which is partly made of an American flag. In the lower photograph a British flag is seen on the right-hand side.[22] The girls perform drills in front of the audience, facing the camera and then lining up (the caption reads: 'Drill'). The photograph on page 50, taken from the upper floor of an adjacent building, shows the girls dancing in circles, probably as part of a performance to the audience.

The audience is composed of well-dressed men and women, sitting on chairs, one of the men patting a small dog next to him.[23] The photographs may have been taken during one of the 4th of July celebrations, hence the American flag that serves as a cover from the sun. (Fig. 2.7) These are the only album pages displaying national symbols. The girls are obviously there to entertain the guests, who may be dignitaries and officials from the British administration, representatives of the American consulate, as well as guests of the American Colony and the sponsoring *Christian Herald* newspaper. The physical setting of this ceremony, and the clothing of the men and women, is similar to a typical colonial photograph, embodying in it the power relations and hierarchies of colonial society. Here, as in many of the other photographs discussed, the role of the photograph in representing social dynamics, social relations and possibly an ideological act, is clear. It also hints at the central role of the American Colony in the city, and possibly to the position of the US during the early years of British colonial role in Palestine.[24]

Throughout the Album we hardly see any men in the photographs. Most of the images feature the girls and their teachers. The men who appear are either officers or officials with few exceptions, one of which is Mr Ernest Forrest Beaumont, the Colony and Orphanage dentist and possibly one of

---

22 Photograph Album, 11.
23 Photograph Album, 50.
24 Sheehi, *The Arab Imago*, xxviii. In this context it is worth mentioning the stormy relations between the Colony and the American Consulate in Jerusalem, especially in the late nineteenth century during the terms of two consuls, Selah Merrill and Edwin Wallace, due to their suspicion of the Colony's messianic beliefs and communal nature. See more on this in Ariel and Kark, "Messianism, Holiness, Charisma and Community: The American-Swedish Colony in Jerusalem, 1881–1933", 653–654.

FIGURE 2.7 *Untitled.* Part of the Christian Herald Orphanage Photograph Album, 50.
IMAGE COURTESY OF THE AMERICAN COLONY ARCHIVE

the administrators, who is seen in several photographs, including one taken in his dentistry office (Fig. 2.8). The dentistry image may allude to the importance placed in the Orphanage on the girls' health and hygiene. It also raises the question of whether oral hygiene may have been a privilege during these years. Another exception is a man seen in some of the photographs, who may be the Orphanage's butler. The Album is hence a clear representation of gender dynamics and reflects the hierarchical colonial division, in which the men featured are in a position of power and authority over the girls. The feminine role is either that of the care-givers (teachers) or the indigenous girls in need of care and support. The central place of women in the Album also goes very much in line with the female-dominated atmosphere of the American Colony and the strong role that the Colony women played within it.

The photographers of the Album are unidentified. However, the original negatives of the Album are held at the American Colony Archive Collection, which suggests that the ACPD produced this Album as well. Exploring the negatives, one can learn about the production process of the Album, as well as the selection of the photographs included in it. The negatives show that some of the photographs were not included in the Album at all. In other cases, photographs were included in part or with some editing work done to them. Such is the case of the Christmas photograph, discussed above (Fig. 2.6). Comparing

FIGURE 2.8 Upper photograph: 'Dentistry'. Part of the Christian Herald Orphanage
Photograph Album, 12. Ernest Forrest Beaumont's wife, Hulda Larsson Beaumont,
was one of the Orphanage teachers. See: Green, 'From Chicago to Jerusalem.'
IMAGE COURTESY OF THE AMERICAN COLONY ARCHIVE

this photograph to its negative one can clearly see that the two are different. On the left-hand side of the negative there is a blurry image of a girl and a woman, both unidentified, who were not included in the photograph that appeared in the Album. Instead of them, the photograph's corner is folded. (Fig. 2.9) One can only speculate why the original image was edited before included in the final Album, due to the poorer quality of the negative.

The Orphanage Album, then, captures the daily life and routine of the girls, as well as exposes us to their indoor and outdoor activities. The Album was not supposed to be sold or circulated. Its sole purpose was to present the Orphanage to the donors and to highlight its main activities and features in order to raise funds. In this, it is similar to the function of photographs that is discussed in Okkenhaug's article, regarding the Swedish School. The selection of photographs and the high-quality of print suggests that much work and talent was also put into the photography, the production and the organisation of the Album.

The main actors in the narrative presented in the Album are the girls, whose portraits appear on pages 18–23.[25] Unlike the small face portraits that are featured in the Record Book album, these photographs show almost a full body image of each girl, in more or less the alphabetical order featured in the Orphanage Record Book. The names of each of the girls are handwritten in black ink under the photographs. The girls are all facing the camera, with serious expressions, and are all wearing more or less the same cotton dress. Most of the portraits were probably taken in a studio, with a dark background; only a few were taken outside. The girls' names are the only indicators to their ethno-religious identity as Muslims and Christians. Not only are they disconnected from the scenery presented in the rest of the Album, they are also dislocated from space and represent a neutral identity.[26] The story of the girls, though, is revealed when looking at the next record available, to which we now turn.

25   Photograph Album, 18–23.

26   Wendy M.K. Shaw, "The Ottoman in Ottoman Photography: Producing Identity through its Negation," in *The Indigenous Lens? Early Photography in the Near and Middle East*, eds. Markus Ritter and Staci G. Scheiwiller (Berlin: De Gruyter, 2018), 189.

FIGURE 2.9 *Christmas at the Christian Herald Orphanage*, 1918. Part of 'Members and Activities of the American Colony and Aid Projects', Negative Collection, series 24_13, American Colony Archive, Jerusalem. (Hereafter: Negative Collection).
IMAGE COURTESY OF THE AMERICAN COLONY ARCHIVE

3   Orphans and Patrons: The Christian Herald Orphanage Record Book

The black leather-bound 55-page sequential Record Book is entitled: *Christian Herald Orphanage, conducted by the American Colony, List of Children*.[27] Reading through the Record Book it is clear that this is much more than simply a list of girls hosted at the Orphanage, but rather more of a social profile of the girls and their donors, a record of correspondence regarding the money donated to the Orphanage. The pages of the Book feature the name of each girl and a small clipping of a facial portrait, alongside a clipping consisting of a short explanation of the girl's background and her donor's name and address, followed by a handwritten record of the money donated on her behalf from

---

27   The Record Book was originally organized alphabetically, with the alphabetical letters replaced with handwritten numbers. These numbers may indicate the order of the girls' attendance at the Orphanage.

her 'patron' to the Orphanage. A newspaper clipping on the first page of the
Record Book, entitled 'Little Orphans of Jerusalem: A Wonderful Opportunity
of Service is Offered', explains the rationale of the Album and its purpose:

> The Christian Herald today presents to its readers an opportunity for
> service that will gladden many hearts. In past years, they have been the
> special patrons of thousands of children in India and China, of hun-
> dreds in Japan and of a number in Africa ... Now, the way is open to
> them to become the godfathers and godmothers of little orphan waifs in
> Jerusalem, the land which of all the world holds the most sacred mem-
> ories of childhood. There are some thirty-six of these little folks in the
> Christian Herald Orphanage in Jerusalem – all girls – in whose behalf we
> appeal to your love and sympathy. [...]
>
> Here is an opportunity for Sunday School classes, Epworth Leagues,
> Christian Endeavour Branches, Baptist Young People's organizations,
> Ladies' Aid Societies and kindred bodies to take up the support of a
> Palestine orphan. Their little protégé will be trained and taught to write
> to her benefactors at regular intervals, and the latter will thus be put in
> personal communication with the children of their adoption. Individual
> members, too, will be welcomed as patrons. There could be no nicer
> opportunity for getting into personal touch with a little Jerusalem child
> and influencing her whole future life. [...]
>
> This is a kind of missionary work that lies closer to the heart than any
> other, because it links the patron to the protégé in a union that grown
> more and more interesting every year. The cost of support, which includes
> shelter, clothing, tuition and food, is estimated at $130.00 a year – equal
> to $2.50 a week, or almost 35 cents a day. This, in view of the importance
> of the work and the great results to be attained, is a very modest figure
> and one which cannot be considered burdensome. [...][28]

The Record Book, then, compliments the Album, discussed above, and also
may shed some light on its purpose. Unlike the Album, the Record Book does
not include photographs, other than those small portrait clippings which were
cut out of the full-body photographs. Each page is divided into two columns,
a left one entitled 'received' and a right one entitled 'sent'. The left column
lists the exact dates in which contributions were sent to the girls (referred
to as 'protégé'), and the right one indicates what the girls sent to the donor

---

28   "Little Orphans of Jerusalem: A Wonderful Opportunity of Service is Offered," Record
      Book, 1. The original article appeared at *The Christian Herald,* January 29, 1921.

(referred to as 'patron'). It seems that the correspondence with the donors was made on behalf of the girls, possibly by Bertha Vester herself. Hence, there was no direct link between the girls and the donors. The audience of the Album and the Record Book seems to be the same: the donors among the readers of the *Christian Herald* newspaper, and possibly also among the supporters of the American Colony. Both can be seen as part of the effort to show 'where the money goes to'.

In his analysis of Ottoman portrait photography, Stephen Sheehi discusses the question of repetition of certain patterns within the portraits he investigates, which represent and enact the ideals of Ottoman modernity.[29] In the case of the Record Book, the pages all contain the same elements, create some repetition and a sense that all the girls are similar to each other. The organisation of the Record Book gives a sense of a catalogue of the girls and does not provide any agency to the girls themselves. It overshadows their identities, the stories of their parents, families and background. The short, and usually tragic, life-story of the girls is revealed only when looking more carefully at the newspaper clipping attached to the girls' images.[30]

This feeling of a catalogue is enhanced when reading the original article from which this piece is taken, published in *The Christian Herald* newspaper on 29th January, 1921. This two-page article presents the stories of all the girls living in the Orphanage. Around the article itself are all the portraits of the girls, with their consecutive numbers, for easy recognition (Fig. 2.10).[31] Two years earlier, on 14th June, 1919, a similar article with children's photographs entitled 'Hear these fifteen little pleaders' appeared in the newspaper, this time referring to an orphanage in China. This display of children in need, then, was not unique only to the Jerusalem Orphanage, but was the way the *Christian Herald* was trying to convince its readers to contribute to charity institutions and welfare projects around the world.[32]

Who, then, are the girls who found refuge in the *Christian Herald Orphanage*? From the short profiles of the girls one can learn something about the traumas and effects of the Great War on them and their families. The girls are of Greek Orthodox, Protestant and Muslim backgrounds. Before joining the Orphanage, they mostly lived in Jerusalem, but some also came originally from Mesopotamia, Hebron, the mountains of Ajloun and Greece. This hints at the population movement of the post-war period. One or both of their parents

---

29   Sheehi, *The Arab Imago*, 14–20.
30   The girls' destiny after the orphanage was closed (between 1922–1923) remains unknown.
31   *The Christian Herald*, January 29, 1921.
32   Ibid., June 14, 1919.

FIGURE 2.10   *Little Orphans of Jerusalem*, 1921. *The Christian Herald,*
29th January, 1921

f Jerusalem

Service Is Offered

Scars

By MARGARET E. SANGSTER

either died or were injured during the war. Some died due to diseases, such as typhus and tuberculosis, some during their work in the labour battalions and one died of snake bite. The father of Fareedy Elias (no. 4), George, for example, deserted his family and travelled to South America, leaving her mother behind to support their two children. Some of the girls were first adopted by relatives or other families, who were usually unable to continue taking care of them and hence sent them to the Orphanage. The girls did not seem to have any pre-existing links with the American Colony.

Some girls, such as Asma Wahabie (no. 36, p. 44), suffer from trachoma, malnutrition or are handicapped. Asma Najla Aish, age 6, for example, is described as partly crippled, and also was 'threatened by tuberculosis, but shows no signs of it now'.[33] In some cases, we can learn about the tragic journeys of some of the girls before they reached the Orphanage. Marie Elias (no. 20), for example, is described as the eight year old daughter of a school teacher of the church missionary society in Gaza, who was forced to leave with his family to al-Salt due to the Ottomans' suspicion that he worked with the British. After the British occupation, and following the mother's death, the father returned to Jerusalem with his daughters, but was unable to support them. His three daughters, described as 'bright, nice girls', are held at the Orphanage. Nellie Elias, one of the sisters (no. 22), has her patron's photograph next to hers (p. 29).

The Orphanage's contribution to the lives of the girls is clear. In some cases, the girls were rescued from 'going to the wrong' or from hunger. In others, the American Colony played a different role. Such was the case of Guldusta Bada, age 10, who, as written next to her portrait, 'is pretty and was asked for in-marriage. The American Colony prevented this and will insist on retaining her until she is of marriageable age'.[34] These descriptions are indicative of the value system of the American Colony and the Orphanage it managed, of the way the Colony perceived its mission, as well as that of the newspaper readership. This language and spirit of protection also go hand in hand with notions from a different context, that of late Victorian England and the Child Protection Movement. The mission of the 'children savers', as they were called, were both to remove children at risk from their families and, at the same time, to protect society at large from their potentially bad influence. In relation to girls, the mission was to protect the girls from being corrupted

---

33   Asma Najla Aish, Record Book, 8 no. 6.
34   Guldusta Bada, Record Book, 15 no. 12.

and turning into prostitutes, and at the same time to protect the society from corruption and disease.[35]

What can we learn about the relations between the donors and the girls? The girls' voice is not heard in this narrative. It seems that there was no direct correspondence between the girls and their donors, as all correspondence went through the American Colony and the Orphanage. From the right-hand ('sent') column of the girls' pages we learn about the thank-you letters that were sent on behalf of the girls to her respective patron, including a postcard for Christmas that was sent by all girls on 8th December, 1921. Sometimes pictures of the girls were sent to the donors as well. We also learn that at the end of December 1922 many of the donors received a letter indicating that the Orphanage was about to close (even though correspondence documented in the Record Book continued in some cases into 1923). There are some cases in which donors sent not only money, however. Mrs J. Edward Davis from Maryland, who supported the 9 year old Evelina Izrak, reported in 1923 about a financial crisis she went through, but wrote that despite her difficulties, she crocheted a luncheon set and sold it for $23, and sent the money to the Orphanage.[36] In February 1922, Mrs Cramer from Warren, Pennsylvania, sent a gold brooch to Naheel Katooha, 8 years old. A year later the Orphanage contacted Mrs Cramer and suggested that she send funds to the Orphanage, not only to the girl she was supporting.[37] It seems that at least some of the donors were involved in the girls' lives and upbringing, possibly after the closing of the Orphanage. In a letter sent to Bertha Vester, attached to the Record Book and dated February 1927, one of the donors enquires about the girl she was in touch with, hoping that she will continue developing and go on to train at nursing school as she desired.[38] The period at the Orphanage and the American Colony, then, may have served as a point of departure for some girls' future development.[39]

The Record Book teaches us not only about the girls, but also about their 'patrons', the donors who supported them. Who are the donors, and, more importantly, what is the connection between the *Christian Herald* newspaper and the Jerusalem-based Orphanage?

---

35   See on this, for example: Barbara Littlewood and Linda Mahood, "Prostitutes, Magdalenes and Wayward Girls: Dangerous Sexualities of Working-Class Women in Victorian Scotland," *Gender & History* 3, no. 2 (1991): 166; Mahood, "The "Vicious" Girl," 549–578.

36   Evelina Izrak, Record Book, 3 no. 1.

37   Naheel Katooha, Record Book, 18 no. 13.

38   Letter from Ellis Jones to Bertha Vester, Feb. 22, 1927, Record Book, 22–24.

39   Unfortunately, I was unable to track any of the girls after they left the Orphanage. Any suggestion about their future is therefore only a speculation.

4   Pictorial Humanitarianism: *The Christian Herald* Newspaper and
         the American Colony

The *Christian Herald* was a New York-based weekly magazine, a pioneer of
pictorial journalism, which used photographic technologies in order to pub-
licise humanitarian crisis in the United States and around the world. Louis
Klopsch, who served as its editor from 1890 until his death in 1910, convinced
the newspaper's readers to open their hearts, hands, and purses, in order to
feed the hungry, send or carry aid to the sick and to spread the Gospel message everywhere.[40] The newspaper became the most widely-read religious
newspaper in the world. As a channel for relief and charity campaigns it was
responsible for raising millions of dollars to aid people suffering around the
world.[41] Unlike some of the well-known charitable foundations, such as the
Rockefeller Foundation, the *Christian Herald* newspaper represented a grassroots effort to practice American evangelical ideals and translate them into
the practice of humanitarian work, using the tools of the popular religious
media.[42] By the turn of the century, the *Christian Herald* had almost a quarter
million subscribers, with its readers coming from all around the United States,
as well as from other countries.[43] Using the language and ideas of evangelical
benevolence, the *Christian Herald* was engaged in hundreds of campaigns to
collect donations for various humanitarian causes, stretching geographically
from Mexico to China and from Turkey to Russia. By 1910, the newspapers'
subscribers had donated more than $3.3 million for domestic and interna-
tional crises.[44]

    The connection between the newspaper and the Orphanage in Jerusalem
was made through the American Colony. The *Christian Herald* had published several articles about the American Colony, in which the newspaper's
enthusiasm about the Christian organisation within the grim realities of
Jerusalem in particular, and the Levant in general, was very clear. In an article
accompanied by photographs, published in the newspaper on February 1919,
the writer Wilbur Williams describes his visit and stay at the American Colony,
writing that:

---

40   Heather D. Curtis, *Holy Humanitarianism: American Evangelicals and Global Aid*
      (Cambridge: Harvard University Press, 2018), 2. The *Christian Herald* was founded origi-
      nally in Britain in 1876 by Reverend Michael Baxter, and purchased in 1890 by Thomas De
      Witt Talmage and Louis Klopsch. Ibid., 7–8.
41   Ibid., 3.
42   Ibid., 5.
43   Ibid., 9.
44   Ibid., 11.

By this time we were exceedingly interested in the history of the American Colony, and marvelled at the sturdy sinews of Christian fortitude which can endure persecutions patiently and meekly and free of hatred, when nurtured by sustaining faith.[45]

Later that year, on 19th April, 1919, the connection between the newspaper and the American Colony was demonstrated more clearly, through Bertha Vester's letter addressing the readers of the *Christian Herald*:

> Can I describe to you the thrill of joy when I read that the generous readers of the Christian Herald were going to continue their beneficent assistance and keep our poor orphans in the Home they have learned to love? Nay, it is more than this; they will, by their Christmas gift, allow us to take more children into the Orphanage, who are pressing us to admit them into "God's House," as they call it. [...] It is with heartfelt gratitude that the American Colony sends these lines to the readers of the Christian Herald, for their generous contributions contained in the Christmas Chest, which will enable us to continue this very successful and necessary work of mothering these motherless, suffering little ones in the land of the Child Jesus.[46]

Many of the children in the Orphanage were Muslims, continued Vester, who were exposed to the Christian ceremonies and atmosphere. According to her, 'the Mohammedans do not object to a change of religion if it is not a change of the 'outer garment' for gain; that they hate'. And indeed, the religious element is clearly addressed in Vester's letter, when she discusses the questions raised by the children at the Orphanage:

> The new surroundings have brought the children new ideas. "Whence all this bounty? Who made the kind friends in America think of the poor little miserable, unattractive, dirty looking children in Jerusalem? Then we tell them of the Child who lived here and who gave his life to save us, and for his sake we remember to be kind to our less fortunate brothers and sisters, for he said that to "love our neighbor as ourselves fulfilled all the law and the prophets". Then they wished to pray and thank this

---

45   "The American Colony at Jerusalem," *The Christian Herald*, February 22, 1919, 210–212.
46   "Christian Herald Orphanage in the Holy Land," *The Christian Herald*, April 19, 1919, 450–451.

new Friend for all they had received. They did not forget their friends in America; they always ask me to send their love and gratitude to them.[47]

On 27th December, 1919, Vester writes again in the newspaper with more news from the Orphanage. This time she updates that with the acceptance of General Arthur Money, the Chief Administrator of the southern district of British military rule (OETA-South), the name of the Orphanage would change to 'The Christian Herald Orphanage in the Holy Land, under the auspices of The American Colony'. But then, as she continues writing, a potential problem arose:

> During his [General Money's] visit at the orphanage, 1 asked him further about the name, and he at that time gave us permission to use the name 'Christian Herald Orphanage' provided the children were all Christian. At present we have about half Mohammedan and half Christian children with us. General Money said there could be no objection brought if Mohammedans chose to bring their children to the Christian Herald Orphanage. They would have to take the consequences. This statement will prove to you, as it did to us, a great relief.[48]

The importance given to the religious aspect is clear, then, as well as the embedded missionary element and the possibility of proselytisation of the girls. This may be why the girls, including the Muslim ones, participated in the Christmas celebration and Easter lunch, and why the Album featured those events as part of its activities. This did not go hand in hand with the mission of the American Colony, but Vester, who clearly needed the money (when the check of $3000 arrived, the Orphanage had $25 left in the account, she said) and the support for the institution, was willing to compromise on this issue. The concern about the influence of the mission on the Orphanage may also explain the absence of any Jewish girls from the Orphanage, despite the fact that they too were among the victims of the war and needed support as well.[49]

---

47   Curtis, *Holy Humanitarianism*, 11.

48   "The Orphans of the Holy Land," *The Christian Herald*, December 27, 1919, 1335.

49   The number of Jewish orphans in Palestine, and mainly in Jerusalem, as a result of the war is estimated at around 4500. There were, however, several orphanages that had already operated within the Jewish community since the late nineteenth century and the early twentieth century, including the Diskin Orphanage, the Weingarten Orphanage, the Sephardi orphanage and others. The Joint Distribution Committee operated the "Orphanage Committee to the Land of Israel," which operated between 1919 to 1927 in Jerusalem and other cities and was in charge of supporting Jewish orphans in particular.

Charity was viewed as a mission uniting the believers.[50] Like other human-itarian projects and welfare efforts, in the United States and beyond, the newspaper used evangelical ideas, mixed with political projects and social agendas, in order to promote what was seen as cosmopolitan charity among the believers.[51] The main motivation was the belief that the US had an obli-gation to support, and possibly educate, distant strangers as well as American citizens. The unique mechanism for this vast grassroots welfare and charitable project was what Heather D. Curtis calls Pictorial Humanitarianism, the power and influence offered by the illustrative magazine.[52] Like other philanthropic projects carried out by the United States at the turn of the century, though, this project too was not benign or devoid of political interests and demonstration of power. In the words of Ian Tyrrell, 'giving was genuine, but never simple'.[53] What, then, is the connection between humanitarianism and photography, as played out in the case of the Orphanage?

5   Humanitarianism, Philanthropy and the Image

Discussing the history and development of modern humanitarianism in the Middle East, Keith Watenpaugh argues that the centre of humanitarianism is the project of *unstrangering* the object of humanitarianism. This process of unstrangering is derived not only from empathy towards the victim, but from the attempt to close the distance between the humanitarian subject ('patron') and the humanitarian object ('protégé').[54] In fact, as Denis Kennedy argues, there is an integral relationship between humanitarian relief and imagery.

See Ella Ayalon, "Mevakrot Yetomin Beyerushalayim," *Zmanim* 124 (2014): 72–83. In rela-tion to photography and the concern about conversion, one may also remember the earlier conversion of Mendel John Diness, a Jew who converted to Christianity in 1849, and is considered by some to be the first professional photographer in Jerusalem. See Dror Wahrman, "Mendel Diness – Hazalam Hayerushalmi Hamikzo'i Harishon?" *Cathedra* 38 (1985): 104–120. Diness' conversion caused a major outcry within the Jewish community in mid-nineteenth century Jerusalem.

50   Curtis, *Holy Humanitarianism*, 47–49.

51   Ibid., 58, 64.

52   Ibid., 283–287.

53   Ian Tyrrell, *Reforming the World: The Creation of America's Moral Empire* (Princeton: Princeton University Press, 2010), 98. In his book Tyrrell discusses the creation of what he calls "America's Moral Empire", and examines the relationship between Protestant reformers' aspiration to create a more Christian and moral world, and the rise of American imperialism and colonialism.

54   Keith David Watenpaugh, *Bread from Stones: The Middle East and the Making of Modern Humanitarianism* (Oakland: University of California Press, 2015), 19, 34.

Because people are less likely to help distant strangers, the challenge facing humanitarian agencies, until today, is to bridge the distance between the victim and donor and attract support. This is done by the use of images and technology.[55] Hence, as Kennedy argues, selling pain and suffering is in fact central to humanitarian fundraising. This close connection brings with it a set of ethical dilemmas, such as the dignity of the victim, and the way that the victims in fact become depersonalised and abstract.[56]

In this regard, the act of unstrangering operates in a way that is parallel to the process of 'biblification'. That is to say, a process of making legible that which is distant and removed from the immediacy of the photographic viewer. Biblified images presented Jerusalem in particular as an empty space, highlighted the presence of Jewish and Christian minorities who needed protection, treated the city as an iconic image and ignored the realities of the living city. Biblification, then, was another mean of discovering the (imagined) country and bringing it closer to the western audience.[57] In the case discussed in this article, though, it is not biblical images that are presented, but images of a philanthropic enterprise.

Photography played an integral part in the extension of American philanthropy abroad from the end of the nineteenth century, argues Curtis. This practice, also termed 'humanitarian photography', served to mobilise photography in the service of humanitarian initiatives across state boundaries.[58] The invention of the portable Kodak camera in 1888 enabled missionaries, aid workers, journalists and tourists to document humanitarian crises in remote places and publish the photographs in different venues, including popular periodicals.[59] The photographs were supposed to arouse sympathy for suffering strangers and to encourage compassion among the readers, which would later translate into financial assistance, as in the case of the Orphanage. This use of images, though, was often used for commercial purposes and for the

55   Denis Kennedy, "Selling the Distant Other: Humanitarianism and Imagery-Ethical Dilemmas of Humanitarian Action," *The Journal of Humanitarian Assistance* (2009), accessed July 16, 2019, available online at: http://sites.tufts.edu/jha/archives411.

56   Ibid., 7.

57   Issam Nassar, "'Biblification' in the Service of Colonialism: Jerusalem in Nineteenth Century Photography," *Third Text* 20, nos 3/4: 317–326.

58   On Humanitarian Photography see Heide Fehrenbach and Davide Rodogno, "The Morality of Sight: Humanitarian Photography in History," in *Humanitarian Photography: a History*, eds. Heide Fehrenbach and Davide Rodogno (Cambridge: Cambridge University Press, 2015), 1–4.

59   Heather D. Curtis, "Depicting distant suffering: Evangelicals and the politics of pictorial humanitarianism in the age of American empire," *Material Religion* 8, no. 2 (2015): 157–158.

creation of calls for humanitarian appeals which were based on 'spectacles of suffering'.[60]

The case of the Christian Herald Orphanage serves as a demonstration of the process that Watenpaugh, Curtis, Fehrenbach, Rodogno and Kennedy describe, but offers a 'twist'. The photographs that are presented in both records, mediated by the *Christian Herald* newspaper, bring the girls closer to the hearts and minds of the newspaper's readership and create the hierarchy and relationship of a patron/protégé. They allow the donors to feel closer to the girl they support, to personalise her and to follow her development and growth by actually becoming her godparent. It is through the image, presented in the Photograph Album, and the ongoing communication with the girls, as documented in the Record Book, that the physical, as well as psychological, distance between Jerusalem and the United States is bridged. But it is also through the image that the girls are made less abstract and more personalised.

The relationship between the donor and the girl, reflected in the photographs and the newspaper, may also shed light on some of the motivations behind the act of charity and benevolence. What seems to be the religious agenda of the donors, as discussed above, is most probably not the only motivation for supporting the orphans. As Beth Baron, Keith Watenpaugh and Nazan Maksudyan, among others, show, the act and discourse of welfare is not benign or free of political agendas and motivations. Patrons, or sponsors, hope to enhance their social capital through supporting the needy and the orphans serve, in certain cases, as a fresh ground for a proselytising and modernising effort. Hence, the donors' motivations may be driven by social, religious, political and sometimes even economic motivations, and not only by a pure desire to save the children.[61]

The case of the *Christian Herald Orphanage*, then, demonstrates the close connection between the humanitarian project and the image, in the context of post-World War I Jerusalem. Regarding the question of context and location, the photographs play a double role here. On the one hand, they aim at bringing the orphans closer to the donors, by personalising them. On the other hand, they present what Shaw portrays as an 'identity dislocated from space' or context, as the girls' images are not positioned in any particular 'classical' Jerusalem scene, have no ethnic or national features and hence

---

60   Ibid., 159–160; Fehrenbach, "The Morality of Sight," 4.

61   See more on this in Beth Baron, "Orphans and Abandoned Children in Modern Egypt," in *Interpreting Welfare and Relief in the Middle East*, eds. Nefissa Naguib and Inger Marie Okkenhaug (Leiden: Brill, 2008), 33–34; Nazan Maksudyan, *Orphans and Destitute Children in the Late Ottoman Empire* (Syracuse: Syracuse University Press, 2014), 10–11, 116.

their photographs, as well as their portraits, are not easily identified as being located in Jerusalem.[62] In fact, with the dresses and their haircuts, the girls do not hold local markers at all and can be mistaken for girls living in any other place, for that matter. The images of the girls, then, are mediated through the photographs, to create a sense of a local-stranger for the American audience and present them as decent, clean and respectable. The role of the American Colony, as the institution running the Orphanage, is central here, as this institution is embedded within the social and political life of Jerusalem, as well as in its scenery. The humanitarian project is hence both general and contextualised, can take place anywhere and at the same time is deeply embedded in the history of Jerusalem and the American Colony. The two records that tell the history of the Orphanage, then, serve as much more than a pictorial evidence, but depict in them a multi-faceted story and complex political realities.

Acknowledgments

I would like to deeply thank Rachel Lev, the archivist and curator of the American Colony Archive in Jerusalem, for her assistance and helpful comments and suggestions on earlier drafts of this paper. I would also like to thank Liat Kozma, Ilanit Chachkes, and Sivan Balslev for commenting on different drafts of this paper.

Bibliography

Primary Sources

American Colony in Jerusalem, and Christian Herald Orphanage. Photograph Album, Christian Herald Orphanage. Palestine, 1919. Unpublished Album, Library of Congress, American Colony Collection Photograph. https://www.loc.gov/item/ mamcol.091/.

Negative Collection, series 24_13. Jerusalem: American Colony Archive.

Spafford Vester, Bertha and Christian Herald Orphanage. *Record book listing girls receiving support through the Christian Herald Orphanage, as supervised by the American Colony.* Library of Congress, American Colony Collection, Manuscript/ Mixed Material. https://www.loc.gov/item/mamcol.092/.

The Christian Herald, New York.

---

62   Shaw, "The Ottoman in Ottoman Photography," 189.

Secondary Sources

Ariel, Yaakov and Ruth Kark. "Messianism, Holiness, Charisma and Community: The American-Swedish Colony in Jerusalem, 1881–1933." *Church History* 65 (1996): 641–658.

Ayalon, Ella. "Mevakrot Yetomin Beyerushalayim." *Zmanim* vol. 124 (2014): 72–83. (In Hebrew)

Bair, Barbara. "The American Colony Photography Department: Western Consumption and "Insider" Commercial Photography." *Jerusalem Quarterly* 44 (2010): 28–38.

Baron, Beth. *The Women's Awakening in Egypt: Culture, Society, and the Press*. New Haven: Yale University Press, 1994.

Baron, Beth. "Orphans and Abandoned Children in Modern Egypt." In *Interpreting Welfare and Relief in the Middle East*, edited by Nefissa Naguib and Inger Marie Okkenhaug, 13–34. Leiden: Brill, 2008.

Curtis, Heather D. "Depicting distant suffering: Evangelicals and the politics of pictorial humanitarianism in the age of American empire." *Material Religion* 8, no. 2 (2015): 157–158.

Curtis, Heather D. *Holy Humanitarianism: American Evangelicals and Global Aid.* Cambridge: Harvard University Press, 2018.

Dudman, Helga and Ruth Kark. *The American Colony: Scenes from a Jerusalem Saga.* Jerusalem: Carta, 1998.

Fehrenbach, Heide and Davide Rodogno. "The Morality of Sight: Humanitarian Photography in History." In *Humanitarian Photography: a History*, edited by Heide Fehrenbach and Davide Rodogno, 1–21. Cambridge: Cambridge University Press, 2015.

Fletcher Geniesse, Jane. *American Priestess: The Extraordinary Story of Anna Spafford and the American Colony in Jerusalem*. New York: Nan A. Talese, 2008.

Gavish, Dov. "The American Colony and its Photographers." In *Zev Vilnay's Jubilee Volume: Essays on the History, Archaeology, and Lore of the Holy Land, Presented to Zev Vilnay*, edited by Ely Schiller. Jerusalem: Ariel Publishing House, 1987. (In Hebrew).

Green, Jack. "From Chicago to Jerusalem (and Back Again): The Untold Story of E.F. Beaumont." *The Oriental Institute News and Notes* 227 (2015): 15–19.

Greenberg, Ela. *Preparing the Mothers of Tomorrow: Education and Islam in Mandate Palestine*. Austin: University of Texas Press, 2010.

Hannoosh, Michèle. "Practices of Photography: Circulation and Mobility in the Nineteenth-Century Mediterranean." *History of Photography* 40, no. 1 (2016): 3–27.

Hirsch, Dafna. *Banu Lekan Lehavi et haMa'arav: Hanchalat Higiena uBniyat Tarbut Bahevra Hayehudit Bitkufat Hamnadat*. Sede Boqer: The Ben Gurion Research Institute, 2014. (In Hebrew).

Kark, Ruth. "Post Civil War American Communes: A Millenarian Utopian Commune Linking Chicago and Nås, Sweden to Jerusalem." *Communal Societies* 15 (1995): 75–114.

Kennedy, Denis. "Selling the Distant Other: Humanitarianism and Imagery-Ethical Dilemmas of Humanitarian Action." *The Journal of Humanitarian Assistance* (2009). Accessed July 16, 2019. Available online at: http://sites.tufts.edu/jha/archives411.

Lev, Rachel. "Visionaries and Creators: Members and Creative Ventures of the American Colony in Jerusalem, 1881–1948" (Exhibition Catalogue). Jerusalem: American Colony Archive Collection, 2014.

Littlewood, Barbara and Linda Mahood. "Prostitutes, Magdalenes and Wayward Girls: Dangerous Sexualities of Working-Class Women in Victorian Scotland." *Gender & History* 3, no. 2 (1991): 160–175.

Mahood, Linda and Barbara Littlewood. "The 'Vicious' Girl and the 'Street-Corner' Boy: Sexuality and the Gendered Delinquent in the Scottish Child-Saving Movement, 1850–1940." *Journal of the History of Sexuality* 4, no. 4 (1994): 549–578.

Maksudyan, Nazan. *Orphans and Destitute Children in the Late Ottoman Empire.* Syracuse: Syracuse University Press, 2014.

Nassar, Issam. *Photographing Jerusalem: The Image of the City in Nineteenth Century Photography.* Boulder: East European Monographs, 1997.

Nassar, Issam. "'Biblification' in the Service of Colonialism: Jerusalem in Nineteenth Century Photography." *Third Text* 20, no. 3/4, 317–326.

Othman, Enaya Hammad. *Negotiating Palestinian Womanhood: Encounters between Palestinian Women and American Missionaries, 1880s–1940's.* Lanham: Lexington Books, 2016.

Seikaly, Sheren. *Men of Capital: Scarcity and Economy in Mandate Palestine.* Stanford: Stanford University Press, 2016.

Shakry, Omnia. "Schooling Mothers and Structured Play: Child Rearing in Turn-of-the-Century Egypt." In *Remaking Women: Feminism and Modernity in the Middle East*, edited by Lila Abu-Lughod, 126–170. Cairo: AUC Press, 1998.

Shamir, Milette. "'Our Jerusalem': Americans in the Holy Land and Protestant Narratives of National Entitlement." *American Quarterly* 55, no. 1 (2003): 29–60.

Shaw, Wendy M.K. "The Ottoman in Ottoman Photography: Producing Identity through its Negation." In *The Indigenous Lens? Early Photography in the Near and Middle East*, edited by Markus Ritter and Staci G. Scheiwiller, 173–192. Berlin: De Gruyter, 2018.

Sheehi, Stephen. *The Arab Imago: A Social History of Portrait Photography, 1860–1910.* Princeton: Princeton University Press, 2016.

Spafford Vester, Bertha. *Our Jerusalem: An American Family in the Holy Land 1881–1949.* Jerusalem: Ariel Publishing House, 1992.

Tveit, Odd Karsten. *Anna's House: A Story from Stavanger to Jerusalem*. Oslo: Cappelen, 2000.

Tyrrell, Ian. *Reforming the World: The Creation of America's Moral Empire*. Princeton: Princeton University Press, 2010.

Wahrman, Dror. "Mendel Diness – Hazalam Hayerushalmi Hamikzo'i Harishon?" *Cathedra* 38 (1985): 104–120. (In Hebrew)

Watenpaugh, Keith David. *Bread from Stones: The Middle East and the Making of Modern Humanitarianism*. Oakland: University of California Press, 2015.

CHAPTER 3

Swedish Imaginings, Investments and Local Photography in Jerusalem, 1925–1939

Inger Marie Okkenhaug

In the fall of 1925, Lord Herbert Plumer (1857–1932), the newly appointed High Commissioner to Palestine, made an official visit to a small school for Arab children in Jerusalem, run by the Protestant organisation the Swedish Jerusalem Society (sjs).[1] Also present was Palestine's Director of Education, Humphrey Bowman (1879–1965). The presence of these British dignitaries made the visit a major event in the history of the school, narrated in text and photographs and published for supporters in Sweden and North America. While the visit ended with tea and conversation in the teachers' comfortable office, a photograph of the meeting shows a formal setting with two women and four men standing in the doorway under a British flag, reminding us of the political realities in Palestine under British Mandate rule. To the left in the photograph stands the *qawās* – the Consular Guard – wearing the official Ottoman *qawās* uniform, hinting at the Middle East context. Next to the *qawās* we see the Swedish Consul in Jerusalem and member of the American Colony, Hol Lars (Lewis) Larsson (1881–1958). To Larsson's right stands High Commissioner Plumer, while Bowman is seen to the right of the picture. In the centre of the photographs, staring at the lens, is Swedish headmistress Signe Ekblad's tall and commanding figure, demanding our attention.[2] The school's Palestinian teachers, Warda Abūdiyya, N. Ḥalabī, Ḥannā 'Abla, Bīdyā Ḥarāmī and Hīlīnā Kāssīsiyya were also present at the official visit. However, in this photograph, taken by a photographer from the American Colony's Photo Department, it

---

1 *Svenska Jerusalemsföreningen.* I would like to thank Sary Zananiri, Karène Sanchez Summerer, Rachel Lev, Issam Nassar, Åsmund Svendsen and anonymous reviewers for insightful comments to various versions of this chapter. I would also like to thank Åsa Henningsson and other staff at the Uppsala University Library for invaluable help and assistance with the sjs-photo collection.

2 Comment by Issam Nassar at conference the "Imaging and Imagining Palestine", Leiden, October 16th 2019. These images of the Swedish school are all from the sjs collection held at the Uppsala University Library. They were printed in the sjs publication *Svenska Jerusalemsföreningens Tidsskrift*, and in Märta Lindqvist's travel book *Palestinska dagar* ("Palestinian Days") (Stockholm: Skoglund Bokförlag, 1931).

© INGER MARIE OKKENHAUG, 2021 | DOI:10.1163/9789004437944_004

is the British Mandate system that is visualised, to the exclusion of the Arab teachers.

During the interwar period the Swedish institution received state funding in a manner similar to other private schools and was part of the British Mandate's educational system. From the early 1920s the school was headed by Signe Ekblad (1894–1952), who had come to Jerusalem as a young woman in 1922.[3] Even so, the school's history went back to Ottoman rule and was established by the SJS in 1902.[4] This organisation was founded in 1900 by members of the Swedish elite, and had strong connections to the Swedish state church and royal family, with King Oscar II as its 'high protector'.[5] The SJS was to be modelled upon the German *Jerusalemsverein*. In a similar manner to the German organisation, SJS focused on welfare and humanitarian work that included a hospital in Bethlehem, (operating from 1903 to 1925), in addition to the school in Jerusalem.[6] The organisation aimed at representing the Swedish nation in Palestine in the same manner as the Great Powers, France, Great Britain, Russia and Germany were represented through national Protestant and Catholic missions. In the Middle East missionaries faced major obstacles in their attempt to convert locals.[7] As a consequence, organisations like the SJS increasingly shifted their focus from evangelisation to health and education. The SJS, active in Palestine from 1900 to 1948, when war forced the school to close down, transformed its vocation to non-proselytising welfare work among the local, Arab population.[8]

By the 1920s, Sweden had long ceased to be an expansionist colonial power, even so, in the inter war period, it is possible to locate Swedish expansionist

3   Lindqvist, *Palestinska dagar*, 62.

4   Inger Marie Okkenhaug, "Scandinavian Missionaries in Palestine: The Swedish Jerusalem Society, Medical Mission and Education in Jerusalem and Bethlehem, 1900–1948," in *Tracing the Jerusalem Code: Christian Cultures in Scandinavia*, vol. 3., eds. Anna Bohlin and Ragnhild J. Zorgati (Berlin: De Gruyter Verlag, 2021). Sune Fahlgren, Mia Gröndahl, and Kjell Jonasson, eds., *A Swede in Jerusalem. Signe Ekblad and the Swedish School, 1922–1948* (Bethlehem: Diyar Publishing and Swedish Jerusalem Society, 2012), 20.

5   During the Mandate period, King Oscar's granddaughter Countess Elsa Bernadotte af Wisborg, head of the Swedish YMCA, became an active supporter of the SJS school in Jerusalem. Gustaf Björk, *Sverige i Jerusalem och Betlehem. Svenska Jerusalemsföreningen 1900–1948* (Uppsala: Svenska Jerusalemsföreningen, 2000), 50–51.

6   Björk, *Sverige i Jerusalem och Betlehem*, 14.

7   Conversion efforts were aimed mainly at the Jewish population, and largely failed.

8   See Inger Marie Okkenhaug, "Signe Ekblad and the Swedish School in Jerusalem, 1922–1948," *Svensk Missionstidskrift* 2 (2006): 147–162 and Inger Marie Okkenhaug, "Att avresa till Jerusalem som lärarinna: Signe Ekblad, jorsalsfarer, lærer og misjonær," in *Religiøse reiser. Mellom gamle spor og nye mål*, eds. Siv Ellen Kraft and Ingvild S. Gilhus (Oslo: Universitetsforlaget, 2007), 121–134.

FIGURE 3.1 *High Commissioner Herbert Plumer and Director of Education, Humphrey Bowman on an official visit to the Swedish School,* 1925. American Colony Photo Department. From left: The Consular Guard, Hol Lars (Lewis) Larsson, Herbert Plumer, Signe Ekblad, unknown woman, unknown man, Humphrey Bowman, unknown man. Swedish Jerusalem Society's Collection, *270068*
IMAGE COURTESY OF UPPSALA UNIVERSITY LIBRARY

ambitions in mission-based welfare projects in colonial (and Mandate) areas.[9] In line with what some historians have labelled 'Nordic colonial thinking',[10] a

---

9   See for example Seija Jalagin, Inger Marie Okkenhaug and Maria Småberg, "Introduction: Nordic Missions, gender and humanitarian practices: from evangelization to development," *Scandinavian Journal of History* 40, no. 3 (2015): 285–297.

10   Peter Forsgren, "Globalization as 'The White Man's Burden': Modernity and Colonialism in a Swedish Travelogue," *Scandinavian Studies* 91, nos. 1–2 (2019): 222–223. See also Johan Höglund and Linda Andersson Burnett, "Introduction: Nordic Colonialism and Scandinavian Studies," *Scandinavian Studies* 91, nos. 1–2 (2019): 1–12.

FIGURE 3.2 *The Arab Teachers and headmistress Ekblad, the Swedish School during the Summer Term, 1926.* Photographer unknown. Swedish Jerusalem Society's Collection, *396359*
IMAGE COURTESY OF UPPSALA UNIVERSITY LIBRARY

humanitarian, Christian, Swedish presence in Palestine, helped boost Sweden's self-image as a modern, European nation. The export of Swedish modernity to Palestine was seen in the fact that the Swedish school was modelled on Swedish educational culture and to a large extent financed from Sweden. Even so, the school had a profound local connection to the Arab community.[11] The staff consisted mainly of Christian Arab teachers and the pupils came from Arab families and, unlike most other mission schools, Arabic was the language of instruction. The connection to the local environment was strengthened with the purchase of land and a building in Jerusalem in June 1926. From renting a house outside the Damascus Gate, the Swedes now owned a property in Musrara, a prosperous Arab neighbourhood close to Prophet Street. The property included a stately villa which was reconstructed into a school for more

---

11   Björk, *Sverige i Jerusalem och Betlehem,* 28–29. The Swedish Jerusalem's Society (*Svenska Jerusalemsföreningen*), started out as a mission to the Jews, but due to Jewish hostility in Palestine the Swedish missionary agenda was very soon transformed into a cultural mission; in practical terms this meant education, health and relief work among the Arab population. The Swedish school opened in October 1902, providing a kindergarten and the first two years of primary school for girls. In 1909, Ottoman authorities officially recognised the school as the *École de la Société de Jérusalem.*

than 100 pupils. In 1928, the sjs added a new school building on their property, expanding the number of pupils to 250. Ten years later, in 1938, as a response to the humanitarian crisis caused by the war-like situation in Palestine, yet another building, a soup kitchen named the Green Hall, was added to the school premises.

This chapter focuses on photographs of the Swedish School, most of them published in the Swedish Jerusalem Society membership journal and the Swedish travel book *Palestinska dagar* (Palestinian Days)[12] from c. 1925 to 1940.[13]

Some of these photographs were taken by Signe Ekblad and printed as illustrations to her articles in the sjs journal. While Ekblad was an amateur photographer, a number of the published photographs were taken by photographers from the American Colony Photo Department (ACPD). The photographic motifs of the Swedish School included official and private guests, pupils and staff, buildings, playground and wider surroundings, and the school's welfare work. The aim here is to examine the social history told in the sjs photographs. Importantly, there was a utilitarian aspect to the photographs: in a similar way to other Protestant missions, photographs were crucial to the funding campaigns. The daily operations of a mission's school or hospital depended on the generosity of 'friends' back home. The fact that the sjs operated in 'The Land of the Bible' where every Christian nation (of some size) longed for a presence was of course a great asset in convincing potential donors. The photographers and the audience, middle- and upper-middle class Swedish men and women with Protestant sympathies and a humanitarian consciousness, desired a Swedish presence in Palestine. This was motivated by religious faith and Swedish national patriotism, but manifested itself in humanitarian work.[14] The Swedish people, wrote Ekblad in the sjs journal, not only had a duty to fulfil their gratefulness to the Holy Land. The people of Palestine expected the Swedes to act on this responsibility.[15] After the closing of the sjs hospital in Bethlehem in 1925, the only way of living up to these expectations was to support the Swedish educational work in Jerusalem. In a similar manner to

---

12   Lindqvist, *Palestinska dagar*.

13   These photographs are now kept at the sjs collection at Uppsala University Library. There is a total of seventeen albums in addition to loose photographs. There is no record of all photographs. Many of the images are found both in the albums and as loose photographs. See http://www.alvin-portal.org/alvin/view.jsf?pid=alvin-record%3A92948&dswid=1023. Personal communication, e-mail from Åsa Henningsson, November 5th 2020.

14   See Okkenhaug, "Scandinavian Missionaries in Palestine."

15   Uppsala University Library, Svenska Jerusalemsföreningen's Archives *Svenska Jerusalems-föreningens Tidsskrift* 2 (1923): 97.

the Swedish-American humanitarianism of the American Colony, as shown by Abigail Jacobson in this volume, photography played an integral part of Swedish welfare enterprise. I thus argue that the photographs, together with printed reports dealing with the Swedish humanitarian efforts in Palestine, visualised the imagined need for a Swedish presence in 'The Holy Land', but even more so the tangible results the Swedish engagement had in the country. Moreover, the article shows that while the photographs are visual documents of religious longing, they do not tend to dwell on ahistorical Biblical motifs. Instead, they reflect the thriving, intense process of modernity taking place in Palestine at the time, a process the Swedes wanted to take part in as a way of manifesting their claim to a national presence in Palestine. In addition, the photographs visualise the extent to which the Swedish enterprise was Palestinian; as mentioned earlier, the staff was mainly Arab and the school was part of a local Jerusalemite neighbourhood. Even so, the people in charge, the headmistress and board members were always Swedish. This external control is embodied in Ekblad's central presence in many of the photographs of the school.

This chapter is divided in three parts. The first part gives a background of the different people who were behind the photographs discussed here. The second part of the chapter focuses on photographs of the building process from 1927 to 1929. The third part focuses on the welfare and relief work of the Swedish institution, in particular the food distribution that took place from 1937 to 1939, during the Arab Revolt, thus offering an understanding of transnational welfare and local practice as imagined by the Swedish actors in Palestine.

1   The Photographers

Most noticeable here is the Colony's photo facility with its excellent laboratory where all photographic work imaginable is carried out. Even Baedeker (Palestine and Syria) says that fine pictures originate here, the best available in the Orient.[16]

This praise of the American Colony's Photo Department was voiced by Swedish Nobel Peace Prize Laureate Klas Pontus Arnoldson (1844–1916) who visited the American Colony in 1911.[17] The American Evangelical Protestants who founded the pre-millennialist community in Jerusalem in 1881 were joined fifteen

16   Mia Gröndal, *The Dream of Jerusalem. Lewis Larsson and the American Colony Photographers* (Stockholm: Journal, 2005), 151.

17   Gröndal, *The Dream of Jerusalem*, 151.

years later by a large group of Swedes and Swedish-Americans. The Colony's Photo department consisted of a collective of men with American, German, Palestinian, Indian and Swedish backgrounds. According to Rachel Lev, there were around fifteen photographers who operated the department between 1896 to 1934.[18] One of them was Jerusalem born John D. Whiting (1882–1951), whose *Diaries in Photos series* is the topic of Rachel Lev's article in this volume. Whiting's peer and colleague Hol Lars (Lewis) Larsson became head of the Colony's Photo department. Larsson and a younger Swede, Eric Matson both photographed the Swedish school at various times.[19] The high professional standard of the Photo department was widely acknowledged locally. In 1916, for example, the Red Crescent appointed Larsson as their head photographer in the region.[20]

The Swedish American Colony photographers were not Jerusalemites by birth. Hol Lars (Lewis) Larsson and Eric Matson had immigrated because their parents had joined a Swedish-American awakening movement. Even so, in a similar manner to Whiting and other photographers at the American Colony, these young Swedish men were fluent in Arabic and got to know Palestine and the region by extensive travels with their cameras.[21] Nada Awad also underlines the local character of the American Colony's photographers: 'Unlike foreign photographers who came for short periods of time, the American Colony Photo department was established and run for more than thirty-seven years in Palestine by photographers who lived in the country, knew the culture; some of them were even born in Jerusalem and spoke Arabic'.[22] Larsson was one of these photographers who spoke both Arabic and English fluently. In 1921 he was to become Swedish vice consul in Palestine and full honorary consul in 1925.[23] Larsson's double identity as local Jerusalemite and official Swedish representative was to be a major asset for the development of the Swedish School.

In the same manner as Larsson, Signe Ekblad would also develop a double identity as a Swede living and working in Jerusalem for most of her adult life. She was both a labour migrant and a religious agent seeking to fulfil her vocation. Before moving to Jerusalem, Ekblad had trained and worked as a teacher in Sweden. Later in life, after several years in Palestine, she received an MA in Semitic languages at Uppsala University. Her religious calling to become a

---

18   Rachel Lev, comment on the draft.
19   Gröndal, *The Dream of Jerusalem*, 161.
20   Gröndal, *The Dream of Jerusalem*, 216.
21   See Edith Larsson, *Dalafolket I Heligt Land* (Stockholm: Natur och Kultur, 1957).
22   Nada Awad, "Waiting for the Second Coming: The New Photographic Collection of the American Colony Archives," *Jerusalem Quarterly* 61 (2015): 101–112, 105.
23   Gröndal, *The Dream of Jerusalem*, 242.

teacher in Jerusalem was inspired by her time working for the Swedish settlement movement's work among poor industrial workers in the settlement
of Birkagården in Stockholm.[24] Birkagården, was inspired by the work of
the British settlement movement in the slums of inner London. It had its
supporters among the radical, Christian, cultural and intellectual elite in
Sweden. Social Christianity, with an emphasis on reconciliation between
the classes and self-help rather than charity, were the central points of this
movement.[25] This ideology, which contributed significantly to the establishment of the welfare state, influenced Ekblad's understanding of her mission
in Palestine.[26] The idea of Christian faith, expressed as practical welfare work,
was something Ekblad had in common with Larsson and other members of the
American Colony.

   Before World War I, connections were not close between the Swedish members of the American Colony and the sjs, as the confessional differences were
too considerable.[27] The high church, elite profile of the sjs (as represented by
the Swedish medical staff in Bethlehem)[28] and the rural and low church background of the Swedish members of the American Colony might also explain
the distant relationship between the Swedes in Palestine.[29] After the First
World War, however, relations between the Colony and the sjs became quite
close. The Swedish School's development under Ekblad's leadership, and her
role in making it into a hub for Scandinavians living or traveling in the region,
would have given the Swedish headmistress a social status that opened doors to
the influential American Colony. Ekblad's friend, the Swedish-Finnish anthropologist Hilma Granqvist (1890–1972), famous for her ethnographic work in
Palestine in the 1920s, describes the matriarchal head of the Colony, Bertha
Spafford Vester, as a beautiful, charming and warm woman. Vester's verve and
connections helped Granqvist establish her field work in the village of Artas,
close to Bethlehem. Spafford Vester's connectedness and talents as a social

---

24   Okkenhaug, "Signe Ekblad and the Swedish School," 147–162.
25   Birkagården, http:www.birkagarden.se.
26   Both Ekblad's and Larsson's official roles and duties meant that they also quite often were
     the object of the photography as main character or part of a group of important figures.
     In this manner the Swedes in Jerusalem could be assured that the prominent roles played
     by Larsson and Ekblad were transmitted to supporters in Sweden without words.
27   Björk, *Sverige i Jerusalem och Betlehem*, 32. Even so, the founder of the sjs, Bishop Henning
     von Schéele, wrote with sympathy about the Colony in several articles in the sjs journal.
28   Okkenhaug, "Scandinavian Missionaries in Palestine".
29   Swedish author and Nobel laurate Selma Lagerlöf's novel *Jerusalem*, based on the history
     of the Swedish members of the American Colony, published in 1902–03, had made the
     American Colony known in the Scandinavian countries. Lagerlöf had visited Jerusalem
     and the American Colony herself.

player would have appealed to Ekblad's professional self.[30] In addition, by the
1920s, the American Colony was no longer a utopian community. The younger
generation was mostly secular.[31] Concerned with commercial ventures and
social relations, their American Colony had become a centre for social events
for the upper strata of all Jerusalem and ex-pat milieus. Ekblad accepted invi-
tations to events at the Colony, and members from the leading families in the
Colony attended Christmas parties and concerts organised by Ekblad and her
staff, thus adding social prestige to the Swedish School.[32]

The links between the SJS and the American Colony contained more than
social interaction, however. Larsson, Matson and other (unnamed) photographers photographed the Swedish School and these photographs were printed
in the SJS membership journal in order for the Swedish supporters to follow
the 'Swedish' cultural (and financial) investment in Palestine. Like Ekblad and
the SJS, the members of the American Colony did not proselytise, but engaged
in economic enterprises as well as welfare work which was open to all religious communities in the city. Even so, in the inter-war period, the Colony
focused mainly on the Arab population.[33] Thus, the younger Swedish members of the Colony shared with Ekblad a yearning to contribute to modernising
Palestinian, Arab society.[34] Both parties took photographs that tell a social history from a local, Palestinian context. This is in accordance with Issam Nassar
who argues that 'Local photography is any photography that represented social
life in Palestine as opposed to biblical landscapes or Zionist photography that

---

30   Sofia Häggman, *Hilma Granqvist. Antropolog med hjärtat i Palestina* (Vasa; SFV, 2017), 55.

31   Comment by Rachel Lev.

32   See Bertha Spafford Vester, *Our Jerusalem: An American Family in the Holy City, 1881–1949*
      (New York: Doubleday, 1950).

33   Abigail Jacobson, "American "Welfare Politics": "American Involvement in Jerusalem
      During World War I," *Israeli Studies* 18, no. 1 (2013): 56–76; Awad, "Waiting for the Second
      Coming," 107–108. See also Heleen Murre-van Den Berg, "Our Jerusalem": Bertha Spafford
      Vester and Christianity in Palestine during the British Mandate", in *Britain, Palestine and
      the Empire: The Mandate Years*, ed. Rory Miller (Farnham/ Burlington: Ashgate, 2010),
      328–331.

34   The American Colony created a School of Handicrafts and Dressmaking for girls in 1918
      and a hospital for children (the Spafford Children's Center). Bertha Spafford Vester,
      Our Jerusalem. An American Family in the Holy City, 1881–1949 (London: Evans Brothers
      Limited, 1951), 328: the School of Handicrafts and Dressmaking had been established
      during the war. "After the war it was enlarged and added plain sewing and dressmaking
      classes. Instruction given in the three R's in Arabic, and English was taught. Needle lace
      and embroidery, using traditional patterns characteristic to the country, were developed.
      Later we added knitting, crocheting, and weaving."

was exclusively representing the Jewish settlement project in Palestine'.[35] Even so, local photographs also dealt in the Biblical, as seen in Rona Sela's chapter in this volume.

The American Colony's Photo Department can be seen as both foreign with photographers like Larsson and Matson who were born in Sweden and local, with its history and roots in Jerusalem.[36] The same might be said of Ekblad who immigrated to Palestine as a young adult and lived and worked in Jerusalem for twenty-six years. I would argue that Larsson, Matson and Ekblad are 'local photographers'. 'It is the context in which the images were produced, exchanged, viewed and assigned meanings that must be placed at the core of our attempt to discern what is local from what is not.'[37] What was the social context in which the SJS images were produced? What stories were they intended to tell the viewer, that is, the supporters in Sweden?

2   'The Great Gift': The Swedish School in Jerusalem

Our hearts are filled with happiness and thankfulness towards God and people for the great gift to us and our work, that are contained in the words "Swedish Jerusalem Society's plot and school building in Jerusalem".[38]

The gift referred to by the SJS secretary in Uppsala was a large testimonial endowment from the founder of the SJS, Bishop Knut Henning G. von Schéele (1838–1920) and his wife, Anna Ekman Schéele (1850–1925).[39] The donation was explicitly assigned to the purchase of a building in Jerusalem suitable for a school and created a financial and psychological base necessary to develop the Swedish school into a competitive primary school. This was the ambition of Signe Ekblad and her ally, Hol Lars (Lewis) Larsson, by now the Swedish Consul in Jerusalem.[40] At the time, Larsson who had been fifteen years old when he left Sweden with his mother and siblings in 1896, had lived thirty years in the American Colony in Jerusalem. Swedish-American connections were, however, not unusual at the time. There were strong links between Sweden and Swedish-American milieus in the United States, not least based

35   Issam Nassar, "Early local photography in Jerusalem," *History of Photography* 27, no. 4 (2015): 325.
36   I thank Sary Zananiri for making this point.
37   Nassar, "Early local photography in Jerusalem," 324.
38   *Svenska Jerusalemsföreningens Tidsskrift* no. 4 (1926): 194–195.
39   *Svenska Jerusalemsföreningens Tidsskrift* no. 3 (1926).
40   Okkenhaug, "Att avresa till Jerusalem som lärarinna," 121–134.

on a shared Lutheran Protestantism. In the United States, Swedish immigrants tended to keep the Lutheran religion and links to the Swedish state church.[41] The importance of Swedish-American ties was also seen among the supports of the Swedish Jerusalem's Society: from the beginning the organisation had a number of Swedish-American members, and Swedish-American congregations funded part of the sjs's new school complex in Jerusalem.[42] Thus, Larsson's American ties did not disqualify him from representing Sweden in Palestine.[43] The previous Swedish Consul in Jerusalem, Professor Gustaf Dalman, a German citizen and thus disqualified to continue his official role in Palestine after 1918, pointed to both the Swedish roots and deep connections to Palestine, when describing Larsson: 'While Herr Hol Lars Larsson was born in Nås, western Dalarna, he has been in Jerusalem since 1896, has worked his way up to becoming the American Colony's most distinguished landscape photographer and head of its Photo store, is married and soon to be 40 years old.'[44]

In a similar manner to John Whiting, Larsson became a popular tour guide. Prominent Swedes visiting Palestine raved about this 'ordinary boy from Nås in west Dalecarlia'.[45] Renowned explorer Sven Hedin travelled with Larsson as his guide during a longer stay in Palestine and was full of praise for Larsson, as one can read in his travel book, Jerusalem. Hedin writes of Larsson:

> [M]y faithful companion, a better cicerone on earth is not to be found ... He knew every corner of Jerusalem city, every road, village and ruin in the whole of Palestine and Syria. If the choice was mine, I would rather have his knowledge than all the wisdom of Baedeker, for he has travelled the country in all directions many, many times, partly to take photographs for sale to travellers and pilgrims, partly as a tourist guide.[46]

---

41   More than one million Swedes migrated to the United States between 1885–1915.

42   Björk, *Sverige i Jerusalem och Betlehem*, 19, 38. In 1913 there were more than 100 members in the United States.

43   John Whiting, born in Jerusalem with American parents, became the American consul during the same period. See Rachel Lev's article in this volume.

44   Gröndal, *The Dream of Jerusalem*, 242.

45   Sven Hedin, *Till Jerusalem* (Stockholm: Bonnier, 1917). 242 of the photographs in the book were taken by Lewis Larsson.

46   Gröndal, *The Dream of Jerusalem*, 214. "He (Lewis Larsson) was at home with the country's various history and knew his Bible by heart, albeit in English only, which he spoke as easily as Swedish. He spoke German and French without difficulty, and perfectly fluent Arabic. And this Lars Larsson ... was an ordinary boy from Nås in west Dalecarlia, having emigrated at 15. During the twenty years since then, he had himself acquired his entire store of knowledge."

Larsson's success as local guide for an increasing number of Swedish tourists, including the Swedish minister in Cairo, Harald Bildt, made the Swedish government offer Larsson the position as official Swedish representative in Palestine.[47]

The Swedish Jerusalem Society was the only Swedish organisation in Palestine and as Swedish Consul Larsson became deeply involved in the development of the Swedish School. Larsson recognised the potential for a larger educational institution catering for the Arab community in Jerusalem.[48] He shared this ambition with Ekblad and with the aid of Larsson, Ekblad managed to convince a highly sceptical board in Uppsala that building a new, large school would be sustainable and worthwhile. Ekblad, who had won the support of the Governor of Jerusalem, Edward Keith-Roach, spent summer vacations fundraising in Sweden.[49] She and Larsson also engaged the architect Hermann Imberger from the German Templar society, who, having grown up in Jerusalem, had invaluable knowledge of local properties, architectural styles and builders.[50]

In early 1926 Larsson came across a house in Musrara, near Prophet Street that was for sale for a reasonable price.[51] The three agents in Jerusalem, Ekblad, Larsson and Imberger, urged the board in Uppsala to make a swift decision before the two different owners (one of the house and plot, and one of the

---

47   Larsson, *Dalafolk i heligt land*, 118–119.
48   *Svenska Jerusalemsföreningens Tidsskrift* no. 4 (1926): 188. Larsson was in charge of the purchase of land for new school, he negotiated with the seller, based in Istanbul, and he acted as a mediator between the sJs board in Sweden and the American Colony regarding a short-term loan that secured the purchase of the property.
49   Okkenhaug, "Att avresa till Jerusalem som lärarinna," 129.
50   See Ruth Kark, "Missions and Architecture Colonial and Post-Colonial Views. – The Case of Palestine, Altruism and Imperialism in the Middle East," in *Occasional Papers*, eds. Eleanor H. Tejirian and Reeva Spector Simon (New York: Middle East Institute, Columbia University, 2002), 183–207. Since this plot was not large enough for a good-sized playground, Larsson recommended that they buy the neighbouring property – a plot without a building which was also for sale, for 2000 Egyptian pounds. It was a very good offer, according to Larsson, and Ekblad agreed, pointing to the good qualities of the house as a school building. Larsson had the support of architect Imberger, who guaranteed that this was a good purchase. *Svenska Jerusalemsföreningens Tidsskrift* no. 4 (1926): 184–185.
51   *Svenska Jerusalemsföreningens Tidsskrift* no. 4 (1926): 182–188. The owner lived in Istanbul and wanted to sell his property in Jerusalem, asking 4000 Egyptian pounds for the house and plot. "I hope the sJs does not miss this unique opportunity," Larsson wrote to the board (19th February 1926). 6000 pounds was 110,000 Swedish kroner. The negotiations were additionally complicated because of the fact that the adjoining property had several owners who all had to agree on the price.

adjoining property with no building on it) received higher offers.[52] On 20th
of June, Larsson was finally able to close the deal on one of the properties,
which cost the sjs board 3,000 Egyptian pounds.[53] The board also gave Larsson
authority to purchase the adjoining property and he was in charge of the formal procedures to finalise the deals. It would have been very difficult to find
and buy a suitable property in Jerusalem without Larsson's experience and
knowledge of the city. The board in Uppsala, overjoyed by the fact that the deal
was completed, thanked both Ekblad and especially Larsson for succeeding in
the difficult negotiations.[54]

Before the building could be used as a school, however, there were repairs
to be done.[55] By mid-October, the Department of Education finally approved
the opening of The Swedish School in the newly purchased building. With four
school classes, and a total of 107 pupils, it was no longer only a kindergarten.
The roof had been repaired, a water tank installed and the area outside was
transformed into a modern playground.[56]

With the purchase of the new building the Swedish School had become a
serious player in the private educational market in Palestine. Due to lack of
state run schools, there was a large number of mission run educational institutions in Palestine.[57] The Arab school system was far from universal and
consisted of government-controlled schools, the large majority being rural
schools for boys.[58] The Mandate authorities did not give priority to education

---

52   *Svenska Jerusalemsföreningens Tidsskrift* no. 4 (1926): 184–185. The process was also
      delayed because the owner of the house wanted to close the deal himself. In order to do
      so, he had to make the journey from Istanbul.

53   *Svenska Jerusalemsföreningens Tidsskrift* no. 4 (1926): 186. Larsson sent a telegram to the
      board in Uppsala: "Send via telegraph 3,000 Egyptian pounds. School building bought".

54   *Svenska Jerusalemsföreningens Tidsskrift* no. 4 (1926): 188. Larsson's connections to the
      American Colony was also of great importance, as 'Vester & Co, American Colony', prom-
      ised to lend sjs the necessary sum of money if the money from Sweden did not arrive
      soon enough.

55   *Svenska Jerusalemsföreningens Tidsskrift* no. 2 (1928): 36. By the opening day, October 6th,
      there were only 60 children attending. The rest had started another school. In
      Jerusalem there was little loyalty to one school and it was not uncommon for parents to
      send their child to a number of different schools.

56   *Svenska Jerusalemsföreningens Tidsskrift* no. 4 (1926): 189–191.

57   In theory open to all religions, there were only Jewish children in the Jewish schools.
      The use of Hebrew as language of instruction enforced this separation. The Jewish sys-
      tem consisted of government supported schools, and schools under the Vaád Leumi
      (the Jewish National Council) and Jewish private schools, from kindergarten up to uni-
      versity level.

58   Bowman 2/2/10, St. AP. "A review of Educational Policy 1920–1932". In Palestine, Bowman
      gave priority to primary schools in the villages. During the Mandate period, there were
      75 missionary schools, fourteen British government schools, 412 Muslim public village

for girls, and especially in urban areas girls' education to a large extent became an arena for private schools (both Christian and Muslim).[59] Ekblad was aware of the lack of schools for Arabs and especially the few educational opportunities for Arab girls. Her passionate reports from Jerusalem, accompanied with snapshots of children in the school yard,[60] convinced Swedish supporters that the Swedes were needed among the Arabs.[61] As we shall see, it was this educational void that would help to fulfil Swedish ambitions and competition against other European powers' humanitarian presence in Palestine. Is it possible to detect something of this in the images?

3   Visualised Emotions: Building a School

In her work on photography and transatlantic migration, Sigrid Lien shows how the photographs migrants sent back to Scandinavia visualised emotions and conditions that would be difficult to express in words.[62] For Signe Ekblad, the process of building a new school house embodied her deep desire to create high quality education for Arab girls. Extremely determined and driven by her professional aspirations, she succeeded. But the fundraising and quarrels with the board,[63] in addition to running a school and learning Arabic, took it tolls.

---

and town schools and more than 400 Vaad Leumi Jewish schools (secular and religious) in Palestine. Thomas M. Ricks, "Remembering Arab Jerusalem, 1909–1989: An Oral History of a Palestininan City, its Schools and Childhood Memories", 1. https://www .academia.edu/15767904/Remembering_Arab_Jerusalem_1909-1989_An_Oral_Histroy _of_a_Palestinian_City_Its_Schools_and_childhood_Memories.

59   The Muslim children in towns who received an education for some period or other was as late as 1935 estimated to be for boys 75 % and for girls 45%, while in the villages, 40% of Muslim boys received any education and only 1% of Muslim girls. Bowman, 2/2, St. AP. "Memorandum by Government of Palestine: Description of the Educational Systems, Government, Jewish and Private, and Method of Allocation of Government Grants, 1936." Enaya Hammad Othman, *Negotiating Palestinian Womanhood. Encounters between Palestinian Women and American Missionaries, 1880s–1940s* (Lanham/Boulder/ New York/London: Lexington Books, 2016), 13: the government schools provided education to approximately 20,288 students, with only 942 of those being girls. Othman quotes an article by Khalil Totah, "Education in Palestine"; *The Annals of the American Academy of Political and Social Science*, 163 (September 1932), 156.

60   Unlike many of the photographs in the *Svenska Jerusalemföreningens Tidsskrift*, these are not credited.

61   *Svenska Jerusalemföreningens Tidsskrift*, no. 1 (1923): 6–7.

62   Sigrid Lien, *Lengselens bilder* (Oslo: Scandinavian Academic Press, 2007), 21. English translation: *Pictures of Longing. Photography and the Norwegian-American Migration* (Minneapolis/London: University of Minnesota Press, 2018).

63   Häggman, *Hilma Granqvist*, 166.

By 1930 Hilma Granqvist noted that 'Signe E. has created an adorable creation, her school, but has herself been damaged'.[64] During her years in Palestine, Ekblad suffered from fever and headaches. These health issues might explain her serious demeanour in most of the photographs she appears in.

Ekblad's passion for her school manifested itself in her reports and articles to the SJS supporters, where she went into great detail about the process of transforming the old building into a schoolhouse. These reports were accompanied by photographs that visualised the transformation of the property into a modern school for young children. This process was made possible by local workmen. In Ekblad's texts, these workmen, when mentioned at all, are described as 'labourers' and not by name (the exception being 'our architect Imberger', who is not seen in any of the photographs). However, in the accompanying photographs, the active people at work are local carpenters and masons. When documenting the erection of a beautiful stone wall that was to encircle the property Ekblad focused on the masons at work. In the text accompanying the picture, it becomes clear that the fence was paid for by money from the sale in Sweden of embroidery, postcards with dried flowers from Jerusalem and other craft items made by the teachers and Ekblad.[65] The photographs gave the readers and donors a tangible impression of their contribution not only to education in a country that lacked state schools for its majority population, but also to Swedish-owned land in Palestine, verifying that Sweden was a confident player among other nations' mission enterprises. In addition, the image of building is not only a documentation of an ongoing process, but also an expression of Ekblad's longing for the future and the completion of a new and competitive Swedish School.[66]

In her written reports Ekblad was often concerned with the aesthetics of life in Jerusalem and her photographs also show an awareness of what she finds beautiful and harmonious, including the new wall around the property, the school's garden with its leafy trees and the new playground.[67] In the caption of a photograph taken by Ekblad printed in the SJS journal, she has written: 'The School's beautiful plot fence and (tomtmur och port) gate under construction. In the background one can see the school house, framed by the leafy trees'.[68]

While Ekblad was an amateur taking pictures, she shared a desire to photograph Palestinian landscapes – rural and urban – with Hol Lars (Lewis)

---

64   Häggman, Hilma Granqvist, 166.

65   Svenska Jerusalemsföreningens Tidsskrift no. 1 (1927): 17–18.

66   Lien, Lengselens bilder, 47.

67   See Okkenhaug, "Att avresa till Jerusalem som lärarinna."

68   Svenska Jerusalemsföreningens Tidsskrift no. 1 (1927): 59.

FIGURE 3.3 *Photograph of the ongoing work at the Swedish School*, Signe Ekblad. Swedish
Jerusalem Society's Collection, *396354*
IMAGE COURTESY OF UPPSALA UNIVERSITY LIBRARY

Larsson.[69] Even so, Larsson's photographs of the Swedish School also include the
building process, the new school building and the garden. In addition, Larsson's
photographs printed in the SJS journal also include a landscape photograph of
the school children on an Easter outing in March 1926.[70] In the foreground is
a large, old olive tree, giving a sense of 'eternity' or reference to Biblical times.
The children and teachers are seen at a distance gathered in a large circle in an
open landscape. Thus, Swedish audiences might see that they were funding
an institution that educated the younger generation of Palestine while at the
same time being located in a biblical landscape.

69   *The Dream of Jerusalem*, 242.
70   *Svenska Jerusalemsföreningens Tidsskrift* no. 2 (1926): 77.

FIGURE 3.4 *Children and teachers from the Swedish School on an Easter outing*, 1926. Hol Lars
(Lewis) Larsson. Swedish Jerusalem Society's Collection, Album No. 9, *293849*
IMAGE COURTESY OF UPPSALA UNIVERSITY LIBRARY

4   The Sense of a Swedish Childhood in Palestine

In 1927 the SJS journal printed a watercolour by the Swedish artist Elsa Beskow,
whose illustrated children's books were extremely popular in the Nordic countries. The picture was made for the Swedish School and it depicted a Palestinian
boy and girl, each holding a Swedish flag, in front of a low stone wall (similar
to the one around the Swedish school). Behind the wall was a Middle Eastern
urban landscape that linked the Swedish School to the city of Jerusalem. On the
bottom of the picture was written 'Welcome to the Swedish Jerusalem Society's
School'. While the motif was Palestinian, the style was distinctly Beskow – the
way she created fairy tales in words and paintings for Swedish children.
The original of the watercolour hung in the St John's hotel, while the SJS sold
copies in order to raise funds for the school.[71]

---

71   *Svenska Jerusalemsföreningens Tidsskrift* no. 1 (1927): 27.

Elsa Beskow was a prominent and active supporter (together with Selma Lagerlöf among others) in Sweden of the SJS work in Jerusalem. She was married to the Swedish minister Nathaniel Beskow, whose leadership of Birkagården, from 1912 to 1946, includes Ekblad's three years there as a social worker (from 1912 to 1915).[72] If it is this connection between Ekblad and Nathaniel Beskow that made Elsa Beskow paint for the Swedish School, is not known. However, her picture of the Swedish School connects Sweden with Palestine in a manner that would have resonated with the Swedish viewers and donors.

There are several photographs taken by photographers from the American Colony that might have been inspired by, if not Beskow's style, at least references to Swedish aesthetics. In connection with the move to the new school building in 1926, the SJS journal printed a photograph taken by Hol Lars (Lewis) Larsson of the youngest children, around 30, and a teacher (probably Ekblad) in the background. The children are all wearing wide, white hats and each child is carrying a large framed picture, poster or basket, helping with the move. They are standing in a relaxed line in the school yard beside the wall. In the background are leafy trees.[73] The small children in their wide hats reminiscent of Beskow's child depictions of 'Putte' in the blueberry woods.

Another image printed in the SJS journal and credited to the American Colony, is from 1928 and the laying of the foundation stone for the new school building, one of the most important events in the SJS' history.[74] In this photograph, Ekblad is seen leaning on the stone together with six young Palestinian children, three girls and three boys. The inscription on the large stone is in Swedish and Arabic and reads: 'Foundation stone laid down the 23rd of March 1928'.[75]

Another of these images eternalised by a photographer from the American Colony was used in both the SJS journal and in *Palestinska dagar*. The photograph is from around 1929, when the new school building was finished. The building, impressive with its two storeys, large windows and a gallery, is seen with a Swedish flag high above the flat roof. There are trees on both sides. A large group of children led by a teacher are seen in the front of the building,

---

72   Okkenhaug, "Att avresa till Jerusalem som lärarinna," 126.

73   *Svenska Jerusalemsföreningens Tidsskrift* no. 3 (1926): 178. The caption underneath the image says: "The caravan of the smallest with pictures and on their way to the school's newly purchased home".

74   *Svenska Jerusalemsföreningens Tidsskrift* no. 1, (1928), 43.

75   Swedish Jerusalem Society's Archives, Uppsala University Library. Published in *Svenska Jerusalemsföreningens Tidsskrift* no. 1 (1928): 43.

FIGURE 3.5 *'Welcome to the Swedish School'*, 1927. Reproduction of a watercolour by Swedish
artist Elsa Beskow with caption. Swedish Jerusalem Society's Collection, *396356*
IMAGE COURTESY OF UPPSALA UNIVERSITY LIBRARY

standing in a half circle doing Swedish gymnastics.[76] It is an aesthetically
pleasing image and one of a few with the Swedish flag.

Yet another photograph taken by an American Colony photographer in 1930,
shows the inside of the new school building where a group of children and two
teachers stand facing the photographer, while a teacher is playing the organ.[77]
The youngest children are standing on the stairs with Ekblad and another
teacher, making a half circle with sunlight coming in from a window above.
The photograph captures white walls with an evergreen plant on a shelf, and a
beautiful tiled floor that dominates the front of the picture.[78] The caption says
'Morning prayer in the hall', thus verifying the Christian character of the school

---

76   *Svenska Jerusalemsföreningens Tidsskrift*, no. 1, 1929, 79.
77   Lindqvist, *Palestinska dagar*, 69.
78   Lindqvist, *Palestinska dagar*, 69. Photograph from American Colony's Publishers.

FIGURE 3.6   *The youngest children and teacher (Ekblad?) in connection with the move to*
the new school building, 1926. Hol Lars (Lewis) Larsson. Swedish Jerusalem
Society's Collection, *92997*
IMAGE COURTESY OF UPPSALA UNIVERSITY LIBRARY

FIGURE 3.7   *Signe Ekblad and children with foundation stone for the new building,*
March 1928. The American Colony Photo Department. Swedish
Jerusalem Society's Collection, Album No. 9
IMAGE COURTESY OF UPPSALA UNIVERSITY LIBRARY

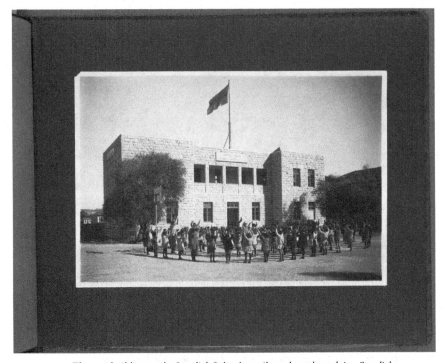

FIGURE 3.8 *The new building at the Swedish School, pupils and teachers doing Swedish gymnastics outside in the school yard*, 1928. The American Colony Photo Department. Swedish Jerusalem Society's Collection, Album No. 9, *194135*
IMAGE COURTESY OF UPPSALA UNIVERSITY LIBRARY

for a Swedish audience. Even so, the image created is a sense of happy Swedish childhood found in Beskow's books for children transferred to a Palestinian setting. It might also remind one of the works of one of Sweden's most popular and internationally known artists, Carl Larsson (1853–1919).[79] Larsson, who was an inspiration for Elsa Beskow's illustrations, is mainly known for his watercolours of idyllic family life. He was hugely influential in Sweden and beyond. Carl Larsson played a prominent role in the Swedish national handicraft movement and the local folklore movement (both ideologically influenced by the arts and crafts movement in England). In Elisabeth Stavenow-Hidemark's words: 'Carl Larsson and his world were considered the height of Swedishness'.[80] Larsson's

---

79   Lena Larsson, "The Larsson Design Legacy: A Personal View," in *Carl and Karin Larsson. Creators of the Swedish Style*, eds. Michael Snodin and Elisabeth Stavenow-Hidemark (Boston/New York/Toronto/London: Little, Brown and Company, 1998), 227.

80   Elisabeth Stavenow-Hidemark, "Carl Larsson's images – mass publication, distribution and influence," in *Carl and Karin Larsson. Creators of the Swedish Style*, eds. Michael

prints and paintings would have been familiar to the Swedish photographers at the American Colony and anyone who visited The Swedish School would have seen reproductions of Carl Larsson's work on the walls of the classrooms.[81]

It is possible that Larsson or Eric Matson or some of the other Swedish-born photographers were influenced by the nostalgia of the Swedish emigrant. A nostalgia underlined by both Beskow and Carl Larson's pictures of idyllic childhood in picturesque images of Swedish forests, lakes and rural homes. Even so, this might also be a form of remaking of Palestine in the image of Sweden that connects Swedish viewers to the Palestinian landscape.[82] Photographs depicting the practical, modern aesthetics of the new school building, for example, can be seen as part of the implementation of Swedish cultural diplomacy. For the viewers in Sweden, this 'Swedish vision of Palestine' would have emphasised the role of the SJs' School as 'Swedish', thus contributing to a feeling of a national and worthy Swedish presence in Palestine.

Carl Larsson's aesthetics might also have inspired images taken of the Sunhut – a shelter for warm or rainy days. Desired by Ekblad and her colleagues, and designed by architect Imberger, the Sunhut was financed by Swedish immigrants in North America. The shelter was constructed by Palestinian workmen and Hol Lars (Lewis) Larsson dealt with all practicalities related to building in Jerusalem.[83] The end result was a pleasing, permanent construction and Ekblad emphasised both its every day, useful sides and its aesthetics when describing it to Swedish supporters: 'It is all very practical, but also particularly nice'.[84]

In this photograph, some teachers are examining schoolgirls' eyes in the Sunhut. Also, here Ekblad has a distinct presence, not at the front, but looking at the camera from the back. Not tending to any of the girls, Ekblad looks as if she is in charge of the whole operation. The majority of the young girls, all wearing the same kind of blue work-dress, are lined up to be checked, but it is not a very orderly line, as some of them are turned away from the camera, while the four girls sitting on the bench to the right of the picture look impatient and two of them have their heads turned towards the fence behind them. The motif of lively children reminds one of the energic children in many of Carl Larsson's pictures. This photograph is hand-coloured: the green leaves outside the hut give a beautiful, subdued light creating a harmonious impression

Snodin and Elisabeth Stavenow-Hidemark (Boston/New York/Toronto/London: Little, Brown and Company, 1998), 218.

81   Okkenhaug, "Att avresa till Jerusalem som lärarinna," 128–129.
82   I would like to thank the reviewer for making this point.
83   Svenska Jerusalemsföreningens Tidsskrift no. 1 (1927): 8, "Solhyddan", The Sun Shed.
84   Svenska Jerusalemsföreningens Tidsskrift no. 4 (1926): 189.

FIGURE 3.9   *The scene is from the hallway of the new building at the Swedish school, with*
children and teachers. Signe Ekblad is standing in the stairs, right, 1930.
The American Colony Photo Department. Swedish Jerusalem Society's Collection,
Album No. 1, *293845*
Note: Held in Uppsala University Library at the Swedish Jerusalem Society's
Collection, Swedish Jerusalem Society's photo album 1, p. 30. Retrieved from
https://www.alvin-portal.org/alvin/imageViewer.jsf?dsId=ATTACHMENT
-0001&pid=alvin-record:293845
IMAGE COURTESY OF UPPSALA UNIVERSITY LIBRARY

FIGURE 3.10   *Teachers examining schoolgirls' eyes in Sunhut.* The American Colony Photo
                Department. Swedish Jerusalem Society's Collection, *293996*
                IMAGE COURTESY OF UPPSALA UNIVERSITY LIBRARY

against the pale blue dresses of the girls and the table with a 'still life' of a white
water-bowl, white napkin and medical equipment.

In a comment on these coloured photographs, Sary Zananari pointed
out that 'Compared to other American Colony hand-coloured photographs
(which aim for realistic/hyper-realistic renderings), these are much softer
and pastel' ... These photographs 'are also much more about something of
an impression, rather than reality, despite the slightly clinical nature of what
is depicted'.[85] This observation speaks to the Swedish aesthetics of both
Beskow's and Carl Larsson's watercolours.

When compared to photographs of other motifs, however, these photographs are very similar to the work of other photographers from the American
Colony.[86] Rachel Lev characterises the creative work of these photographers
as art photography. In other words, it is not possible to know if these

---

85   Sary Zananari commenting on a draft version of this article, 10th of November 2019.
       I thank Sary Zananari for his important insights.
86   For example, two women creating lace artifacts with the view of the Dome of the Rock in
       the background, at the American Colony Industrial School, in Jerusalem circa 1930. See
       Pelletier, "Jerusalem's religious pilgrims."

photographs were inspired by Swedish artists, but it is possible that Larsson or Eric Matson or some of the other Swedish-born photographers were influenced by the nostalgia of the Swedish emigrant. Even so, this might also be a form of remaking of Palestine in the image of Sweden that connects Swedish viewers to the Palestinian landscape.[87] Photographs depicting the practical, modern aesthetics of the new school building, for example, can be seen as part of the implementation of Swedish cultural diplomacy.

Ten years later, photographs from the Swedish School have a totally different rendering, as black-and white documentary photographs of relief work for children on the school premises. No longer a time for yearning for an imagined rural Scandinavian idyll, the war-like situation in Palestine (and in parts of Europe) called for different images and ways of portraying Swedish welfare in Jerusalem.

5   The Green Hall: Relief, Food and Care

During the Arab Revolt from 1936 to 1939 the Swedish school added relief and food distribution to its activities.[88] This humanitarian work is the motif of several photographs. In the fall of 1937, since the food provision in the Old City did not meet the local population's needs, Ekblad and some of the female Arab staff decided to build a soup kitchen on the school grounds.[89] While not receiving news from the board in Uppsala, Ekblad interpreted the lack of response as approval for building a soup kitchen. She raised the money that was needed and again Palestinian carpenters and other workers were able to realise the headmistress' ambitions. Painted green inside and out, the timber hall was formally named *the Green Hall* on King Gustav's 80th birthday on 22nd June, 1938.[90] Originally open only to the school's poorest pupils, the soup kitchen was soon extended to include younger sisters and brothers. The photographs from

---

87   I would like to thank the reviewer for making this point.

88   Letter from Signe Ekblad to her brother Martin Ekblad, the Swedish School, Jerusalem, 23 April, 1936. I would like to thank Signe Ekblad's family for kindly giving me access to these sources.

89   Uppsala University Library, Svenska Jerusalemsföreningen's Archives. Letter from S. Ekblad to the SJF Board, December 21, 1936. Already in December 1936, Ekblad had written to Uppsala suggesting that she use some of the school's savings to assist 'Arab and Jewish children in distress'. Uppsala University Library, Svenska Jerusalemsföreningen's Archives. Letter from S. Ekblad to the SJF Board, December 7, 1937.

90   Inger Marie Okkenhaug, "Setting the Table at the Swedish School in Jerusalem: Food Distribution and Transnational Humanitarianism in Mandatory Palestine," in *Food and Foodways in the Middle East*, ed. Nefissa Naguib (Ramallah: Bir Zeit University and Lower Jordan Series, 2009), 121–127.

the Green Hall depict a vital part of the attempt at bringing Swedish modernity to Palestine. In several photographs children and their mothers are seen sitting by tables, row after row in the Green Hall, waiting to be fed. These images give the impression of an efficient and well-organised Swedish relief effort. Ekblad is the dominant individual distributing food tickets and guarding access to the food. However, the educational aspect of the project was important and the girls learned how to cook and eat nutritious food.[91] This is reflected in some of the photographs where girls are the main actors. In a similar manner to photographs of girls in the American Colony's Orphanage, as shown by Jacobson in this volume, in the sjs photographs Palestinian girls are laying the table, eating and drinking and washing dishes. Thus, conveying to the Swedish supporters that these young girls who put in their share of work, were exposed to the Protestant work ethic and thus were deserving of Swedish aid. In addition, the photographs document that the poorest of girls at the Swedish School were taught 'home economics', a subject familiar to Swedish and as well as Swedish-American supporters. Ellen Fleischmann, in her work on American mission and home economics teaching in Lebanon in the interwar period, points to the global character of this 'educational, social and vocational movement that aimed to modernise, professionalise, and make scientific female domesticity'.[92] Teaching home economics was part of the wider welfare provided by the Swedish School. In Fleischmann's words: 'the praxis involved in implementing home economics resembled social work'.[93] Thus the soup kitchen was more than charity: in the photographs we see young Palestinian girls being taught domesticity by a Swedish woman, ensuring Swedish home audiences that what was seen as Nordic values of modern housekeeping were transmitted to the Middle East. These photographs, capturing the humanitarian Swedish presence in Palestine exemplify the implementation of Swedish cultural diplomacy. In this instance it is a female who mediates Swedish cultural values and customs to young Palestinian girls. The image thus emphasises that interwar Nordic colonial practice was not only a male arena.

91   Signe Ekblad, *Lyckliga Arbetsår i Jerusalem* (Uppsala: J.A. Lindblad, 1949), 18–19.

92   Ellen Fleischmann, "At Home in the World: Globalizing Domesticity through Home Economics in the Interwar Years," in *Transnational and Historical Perspectives on Global Health, Welfare and Humanitarianism*, eds. E. Fleischmann, S. Grypma, M. Marten and I.M. Okkenhaug (Kristiansand: Portal Academic, 2013), 158–159, 161.

93   Ibid.

FIGURE 3.11   *Girls and teachers (Signe Ekblad to the front) washing up at the Swedish school's*
soup kitchen the Green Hall, 1939. Eric Matson. Swedish Jerusalem Society's
Collection, *293998*
Note: Held in Uppsala University Library at the Swedish Jerusalem Society's
Collection. Retrieved from https://www.alvin-portal.org/alvin/imageViewer
.jsf?dsId=ATTACHMENT-0001&pid=alvin-record:293998.
IMAGE COURTESY OF UPPSALA UNIVERSITY LIBRARY

6   Conclusion

Photographs of the Swedish School in Jerusalem in the interwar period were
intended for a Swedish audience of potential donors. The photographs visualised the imagined need for a Swedish presence in 'The Holy Land' and the
tangible results the Swedish engagement had in the country, thus manifesting
Swedish claims to a national presence in the Palestine. While the written texts
to some extent convey a Christian motivation for a Swedish presence in the
Holy Land, the photographs do not tend to dwell on ahistorical Biblical motifs.
Instead, they convey a message of Swedish modernity. Complementing printed
reports, the photographs underlines the message that Sweden as a European
nation had a mission to develop Palestine. This at the same time as motives
seem to have been inspired by the late romantic style of Swedish artists Elsa

FIGURE 3.12   *Signe Ekblad giving out tickets to mothers and children at the soup
              kitchen Green Hall, Jerusalem,* May 1939. Eric Matson. Swedish
              Jerusalem Society's Collection, *92985*
              IMAGE COURTESY OF UPPSALA UNIVERSITY LIBRARY

FIGURE 3.13   *Mothers and children at the food distribution for children at the Swedish
              School,* May 1939. Eric Matson. Swedish Jerusalem Society's Collection,
              93033
              Note: Held in Uppsala University Library at the Swedish Jerusalem's
              Society's Collection. Retrieved from https://www.alvin-portal.org/alvin/
              imageViewer.jsf?dsId=ATTACHMENT-0001&pid=alvin-record:93033.
              IMAGE COURTESY OF UPPSALA UNIVERSITY LIBRARY

Beskow and Carl Larsson, both representing the ultimate 'Swedishness' at the time. Even so, this was not only about a romantic longing, but a form of remaking of Palestine in the image of Sweden that connected Swedish viewers to the Palestinian landscape and people. Photographs depicting the practical, modern aesthetics of the new building at the Swedish School were part of the implementation of Swedish cultural diplomacy. For the viewers in Sweden, this 'Swedish vision of Palestine' would have emphasised the role of the sjs' School as 'Swedish' and underlining that the Swedish presence in Palestine was legitimate and worthy of support.

While some of the photographs visualise the extent to which the Swedish enterprise was Palestinian with Arab pupils and an Arab staff, the people in charge were always Swedish. This uneven relationship is seen in the photographs, with headmistress Signe Ekblad often in the background, as the matriarch in charge. Her presence underscores the colonial aspect of the Swedish humanitarian enterprise in Palestine. Even so, on a personal level, Ekblad's photographs, visualising her emotional investment in female education, were instrumental in finding necessary Swedish support for developing a school that prospered in Jerusalem's highly competitive market of mission schools.

Bibliography

Ariel, Yaakov and Ruth, Kark. "Messianism, Holiness, Charisma, and Community: The American-Swedish Colony in Jerusalem, 1881–1933." *Church History* 65, no. 4 (1996): 641–657.

Awad, Nada. "Waiting for the Second Coming: The New Photographic Collection of the American Colony Archives." *Jerusalem Quarterly* 61 (2015): 101–112.

Björk, Gustaf. *Sverige i Jerusalem och Betlehem. Svenska Jerusalemsföreningen 1900–1948*. Uppsala: Svenska Jerusalemsföreningen, 2000.

Ekblad, Signe. *Lyckliga Arbetsår i Jerusalem*. Uppsala: J.A. Lindblad, 1949.

Fahlgren, Sune, Mia Gröndahl, and Kjell Jonasson, eds. *A Swede in Jerusalem. Signe Ekblad and the Swedish School, 1922–1948*. Bethlehem: Diyar Publishing and Swedish Jerusalem's Society, 2012.

Fleischmann, Ellen. "At Home in the World: Globalizing Domesticity through Home Economics in the Interwar Years." In *Transnational and Historical Perspectives on Global Health, Welfare and Humanitarianism*, edited by E. Fleischmann, S. Grypma, M. Marten, and I.M. Okkenhaug, 158–181. Kristiansand: Portal Academic, 2013.

Forsgren, Peter. "Globalization as "The White Man's Burden": Modernity and Colonialism in a Swedish Travelogue." *Scandinavian Studies* 91, nos. 1–2 (2019): 222–223.

Gröndal, Mia. *The Dream of Jerusalem. Lewis Larsson and the American Colony Photographers*. Stockholm: Journal, 2005.

Häggman, Sofia. *Hilma Granqvist. Antropolog med hjärtat i Palestina*. Vasa; SFV, 2017.

Hedin, Sven. *Till Jerusalem*. Stockholm: Bonnier, 1917.

Höglund, Johan and Linda Andersson Burnett. "Introduction: Nordic Colonialism and Scandinavian Studies." *Scandinavian Studies* 91, nos. 1–2 (2019): 1–12.

Jacobson, Abigail. "American "Welfare Politics": American Involvement in Jerusalem During World War I." *Israeli Studies* 18, no. 1 (2013): 56–76.

Jalagin, Seija, Inger Marie Okkenhaug and Maria Småberg. "Introduction: Nordic Missions, gender and humanitarian practices: from evangelization to development." *Scandinavian Journal of History* 40, no. 3 (2015): 285–297.

Larsson, Edith. *Dalafolket i Heligt Land*. Stockholm: Natur och Kultur, 1957.

Larsson, Lena. "The Larsson Design Legacy: A Personal View." In *Carl and Karin Larsson. Creators of the Swedish Style*, edited by Michael Snodin and Elisabeth Stavenow-Hidemark, 220–229. Boston/New York/Toronto/London: Little, Brown and Company, 1998.

Lien, Sigrid. *Lengselens bilder*. Oslo: Scandinavian Academic Press, 2007.

Lindqvist, Märta. *Palestinska dagar*. Stockholm: Skoglund Bokförlag, 1931.

Murre-van den Berg, Heleen, "Our Jerusalem": Bertha Spafford Vester and Christianity in Palestine during the British Mandate. In *Britain, Palestine and the Empire: The Mandate Years*, edited by Rory Miller, 328–331. Farnham/Burlington: Ashgate, 2010.

Nassar, Issam. "Early local photography in Jerusalem." *History of Photography* 27, no. 4 (2015): 320–332.

Okkenhaug, Inger Marie. "Scandinavian Missionaries in Palestine: The Swedish Jerusalem's Society, Medical Mission and Education in Jerusalem and Bethlehem, 1900–1948." In *Tracing the Jerusalem Code: Christian Cultures in Scandinavia*, vol. 3., edited by Anna Bohlin and Ragnhild J. Zorgati. Berlin: De Gruyter Verlag, 2021.

Okkenhaug, Inger Marie. "Att avresa till Jerusalem som lärarinna: Signe Ekblad, jorsalsfarer, lærer og misjonær." In *Religiøse reiser. Mellom gamle spor og nye mål*, edited by Siv Ellen Kraft and Ingvild S. Gilhus, 121–134. Oslo: Universitetsforlaget, 2007.

Okkenhaug, Inger Marie. "Setting the Table at the Swedish School in Jerusalem: Food Distribution and Transnational Humanitarianism in Mandatory Palestine." In *Food and Foodways in the Middle East*, edited by Nefissa Naguib, 121–127. Ramallah: Bir Zeit University and Lower Jordan Series, 2009.

Okkenhaug, Inger Marie. "Signe Ekblad and the Swedish School in Jerusalem, 1922–1948." *Svensk Missionstidskrift* 2 (2006): 147–162.

Othman, Enaya Hammad *Negotiating Palestinian Womanhood. Encounters between Palestinian Women and American Missionaries, 1880s–1940s*. Lanham/Boulder/New York/London: Lexington Books, 2016.

Pelletier, Mary. "Jerusalem's religious pilgrims who built a photographic empire." *The Middle East Eye* 16 February 2017. https://www.middleeasteye.net/features/jerusalems-religious-pilgrims-who-built-photographic-empire.

Stavenow-Hidemark, Elisabeth. "Carl Larsson's images-mass publication, distribution and influence." In *Carl and Karin Larsson. Creators of the Swedish Style*, edited by Michael Snodin and Elisabeth Stavenow-Hidemark, 220–229. Boston/New York/Toronto/London: Little, Brown and Company, 1998.

Vester, Bertha Spafford. *Our Jerusalem. An American Family in the Holy City, 1881–1949*. London: Evans Brothers Limited, 1951.

The Dominicans' Photographic Collection in Jerusalem: Beyond a Catholic Perception of the Holy Land?

Norig Neveu and Karène Sanchez Summerer

> The Arabs, and chiefly the young among them who are cultivated, are becoming aware of their right to be considered indigenous. We need to remember that. Zionism could be the catalyst to bring about the fusion of Arab society in Palestine.
>
> 15 June 1918, ANTONIN JAUSSEN[1]

∴

At the end of the First World War, having lived in Palestine for more than thirty years, at the *École Biblique et archéologique française de Jérusalem* (EBAF), the Dominican Antonin Jaussen was an expert observer of the local situation as well as the international engagement in Palestine, challenging what he considered to be the international lack of respect for local populations and elites in the region.[2] Many Dominicans from his generation made an important contribution to visual production during the British Mandate in Palestine, given the strong relationship to their mission field and their training in historical and archaeological methodology, along with the increasing availability of light, transportable cameras.

---

1 Dispatch from Antonin Jaussen du 15 juin 1918, in Jean-Jacques Pérennès, *Le Père Antonin Jaussen, o.p., (1871–1962). Une passion pour l'Orient musulman* (Paris: Le Cerf, 2012), 76. We are grateful to Emeritus Professor at the École biblique et archéologique française de Jérusalem, Jean Michel de Tarragon and to the Professor of Archaeology Jean Baptiste Humbert for opening the photographic collection, their multiple answers, the several and 'chaleureux' coffee breaks with many discussions in December 2018 and April 2019, as well as the many visits in recent years and for his precious advice on our article. We remain the only persons responsible for the content.

2 H. Laurens, "Jaussen en Arabie," in *Photographies d'Arabie, Hedjaz 1907–1917*, ed. Brahim Alaoui (Paris: IMA, 1999), 32.

The EBAF was founded in 1890 within the Dominican priory of St Stephen[3] by Marie-Joseph Lagrange O.P. (1855–1938) as a research institution.[4] The school was first called the *École pratique d'études bibliques*, inspired by the recently-created institution in Paris (1868).[5] For Lagrange, members of the school were to collect and produce information regarding Palestine and the Holy Land. The methodological specificity he encouraged was the study of the Bible in its physical and cultural context. The Dominicans of the 'first generation'[6] (1890–1940) on whom this article will focus were specialised in different subjects, from epigraphy to Assyriology and geography to ethnology. From 1920, the institution became the *École biblique et archéologique de Jérusalem* (French Archaeological and Biblical School of Jerusalem) with the support of the French *Académie des Inscriptions et Belles-Lettres* (Paris).[7] In 1892, the Biblical school launched its journal, *La Revue Biblique*, where scholarly results were published, including photographs.[8]

From the early twentieth century, photographs became embedded as evidence for the Dominicans of the Biblical school the development of their scholarly methodology. This echoes the attempt to develop a scientific method promoted by Salzmann from the 1850s for documenting archaeological sites.[9] However, the photograph taken by the EBAF Friars reveal to a semantic turn in the use of photography, no longer as a tool for representing projection over a territory but as scientific evidence about it. Unlike commercial photographers

---

3 St Stephen's was established in 1882 in Jerusalem as a Dominican priory.

4 Marie-Joseph Lagrange, a Dominican exegete, was a central figure in the development of Biblical studies in the nineteenth century. He is especially well known for being one of the precursors of the historical method in Catholic exegesis. See Bernard Montagnes, *Marie-Joseph Lagrange, Une biographie critique* (Paris: Le Cerf, 2005).

5 T.N. Clark, *Prophets and Patrons: the French University and the Emergence of the Social Sciences* (Cambridge: Harvard University Press, 1973), 42–45; Jacques Revel, ed., *Une école pour les sciences sociales. De la VIe section de l'EPHE, à l'École pratique des hautes études en sciences sociales* (Paris: Le Cerf, 1996), 11–12.

6 Marie-Antonin Jaussen (1871–1962), Antoine-Raphaël Savignac (1874–1951), Louis-Hugues Vincent (1872–1960), Felix-Marie Abel (1878–1953), Édouard-Paul Dhorme (1881–1966). On the history of the EBAF, D. Trimbur, *Une école française à Jérusalem. De l'École Pratique d'Etudes bibliques des Dominicains à l'École Biblique et Archéologique Française de Jérusalem* (Paris: Le Cerf, 2002). The author does not mention the photographic collection.

7 French learned society devoted to Humanities, created in 1663, one of the five academies of the *Institut de France*.

8 Up to 1923, the editor of the journal was Marie-Joseph Lagrange, followed by Édouard-Paul Dhorme (until 1931), then by Louis-Hugues Vincent (until 1938) and Roland de Vaux (until 1953) and others after the Mandate period.

9 Sary Zananiri; "From Still to Moving Image: Shifting Representation of Jerusalem and Palestinians in the Western Biblical Imaginary", *Jerusalem Quarterly* 67 (2016): 64–81.

so prevalent in the region, photography was used to document the findings of the archaeological expeditions much like the rubbings, drawings and sketches had previously. In this vein, they were projected during lectures or published in the *Revue Biblique*. The continuous interest of the Dominican Friars in photography throughout the twentieth and twenty-first centuries resulted in the current photographic collection of the EBAF. Besides pictures taken by the Dominicans, the current collection also includes digitised photographs from the other Catholic institutions in Palestine.[10] With more than 30,000 glass plates, photographs and black and white and coloured slides, the collection of the EBAF is one of the most extensive photographic collections of the so-called 'Holy Land' (Palestine and the Middle East more broadly) preserved today.

Research on Palestine has been influential in the way visual iconography has been regarded as a valuable source for historians.[11] The EBAF photographs presented in the recent historiography on Ottoman and British Mandate Palestine dealt mainly with archaeological sites, landscapes and monuments, with only a few focused on people.[12] The main publications concern the his-

---

10   Latin Patriarchate of Jerusalem, Assumptionists, White Fathers, Salesians, Jesuits of the Pontifical Biblical Institute, Lazarists, Betharram Fathers, Rosary Sisters, Sisters of Zion, St Joseph Sisters, the German Paulus Haus and the Albright Institute of Archaeology.

11   Eyal Onne, *The Photographic Heritage of the Holy Land, 1839–1914* (Manchester: Manchester Polytechnic, 1980), Sarah Graham-Brown, *Palestinians and their Society, 1880–1946. A photographic Essay* (London: Quarter Books, 1980); Mounira Khemir, *L'orientalisme. L'Orient des photographes au XIXe siècle* (Paris: Photo-Poche, 1994); Nissan Perez, *Visions d'Orient* (Jerusalem: Israel Museum, 1995); Pierre Fournié and Jean-Louis Riccioli, *La France et le Proche-Orient, 1916–1946, Une chronique photographique de la présence française en Syrie et au Liban, en Palestine au Hedjaz et en Cilicie* (Paris: Casterman, 1996); Issam Nassar, "Familial Snapshots: Representing Palestine in the Work of the First Local Photographers," *History & Memory* 18, no. 2 (2006); 139–155; Zeynep Çelik, "Photographing Mundane Modernity," in *Camera Ottomana: Photography and Modernity in the Ottoman Empire, 1840–1914*, eds. Zeynep Çelik and Edhem Eldem (Istanbul: Koç University Press, 2015), 154–200.

12   The EBAF published catalogues deal mainly with the Ottoman period. *Itinéraires bibliques* (1995), catalogue of the exhibition at the Institut du monde arabe, Paris 17/01–30/04/1995. The only EBAF catalogue dealing with the post-Ottoman period is *Chrétiens d'Orient*, Institut du monde arabe & Centre régional de la photographie Nord Pas-de-Calais (60 photographs from EBAF), first catalogue to present photographs that were non-archaeological and dealing with all indigenous populations. Walid Khalidi, *Before Their Diaspora, A Photographic History of the Palestinians 1876–1948* (Washington D.C.: Institute for Palestine Studies, 1991); Elias Sanbar, ed., *Jérusalem et la Palestine, Photographies de l'École Biblique de Jérusalem* (Paris: Hazan, 2013); Elias Sanbar, *Les Palestiniens. La photographie d'une terre et de son peuple de 1839 à nos jours* (Paris: Hazan, 2004).

tory of Jordan, Oriental Christianity, the Holy Land or Palestine.[13] Beyond a
Biblical studies focused approach that favoured archaeological photographs,
the Dominicans and the Catholic missionaries showed an interest across different segments of society, through the lens of Europeans in daily contact with
the Arab populations of the region. How did photographs present scholarly
actions of collecting local knowledge, theatre and music, education and medicine developing in these Catholic institutions? Is an Arabisation of the clergy
noticeable from the photographers' points of view?

During two research projects on Christian communities at the end of the
Ottoman Palestine and the British Mandate,[14] we came across an exhibition
organised by J.-M. de Tarragon and J.-B. Humbert 'Visages d'Orient' tackling
the question of the indigenous population. Reflecting with them on the reasons for such an exhibition and the relations of Jaussen to his Arab fellows, the
questions that progressively came to our mind were the ways to 'think *about*
and to think *with* images'[15] within our historical approach. How can we capture, through visual representations, the historical changes in Palestine but
also within the scientific perspective of EBAF and other Catholic institutions in
Palestine? To what extent did the First World War and the Balfour Declaration
change the Dominican perception of Palestinian society and communities?
How can we view the photographic collections through the lens of ethnography from the current day, given the different approaches to the production of
photography at the time they were produced? From this perspective, how did
the Dominican's view – with the example of Jaussen – differ from that of other
Catholic organisations? These collections will be decoded as 'action-sources',
bearers of a discourse on the history of Palestine at the beginning of the twentieth century. We shall first analyse the history of the photographers and the
collection itself, then discuss the Dominican ethnographic approach via
the anthropological and photographic study of Nablus. Finally, we will envis-
age the evolution of the broader corpus of Catholic missionary photographs
and the missionaries' perception of Palestinian Arab society.

---

13   Géraldine Chatelard and Jean-Michel de Tarragon, *L'Empire et le royaume. La Jordanie
      vue par l'École biblique et archéologique française de Jérusalem (1893–1935)* (Amman:
      Centre culturel français d'Amman, 2006); Sanbar, *Jérusalem et la Palestine*; Sanbar, *Les
      Palestiniens.*

14   The NWO project Van Morsel (the Dutch Research Council), thanks to which we could
      help in acquiring specific material for photographic preservation and classification,
      helping data management, and the international research consortium MisSMO, https://
      missmo.hypotheses.org/research-program.

15   Gregory Stanczak, *Visual research methods: Image, Society and Representations* (Thousand
      Oaks, CA: SAGE Publications, 2007), 1–22, 83–120.

1   The Constitution of the EBAF Photographic Collection

The constitution of today's collection draws together a multiplicity of views of Palestine and the broader region. As well as the collections produced by the Dominican Friars of the Biblical School, it includes collections by a number of different Catholic institutions present in the region, including the Assumptionist Fathers of Notre-Dame de France, Betharram Fathers, Médebielle collection, White Fathers of Saint Anne of Jerusalem, the Salesians, Catholic order of the Rosary Sisters, the Sisters of Sion as well as some images produced by commercial photographers like Khalīl Ra'ad and the American Colony Photographic Department.

The photographic collection of the Biblical school is mainly composed of glass plates. This illustrates, according to Jean-Michel de Tarragon, Professor Emeritus and archivist of the photographs at the EBAF:

> A particularity of the Dominican collection: at this time, it was not con-
> sidered as a collection, offered to an audience. It was a scientific tool for
> internal use. Between colleagues, with a simple conversation, one was
> able to find this or that series of negative glasses [...]. Originally, the build-
> ing did not house a photographic library as such: the plates remained in
> the cells of the Friars according to the subjects they had treated. After
> their death, a centralised archiving process was decided.[16]

The fact that the Dominicans kept their photographs in their cells explains why they rarely signed their photographs and did not date them. This is one of the difficulties faced by the archivist and the historian while using this collection. Some answers can be found in the *Revue Biblique* or the volumes published by the Dominicans.

In many ways, the broader context of the collection points to some of the complexities of how to address them. On the one hand, the collection is vested in the context of missionaries in and their activities in Palestine. On the other, they are also a form of scientific engagement as part of historical and archae-ological methodologies. Overlapping this division is of course the question of ethnography. Whether images where taken as part of the documentation of

---

16   Interview with Jean-Michel de Tarragon, April 2019, Karène Sanchez Summerer and Norig
       Neveu. 'Those include 2,448 stereoscopic glass negatives. Then, we could add 1,003 ste-
       reoscopic glass positives, for projection or 3D viewing through a viewing machine, not
       scanned because 95 percent are duplicates of negatives included among the bulk of the
       twelve thousand scans.'

missionary activities or scientific endeavour, where populations are concerned, the collections of EBAF that image people constitute a useful record of interactions.

The tensions at play between documenting missionary activities and scholarly documentation also point to the multiple frameworks that enable an understanding of European Catholic networks and indigenous communities across multiple genres of photography. Given the complete and comprehensive nature of the photographic archive, we also have a rare opportunity to address this relationship with knowledge that all available material is present. Further, we can regard missionaries' adoption of photography and the transformations of modernity not just as affecting the indigenous communities with which the missionaries worked, but indeed transforming the missionaries themselves and the nature of their work. In many regards, the multiple photographic lenses of these Catholic collections give us as much information about the photographers as they do about the photographic subjects.

The digitisation process started in 2001 with the glass plates; many Catholic communities accepted the offer to scan their collections free of charge, receiving back their originals and a CD set. In exchange, the EBAF obtained an official written agreement for the Right of Use to the scans.[17] J.-M. de Tarragon chose to include the imperfections, damage, captions, and in some cases handwritten notes on the surfaces of the prints – editorial comments, for example, or simply informal notes jotted down by previous owners or viewers. The vast majority of the Dominican collection and the Catholic missionaries' collections have been scanned. Many pictures, glued into albums, were first dismounted before they were scanned and duplicated. The structuring of the photographic collection does not correspond to the ordering of the photographers. The notion of 'author/photographer' seems of no importance here. Photographs are inventoried and organised according to a geographical classification (by mission fields) and thematic (according to categories such as 'Churches', 'School', 'Medico-social', 'Youth', etc.).

Four thousand positive square glass plates (non-stereoscopic) are in the collection, some of them genuine American Colony photographs from before the time of Eric Matson, and independent from the collection available in the Library of Congress in Washington, DC. The twelve thousand negatives

---

17   J.-M. de Tarragon also scanned two albums stolen in 1948 from the Ra'ad Studio, on loan from Elli Schiller, the Israeli historian who was interested in the photographic collection of the EBAF (the albums subsequently perished in an accidental home fire later). The photographs were small paper prints, not such high quality (many were scratched), but many of them included English captions. The collection also includes 285 pictures taken by Bonfils.

are private, being the work of the Dominicans during a period spanning from 1890 to around 1952. Since the 1990s, the EBAF photographic collection has been expanded. In 1994, the Assumptionist Fathers of Notre Dame de France transferred to the EBAF 1,603 glass plates of different sizes, taken between 1888 and 1930 in Palestine and neighbouring countries. A few years later, the contemporary Assumptionists of St Pierre-en-Gallicante authorised Jean-Michel de Tarragon to digitise the 302 paper prints from the large Notre Dame de France photograph albums (the original glass plates are missing). Several Catholic missionary institutions progressively asked J.-M. de Tarragon to digitise their photographs (Fig. 4.1).[18] We consider, in this article, all the Catholic institutions' photographs present in the EBAF collection.

The Catholic missionaries' photographs range from uncatalogued boxes or albums at one end of the scale to carefully preserved, well-organised and semi-professionally documented collections numbering hundreds of thousands of photographs at the other. That makes the EBAF photographic collection a valuable testimony of the social, political and religious history of Palestine. Many photographs concern the period of the British Mandate, although J.-M. de Tarragon has initially chosen to focus on photographs from the Ottoman period.

Unlike other photographic archives in the region,[19] the Dominican photographs were never destroyed or looted, in spite of their proximity to the conflict zone in 1948. It is in this context, aware that the Dominicans had never sold their pictures, that J.-M. de Tarragon started the digitisation. However, the action was not always understood by his peers as the EBAF as an academic

---

18   They include the Schmidt school photographs, the former German Paulus Hospiz (139 unpublished photographs, dated between 1907 and 1911). In 2008, the glass plates of the White Fathers of St Anne were digitised (701 glass plates). Most of them are unpublished, and the oldest date from before the foundation of the EBAF (from about 1875 to 1939). In this collection, in addition to the glass plates, there are about 872 old photographs on paper (digitised), dealing mainly with the Melkite community. Later, an important addition was made to the collection with the digitisation of the pictures of the Latin Patriarchate and the seminary of Beit Jala and the photographs taken by the Latin Patriarchate's former historian, Pierre Médebielle (so far 2,553 photographs). The collection also includes 366 prints from the album of the Italian Salesian fathers of Beit Jimal (from 1930 to 1940) and the 1,740 photographs, negatives and glass plates and acetate photographs from the Jesuits. This collection or donation process is currently continuing; some feminine orders have recently accepted to share their entire photographic collection (Sisters of Zion, Rosary Sisters).

19   About destruction and dispersion of photographic fund, see in this volume Rona Sela about Khalīl Ra'ad's collection and Rachel Lev about the American Colony collection.

FIGURE 4.1   Preservation, scanning and cataloguing of the EBAF photographs by
              J.M. de Tarragon, April 2015. Latin Patriarchate archives digitisation

institution has focused on textual archives.[20] It thus had no image 'policy', nor
image 'spaces' in the sense of a place devoted to preservation and consultation. Linked to some French and later Palestinian historians, J.-M. de Tarragon
promoted his initiative among his peers and wider audiences in France. He
initiated several exhibitions, collaborated occasionally with researchers and
obtained financial support to start the digitisation.

As far as the posterity of the EBAF *photothèque* is concerned, J.-M. de Tarragon
has addressed the next challenge: namely, the need to consolidate searches
across several physically and administratively separate collections. He is thinking of a potential platform, a 'confederation' of archival source materials, that
would, at a later stage, possibly collate what is learned in one mission collection with what can be found in another. Photographs are inevitably linked to
many text-based historical records which contain information that can often
be linked to the individuals, events, and subjects depicted in the missionary
photographs (eg. the diaries/daily life reports of the Dominican priory and

---

20   The EBAF photographs are not part of the recent initiative by the BNF (National
      French Library) *Bibliothèques d'Orient*, like many other missionary congregations,
      though A. Jaussen is mentioned as an important actor, "Antonin Jaussen (1871–1962),"
      Bibliothèques d'Orient.

activities). They can function as meta-data and allow a finer view of the photographers and the context of their approaches. The potential users would be able to define the search by time, place and theme, sorting the results according to the categories, descriptors and keywords used when photographs were scanned and added to the record. Later on, the viewers familiar with the time, place and people involved would be able to contribute information that the EBAF could consider for incorporation into the electronic record. Another step, linked to the memorial challenges, data availability, the need of preservation and the property/copyrights issues of private institutions.

1.1   The History of the Photographers: Looking for Biblical Lands

The first pictures of the Bible School were taken by M.-J. Lagrange during a trip from Egypt to Jerusalem, during the Spring of 1890. Dominicans of the first generation were encouraged by Lagrange to use photography during their investigations. From 1900, with a peak between 1905 and 1907, Antonin Jaussen, Raphaël Savignac, Louis-Hugues Vincent, and Felix-Marie Abel started to take up photography.[21] It was used as scientific evidence which determined its composition. This appears clearly in comparing the pictures taken by the Dominicans and the Assumptionists in the early twentieth century. The latter would focus on the representation of a romanticised Holy Land as Bonfils had done earlier.[22] This asymmetrical use of photography between the different orders had technical reasons: the Dominicans rarely printed their photographs as they were not produced to be sold to pilgrims. As they aimed to document the Bible in its context, the pictures taken by the Dominicans proposed an alternative representation to the Biblical iconography so common to the photographic milieus in Jerusalem.[23]

Dominicans usually worked in pairs, for instance Jaussen and Savignac or Abel and Vincent. Jaussen and Savignac held a special place because of both the quality and the quantity of their photographic productions.[24] Most of the

21   Jean-Michel de Tarragon, "The photographic-library of the Dominican of Jerusalem," in *Jérusalem et la Palestine, Photographies de l'Ecole Biblique de Jérusalem*, ed. Elias Sanbar (Paris: Hazan, 2013), 163–175; "Antonin Jaussen (1871–1962)," Patrimoines partagés, Bibliothèques d'Orient, accessed 12/01/2020, https://heritage.bnf.fr/bibliothequesorient/ fr/antonin-jaussen-article.

22   Estelle Villeneuve, Jacques Nieuvarts, Alain Marchadour and Benoît Grière, *Terre sainte. Les premières photographies* (Paris: Bayard, 2010); Gavin Carney, "Bonfils and the Early Photography of the Near East," *Harvard Library Bulletin* 26, no. 4 (1978): 442–470.

23   Issam Nassar, "'Biblification' in the Service of Colonialism. Jerusalem in Nineteenth-century Photography," Third Text 20 (3): 317–326.

24   The other Dominicans who took photographs were Paul-Marie Séjourné, Raphaël Tonneau, Bertrand Carrière, Pierre Benoit and Roland de Vaux.

photographs in the collection are theirs, especially the glass plates. Jaussen specialised in stereoscopic views while Savignac mostly produced classical glass-negative photographs.[25]

Jaussen's first photographs were probably taken in Damascus in 1897 during the School's study trip. The history of the photographic collection is intimately linked to that of the EBAF, whose programme of studies included annual trips, the 'Biblical Caravan', to discover the lands of the Bible (Fig. 4.2). They started in and around Jerusalem and gradually concerned visits to the 'Holy Land' and the region (as far as Transjordan, Egypt, Hauran, *Bilād al-Shām*). The purpose of the caravan, made by camel or horseback, was to observe ancient archaeological sites as well as the natural environment and populations of the region.[26] This approach was associated with many other techniques for scientific recording, including note-taking, drawing, rubbings and, very soon, photography. The function of photography, in the context of a positivist approach, was considered as valuable as rubbings was to provide evidence to illustrate or justify discoveries or observations. The photographs of the EBAF collection were taken by scientific amateurs who did not cultivate an artistic practice, even if the latter is appreciable in some photographs.

The Dominicans of EBAF also made expeditions for other scientific purposes, as for example Jaussen's exhibition to Petra in 1896 or to the Negev in 1904 sponsored by the Académie des Inscriptions et Belles-lettres. Some expeditions are well documented in the photographic collection, such as the one to Ḥijāz (1907, 1909, 1910) or to the Dead Sea (1908–1909). Until the First World War, most of the pictures focused on archaeological sites, landscapes and general views of cities. Individuals usually appeared in support of scientific knowledge, notably as scale markers indicating the size of an archaeological site.[27] Apart from Jaussen's famous portraits of some members of the Azayzāt tribe of Mādabā, few photographs are portraits of local people. Most of the time during their expeditions, the Dominicans would be hosted by Latin Catholic missionaries. The pictures document the expansion of these missions, their schools and hospitals. The photographic collection constitutes precious

25   Jean-Michel de Tarragon, "Holy Land Pilgrimage through Historical Photography," *Jerusalem Quarterly* 78 (2019): 93–111, available via https://www.palestine-studies.org/sites/default/files/jq-articles/Pages_from_JQ_78_-_Tarragon_1.pdf.

26   Conferences attended by a big audience, Diaries of St Stephen's priory, Biblical and Archaeological School of Jerusalem, for example: 19/02/1919: Savignac on Nabatean art; 5/051920, Savignac on Palmyre.

27   E. Barromi, "Archeology, Zionism and Photography in Palestine: Analysis of the Use of Dimensions of People in Photographs", *Journal of Landscape Ecology* 10, no. 3 (2017): 49–57.

FIGURE 4.2 *Biblical caravan*, 1913. Photographer unknown
          IMAGE COURTESY OF EBAF

sources about the history of missionary institutions from the late nineteenth
century especially the EBAF (the Friars, the students, the library, the expansion
of the priory), but also St Anne's Melkite seminary[28] or the Sisters of Sion's
educational activities.

The photographic collection also provides important evidence for the period
of the First World War as some Dominicans including Jaussen and Savignac
served as intelligence officers for the French Navy. Based in Port Saʿīd, they
met their British counterpart, T.E. Lawrence. The collection also includes the
famous picture of Allenby entering Jerusalem in 1917. After the end of the War,
the activity of St Stephen's priory started anew in 1920. EBAF members focused
on archaeology and Palestinian cities. During the first years of the Mandate,
Dominicans could access the two major Palestinian holy sites: the Dome of the
Rock (Ḥarām al-Sharīf) in Jerusalem and the Cave of the Patriarchs (Ḥarām
al-Ibrahīmī) in Hebron. They focused less on pilgrimages and processions and
more on the interiors of the sites, their architecture and ornaments.

---

28   The Melkite Church follows the dogmas of the Roman Church and the Byzantine or
       Eastern rite.

The Dominicans were self-taught photographers. For their training, they received the help of the Assumptionists of Notre-Dame de France (NDF). By the end of the nineteenth century, the Assumptionists had established a press service in Jerusalem. In the 1890s, they 'contributed to immortalising Palestine and Jerusalem as pilgrimage sites through a photography service'.[29] From the end of the nineteenth century the Dominicans and the Assumptionists developed scientific collaborations regarding archaeology, especially during the excavations of St Peter in Gallicantu.[30] These collaborations extended to technical training in photography.

The techniques and training of the Dominicans had an impact on the way they took photographs. Conversely, their approach also conditioned each Friar's choice of photographic equipment.[31] As lighter, more robust and more portable cameras were developed, and factory-made negatives became available, some photographs give the impression of the photographers' being closer to the subjects photographed. While Savignac had a more static and frontal approach due to the tripod chambers, the installation of the camera in the field and the treatment of glass plates, Jaussen made reports with more easily manoeuvrable equipment, which allowed him to obtain stereoscopes, which were more vivid, and to photograph people in situ. The very composition of the photographs also depended on the scientific goals of the Friars. Many of Jaussen's photographs reveal a desire to represent Middle Eastern social dynamics. He did not hesitate to take his camera into crowds to capture social events such as pilgrimages.

The plurality of visual narratives offered to the historian is one of the riches of the EBAF photographic collection. During the Dead Sea Expedition, for instance, Jaussen was photographing the encampments, the men on the ship's decks and so on, while Savignac was scientifically composing photography of landscapes.[32] One can hardly argue that Jaussen restored 'the individual identity of the people portrayed',[33] as the subalternity of the relationships between the Dominicans and the workers accompanying their expedition appears in many respects in the photographs.

---

29   Dominique Trimbur, "A French Presence in Palestine – Notre-Dame de France," *Bulletin du Centre de recherche français à Jérusalem* 3 (1998): 117–140.

30   Trimbur, "A French Presence in Palestine."

31   For a detailed list of the cameras used before the 1950s by the Dominicans see, De Tarragon, "The photographic library of the Dominicans of Jerusalem" and Renaud Escande, "Un jeu de regards: la photographie de Jaussen et Savignac à travers la croisière de l'École pratique d'Études bibliques autour de la mer Morte," in *Antonin Jaussen. Sciences sociales occidentales et patrimoine arabe*, eds. G. Chatelard and M. Tarawneh (Beirut: CERMOC, 1999), 109–110, available online https://books.openedition.org/ifpo/5326?lang=fr#bodyftn14.

32   Escande, "Un jeu de regards," 110–111.

33   Nassar, "Familial Snapshots," 147.

The originality of these photographs in comparison to other visual productions of the time – in particular that of Raʿad or the American Colony – relates to its scholarly function as opposed to more popular commercial visual narratives. Thus, what can missionary, but also scholarly, photography teach us about social history? How can we trace the social history of Palestinian Arabs in these Catholic missionary archives? The diaries of St Stephen's priory covering the Mandate period reveal an intense activity of the Dominicans in terms of lecturing in the various scientific societies of Palestine especially the Catholic ones,[34] but also in Europe. These thematic lectures were accompanied by the projection of photographs. Although these photographs were circulated in a number of scientific societies their influence on representations of Palestine within the scholarly community or a wider cultured public remains uncertain.

2   Picturing Palestine, Picturing the Holy Land: A Dominican
       Ethnography?

Jaussen holds a special place in the Dominican scientific production of the time that must be considered in terms of the complementarity of skills. He is the precursor of a comprehensive approach to local societies and the production of ethnographic knowledge. His photographs are therefore both original compared to those of the other friars, while embodying the academic ambitions of his institution. Until the First World War, Jaussen's observations were mainly focused on Transjordan.[35] Afterwards, he focused on urban dynamics and Palestine.[36] If Jaussen's involvement as an intelligence agent during the First World War was considered as evidence of his link with the imperialist powers,[37] his approach to collecting data and iconography was originally as an

---

34   For example: Catholic Club of Jaffa (Jaussen, 22 January 1927), students of St. Joseph (Abel, 11 April 1935, on the various monuments of the Haram eš-Šérif in Jerusalem) or the Palestine Oriental Society (8 April 1936). Diaries of St Stephen's priory, Biblical and Archaeological School of Jerusalem, Jerusalem.

35   Antonin Jaussen, *Coutumes des Arabes au pays de Moab* (Paris: Adrien-Maisonneuve, 1948).

36   See for instance Antonin Jaussen, "Trois inscription arabes inédites, du Haram d'Hébron," *Revue Biblique* (January 1923); Antonin Jaussen, "Inscriptions coufiques de la chaire du martyr al-Husayn, à Hébron," *Revue Biblique* (October 1923); Antonin Jaussen, "Inscription arabes de la ville d'Hébron," *BIFAO* (1924); Antonin Jaussen, "Inscriptions arabes de Naplouse," *BIFAO* (1924).

37   Roberto Mazza and Idir Ouahes, "For God and la Patrie: Antonin Jaussen Dominican and French Agent in the Middle East 1914–1920," *First World War Studies* 3, no. 2 (2012): 145–164.

intermediary between ethnology, Biblical studies and Orientalist influences. How did the post-war period mark a change in his approach?

2.1 *Antonin Jaussen and Nablus, an Ethnographic Turning-point?*

Antonin Jaussen (1871–1962) settled in Jerusalem in 1890 where he was one of the first to become a professor at the EBAF. A specialist in Semitic languages, he began as an epigraphist. He carried out several periods of field research among the nomadic Arab tribes of the East of the River Jordan with an ethnographic interest. He pioneered work by studying the tribes and Bedouins of Transjordan, among whom he lived between 1901 and 1905. He published several articles in the *Revue Biblique, Coutumes des Arabes au pays de Moab* (Customs of the Arabs in the Land of Moab, Paris, 1908) and took several pictures of the life of the tribes of Transjordan.

In 1909, Max van Berchem[38] described Jaussen's approach: 'Jaussen [investigator] prefers the discussion led by the investigator, in the middle of a group of interlocutors'.[39] In this article, Max van Berchem refers to the works of Jaussen as ethnology. The question of Jaussen's inclusion among the first defenders of this discipline at the end of the nineteenth century is a matter of academic debate.[40] This is due to the originality of his approach: the definition of a scientific protocol:

> Wishing to know the nomads, I decided to go straight to the source and went to the desert to study the Bedouins. This work is therefore the result of my personal observations; it only contains data drawn directly from the Arabs. [...] I did not intend to defend a thesis or support a system; I wanted to see the facts and record observations [...] If I have reported certain laws or certain facts from the Bible, it is simply as a marker, not having as my aim to treat such an interesting subject.[41]

---

38   Max van Berchem (1863–1921) established Arabic epigraphy as a discipline. Trained in Leipzig, he had a doctorate. He also studied in the universities of Strasbourg and Berlin. He made his first voyage to the Orient in 1886, visiting Alexandria and Cairo. In 1888, he visited Palestine and Syria. From then on, he visited the Near East annually. See Sophie Makariou, "Van Berchem Max," in *Dictionnaire des orientalistes de langue française*, ed. François Pouillon (Paris: IISMM/Karthala, 2008), 948–949.

39   Max van Berchem, "Aux pays de Moab et d'Edom," Extract from *Journal des Savants* (Paris: Imprimerie nationale, 1909): 33–35.

40   Géraldine Chatelard and M. Tarawneh, eds., *Antonin Jaussen. Sciences sociales occidentales et patrimoine arabe* (Beirut: CERMOC, 1999).

41   Jaussen, *Coutumes des Arabes au Pays de Moab*, 2–3.

Jaussen presents here a scientific method which was an innovation at the time. Jalabert states, that 'this Dominican's approach was part of a long tradition that considered the Arabic language, then Islamology and Bedouin ethnography as a means to a better understanding of the Bible'.[42] Jaussen's approach paradoxically claimed to be detached from Biblical exegesis, but only refers to its representatives rather than quoting the precursors of ethnographic studies such as Lane.[43] Thus, until the First World War, Jaussen's work was at the crossroads of a nascent ethnography and reminiscences of Biblical and Orientalist scholarship productions. This was reflected in the themes he chose such as Bedouins, nomads and tribal social and religious dynamics. This ethnographic work represented an important turning-point within the academic activity of the EBAF.[44]

After serving as an intelligence agent for the French services,[45] Jaussen returned to Jerusalem in 1918. He stayed there until 1927 when he was sent to Cairo by Lagrange to open a Dominican priory. In 1933, he founded the Dominican House of Oriental Studies in Cairo (IDEO). In Palestine under British Mandate, he no longer worked on Bedouins and tribes but started focusing on the social dynamics of Nablus and its surroundings which led to the publication of his book *Coutumes palestiniennes. I. Naplouse et son district* in 1927. He was familiar with the city where he had stayed during his travels and on which he had written an article in the *Revue Biblique* in 1905 about one of the sheikhs, Saad, an amulet producer.[46] In the introduction of *Coutumes palestiniennes*, Jaussen mentions that:

Being unable to undertake a study of the whole of Palestine with its multiple contours and aspects, I have limited my observations to the region, and especially the town, of Nablus: a territory largely sheltered from foreign influence. [...] The method, already used in "Coutumes des Arabes", is the same here: an objective study of the facts; personal verification;

---

42   Cyrille Jalabert, "De l'exégèse biblique au monde arabe," in *Antonin Jaussen. Sciences sociales occidentales et patrimoine arabe*, eds. Géraldine Chatelard and Mohammed Tarawneh (Beirut: CERMOC, 1999), 69.

43   Ibid.

44   Jean-Michel de Tarragon, "Ethnographie," in *L'Ancien testament. Cent ans d'exégèse à l'École biblique. Cahier de la Revue Biblique* 28 (Paris: Gabalda, 1990), 19–44.

45   See Henry Laurens, "Jaussen et les services de renseignement français (1915–1919)," in *Antonin Jaussen. Sciences sociales occidentales et patrimoine arabe*, eds. Géraldine Chatelard and Mohammed Tarawneh (Beirut: CERMOC, 1999): 23–35.

46   Antonin Jaussen, "Le Cheikh Sa'ad ad-Din et les "djinn" à Naplouse," *Revue Biblique* (1905): 145–157.

discussion with the indigenous people concerning some rather extraordinary assertions in order to get at the truth.[47]

The study on Nablus was conducted between 1923 and 1926. He observed the social dynamics in and around the city, conducted interviews with privileged interlocutors about the collective memory, habits and customs of the city dwellers. In an ethnological perspective, most of the cases mentioned by Jaussen are anonymised and only the first letters of the names are mentioned. In the study on Nablus, Jaussen confirms and refines his ethnographic approach and method. It is by its thematic, a study of a Palestinian city and its urban dynamics that his work on Nablus marks a turning-point.

2.2   A French Pictorial and Ethnographic Study of an Historic 'Islamic City'?

The result of Jaussen's research was published in 1927. The book is divided into 10 chapters focusing on the social dynamics of the city and its region. Several photographs were taken during the fieldwork with the help of Savignac, representing the urban landscape, the surroundings of the city, its workers and women (Fig. 4.3). Jaussen chose Nablus for a practical reason: his good relations with the French person in charge of the Catholic mission which opened in the 1860s.[48] In 1904, three French sisters from Saint-Joseph settled in Nablus and opened a dispensary.[49] Jaussen used it as an observatory of urban life where he conducted observations and took photographs. He also chose Nablus because he pictured the city as protected from the upheavals that were transforming Palestine, including the British Mandate and Zionism:

> A city lost in the mountains and off the beaten track, a city that is almost cut off from the movement of the world and which has no local resources: such a town does not feel the need for hard work. Under the pressure of modern times, it may tend to change; but today it has still kept its ancient

---

47   Antonin Jaussen, *Coutumes palestiniennes. I. Naplouse et son district* (Paris: Geuthner, 1927).

48   Jean Jacques Pérennès, *Le Père Antonin Jaussen*. At this period the mission was organised around a chapel, a school for boys and with the help of the Rosary Sisters, a school for girls; Karène Sanchez Summerer, "Réception et impacts de l'action éducative et sanitaire des sœurs de Saint Joseph (Naplouse) et des sœurs de Sion (Jérusalem) par les populations musulmanes rurales et urbaines (1870–1940)," in *Histoire et Missions chrétiennes* 22, eds. Nadine Beligand and Philippe Bourmaud (Paris: Karthala, 2012): 163–196.

49   Jean Métral, "*Naplouse et son district: un essai de monographie urbaine*," in *Antonin Jaussen. Sciences sociales occidentales et patrimoine arabe*, eds. Géraldine Chatelard and Mohammed Tarawneh (Beirut: CERMOC, 1999), 121–135.

FIGURE 4.3 *General view of Nablus*, early 1920s. Antonin Jaussen. Digitised glass plate,
00248-J0253
IMAGE COURTESY OF EBAF

organisation of work. [...] To a certain extent this organisation may evoke
for us what industry was like in Samaria.[50]

Jaussen focuses on the traditional life of a Palestinian city rather than the profound transformations of the urban economy in the 1920s.[51] The city seems
detached from its historical evolution. If the book opens with a description of
the topography of Nablus, it focuses mainly on its social structures, religion
and mentality: women, family, important families and notables, work and religion. The importance given to the family as the basic social structure of urban
social dynamics recalls his analysis of tribes in Ottoman Transjordan. For
Jaussen, the urban identity of Nablus was inherited from its long-term history.
This timeless dimension of urban dynamics echoes the Biblical perception of
the Palestinian territory, but here with an emphasis of the Islamic heritage.

Since the early 18th century, Jabal Nablus had been experiencing a process of
social and economic integration between the city and the countryside.[52] At the
beginning of the Mandate period, Nablus remained the centre of a *mutasar-
rifiyya* (region) of 168 villages whose peasants depended on the important

50   Antonin Jaussen, *Coutumes palestiniennes*, 277.
51   Sarah Graham-Brown, "The Political Economy of Jabal Nablus, 1920–1948," in *Studies
      and Social History of Palestine in the Nineteenth and Twentieth Centuries*, ed. Roger Owen
      (London/Basingstoke: Macmillan, 1982) 88–176.
52   Bishara Doumani, *Rediscovering Palestine: Merchants and Peasants in Jabal Nablus, 1700–
      1900* (Berkeley: University of California Press, 1995).

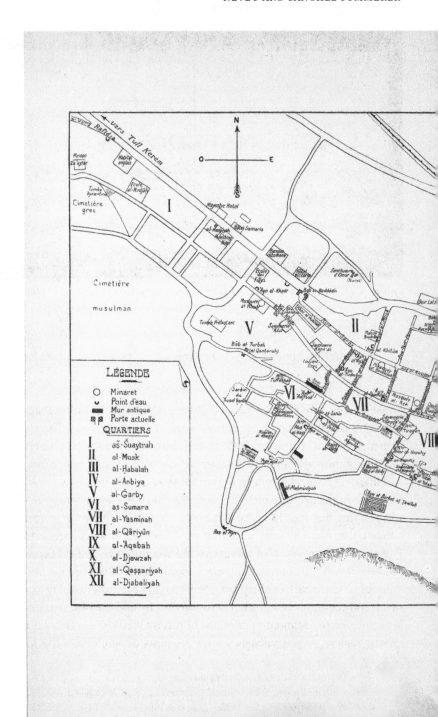

FIGURE 4.4 *Plate IV Map of Nablus.* Jaussen, *Coutumes palestieniennes*, 1927

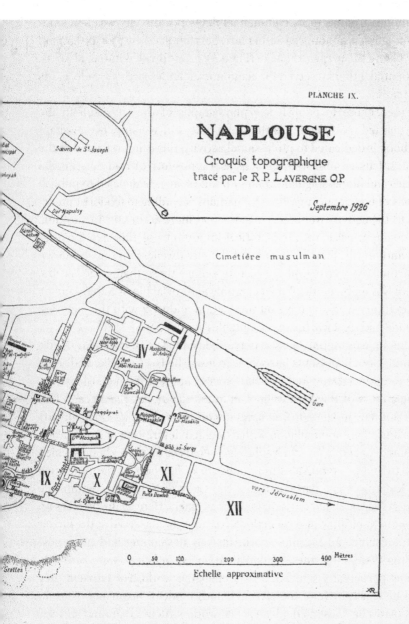

PLANCHE IX.

NAPLOUSE

Croquis topographique
tracé par le R. P. LAVERGNE O.P.

Septembre 1926

Cimetière musulman

Echelle approximative

Nablusi families. Thanks to its commercial networks, the city was less land-locked than Jaussen announced in his introduction. Jaussen provides a map of the city before the 1927 earthquake (Fig. 4.4): it was divided into 12 districts, some residential, others reserved for economic activities such as trade, crafts and industry.

Yet, Jaussen chose to publish few photographs of the city itself in the book and insisted on depicting shrines and places of worship. If one chapter of the book is dedicated to professional activity, this is not reflected in the book's plates. Jaussen observed the suqs as a repository of traditional crafts and factories and not as singular urban or public space He decided to publish photographs of craftsmanship (Fig. 4.5), perhaps according to folklorist preoccupations as the activity would be considered as more authentic. In addition, if the monograph insists on the historical importance of the soap factories in Nablus and on the shared concerns of the city dwellers on the slowdown in activity after the war period, no picture echoes those thematics. Yet, the soap factory was emblematic of the economic and social life of Nablus and its region: agriculture with the olive oil production, industry with the factories, regional trade and the local history of notables' families.[53]

According to Jean Métral, Jaussen perceived Nablus as an exemplary traditional Islamic city. He presents Jaussen as follows: 'he is a Catholic, and seeks to understand in what way, and by what process, another religion, Islam, permeates the culture of the city dwellers and their day-to-day practices'.[54] This concern is not new to Jaussen. *Coutumes des arabes au pays de Moab* already included a long chapter on religion with a detailed description of sanctuaries, religious practices and beliefs. In Nablus, Jaussen takes up these themes which were also studied by some Palestinian folklore researchers of the time such as Tawfīq Kanaʿān.[55] The particularity of the study of Nablus lies within the theme of amulets and what Jaussen qualifies as magic. Here again, he takes up themes dear to Kanaʿān whose collection of amulets is conserved at the Birzeit University Museum. As Muslim reformism was developing and modernist thinking was flourishing, these endangered social practices were probably perceived as particularly significant of a changing world. For Jaussen, they seemed to be constitutive of the city's religious mode of belonging. Thus, in the book's plates he chose to depict a social world structured around shrines,

---

53   Véronique Bontemps, *Ville et patrimoine en Palestine. Une ethnographie des savonneries de Naplouse* (Paris: Karthala, 2012).

54   Métral, "*Naplouse et son district: un essai de monographie urbaine,*" 133.

55   Tawfīq Canaan, *Mohammedan Saints and Sanctuaries in Palestine* (Jerusalem: Ariel Publishing House, 1927).

FIGURE 4.5 *Nablus and its craftsmanship, the weaver,* 1920s. Antonin Jaussen. Digitised glass
plate, 00321-J0326
IMAGE COURTESY OF EBAF

mostly located outside the city, sanctuaries and religious ceremonies. The photographs mostly represent buildings, without worshippers, clerics or guides
(Fig. 4.6).

The unpublished photographs of Nablus mirror another social depth
of the city and its inhabitants including: prayer in one of the city's mosques
(Fig. 4.7), scenes from the daily life in the city's souks with men wearing the
tarboosh (fez) (Fig. 4.8), the olive harvest in the city's surroundings (Fig. 4.9)
and photographs of women. In these photographs, Jaussen also takes up more
classic themes, such as the Samaritans, already represented by other photographers. Beyond Jaussen's bias in this monograph and its accompanying
plates – depicting Nablus in its tradition and timelessness – the question arises
as to the possibility of a visual ethnography at the time and its methodology,
both ethical and material. Jaussen's photographs suggest a certain sensitivity
in this regard as, for instance, in the picture representing the preparation of
the *qirāb* (water bags) (Fig. 4.10). If using video and photography as a tool for
anthropologists progressively became a concern from the 1970s onwards, in
some of his photographs, Jaussen seems to have already, at least in some of
his visual production, in the 1920's 'both implicitly and explicitly accepted the
responsibility of making and preserving records of the vanishing customs and
human being'.[56]

---

56   Paul Hockings, *Principles of Visual Anthropology, ed. World Anthropology Series* (The
      Hague: Mouton; Chicago: Aldine, 1975).

FIGURE 4.6 *Plate VIII*, 1920s. Jaussen, *Coutumes palestiniennes*, 1927

FIGURE 4.7 *Prayer in one of the Nablus' mosques*, 1920s. Antonin Jaussen. Digitised glass plate, 00274-J0279
IMAGE COURTESY OF EBAF

FIGURE 4.8 *The suq of Nablus before the 1927 earthquake*, 1920s. Antonin Jaussen. Digitised glass plate, 00262-J0267
IMAGE COURTESY OF EBAF

FIGURE 4.9 *Olive harvest in the region of Nablus*, 1920s. Antonin Jaussen. Digitised glass plate, 00256-J0261
IMAGE COURTESY OF EBAF

FIGURE 4.10 *Preparation of the qirāb in Nablus*, 1920s. Antonin Jaussen. Digitised glass plate, 00322-J0327
IMAGE COURTESY OF EBAF

These photographs, whether published or unpublished, are valuable sources since they document the state of the city before the earthquake of 1927. Jaussen's bias to depict a timeless city contrasts sharply with the series of photographs taken some fifteen years later, in 1940, by the American Colony that instead aimed at documenting the industrialisation of the city.[57]

2.3 An Ethnography of Intimacy?

In the study on Nablus, the place given to the study of women and women's sociability is noteworthy. Two chapters of the book are devoted to women (private and domestic lives), whereas this theme occupied only a sub-section of the book Coutumes des Arabes au pays de Moab. Jaussen explains this structure as follows: 'A woman is educated twice: the first time in her family, the second with her husband'.[58] The study of Nablus devotes a significant part to urban intimacy and household life.

Jaussen analyses the social dynamics of the city through a gendered perspective. In his perspective, the public space is reserved for men and marked by buildings and equipment of power (seraglio and municipality); of trading, crafts and industry (the souks, the soap factories); the khans and the courts. 'The law of confinement and separation'[59] limits the access of women to these public spaces. He qualifies the feminine city dwelling through the ritualisation of their mobility around some places such as the hammam, the cemetery or events such as weddings or gatherings around olive trees during the summer season. He also gives some descriptions of their ritualised urbanity[60] and different forms of 'sociability' between women, through the description of parties and ceremonies. The book also deals with issues related to intimacy, female genital circumcision and sexuality.

How did Jaussen investigate women in Nablus, since he stipulated: 'It is difficult for a stranger to know the habits of Nablusi women who can never be questioned directly. The obstacle is even greater if the survey concerns intimate lifestyles'.[61] Jaussen collected information during his surveys of Arab inscriptions in the city or at the St Joseph Sisters' dispensary. Part of the data also come from women's testimonials and interviews with Jaussen's privileged

---

57   See the series Arab factories & gen[eral] improvements in Nablus, https://www.loc.gov/ item/2019711122/ttps://www.loc.gov/item/2019711122/.
58   Jaussen, Coutumes palestiniennes, 85, 'La femme reçoit deux éducations: la première dans sa famille, la seconde chez son mari.'
59   Jaussen, Coutumes palestiniennes, 114.
60   Métral, "Naplouse et son district: un essai de monographie urbaine," 126.
61   Jaussen, Coutumes palestiniennes, 40.

male interlocutors, in particular sheikhs. The latter potentially take up the fantasy projections of female socialisation by men in the city, but was an attempt to overcome the methodological limitations imposed by the fieldwork.

The photographic plates of the book echo the focus given to women. Female portraits were commonplace for photographers at the time. One thinks in particular of Bonfils' portrait of a woman from Nablus – very likely a model that posed – representing a young woman sitting, dressed for the occasion, the lower part of her face covered by a veil. Postcards[62] and family portraits[63] were also widely used to depict women, with different perspectives and objectives. In addition, colonial fantasies about the 'Oriental' harem are the result of the difficulties Europeans had in understanding female spaces in Islamic societies.[64] The issue of the representation of women in the colonial context has been the subject of significant literature emphasising their eroticisation. In a context of growing nationalism, portraits of women have also contributed to national or activist iconographies, as in Egypt.[65] What narrative do Jaussen's portraits of women carry?

The discrepancy between Jaussen's description of social dynamics and the portraits presented in the book's plates is insightful. He states:

> The black veil (al-burqa') which, like a thick curtain, falls from the top of the head to the chest, completely obscures the view of the woman's features from the curious eye. Describing the physiognomy of a Nablus woman seems an impossible attempt for the visitor, who is necessarily kept at a distance.[66]

However, photographs of three women with uncovered faces within their house are reproduced in plate II (Fig. 4.11). On the lower right, a posed portrait of a woman obviously belonging to the Christian bourgeoisie of Nablus (Fig. 4.12). The composition of the picture recalls that of the wife of Ibrāhīm al-Tuwāl, from Mādabā (Fig. 4.13), photographed by Savignac in 1905, especially

---

62   Annelies Moors, "From 'Women's Lib.' to 'Palestinian Women': The Politics of Picture Postcard in Palestine/Israel," in *Visual Culture and Tourism*, eds. David Crouch and Nina Lubbren (Oxford and New York: Berg Publishers, 2003), 23–39.

63   Nassar, "Familial Snapshots."

64   Jocelyne Dakhlia, "Entrées dérobées: l'historiographie du harem," *Clio. Histoire, femmes et sociétés* 9 (1999): 1–13, online available via http://journals.openedition.org/clio/282.

65   Beth Baron, *Egypt as a Woman. Nationalism, gender and politics* (Berkeley: University of California Press, 2005).

66   Jaussen, *Coutumes palestiniennes*, 270.

COUTUMES PALESTINIENNES : NAPLOUSE PLANCHE II

1. La reine de la fête.

2. "... Les bandes de la tiare descendent le long du dos..."

3. "...collier au cou..., bracelets aux bras...".

FIGURE 4.11 *Plate II, 1920s. Jaussen, Coutumes palestiniennes, 1927*

FIGURE 4.12   *Christian Palestinian lady of Nablus*, 1920s. Antonin Jaussen. Digitised glass
plate, 11 × 15 cm, 00300-J0305
IMAGE COURTESY OF EBAF

the disposition of the arms. Clearly, the purpose of the photograph is to depict
the clothing and jewellery – which is carefully described in the book – but
also the atmosphere within the house. It is more as a model and not as a
subject-actor that this woman is represented in an almost folklorist perspective.
This portrait does not reveal much exoticisation, but rather the valorisation of
a certain urban bourgeoisie.

On the other two photographs of plate 11, the folklorist interest in the materiality of womanhood also appears clearly with a focus on women's clothing
and headdresses. All the pictures seem to have been taken in the same house.
Moreover, for those two photographs and others unpublished (Fig. 4.14), the
same woman poses to illustrate different situations. Probably confronted with
the impossibility of taking portraits of women from various social backgrounds,
Jaussen opted for, posed and composed portraits. This seems quite far from the
intimacy of female sociability presented in the text. At the top of the page,
the elongated portrait takes up the Orientalist codes of female representation
(Fig. 4.15). The composition of the photograph recalls odalisque paintings. This

FIGURE 4.13 *The wife of Ibrāhīm al-Tuwāl of Mādabā*, c. 1905. Raphaël Savignac. Digitised
glass plate, 11 × 15 cm, 00300-J0305
IMAGE COURTESY OF EBAF

FIGURE 4.14   *Portrait of a Nablusi woman*, 1920s. Antonin Jaussen. Digitised glass
plate, 11 × 15 cm, 00302-J0307
IMAGE COURTESY OF EBAF

FIGURE 4.15   *Portrait of a Nablusi woman lying down*, 1920s. Antonin Jaussen.
Digitised glass plate, 11 × 15 cm, 00302-J0308
IMAGE COURTESY OF EBAF

FIGURE 4.16   *Nablusi woman with her baby on her knees*, 1920s. Antonin Jaussen. Digitised
glass plate, 11 × 15 cm, 00304-J0309
IMAGE COURTESY OF EBAF

reveals that the circulation of harem iconography contributed to the creation
of a historically distorted world in which gendered, staged images of anonymous models were attributed to Moorish, Bedouin, Jewish and Arab identities.
The subject poses lying down, sideways on a makeshift bench installed on the
floor. The photograph is taken near stairs, far from the intimacy of a bedroom
or private room. It reveals the impregnation of an Orientalist imaginary and
the methodological and technical inability to represent feminine intimacy
differently.

For his book, Jaussen chose posed and highly composed photographs. Yet
other pictures may show this feminine intimacy differently. For instance, one
posed picture shows a woman with her baby on her knees. This representation echoes the symbolic universe and the canon of representation of the
Virgin with the child and recall Biblical themes. (Fig. 4.16). Several photographs represent women visiting the Sisters' dispensary. In his book, Jaussen
depicts women in what he projected to be the intimacy of their homes. To do
so, in some respects, as experimenting with ethnographic portraits, he did not
necessarily detach himself methodologically or artistically from Orientalist
representations or other artistic codes.

3   A Plurality of Perception?

If Jaussen's photographs stand out within the EBAF's collection, they embody some of the scientific ambitions of this specific Catholic institution. How do we find, in the photographs of other Catholic institutions, concerns that *a posteriori* can be read as ethnographic? Along with a visual production directly linked to religious objects and events in the different European Catholic communities in Palestine, the EBAF photographic collection provides insights into the Arab Palestinian communities and invites us to reflect on the role of missionary photography within social history. As observers of political tensions and social change, the missionaries' lenses captured more than what was explicitly and deliberately religious in nature. What representations emerge from this collection?

3.1   *Catholic Missionary Photographs and the Social History of Palestine*
We returned to the diversity of missionary images often, during and after our stay at the EBAF, and asked ourselves what they conveyed; what types of relationships might be inferred or imagined between the photographer and the people in the photographs. For us, as historians, the visual archives of missions must be approached with the same critical scrutiny as any other organisational record. How do photographs taken by missionaries constitute a distinct category of information that can be used alongside the more familiar text-based materials?

We expected the corpus of photographs of the other Catholic missionaries to include 'Holy Land' sites, archaeology, transnational movements of pilgrims during the interwar period, views on different aspects of what was presented as modernity/modernisation propelled by empires.[67] Many of the photographs in the Catholic missionary collections we consulted for this article deal with what could be described as the physical influence of the missionaries: roughly one third of the photographs depict school buildings, mission compounds, construction projects, dispensaries and hospitals; one third (mainly those of the EBAF) archaeological sites. The other third depicts spaces of religion (dealing with Western and local religious events in Palestine) and spaces of power (related to consulates, local Arab elites or linked to specific political events).

---

67   Mary Roberts and Jocelyn Hackforth-Jones, "Introduction: Visualizing Culture across the Edges of Empires," In *Edges of Empire: Orientalism and Visual Culture*, eds. Jocelyn Hackforth-Jones and Mary Roberts (Oxford: Blackwell Publishing, 2005), 1–19; Michelle Woodward, "Between Orientalist Clichés and Images of Modernization," *History of Photography* 27, no. 4 (2003): 363–374.

The collections document the religious endeavours of the missionaries as they reflect their experiences and agenda. These archives record their views of communities and the religious and political environment of British Mandate Palestine. Missionaries had both religious and mundane reasons to take photographs: they were record keepers and, with the advent of photography, they began to use photography to compile a visual record of their activities. They became more sophisticated about the educational and fundraising potential of photography. They also kept detailed records and photographs for their hierarchy and for missionary events within their correspondence with the Vatican. As a consequence, most Catholic missionary orders keep their archives, where they have an accumulation of historical photographs, taken for a variety of purposes, and in various styles and levels of technical skill.

When dealing with missionary photographs, inevitably comes the question of the 'propaganda'[68] discourse these photographs convey. As Anne Hugon pointed out, it would be necessary to 'recover the intention of the producer' and 'understand how these images were perceived',[69] which is very often difficult to grasp. The photographs in various missionary journals reflect the changes affecting missionary work, especially in their relations with indigenous peoples.[70] The 'transformative' photographs, i.e. those that reflect the changes that people have undergone in contact with missionaries, are recurrent.[71] But

---

68   Jean Pirotte, "La mobilisation missionnaire, prototype des propagandes modernes," in *La mission en textes et en images*, ed. Christine Paisant (Paris: Karthala, 2004), 213; Christraud Geary, "Missionary photography: private and public readings," *African Arts* 24, no. 4 (1991): 48–59; Paul Jenkins, "On using historical missionary photographs in modern discussion," *Le Fait Missionnaire* 10 (2001): 71–87; Paul Jenkins, "Sources of unexpected light. Experiences with old mission photographs in research on overseas history," *Jarhbuch für Europaische Uberseegeschichte* 1 (2001): 157–167; Jack Thompson, "Xhosa missionaries to Malawi: Black Europeans or African Christians?," *International Bulletin of Missionary Research* 24, no. 4 (October 2000): 168–170; Jack Thompson, *Light on Darkness?: Missionary Photography of Africa in the Nineteenth and Early Twentieth Centuries, Studies in the History of Christian Missions* (Grand Rapids, MI: Wm. B. Eerdmans Publishing, 2012).

69   Anne Hugon, "Aspect de la propagande missionnaire," in *Images et colonies. Nature, discours et influence de l'iconographie coloniale liée à la propagande coloniale et à la représentation des Africains et de l'Afrique en France, de 1920 aux Indépendances*, eds. Pascal Blanchard and Armelle Chatelier (Paris: ACHAC et Syros, 1993), 77–84.

70   Françoise Raison-Jourde, "Image missionnaire française et propagande coloniale," in *Images et colonies. Iconographie et propagande coloniale sur l'Afrique française de 1880 à 1962*, eds. Nicolas Bancel, Pascal Blanchard and Laurent Gervereau (Nanterre: BDIC, 1993), 50–57; Judith Becker, *Menschen – Bilder – Eine Welt: Ordnungen von Vielfalt in der religiösen Publizistik um 1900* (Veröffentlichungen des Instituts für Europäische Geschichte Mainz – Beihefte, Band 118).

71   In a comparative perspective, we questioned the main differences between Protestant and Catholic missionaries' photographs for the Mandate and noticed the Protestant

most of these Catholic missionaries' photographs were not intended for missionary journals.[72]

The acknowledged motive of the missionaries may have been to record their own evangelical activities, to inform their superiors and ensure continued public support from their home nations. However, some seem to have been curious about what happened around them, whether or not those objects and events were specifically religious. The result is that the themes illustrated by the pictures in these collections are not limited to photographs that display or validate the missionary agenda. These images help in capturing the broader developments of cultural, economic, political and technological transformation of societies. They also show the international platform that was Palestine and the dynamics of power between European countries and different Christian communities, the growing Arab Latin Catholic communities in Palestine, their traditional celebrations as well as their trans-regional links, particularly to Transjordan.[73]

Looking at missionaries as photographers questions situations of complicity/distancing/spontaneity in the photographs, though this is often difficult to tackle. It also questions the bodies in the photographs. Within the context of a renewed interest in photography as an object, source and method in anthropology since the 1990s,[74] missionary photography was analysed within a colonial framework. It was approached via the anthropology of the body or even an anthropology of aesthetics/otherness developed by missionaries[75] that made these colonised bodies meaningful (mainly in the context of Africa). In this article, we tried to question the straightforward documentation, the 'counterintuitive events, [...] scenes that go against common stereotypes' [...]

---

missionary work in the school field for example, aimed mainly at enabling the formation of an indigenous clergy and a certain secular elite; images of the child and the nun are major figures used as metaphors for Protestant missionary work. Norbert Friedrich, Uwe Kaminsky, and Roland Löffler, eds., *The Social Dimension of Christian Missions in the Middle East. Historical studies of the 19th and 20th Centuries* (Stuttgart: Franz Steiner Verlag, 2010).

72   'It would be a pity, of course, if analysis of missionary photography only concerns themselves with photographs as propaganda', Jenkins Paul, "The earliest generation of missionary photographers in West Africa: The portrayal of Indigenous people and culture," *Visual Anthropology* 7 (1994): 137.

73   De Tarragon, "Holy Land Pilgrimage through Historical Photography."

74   Gilbert Beaugé and Jean-Noël Pelen, eds., "Photographie, ethnographie, histoire. Présentation," *Le monde alpin et rhodanien* 2–4 (1995): 7–17; Emmanuel Garrigues, "Le savoir ethnographique de la photographie," *L'Ethnographie* 109, 87–1 (1991): 11–54.

75   Dahbia Abrous and Hélène Claudot-Hawad, *Mimétisme des corps et conquêtes des âmes. Les photographies des Missionnaires d'Afrique (Kabylie, Aurès, Sahara)* (Paris: Non-lieu, coll; Entre-Rives, 2017), 14.

challenging 'taken-for-granted presuppositions and stimulat[ing] new ways of looking at social change'.[76]

By the First World War, male and female Catholic mission agents had succeeded in establishing outposts wherever the influence of European countries had penetrated Palestine: in the main cities, but also in rural areas, reaching remote regions. They were significant non-Arab witnesses to events in those places. Some were alert observers of the political, social and economic transformations of the period, though these evolutions were not at the heart of their albums/photographic collections.

3.2   *What Representation of Palestinian Society and Its Evolution?*
There are more photographs dealing with indigenous people for the Mandate period than for the period from the EBAF's establishment in 1890 to the fall of the Ottoman Empire. Some photographers seem to have sought to document the daily lives and traditions of Palestinian Arabs, while others seem to have been more interested in the changes that the mission brought. Many pictures were taken in diverse places, from the neighbourhood of the EBAF to coastal cities and remote villages of Palestine. Those pictures – as ethnographic evidence – represent different social groups,[77] not only the employees of the EBAF and the workers on the archaeological sites. They also show a good knowledge of some of the elites, as explained above (Fig. 4.17), the quality glass plate used to photograph this couple indicates that they were close to Savignac). They document the diversity of the missionaries' activities, of the Arab population and different types of events. Those multiple lenses also interact with the multiple agendas of the photographers so as to constitute situated testimonies on the Palestinian society of the time. Here (Fig. 4.18), a Christian family from Mādabā visiting the Dominican Friars, in the courtyard of St Stephen convent, just before or after WWI, illustrating the mobility and the transregional exchanges in the zone up to the early 1920s.

We targeted a few subcategories from the many intended and unintended cultural impacts[78] of the missions rooted in the early development of

---

76   Stanczak, *Visual research methods Image Society and Representations*, 83–120.

77   *The First Century of Photography: Photography as History/ Historicizing Photography in Ottoman territories (1839–1939)*, workshop organized by Boğaziçi University Archives and Document Center, RCAC (Research Center for Anatolian Civilization), and IFEA (Institut Francais d'Études Anatoliennes), İstanbul and Aix Marseille University, LabExMed & IDEMEC, 19–21 June 2018, https://anamed.ku.edu.tr/wp-content/uploads/2018/08/The _First_Century_of_Photography_ANAMED-1.pdf.

78   Heather Sharkey, *Unexpected Consequences of Christian Missions in the Middle East, Africa and South Asia* (Syracuse: Syracuse University Press, 2013).

FIGURE 4.17   *Couple levantin*, after 1920. Raphaël Savignac. Digitised glass plate, 11 × 15 cm,
5601-6644
IMAGE COURTESY OF EBAF

missionary-founded congregations. They are by no means exhaustive or representative of the diversity of this collection.

The Dominicans commented on the political situation and were conscious
of witnessing formative events for the Arab population. This is also true for
some of the other Catholic missionaries. Though the Dominicans did not
share the same time/space scales to Palestine as the indigenous Arab population. Jaussen was a witness of Arab frustration in Palestine during and after
the First World War as evidenced in his reports to the French authorities.
The silence about Zionist activities is remarkable. Jewish religious communities and celebrations do appear in the photographic collection, but not the
Zionist associations, leaders or activities. This can be interpreted as a negation,
either of their activities and impact in the missionaries' local environment at a
proto-national level; or as situated outside missionary reality. Several missionaries did however reflect on the political events in different archives.

Indeed, during the political turmoil, missionaries were in the front row. For
example, from the Old City of Jerusalem, where most Catholic missionaries
had their compounds, they witnessed riots, curfews, their social and economic

FIGURE 4.18   *Catholic family of Mādabā visiting EBAF*, early 1920s. Raphaël Savignac.
Digitised glass plate, 11 × 15 cm, 5468-2484
IMAGE COURTESY OF EBAF

impact. Cross-analysed with their diaries when available, the image of
Jerusalem that emerges from this collection is not a sleeping city, resting on its
mythical and biblical reputation during the Mandate, but a worldly and political Jerusalem. This might have resulted from the need to record and display
Jerusalem, whether for specific religious audiences, or for French and Italian
diplomats as well as for Vatican interlocutors. But also as a personal testimony,
as confirmed in the diary entries of some missionaries.[79] The following two
photographs, likely taken spontaneously, most probably from the building of
the Betharram Fathers in the Old City of Jerusalem, deal with the beginning of
a riot on 13th October 1933,[80] when the Arab Executive Committee planned a

79   Archives of the Collège des frères des écoles chrétiennes of Jerusalem ACJ, Bethlehem ACB
     and Caiffa (Haifa) ACH, Sisters of Zion diaries ASZ, Archives of Saint Anne of Jerusalem
     diaries ASAJ.
80   The riots came as the culmination of Arab resentment at Jewish migration after it surged
     to new heights following the rise of Nazi Germany, and at the British Mandate authorities
     for allegedly facilitating Jewish land purchases. Rashid Khalidi, *The Iron cage. The Story of
     the Palestinian Struggle for Statehood* (Boston: Beacon Press, 2007), 32, 36.

strike accompanied by a procession to take place from the Ḥarām al-Sharīf to the Government Offices. The High Commissioner banned the demonstration, but it went ahead, regardless. British police officers stationed themselves at all the gates of the Old City and locked the gates to keep the rioters inside and dispersed them (Fig. 4.19 and Fig. 4.20).

Some photographs show other aspects of political events though not a priori dealing with them directly. The seminary of Saint Anne for the Melkites maintained by the White Fathers since 1882[81] for example, has more than 200 photographs dealing with different political/religious events. The brass band of Saint Anne (*fanfare*) (Fig. 4.21), created in 1887, was requested by the Consulate General of France for notable events such as the Mass of 14 July (Bastille Day), the Mass of Joan of Arc or for the arrival of the first plane in Jerusalem on 31 December 1913. Different parts of Arab Palestinian society appear in this type of photograph. In this photograph of 1932, only the professor is French, Armand Laily. Saint Anne was also on the route followed by pilgrims during the celebrations of Nabī Mūsā, near the Ḥarām and the Lions' Gate (Fig. 4.22, Fig. 4.23). During the Mandate period, the Mawsim al-Nabī Mūsā (the Prophet Moses festival), honouring the shrine of the Prophet Moses (7 kilometres from Jericho) was both a religious celebration and a national gathering for pilgrims from all Palestine.[82] The riots during the Nabī Mūsā festival in Jerusalem in 1920 was an expression of opposition both to Zionism and to the British rule. These images were probably taken from one of the furthest rooms of the White Fathers' building on the Via Dolorosa. Several photographs concern Nabī Mūsā pilgrims in different parts of Jerusalem, during the different moments of the celebration. The photographer, a White Father, captured many moments while being among the crowd of pilgrims until the beginning of 1920, then more from Saint Anne's balconies (for instance in 1922; a British officer on horse, Fig. 4.22). The comments in the Saint Anne diaries and personal notes of some French Melkite Fathers reveal their understanding of the political repercussions and

---

81   Archives of Saint Anne of Jerusalem ASAJ, diaries of the junior and senior seminary, 1919 until 1933 and Central White Fathers archives, Rome, Saint Anne of Jerusalem reports, statistics and programmes of events. Dominique Trimbur, "Sainte Anne, lieu de mémoire et lieu de vie français à Jérusalem," *Chrétiens et sociétés XVIe–XXe*, Bulletin 7 (2000): 39–69.

82   Awad Halabi, "Islamic Ritual and Palestinian Nationalism: al-Hajj Amin and the Prophet Moses Festival in Jerusalem, 1921 to 1936," in *Jerusalem Interrupted: Modernity and Colonial Transformation 1917-Present*, ed. Lena Jayyusi (Northampton, MA: Interlink Publishing, 2013), 139–161; Emma Aubin-Boltanski, *Pèlerinages et nationalisme en Palestine. Prophètes, héros et ancêtres* (Paris: EHESS, 2007); Roberto Mazza, "Transforming the Holy City: From Communal Clashes to Urban Violence, the Nebi Musa Riots 1920," in *Urban Violence in the Middle East Changing Cityscapes: The Transition from Empire to Nation State*, eds. Ulrike Freitag, Nelida Fuccaro, Claudia Ghrawi and Nora Lafi (New York: Bergham, 2015), 179–94.

FIGURE 4.19   *Riot*, 13th October 1933. Caption (in French) on the top part: "Émeutes du 13 octobre 1933", bottom: "Avant: la police approche ..." Betharram Fathers, Médebielle collection; 22547-LPJ, 1644
IMAGE COURTESY OF EBAF

FIGURE 4.20   *Riot,* 13th October 1933. Caption on the top part: "La charge ..." bottom: "Après:
le débloquement ..." Betharram Fathers, Médebielle collection; 22547-
LPJ, 1645
IMAGE COURTESY OF EBAF

FIGURE 4.21   *Brass band of Saint Anne (fanfare)*, early 1920s. White Fathers collection,
15977-SteA-0146
IMAGE COURTESY OF EBAF

the nationalist nature of this pilgrimage. They discuss the diversity of its participants (from Arab peasants to young nationalist activists) and the rivalry
between the Ḥusaynīs and the Nashāshībīs.

Several photographs concern the Arab clergy, its role within the different
Oriental Churches, the cultural and religious influence around them and the
ecclesiastical relationships between European missionaries and indigenous
church members. Some photographs bring to the fore simple congregants, like
in this photograph (Fig. 4.24) of a Melkite priest and his wife with their two
daughters (until the 1920s they were not dressed in the Western style). The
Saint Anne collection also addresses the rural Melkite communities. The following photograph of Nīcūlā Dāhbār (Fig. 4.25), a future Melkite priest and his
father, taken in the garden of Saint Anne, at the beginning of the 1920s, is interesting on different levels. Dāhbār attended the Senior Seminary. He had already
received minor orders (deacon in 1916) as he is wearing the Greek cassock and
the cylindrical hat (without the edges at the top reserved for priests). Born in
1891 in Yabrūd (Syria, near Ḥums), he stayed twice at Saint Anne's because of
the 1914–1918 war. In 1904 he arrived there as a junior seminarian at the age of
13; he remained there until 1914. During the war he taught in Damascus and
returned to Saint Anne's, after the armistice. He was ordained in 1920. Friars

FIGURE 4.22   *Nabi Mouça* (sic) *festival,* 1922. White Fathers collection, 19348-Ste A-Cont.1275
IMAGE COURTESY OF EBAF

FIGURE 4.23   *Nabi Mouça* (sic) *festival*, 1922. White Fathers collection, Nabī Mūsā
19355-Ste A-Cont.1282
IMAGE COURTESY OF EBAF

wore the traditional dress of the cities and urban periphery.[83] Later on, Dāhbār
played an important role in the quarrels with the Bishop concerning the impact
of French diplomacy and language on the Melkite communities.

Education was one of the means of social progression in Palestine; missionaries had been very active in this field since the last quarter of the nineteenth
century. The photographic collections deal with different types of education
provided for different groups, from the growing Arab Palestinian middle
class to vocational education like that of the Salesian schools (Fig. 4.26). The
Salesians maintained vocational schools mainly oriented towards agriculture,
but also other manual trades according to the tradition they had inherited from
Don Bosco. Initially created for orphans they rapidly admitted non-orphan
children. The vocational schools welcomed children beyond the borders of
Mandate Palestine. For the agriculture section, they recruited throughout
the region. As in the case of the Melkite photographic collection, they show
trans-regional relationships. The estate of Bayt Jamāl owned vineyards, had

83   Réseau Barnabé, "*Regards sur l'éducation chez les Chrétiens d'Orient, A travers le fonds
photographique ancien (1890–1930) de l'Ecole biblique et archéologique française de
Jérusalem*," 68.

FIGURE 4.24   *A melkite priest with his wife and daughters*, 1920s. F. Jules Riffier, photographer
of Saint Anne until 1926, White Fathers collection, from, 18325 Ste A 238
IMAGE COURTESY OF EBAF

developed the production of wine, and taught their pupils how to make good
wine. The technical equipment and knowledge also echoes the Zionist equipment in agricultural outposts (here, a Fordson tractor with metallic wheels, in
a region where harvest was difficult due to the stones).

Within missionary stations, students are mainly presented through class-
room portraits, where they are organised in successive rows according to their
gender. From the 1940s onwards, this aesthetic tends to disappear in favour of
interactions between missionaries and Arab Palestinians. Schoolchildren are
always photographed outdoors, but more often in less organised groups, with
photographs taken 'on the spot'. In the class photographs for example, one
perceives situations of collusion, spontaneous exchanges, the type of relationships that texts addressed to superiors do not always evoke (Fig. 4.27). Multiple
influences on the Arab Palestinian population are revealed by clichéd gestures
or practices. Appearances show the complexity of the influences: adoption of
another costume, abandonment of local clothing with a strong symbolic charge
(such as the *tarbush*). The 1930s also present the student's cultural activities,

FIGURE 4.25
Nīcūlā Dāhbār and his
father from Yabroud,
1920s. White Fathers
collection, 18291-Ste
A-Cont.204
IMAGE COURTESY OF
EBAF

places of sociability and events in which Scouts participated in the competitive educational arena, (Fig. 4.28) offering cultural activities for youth. Catholic
institutions competed the establishment of the YMCA with its multiple activities. The photographs also reveal the travels of pupils around Palestine and
a comprehension of the 'national'[84] and religious heritage (no captions, but

84   Though the Catholic hierarchy prevented missionaries from taking part in local national
      agenda (Apostolical Letter *Maximum Illud* in 1919 and Encyclic *Rerum Ecclesiae* in 1926),
      the Latin Patriarch Barlassina, pro-Italian, emphasised the importance of the teaching of

FIGURE 4.26   *Salesian school, tractor Fordson*, 1938. Collection of the Salesians
               Fathers, 17165-Sal.196, Beit Jimal, 1935–38
               IMAGE COURTESY OF EBAF

FIGURE 4.27   *A class outside, Ain Karim*, 17th February 1934. Latin Patriarchate
               archives, 22572-LPJ, 1669
               IMAGE COURTESY OF EBAF

FIGURE 4.28   *Catholic scouts of Beit Jala*, 1925. Caption behind, 'À Sa Béatitude Mgr.
le Patriarche Latin, Jérusalem'. Blue stamp, 'Palestine Catholic Scouts
Association. Beit-Jala'. On the sticker: 'I giovani esploratori col loro
Parroco D. Bonaventura Habase – 1925'. Latin Patriarchate archives,
21420-LPJ, 0524
IMAGE COURTESY OF EBAF

FIGURE 4.29   *Catholic scouts in a trip around Palestine, Lydda junction station*, 1930s.
Salesians archives, 26489-scouts 28
IMAGE COURTESY OF EBAF

FIGURE 4.30   *Alumni of the Sisters of Sion, charity for the poor of the Bab Hutta neighbourhood*, 1926. Sisters of Sion Archives
IMAGE COURTESY OF EBAF

FIGURE 4.31   *Rosary sisters and their pupils, Zababdeh*, 1933. Archives of the Rosary Sisters,
22188-LPJ, 1293
IMAGE COURTESY OF EBAF

the expressions 'patrimoine', 'patrie' appear in the textual archives) (Fig. 4.29),
Salesians scouts in their 'tour of Palestine' in the mid-1940s).

The various schools' photographs also convey views on girls'/women's education and role in Palestinian society. The alumni photographs of the three
main Catholic women orders offer glimpses of the activities of women's associations, sometimes linked to political activism or welfare actions (Fig. 4.30,
Sisters Sion alumni, charity for the poor families of the neighbourhood of Bab
Hutta, Jerusalem). These archives often contain lists of people that can be
cross analysed with other archives to understand the activities and potential
impact of alumni associations[85] and trajectories of girls enrolled in these missionary schools. They also reveal the impact of the indigenous Catholic order
of the Rosary Sisters (Fig. 4.31 and Fig. 4.32, Rosary Sisters pupils and alumni in
Zababdeh in 1933). Created in 1886 by D. Tannous, a local priest, and the only

Arabic as the national language of Palestine (*Ordonnance*, 1920, LPA) and the knowledge
of the geography and history of the region for pupils of Catholic schools.

85   Ellen Fleischmann, *The Nation and Its "New" Women: The Palestinian Women's Movement,
1920–1948* (Berkeley: University of California Press, 2003).

FIGURE 4.32   *Rosary Sisters with Alumni and priest, Zababdeh*, 1933. Archives of the Rosary
sisters, 22189 LPJ 1294
IMAGE COURTESY OF EBAF

Palestinian Catholic congregation, the Rosary sisters expanded in the region
and reached remote rural areas.[86] They promoted girls' education, going further than the Latin Patriarchate schools by teaching all topics in Arabic (here,
Fig. 4.33 at Yāffā al-Nāṣariyya, 1922–23).[87]

Other photographs deal with inter-rituality among Catholic communities.
The Catholic Procession at Beit Jimal (Fig. 4.34) took place at Corpus Christi.
The students from the vocational school frame the canopy under which the
priest carries the Blessed Sacrament in procession. The rite is Latin Catholic,

---

86   Vatican Archives of the Oriental Congregations, Rome, Latini Propaganda Fide, file 451,
     Suore del Rosario (in Zabaddeh since 1884; in Yāffā al-Nāṣariyya since 1885, school and
     professional school 'ouvroir') and *La congrégation des sœurs du Rosaire de Jérusalem*
     (Paris: J. Gabalda, 1913).

87   In the 1922 census of Palestine conducted by the British Mandate authorities, Yāffā
     al-Nāṣariyya had a total population of 615; 215 Muslims and 400 Christians; J.B. Barron,
     ed., *Palestine: Report and General Abstracts of the Census of 1922. Government of Palestine;*
     Barron, 1923, Table XI, Sub-district of Nazareth, 38. The population had increased at the
     1931 census, when Yafa had a population of 833; 456 Muslims and 377 Christians, in a
     total of 213 houses, E. Mills, ed., *Census of Palestine 1931. Population of Villages, Towns and
     Administrative Areas. Jerusalem: Government of Palestine (1932).*

FIGURE 4.33   *School for girls in Yaffa en-Nasariyye*, 1922–1923. Caption on the back, 'Jaffa
de Nazareth. 1922–1923', 'La scuola feminile nel 1920'. Latin Patriarchate
archives, 21617-LPJ 0721
IMAGE COURTESY OF EBAF

FIGURE 4.34   *Latin procession at Beit Jimal*, 1935, with Greek-Catholic, Maronite, Armenian
Catholic and Syriac Catholics. Salesians archives, 17098 Sal. 100
IMAGE COURTESY OF EBAF

although the students are Greek-Catholic, Maronite, Armenian Catholic and Syriac Catholic.

Catholic missionaries witnessed the social changes in Palestinian society. They were present in Palestine since the last quarter of the nineteenth century for most of them. For some, they maintained close relations with different parts of Arab Palestinian society, partly reflected on the changes in their diverse visual productions. Producing diverse photographs about rural and urban Palestine and Palestinians, the missionaries also underlined 'the emergence of a cultural divide between mercantile coastal communities and mountain-dwelling smallholder peasants'.[88] The visual language used during the Ottoman period was still influencing their visual production at the beginning of the 1920s, but they transformed it as society faced rapid changes. At the end of the Mandate period, missionaries documented the social history of Arab Palestinian refugees during and after the Arab-Israeli War and many missionary outposts served as refuge zones: Jerusalem, Jaffa, Bethlehem and Gaza areas (Fig. 4.35 here at the Latin Patriarchate school courtyard in Gaza, food and clothes distribution).[89]

4   Conclusion

By attempting to analyse the constitution of Catholic missionaries' photographic archives at the EBAF – images not disseminated through the illustrated press, postcards, so not well-known by researchers and wider audiences – we hope to contribute to a broader and nuanced redefinition of the British Mandate visual space. To a certain extent, this responds to the call of Ali Behdad for archival awareness in the study of photography. Behdad contends that:

> Faced with a seemingly endless, dispersed corpus of visual materials, photographic historians must remain vigilant about the internal differences and histories of archives and about their modes of production and

---

88   Salim Tamari, *Mountain against Sea. Essays on Palestinian Society and Culture* (Berkeley: University of California Press, 2008).

89   Maria Chiara Rioli, "Catholic Humanitarian assistance for the Palestinian refugees: The Franciscan Casa Nova of Jerusalem in the 1948 Storm," in *Christian Missions and Humanitarianism in the Middle East, 1850–1950. Ideologies, Rhetoric and Practices*, eds. Inger Marie Okkenhaug and Karène Sanchez Summerer (Leiden: Brill, 2020), 253–275.

FIGURE 4.35   *Food distribution in Gaza*, 1948. Caption 'D. Sourour with refugee children'.
Latin Patriarchate archives, 21763-LPJ 0868
IMAGE COURTESY OF EBAF

intended purposes, lest the sheer mass of material impose its own logic
that occludes the complexities of its subject matter'.[90]

This overview resulted from time spent at the EBAF when for the first time our
research agendas prompted us to rethink what the EBAF images were telling
us about the image maker, the viewer, the way in which images were shared,
talked about and the impact of missionary photography on social history.[91]

    The way observers such as missionaries have looked at, perceived and under-
stood Arab communities remains largely unknown. Missionary photography
cannot therefore be analysed from a single point of view. On the contrary, it
must be read from different perspectives. Interest in Palestinian Arab society
became progressively more important among Catholic missionaries during
the Mandate period. If Palestine is compared to the rest of the 'Holy Land', the

90   Ali Behdad and Luke Gartlan, eds. *Photography's Orientalism: New Essays on Colonial
Representation* (Los Angeles: Getty Publications, 2013), 5.
91   Friedrich, *The Social Dimension of Christian Missions in the Middle East.*

position of the Catholic missionaries as photographers, is of an idiosyncratic character: it interprets local architectural traditions in a proto-regionalist manner and, to a certain extent, populations, through a plurality of visual narratives. The Mandate period corresponds to an in-between period for Catholic missionaries, adapting their visual approach and production to their adjustment to the mandated control of a non-Catholic European power and to Arab nationalism.

References

Archives and Sources

Photographic collection of the EBAF (*photothèque*)

Diaries of St Stephen priory

ACJ   Archives of the Collège des frères des écoles chrétiennes of Jerusalem
ACB   Archives of the Collège des frères des écoles chrétiennes of Bethlehem
ACH   Archives of the Collège des frères des écoles chrétiennes of Caiffa (Haifa)
AMGPB   Archives of the Maison Généralice des Pères Blancs – Rome
ASAJ   Archives of Saint Anne of Jerusalem
ASSJ   Archives of Saint Joseph Sisters
ASZ   Archives of Sisters of Zion

Berchem, M. van. "Aux pays de Moab et d'Edom." Extracted from *Journal des Savants*. Paris: Imprimerie nationale (July-August- 1909): 33–35.

Canaan, T. *Mohammedan Saints and Sanctuaries in Palestine*. Jerusalem: Ariel Publishing House, 1927.

Jaussen, A. "Le Cheikh Sa'ad ad-Din et les 'djinn' à Naplouse." *Revue Biblique* (1905): 145–157.

Jaussen, A. "Trois inscription arabes inédites, du haram d'Hébron." *Revue Biblique* (January 1923).

Jaussen, A. "Inscriptions coufiques de la chaire du martyr al-Husayn, à Hébron." *Revue Biblique* (October 1923).

Jaussen, A. "Inscription arabes de la ville d'Hébron." *BIFAO* (1924).

Jaussen, A. "Inscriptions arabes de Naplouse." *BIFAO* (1924).

Jaussen, A. *Coutumes palestiniennes. I. Naplouse et son district*. Paris: Geuthner, 1927.

Jaussen, A. *Coutumes des Arabes au pays de Moab*. Paris: Adrien-Maisonneuve, 1948.

La congrégation des sœurs du Rosaire de Jérusalem. Paris: J. Gabalda, 1913.

Vincent, L.-H., and F.-M. Abel. *Hébron. Le Haram el-Khalîl, sépulture des Patriarches*. Paris: Leroux, 1923.

Bibliography

Abrous, Dahbia and Claudot-Hawad, Hélène. *Mimétisme des corps et conquêtes des âmes. Les photographies des Missionnaires d'Afrique (Kabylie, Aurès, Sahara)*. Paris: Non-lieu, coll. Entre-Rives, 2017.

Aubin-Boltanski, Emma. *Pèlerinages et nationalisme en Palestine. Prophètes, héros et ancêtres*. Paris: EHESS, 2007.

Baron, Beth. *Egypt as a Woman. Nationalism, gender and politics*. Berkeley: University of California Press, 2005.

Barromi, Edna. "Archeology, Zionism and Photography in Palestine: Analysis of the Use of Dimensions of People in Photographs." *Journal of Landscape Ecology* 10, no. 3 (2017): 49–57.

Beaugé, G., and Pelen, Jean-Noël, eds. "Photographie, ethnographie, histoire. Présentation." *Le monde alpin et rhodanien* 2–4 (1995): 7–17.

Becker, Judith. *Menschen – Bilder – Eine Welt: Ordnungen von Vielfalt in der religiösen Publizistik um 1900*. Veröffentlichungen des Instituts für Europäische Geschichte Mainz – Beihefte, Band 118.

Behdad, Ali and Gartlan, Luke, eds. *Photography's Orientalism: New Essays on Colonial Representation*. Los Angeles: Getty Publications, 2013.

Bontemps, Véronique. *Ville et patrimoine en Palestine. Une ethnographie des savonneries de Naplouse*. Paris: Karthala, 2012.

Carney, Gavin. "Bonfils and the Early Photography of the Near East." *Harvard Library Bulletin* vol 26, no. 4 (1978): 442–470.

Çelik, Zeynep. "Photographing Mundane Modernity." In *Camera Ottomana: Photography and Modernity in the Ottoman Empire, 1840–1914*, edited by Zeynep Çelik and Edhem Eldem, 154–200. Istanbul: Koç University Press, 2015.

Chatelard, Géraldine and Tarawneh, Mohammed, eds. *Antonin Jaussen. Sciences sociales occidentales et patrimoine arabe*. Beirut: CERMOC, 1999.

Chatelard, Géraldine and de Tarragon, Jean-Michel. *L'Empire et le royaume. La Jordanie vue par l'École biblique et archéologique française de Jérusalem (1893–1935)*. Amman: Centre culturel français d'Amman, 2006.

Clark, Terry. *Prophets and Patrons: the French University and the Emergence of the Social Sciences*. Cambridge: Harvard University Press, 1973.

Dakhlia, Jocelyne. "Entrées dérobées: l'historiographie du harem." *Clio. Histoire, femmes et sociétés* 9 (1999): 1–13. Available via http://journals.openedition.org/clio/282.

Depaule, Jean-Charles. "Archiver des photographies au Proche Orient: La Fondation arabe pour l'image." In *Archiver au Moyen-Orient, Fabriques documentaires contemporaines*, edited by Christine Jüngen and Jihane Sfeir, 157–190. Paris: Karthala, 2019.

Doumani, Bishara. *Rediscovering Palestine: Merchants and Peasants in Jabal Nablus, 1700–1900*. Berkeley: University of California Press, 1995.

Escande, Renault. "Un jeu de regards: la photographie de Jaussen et Savignac à travers la croisière de l'Ecole pratique d'Etudes bibliques autour de la mer Morte." In *Antonin Jaussen. Sciences sociales occidentales et patrimoine arabe*, edited by G. Chatelard and M. Tarawneh, 107–120. Beirut: CERMOC, 1999.

Eyal, Onne. *The Photographic Heritage of the Holy Land, 1839–1914*. Manchester: Manchester Polytechnic, 1980.

Fleischmann, Ellen. *The Nation and Its "New" Women: The Palestinian Women's Movement, 1920–1948*. Berkeley: University of California Press, 2003.

Fournié, Pierre. and Riccioli, Jean-Louis. *La France et le Proche-Orient, 1916–1946, Une chronique photographique de la présence française en Syrie et au Liban, en Palestine au Hedjaz et en Cilicie*. Paris: Casterman, 1996.

Friedrich, Norbert, Kaminsky, Uwe, and Löffler, Roland, eds. *The Social Dimension of Christian Missions in the Middle East. Historical studies of the 19th and 20th Centuries*. Stuttgart: Franz Steiner Verlag, 2010.

Garrigues, Emmanuel. "Le savoir ethnographique de la photographie." *L'Ethnographie* 109, 87–1 (1991): 11–54.

Geary, Christraud. "Missionary photography: private and public readings." *African Arts* 24, no. 4 (1992): 48–59.

Geary, Christraud, and Jenkins, Paul. "Photographs from Africa in the Basel Mission archive." *African Arts* 18, no. 4 (1985): 56–63.

Graham-Brown, Sarah. *Palestinians and their Society 1880–1946. A photographic Essay*. London: Quarter Books, 1980.

Graham-Brown, Sarah. "The Political Economy of Jabal Nablus, 1920–1948." In *Studies and Social History of Palestine in the Nineteenth and Twentieth Centuries*, edited by Roger Owen, 88–176. London/Basingstoke: Macmillan, 1982.

Halabi, Awad, "Islamic Ritual and Palestinian Nationalism: al-Hajj Amin and the Prophet Moses Festival in Jerusalem, 1921 to 1936." In *Jerusalem Interrupted: Modernity and Colonial Transformation 1917-Present*, edited by Lena Jayyusi, 139–161. Northampton, MA: Interlink Publishing, 2013.

Hugon, Anne. "Aspect de la propagande missionnaire." In *Images et colonies. Nature, discours et influence de l'iconographie coloniale liée à la propagande coloniale et à la représentation des Africains et de l'Afrique en France, de 1920 aux Indépendances*, edited by P. Blanchard and A. Chatelier, 77–84. Paris: ACHAC et Syros, 1993.

Jalabert, Cyrille. "De l'exégèse biblique au monde arabe." In *Antonin Jaussen. Sciences sociales occidentales et patrimoine arabe*, edited by G. Chatelard and M. Tarawneh, 65–72. Beirut: CERMOC, 1999.

Jenkins, Paul. "The earliest generation of missionary photographers in West Africa: The portrayal of Indigenous people and culture." *Visual anthropology* 7 (1994): 99–118.

Jenkins, Paul. "On using historical missionary photographs in modern discussion." *Le Fait Missionnaire* no. 10 (January 2001): 71–87.

Jenkins, Paul. "Sources of unexpected light. Experiences with old mission photographs in research on overseas history." *Jarhbuch für Europaische Uberseegeschichte* 1 (2001): 157–167.

Khalidi, Rashid. *The Iron cage. The Story of the Palestinian Struggle for Statehood.* Boston: Beacon Press, 2007.

Khalidi, Walid. *Before Their Diaspora, A Photographic History of the Palestinians 1876–1948.* Washington D.C.: Institute for Palestine Studies, 1991.

Khemir, Mounira. *L'orientalisme. L'Orient des photographes au xixe siècle.* Paris: Photo-Poche, 1994.

Laurens, Henry. "Jaussen en Arabie." In *Photographies d'Arabie, Hedjaz 1907–1917*, edited by Brahim Alaoui, PAGE NUMBERS. Paris: IMA, 1999.

Laurens, Henry. "Jaussen et les services de renseignement français (1915–1919)." In *Antonin Jaussen. Sciences sociales occidentales et patrimoine arabe*, edited by Géraldine Chatelard and Mohamed Tarawneh, 23–35. Beirut: CERMOC, 1999.

Makariou, Sophie. "Van Berchem Max." In *Dictionnaire des orientalistes de langue française*, edited by François Pouillon, 948–949. Paris: IISMM/Karthala, 2008.

Malti-Douglas, F. *Woman's Body, Woman's Word: Gender and Discourse in Arabo-Islamic Writing.* Princeton: Princeton University Press, 1991.

Mazza, Roberto. "Transforming the Holy City: From Communal Clashes to Urban Violence, the Nebi Musa Riots 1920." In *Urban Violence in the Middle East Changing Cityscapes: The Transition from Empire to Nation State*, edited by Ulrike Freitag, Nelida Fuccaro, Claudia Ghrawi and Nora Lafi, 179–94. New York: Berghahn, 2015.

Mazza, Roberto and Ouahes, Idir. "For God and la Patrie: Antonin Jaussen Dominican and French Agent in the Middle East 1914–1920." *First World War Studies* 3, no. 2 (2012): 145–164.

Merli, Andrea. "A New Art in an Ancient Land: Palestine through the lens of early European Photographers." *Jerusalem Quarterly* 50 (2012): 23–36.

Métral, Jean. "Naplouse et son district: *un essai de monographie urbaine.*" In *Antonin Jaussen. Sciences sociales occidentales et patrimoine arabe*, edited by Géraldine Chatelard and Mohammed Tarawneh, 121–135. Beirut: CERMOC, 1999.

Montagnes, Bernard. *Marie-Joseph Lagrange, Une biographie critique.* Paris: Le Cerf, 2005.

Moors, Annelies. "From 'Women's Lib.' to 'Palestinian Women': The Politics of Picture Postcard in Palestine/Israel." In *Visual Culture and Tourism*, edited by David Crouch and Nina Lubbren, 23–39. Oxford and New York: Berg Publishers, 2003.

Nassar, Issam. "Familial Snapshots. Representing Palestine in the Work of the First Local Photographers." *History & Memory* 18, no. 2 (2006): 139–155.

Nassar, Issam. "'Biblification' in the Service of Colonialism. Jerusalem in Nineteenth-century Photography." *Third Text* 20, no. 3 (2007): 317–26.

Palestine Exploration Fund. "Christ Church archives Shimon Gibson." *Jerusalem in Original Photographs, 1850–1920*. London: Stacey International, 2003.

Pérennès, Jean-Jacques. *Le Père Antonin Jaussen, o.p., (1871–1962). Une passion pour l'Orient musulman*. Paris: Cerf, 2012.

Perez, Nissan. *Visions d'Orient*. Jerusalem: Israel Museum, 1995.

Pirotte, Jean. "La mobilisation missionnaire, prototype des propagandes modernes." In *La mission en textes et en images*, edited by C. Paisant. Paris: Karthala, 2004.

Raison-Jourde, Françoise. "Image missionnaire française et propagande coloniale." In *Images et colonies. Iconographie et propagande coloniale sur l'Afrique française de 1880 à 1962*, edited by Nicolas Bancel, Pascal Blanchard, and Laurent Gervereau, 50–57. Nanterre: BDIC, 1993.

Réseau Barnabé. *Regards sur l'éducation chez les Chrétiens d'Orient, À travers le fonds photographique ancien (1890–1930) de l'Ecole biblique et archéologique française de Jérusalem*. Publication à l'occasion de l'exposition, Héritage architectural, Réseau Barnabé, 2014.

Revel, Jacques, ed. *Une école pour les sciences sociales. De la VIᵉ section de l'EPHE, à l'École pratique des hautes études en sciences sociales*. Paris: Le Cerf, 1996.

Rioli, Maria Chiara. "Catholic Humanitarian assistance for the Palestinian refugees: The Franciscan Casa Nova of Jerusalem in the 1948 Storm." In *Christian Missions and Humanitarianism in the Middle East, 1850–1950. Ideologies, Rhetoric and Practices*, edited by Inger Marie Okkenhaug and Karène Sanchez Summerer, 253–275. Leiden: Brill, 2020.

Roberts, Mary, and Hackforth-Jones, Jocelyn. "Introduction: Visualizing Culture across the Edges of Empires." In *Edges of Empire: Orientalism and Visual Culture*, edited by Jocelyn Hackforth-Jones and Mary Roberts, 1–19. Oxford: Blackwell Publishing, 2005.

Sanbar, Elias, ed. *Jérusalem et la Palestine. Photographies de l'Ecole Biblique de Jérusalem*. Paris: Hazan, 2013.

Sanbar, Elias. *Les Palestiniens. La photographie d'une terre et de son peuple de 1839 à nos jours*. Paris: Hazan, 2004.

Sanchez Summerer, Karène. "Ouvrir les trésors de la charité aux enfants dévoyés d'Abraham – L'action éducative des sœurs de Sion en Palestine ottomane et mandataire (1860–1948)." In *Judaïsme, école et mission en Méditerranée à l'heure coloniale*, edited by Jérôme Bocquet, 207–238. Rennes: Presses universitaires de Rennes, 2010.

Sanchez Summerer, Karène. "Réception et impacts de l'action éducative et sanitaire des sœurs de Saint Joseph (Naplouse) et des sœurs de Sion (Jérusalem) par les populations musulmanes rurales et urbaines (1870–1940)." In *Histoire et Missions chrétiennes* no. 22, edited by Nadine Beligand and Philippe Bourmaud, 163–196. Paris: Karthala, 2012.

Sanchez Summerer, Karène. "Entre négligence et secret. Entreprises archivistiques en Palestine." In *Archiver au Moyen-Orient, Fabriques documentaires contemporaines*, edited by Christine Jüngen and Jihane Sfeir, 79–102. Paris: Karthala, 2019.

Sanchez Summerer, Karène and Turiano, Annalaura. "Les archives de *l'Associazione nazionale per soccorrere i Missionari italiani all'Estero (ANSMI)*: (Re) découverte d'un fonds, projet de préservation et perspectives de recherche." *MEFRIM*, 132, no 2 (2020).

Sharkey, Heather. *Unexpected Consequences of Christian Missions in the Middle East, Africa and South Asia*. Syracuse: Syracuse University Press, 2013.

Stanczak, Gregory. *Visual research methods Image Society and Representations*. Thousand Oaks, CA: SAGE Publications, 2007.

Tamari, Salim. *Mountain against Sea. Essays on Palestinian Society and Culture*. Berkeley: University of California Press, 2008.

Taraud, Christelle. *Mauresques: femmes orientales dans la photographie coloniale 1860– 1910*. Paris: Albin Michel, 2003.

Tarragon, Jean-Michel de. "Ethnographie." In *L'Ancien testament. Cent ans d'exégèse à l'École biblique. Cahier de la Revue Biblique* 28, 19–44. Paris: Gabalda, 1990.

Tarragon, Jean-Michel de. "The photographic library of the Dominicans of Jerusalem." In *Jérusalem et la Palestine, Photographies de l'Ecole Biblique de Jérusalem*, edited by Elias Sanbar, 163–175. Paris: Hazan, 2013.

Tarragon, Jean-Michel de. "Holy Land Pilgrimage through Historical Photography." *Jerusalem Quarterly* 78 (2019): 93–111. Available via https://www.palestine-studies. org/sites/default/files/jq-articles/Pages_from_JQ_78_-_Tarragon_1.pdf.

The First Century of Photography: Photography as History/ Historicizing Photography in Ottoman territories (1839–1939). Workshop organized by Boğaziçi University Archives and Document Center, RCAC (Research Center for Anatolian Civilization), and IFEA (Institut Francais d'Études Anatoliennes), İstanbul and Aix Marseille University, LabExMed & IDEMEC, 19–21 June 2018, https://anamed.ku.edu.tr/ wp-content/uploads/2018/08/The_First_Century_of_Photography_ANAMED-1.pdf.

Thompson, T. Jack. "Xhosa missionaries to Malawi: Black Europeans or African Christians?" *International Bulletin of Missionary Research* 24, no. 4 (2000): 168–170.

Thompson, T. Jack. *Light on Darkness?: Missionary Photography of Africa in the Nineteenth and Early Twentieth Centuries, Studies in the History of Christian Missions*. Grand Rapids, MI: Wm. B. Eerdmans Publishing, 2012.

Trimbur, Dominique. "A French Presence in Palestine – Notre-Dame de France." *Bulletin du Centre de recherche français à Jérusalem* no. 3 (1998): 117–140.

Trimbur, Dominique. "Sainte Anne, lieu de mémoire et lieu de vie français à Jérusalem." *Chrétiens et sociétés XVIe–XXe siècles* Bulletin 7 (2000): 39–69.

Trimbur, Dominique. *Une école française à Jérusalem. De l'École Pratique d'Etudes bibliques des Dominicains à l'Ecole Biblique et Archéologique Française de Jérusalem.* Paris: Le Cerf, 2002.

Varisco, Daniel. "Orientalism and Bibliolatry. Framing the Holy Land in Nineteenth Century Protestant Bible Customs Texts." In *Orientalism Revisited: Art, Land and Voyage*, edited by Ian Richard Netton, 187–204. London: Routledge, 2013.

Villeneuve, Estelle, Nieuvarts, Jacques, Marchadour, Alain, and Grière, Benoît. *Terre sainte. Les premières photographies.* Paris: Bayard, 2010.

Woodward, Michelle. "Between Orientalist Clichés and Images of Modernization." *History of Photography* 27, no. 4 (2003): 363–374.

Zananiri, Sary. "From Still to Moving Image: Shifting Representation of Jerusalem and Palestinians in the Western Biblical Imaginary", *Jerusalem Quarterly* 67 (2016): 64–81.

CHAPTER 5

Bearers of Memory: Photo Albums as Sources of Historical Study in Palestine

Issam Nassar

This chapter can be generally described as an attempt to engage with three themes that have been pushed to the margins in the study of the history of photography. The first of these themes is the study of the photographic production of, and by, the Palestinians. Although in the recent years, a growing number of studies have come to light regarding certain native Palestinian photographers, they remain marginal if looked at in comparison with studies of the photographies of Europe or its colonial expansions abroad. This is partly due to the fact that all non-European histories of photographies have been relegated to inferior status, and never seriously considered when studying what is deemed to be the history of the practice. Suffice to remember that when studies appear about photography in the *majority world*, to use the concept introduced by Shahidul Alam,[1] they do not appear with titles that places them within the general history of photography, instead with hyphenated titles that connects them with the specific country or region which they depict, such as Indian photography, Palestinian, Egyptian, Ottoman, etc. But books on French, British or American photographies usually appear with titles that places them into the larger history of the discipline. Furthermore, because the particular history of Palestine has become a contested subject due to its colonisation and the uprooting of its people, very little attention is ever given to its photographic history outside the narrow circle of Palestinians and a few other academic specialists.

The second theme with which this chapter deals, that has also been pushed to the margins, is that of the study of the photographic album as a compilation of images fashioned together to produce certain visual narratives. For albums are, after all, not only containers that preserve individual photographs, but

---

1 "Majority world" is the term popularised by the Shahidul Alam as an alternative to the often used "third World." See Maia Hibbett, "Free Shahidul Alam, the Photographer of the 'Majority World' in The Nation (August 24, 2018): https://www.thenation.com/article/archive/free -shahidul-alam-the-photographer-of-the-majority-world/, accessed November 9, 2020.

pictorial narratives organised by their owners to tell stories about their own lives and adventures.

The third of the marginalised themes relates to the fact that vernacular photography is rarely considered as a subject worthy of serious study in contrast to professional or artistic work. Albums, more often than not, are composed of pictures that belong to this kind of photography, even if more professional images can also be found within their leaves.

The study at hand is, therefore, concerned with both the attempt to reclaim Palestinian life in Palestine and to interrogate the various possibilities in which albums of vernacular photographs could enable us to further our knowledge of that life. Of course, a short chapter such as this, cannot cover all aspects of the subject, but the hope is that it will be a starting point for further studies. This essay, therefore, will limit itself to examining three Palestinian albums from the first half of the twentieth century, before Palestine was removed from the map as a country and its people were deemed illegitimate Arab refugees.

The examined albums constitute three different types of compilations, not merely due to the differences in ways of collecting, but also in the fact that they were put together by very different kinds of individuals, with different photographic and social intentions. A person who saw himself as the storyteller of Jerusalem and its historian, Wāṣif Jawhariyya, produced the first of the albums under study. The second, crafted by an upper-class woman named Julia Luci, was clearly intended to narrate – whether intentionally or not – the highlights in her life and that of her family. A playful young athlete named George Mushabek produced the third, in which he documented a very specific event, that of his trip to attend the Olympics in 1936.[2] While Jawhariyya collected images from professional photographers that were often given to him by friends and dignitaries, Mushabek's photographs were snapshots taken with the camera of an amateur traveller. At the same time, the album of Luci was compiled largely from studio portraits in which she or a relative of hers appeared in front of the camera in a setting that was carefully planned. Still, we find exceptions in all of the albums that do not conform to the rest of the included photographs. The albums, therefore, can be said to represent both the public and the private spheres. The three albums were rescued either through the fact that their owners took them on their journeys to exile in 1948, or were reclaimed from where they were left after the occupation of the rest of Palestine in 1967. All three albums were put together in the part of Jerusalem that fell to Israeli control in 1948 during the Palestinian *Nakba*.

---

2   The Albums of Wāṣif Jawhariyya are kept in the archives of the Institute for Palestine Studies in Beirut and the other two are with relatives of the two original owners of the albums.

Before delving into a discussion of the albums at hand, I would like to state three elementary observations that are of great significance for studying pictures. The first is that photographs are never static objects, even if they are physically so. Rather, they are dynamic artifacts that continue to acquire new meanings socially and historically, as Elizabeth Edwards argues. In her words, photographs are 'not merely passive and inert entities to which things happen and things are done', rather, they 'remain socially and historically active' shifting between different contexts and open to 'multiple performances and the making of multiple meanings'.[3] Viewing the photographs affixed in the albums, a century later and in a dramatically different historical and social circumstance, one cannot escape imposing new meanings and removing the intimacy which the people in the photograph and the owners of the albums must have had with each and every image.

It is through such a process that we neutralise the images at hand and rub out of them any temporal, personal attachments that led those particular photographs to be included in the albums. In a sense, we exercise our own power over the photos, disregarding the power of those who appear in the photographs. One example that could illustrate this point comes from the album of Wāṣif Jawhariyya, which he devoted to the late Ottoman period in Jerusalem. In the album, Wāṣif included a photograph of the infamous Jamāl Pāshā, the ruler of Bilād al-Shām during the Great War. The Pasha was such a brutal authoritarian figure, at least in the eyes of his Syrian subjects, that he was given the name al-Safāḥ, meaning the blood shedder. It is very likely that a person living in Jerusalem or Damascus during the Pasha's reign would never have dared to look Jamal in the eyes. But now, a century later, I am able to fix my gaze on his eyes as they appear in the photograph for as long as I want, totally free from any feeling of fear.

The second observation that I would like to make relating to the nature of family pictures is in line with Marianne Hirsch's observation that 'recognizing an image as familial elicits a specific kind of readerly or spectorial look, an *affiliative* look through which we can be sutured into the image and through which we adopt into our own familial narrative'.[4] In other words, the familial gaze that she is referring to relates to the sense of familiarity that a viewer has when looking at family pictures of other people that bear some resemblance to their own family photographs. In a sense, gazing at another family's photograph – be it a

---

3   Elizabeth Edwards, *Raw Histories: Photographs, Anthropology and Museums* (Oxford: Berg., 2001), 13–14. Also cited in Nawal Musleh-Motut, "From Palestine to the Canadian Diaspora: The Multiple Social Biographies of the Musleh Family's Photographic Archive," *Middle East Journal of Culture and Communication* 8 (2015): 308.

4   Marianne Hirsch, *Family Frames: Photography, Narrative, and Postmemory* (Cambridge: Harvard University Press, 1997), 93.

portrait or a snapshot – we project familiarity from our own family into the one in the picture, recognising those present in it as a family and assigning roles to them within the household structure based on the semblance with our own.

The third observation I would like to highlight relates to the nature of photography albums, treated in this chapter as primarily narratives that recount a story authored by the people organising them. It is worth remembering that even if the owner of each of the albums desired to present a certain tale through the pictures included and the sequence in which they are presented, the materiality of the album itself often dictates certain elements relevant to the story being told. By that I mean the album, as a commercial product sold in the market, already limits the space available for the photographs and their numbers on each page. Sometimes, the albums have certain designs that might impose certain additional meanings and artistic touches that could potentially intertwine with the narrative being told. One example from the three albums under study is Mushabek's, who used an album designed and sold at the Olympics and ornamented with the logo of the games, scenery from the host country and even a picture of the leader of that country.

1   Palestinian Worlds

1.1   *Wāṣif Jawhariyya*
Moving on to the albums themselves, the subject of this study, we will start with one of the seven albums of Wāṣif Jawhariyya. The album in question is that which Wāṣif devoted to Ottoman Jerusalem and numbered album one in his collection. The album is divided thematically, when it comes to the portraits, and chronologically, when the photographs are of events. It centred on life in the city, including the political changes that were taking place in each period. Wāṣif kept a separate notebook for each of the albums, in which he described every picture included.

The album is filled with professional photographs of the leaders and elites in Jerusalem during the last two decades of Ottoman rule over Palestine. As an archive, the album is unique in terms of the images it contains. Interestingly enough, Wāṣif fashioned it as if it was an official album produced by an Ottoman authority in the city. He even states on the first page that he dedicates it to both the sultan and the governor of the city, both of whom were no longer in position, or even alive, when the album was constructed in 1924.

As peculiar as that may seem, it does constitute an indication of Jawhariyya intention in collecting the photographs and fashioning them into an album. For there is no chance whatsoever that he had any kind of relations

FIGURE 5.1 *A page from the album showing the mayors of Jerusalem.* Album 1,
Wāṣif Jawhariyya
IMAGE COURTESY OF THE INSTITUTE FOR PALESTINE STUDIES

with the sultan, nor that the sultan would have had the opportunity to ever
see the albums. In addition, it is clearly a dedication written after the fact, with
the intent of giving merit to the album as a public work as if it was a published book. Moreover, the specific sultan to whom he dedicated the album
was removed from power in 1909, when Jawhariyya himself would have been
no more than a teenager. In addition, in his own memoirs Jawhariyya showed
disapproval, if not outright animosity, towards this specific sultan. The dedication read as follows:

> Sulṭān ʿAbd al-ʿAzīz
> I adorn this book with the logo of the Ottoman state [...] his royal maj-
> esty Sulṭān ʿAbd al-ʿAzīz, one of the great kings of the Ottoman State who
> was followed in the high position by his brother Sultan Abdul Hamid. And
> with a photo of his Excellency Raʾuf Pāshā, the *mutaṣarrif* of Jerusalem.

As in the case of the sultan, Raʾuf Pāshā was not the governor of the city at
the time Wāṣif put together this particular album. It is more likely that by not
making the dedications to the last sovereign sultan of the empire, but to two

FIGURE 5.2 *A photograph of Ottoman mutaṣarrif* Ra'uf Pāshā. Album 1,
Wāṣif Jawhariyya
IMAGE COURTESY OF THE INSTITUTE FOR PALESTINE STUDIES

previous ones, as well as to a previous governor, Jawharriyya was echoing his father's admiration of the specific regime that was overthrown and replaced by one that was significantly different and perhaps had more elements of Turkish anti-Arab xenophobia than its predecessor. Jaryas Jawharriyya, the father of Wāṣif, was a judge in the Sharīʿa court in Jerusalem, despite being a Christian subject of the state, during the period of both Sulṭān ʿAbd al-Ḥamīd and governor Raʾuf Pāshā.[5] Hence, the dedication could be read more as honouring his own father than reflecting his own politics in which, based on his published memoirs, he appears to have been an opponent of the Hamidian *regime*. Still, there is another possibility that could explain such a dedication: namely that the compiler of the album aimed at reflecting the dominant discourse relating to the periods he was documenting. A sign of such an act can be seen in the photographs of the other authority figures that he included in his albums, such as Jamal Pasha, the head of the Fourth Ottoman Army in Palestine during the Great War, to whom he often referred in his memoirs as 'the blood shedder,' even as he was proudly announcing that he saw or encountered him at some point. The same is true of portraits of British governors and High Commissioners, whose pictures he included in the other albums in a rather celebratory fashion, appearing with their wives or entourages, despite his clear opposition to them in his memoirs as enablers of the Zionist colonisation of Palestine.[6] Jawharriyya, like many Palestinians, celebrated the end of Ottoman rule in Palestine hoping that it would be a step towards Arab independence. Writing in his memoirs about the day Jerusalem fell to the British, he stated: '[w]e began to breathe relief and praised the Almighty for this blessing', adding 'little did we know at the time that this cursed occupation was in fact a curse for our dear country'.[7]

What is clear is that Jawharriyya fashioned his albums to reflect the historical record more than to display his personal feelings or the ties he might have had with the leaders whose photographs adorned his albums. In the captions, the notebooks that accompanied the albums as well as in his memoirs, Wāṣif often referred to his relationship to some of the individuals depicted. Was he trying to place himself, or his family, within the echelons of high society in the city?

---

5 For a more detailed account on Jaryas Jawhariyya see: Wasif Jawharriyyeh, *The Storyteller of Jerusalem: The Life and Times of Wasif Jawhariyya*, eds. Salim Tamari and Issam Nassar (Northampton, MA: Interlink Publishing Group, 2014), 10–12.

6 Jawharriyya's album 2 devoted to British rule in Palestine includes a large number of portraits of British officials.

7 *The Storyteller of Jerusalem*, 99.

الجنرال والليدي ادموند اللنبي

FIGURE 5.3 *General and Lady Allenby in Jerusalem.* Album 1, Wāṣif Jawhariyya
IMAGE COURTESY OF THE INSTITUTE FOR PALESTINE STUDIES

FIGURE 5.4 *The Ottoman pilots in Jaffa.* Album 1, Wāṣif Jawhariyya
IMAGE COURTESY OF THE INSTITUTE FOR PALESTINE STUDIES

The answer to this question is in the affirmative for, in his notebooks, Wāṣif stated that he acquired many of the photographs (carte de visites) as gifts from the notables they depict. He inserted himself into the photographs as an eye witness to history, not through actually being one of the people depicted in the photographs, but through a narration that places him either in the vicinity of the events depicted or explains his relationship to those present in the pictures. Several examples can be provided to illustrate this point. They include his lengthy description of what he witnessed in 1914 when an Ottoman plane was due to land in Jerusalem. The plane never arrived as it crashed in northern Palestine on its way to the city, but Wāṣif described how the people were waiting in the sun for the arrival of the plane, and how some sold water or other drinks to make some money and cool off those waiting in the heat. He inserted a photograph of the plane and its crew before they departed from Jaffa and described the gloomy feelings that dominated the city upon receiving the news.

FIGURE 5.5 *The surrender of Jerusalem.* American Colony Photo Department. Album 1,
Wāṣif Jawhariyya
IMAGE COURTESY OF THE INSTITUTE FOR PALESTINE STUDIES

Another example relates to his narration of the last photograph in
the album, the famous photograph showing the surrender of Jerusalem to the
British forces on 9th December, 1917, in which the mayor of the city and his
entourage posed with the white flag of surrender next to the two soldiers that
they encountered on that day. Wāṣif named those appearing in the photograph,
highlighting his personal or family relationship to them,[8] and even made the

---

8 According to Wāṣif's memoirs those present in the photograph include: Tawfiq Muhammad
Saleh al-Ḥusaynī; Ahmed Sharaf, police commissioner; Hajj Abdul-Qader al-Alami, police
commissioner – lancers; Shamseddine, policeman; Amin Tahboub, policeman; Jawwad Bey
bin Ismail Bey al-Ḥusaynī, who was wearing short trousers; Burhan, son of the late Taher Bey
al-Ḥusaynī; and behind Husayn Bey, the white flag of surrender, held by Jamāl Pāshā's driver,
a Lebanese man called Salim who was married to the sister of Hanna al-Lahham. The latter
was standing by his side. Only two individuals were present from the other party (the British
army). See *Wasif Jawharriyyeh, The Storyteller of Jerusalem*, 100.

claim that the surrender flag was a bed sheet brought from his family's home in the Old City.[9]

This photograph, taken by Lars Larsson, a photographer from the American Colony group in Jerusalem, is a famous image that had already appeared in numerous publications with captions which usually highlighted the names of the two British officers. It constitutes a strong example of simultaneous, non-intersecting histories from which the people of the city are often left out, but Wāṣif reverses that process completely. Not only does Jawharriyya fail to mention the names of the two officers and list the names of everyone else present, but he even describes in his caption what he was doing and where he was at the time of the event, despite his not being in the photograph, or even in the vicinity of the location in which it was shot. While it is possible to read Wāṣif's description as inscribing the natives into the historical narrative, in my view it is more about placing himself individually within the historical context.

Sometimes, Jawharriyya is actually present in the image; a few photographs show Wāṣif among a crowd – sometimes with his father or the mayor of Jerusalem – and in such cases he made sure to draw an arrow pointing to himself or, as in one case, to the location of his house in a panoramic view of Jerusalem.

The great figures that appeared in his albums always looked their best in portraits which gave them the aura of authority rather than in images that showed them behaving ruthlessly. Despite stating in his notebook that he acquired pictures from certain notables, in the album Wāṣif does not provide information about the sources of each photograph or about its photographer. This stands in contrast to the careful documentation that accompanied his memoirs that were recently published, decades after his death.

1.2   *Julia Luci*

Julia Luci's album, in contrast to Jawharriyya's focus on the public sphere, constitutes a private archive of personal and familial life. The photos in the album are a combination of studio portraits of her and of her family and friends. But the album also includes snapshots of family events. Gisèle Freund pointed out that the emergence of photographic portraits corresponded historically 'with the rise of middle class and their increased social, political and economic

---

9   In her book Our Jerusalem, Bertha Spafford Vester claimed that the white flag came from the American Colony hospital. See Bertha Spafford Vester, *Our Jerusalem* (Garden City, N.Y., 1950), 255.

power.[10] The portrait enabled the members of the middle class to visually affirm their social status. A Jerusalem-raised woman from rather humble origins, married to a Bethlehemite of similar background, Julia and her husband Jaryas migrated to Haiti early in their marriage, where they opened up a business venture that expanded in the late 1920s and the 1930s. After accumulating enough wealth in Haiti, the couple returned to Palestine and decided to settle in the upscale neighbourhood of Jerusalem, *al-Baqa'a*, where they built a house and opened various new business ventures. Among the different enterprises that they engaged in was a building of several storeys on Ben Yehuda street in the new part of the city.

The album visually reflects and affirms the new status of the couple as part of the social and economic elite, not unlike Jawharriyya's albums, albeit different in scope due to it belonging to the private sphere of the home. The first few pages of the album were devoted to portraits of the couple, individually and together, along with portraits of relatives – mostly on Julia's side. This can be an indication that the album was a project of Julia alone without much, or perhaps any, input from her husband. Still, it might also be an indication of who the potential viewers of the album would be. While the Bethlehemite husband's relatives remained living in their houses in one of the old quarters of Bethlehem, Julia's were moving into the new suburbs of Jerusalem and expanding their business ventures significantly. She was known for her Tuesday gatherings for women friends known as *istiqbāl*, or reception, when her friends from the neighbourhood would come and spend the entire afternoon visiting, and perhaps looking at the album which would have been placed on the coffee table in the middle of the guest room, as was the habit on middle class homes at the time. Her new social status was continuously asserted not only through the delicacies she offered her guests, but also through the images that appeared in the album. In her study of the construction of journals by Russian women, Gitta Hammarberg made the observation that a 'woman (and occasionally a man) was the owner, main reader, and addressee of an album; she determined who inscribed and read it, and her social context both produced it and was reproduced in it; she 'edited' it by erasure or commentary'.[11] Julia's album illustrates Hammarberg's point clearly, as it was fashioned by her not only as its main 'reader', but as the addressee of the album as a

---

10   Gisèle Freund, '*Precursors of the photographic portrait*', in *The Nineteenth-Century Visual Cultural Reader*, eds. Vanessa Schwartz and Jeannene Przyblyski (New York: Routledge Publication, 2004), 79.

11   Gitta Hammarberg, "The First Russian Women's Journals and the Construction of the Reader," in *Women in Russian Culture and Society, 1700–1825*, eds. Wendy Rosslyn and Alessandra Tosi (New York: Palgrave McMillan, 2007), 84.

woman of certain social class which is affirmed through each and every picture inside it as well as through its entirety as a journal of sort.

The social class that Julia belonged to was that of the new and aspiring bourgeoisie in Palestine of the period, not the old landed aristocracy. The new bourgeoisie class saw itself as part of the world of wealth and leisure based on accumulation not only of capital, but of material goods and the latest innovations coming from abroad. They distinguished themselves through their embrace of, and affinity with, the bourgeois European lifestyle and latest trends in consumption and leisureliness as well as their embrace of the new ideas that the *Nahda*, or Arab renaissance, thinkers were preaching.[12] Producing a family album was perhaps a sign of belonging to the new class, as peasant women certainly did not produce such artifacts.

Among the studio portraits that appear in the album, we find several in which Julia, or one of her female friends, appear in traditional village dresses. The photograph below is perhaps the best among them technically. Although the photograph is signed by 'Paramount Photo, J. Solomon', we have no information on this particular photographer, though the name might suggest that the photographer was Jewish, not Arab. In it, Julia appears with her sister in-law, both dressed in embroidered *thawb* that recall those of the Ramallah peasantry, and perhaps of Bedouins from southern Palestine. Considering that Julia hailed from an urban Jerusalem family, and her sister in-law from a Bethlehemite one, the outfits reflect neither how they normally dressed, nor the traditional dresses of their hometowns. Such an image is in line with a tradition that existed in early local photography of Palestine, where studios had 'exotic' attire readily available for the benefit of the European tourists who wanted to appear in oriental dress, as the advertisement by Ḥannā Tūmāyān, below, clearly illustrates. Members of the upper classes in Palestine started to imitate the European visitors and sometimes had their pictures taken in the studio in traditional dresses, adopting, perhaps, the orientalist tradition as a sign of their difference from the rural or Bedouin population of Palestine.[13] Taking a portrait in peasant dresses was perhaps their way of showing affinity with the western tradition and a statement that 'proved' their special social

12   Sherene Seikaly wrote an excellent study on the rise of the new bourgeois class in Palestinian society. See Sherene Seikaly, *Men of Capital: Scarcity and Economy in Mandate Palestine* (Stanford: Stanford University Press, 2016).

13   Perhaps the various self-portraits of the English photographer Francis Frith (1822–1898) dated 1857 provide good examples of such early European practice. Many of such images are available online. See: https://sites.hampshire.edu/reorient/works/frontispiece -portrait-of-turkish-summer-costume/ and https://commons.wikimedia.org/wiki/File: FrancisFrith.png.

FIGURE 5.6 *Julia and sister in-law.* Julia Luci's album
IMAGE COURTESY OF THE LUCI FAMILY

status in society. Still, we cannot fully dismiss the possibility that the picture of Julia and her sister in-law were also celebrating and showing pride in their Palestinian heritage as they both had enough distance from the peasantry that they see them and their attire as part of their own past.

The album also included studio photographs of child relatives seated on sheepskin rugs, sometimes in the nude – another trope popular at the time, especially among the *nouveaux riches*. Such images are interesting not only in showing the status to which the family of the child aspired, but also because they could relate to what Lacan called the mirror stage through which the child recognises him or herself as an independent person from the mother.[14] An example of such images is that of her nephew, Sami, in a studio portrait on his first birthday sitting on a lambskin.

Among the photographs in the album, we also see pictures of the vacations Julia and her husband took to places in Lebanon and elsewhere. Pictures of the new houses built by her siblings in the same neighbourhood were also present, as well as photographs of the younger relatives taken to mark certain special occasions.

---

14   Jane Gallop, "Observation of a Mother," in *The Familial Gaze*, ed. Marianne Hirsch (Dartmouth: University Press of New England, 1999), 79.

FIGURE 5.7 *Julia's nephew Solieman Salti.* Julia Luci's album
IMAGE COURTESY OF THE LUCI FAMILY

FIGURE 5.8 *Julia and husband on vacation in Lebanon.* Julia Luci's album
IMAGE COURTESY OF THE LUCI FAMILY

Luci's album largely represents the private life of her family, emphasising the highlights in her own life, including the trips she and her husband took, or the new house they built. However, what stands out is the very last picture of the album, in which the building her husband owned on Ben Yehuda street in Jerusalem is shown after its destruction as a result of a bomb placed by Palestinian fighters. The bombing was due to the fact that in the building there were offices of a Zionist organisation – not known to this author – and the street was the hub of Jewish economic activities.[15]

The fact that this was the last picture in the album is an indication, perhaps, of the burden of the trauma of loss, both financially as well as in social status, which must have weighed heavily on Julia Luci. Following her exile from Jerusalem, she and her husband lost their property and with it their social standing. Her husband passed away shortly after the *Nakba* while he was standing on a hill south of Jerusalem, trying to look at the part of the city where he once lived. Julia never added any pictures from the last three decades of her life after the destruction of Palestine in 1948. Sadly enough, the album in retrospect shows us now not where she once was, but who she once was. For us today, it evokes collective memories that might not be about what appears in it, but the life that was lost with the *Nakba*.

1.3   *George Mushabek*

The third album that this paper tackles is of a journey taken by five young friends from Jerusalem to attend the 1936 Olympics in Germany. The album belongs to George Mushabek, who also lived in the part of the city that fell to Zionist control in 1948. It documents the trip the five friends took from Jerusalem to Berlin by sea. Along with Mushabek, the other four; Ghabī and Raymūnd Dīb, Attāla Kidās and Frītz Marrūm, were also Jerusalemite, Christian member of the YMCA.[16] The album itself is an item of memorabilia from the

---

15   The information about the Luci's ownership came from various oral interviews conducted with relatives on different dates. The bombing that occurred on February 22, 1948 is well documented and according to the Palestine Post of February 23, 1948, it took place in front of the Atlantic Hotel building, owned by an [unnamed] Christian Arab, possibly Luci. The hotel, according to a report by a British Palestine police source, housed the headquarters of the elite Palmach troops. See http://britishpalestinepolice.org.uk/polhist50.html (accessed on October 20, 2020).

16   Special thanks to Mona Halaby for her help in identifying the individuals. It might be worth mentioning that Attallah Alexander "Ted" Kidess (1910–1999), was a leading figure in the Jerusalem YMCA as he served as its physical director. See San Charles Haddad, "Rise of the Reich in Mandate Palestine: The NSDAP, Jerusalem YMCA, and 'Participation' of Attallah Kidess in the 1936 Berlin Olympic Games," *Journal of Olympic History* 28, no. 2, 2020: 20–33.

FIGURE 5.9 *Bombing on Ben Yehuda St*, 1948. Julia Luci's album
IMAGE COURTESY OF THE LUCI FAMILY

FIGURE 5.10   *Cover of the album.* Olympic Album, George Mushabek
IMAGE COURTESY OF THE MUSHABEK FAMILY

FIGURE 5.11   *The inside cover of the album.* Olympic Album, George Mushabek
IMAGE COURTESY OF THE MUSHABEK FAMILY

Olympics with the logo of the games on the cover and imprinted images within from the preparations for the games. The imprinted photographs include an aerial photograph of a stadium, a map of a stadium, views from Berlin, where the games were held, and a photograph of Adolf Hitler talking with members of the German team. On the inside cover of the album, Mushabek placed the faces of the five friends within the five circles of the Olympic logo, although two of the photographs have been lost.

The photographs in the album were taken using a handheld camera and could be classified as amateur snapshots, rather than professional photographs, and thus are more spontaneous and freer of the constrictions of the studio portraits seen in the previous two albums. The album is organised chronologically, detailing the journey of the five friends, their departure from Jerusalem through to their attendance at certain games during the Olympics. In this sense, the album is a visual travelogue of the trip. The return journey to Palestine was not included in the photographs. In this sense, it does resemble an inversion of European tour albums most famous since the end of the nineteenth century where Western tourists and pilgrim took one of Thomas Cook's excursions to the Orient including Greece, Palestine and Egypt.

Tourists also fashioned their albums in chronological order and included snapshots of themselves in front of the monuments and sites they visited. But unlike such albums, Mushabek's does not have captions, though at times a short description is inscribed directly on some photographs, giving a date and location. Unlike the European tourists, who often included a reference to some Biblical verse or another in their captions, no references to historical texts appear in our album. The five friends were on a fun trip, not on a pilgrimage. This fact becomes clear when we notice a complete lack of interest in the politics of the places they visited.

There is also no indication that the group had any interest in the politics of this particular Olympics, which came to be known as Hitler's Olympics by historians and politicians later on. Aside from the embedded picture of Hitler with the team that came with the album, there are no signs of Nazi influence of paraphernalia anywhere in the album – though the Nazi flag appears in some of the pictures of the streets of Berlin included in the album. In any case, although Zionist propaganda often made the Palestinians appear to be on the side of Hitler and the Nazis due to the visit of Palestine's Grand Mufti Ḥājj Amīn al- Ḥusaynī to Berlin and his meeting with Hitler in November 1941, the general mood in Palestine at the time was wary of the rise of Hitler and what it might mean for the country as attested to in the various articles that appeared in the Arab newspapers at the time. Anticipating how Hitler's policy towards to the Jews would affect Palestine, the Jerusalem based al-Jamāʿa al-Islāmīyya newspaper warned as early as March 1933 that:

FIGURE 5.12   *Page from album that has an imprint of Hitler with the German team and Mushabek at a game*, 1936. Olympic Album, George Mushabek
IMAGE COURTESY OF THE MUSHABEK FAMILY

Hitler's victory is a dangerous development for the Arabs in Palestine; his plans regarding the Jews are well known. He will not hesitate to realize these plans and we will witness waves of refugees to [Palestine]. The German Jews are rich industrials and they will be the first, who will take the land from our hands.[17]

The same sentiment was echoed by *al-Difaʿ*, another Palestinian newspaper in 1936, the same year in which the as the Olympics were held, by stating that 'there will be no peace in Europe until the spirit of the Swastika, ruling Germany today, will be overcome'.[18] It is, therefore, rather doubtful that the five visitors to Berlin were sympathetic to Nazism.

The visual travelogue, which is the album, starts with the departure of the friends from Jerusalem by train. They were local athletes, hailing from the

---

17   *al-Jamāʿa al-Islāmīyya*, March 8, 1933, cited by René Wildangel's chapter entitled "More than the Mufti: Other Arab-Palestinian Voices on Nazi Germany, 1933–1945, and Their Postwar Narrations," in *Arab Responses to Fascism and Nazism: Attraction and Repulsion*, ed. Israel Gershoni (Austin: University of Texas Press, 2014), 108.

18   Cited in ibid., 108.

Christian community of Palestine, at the Jerusalem YMCA, located on King
George Street in the new section of the city. It was established in 1924 and
the building was dedicated in 1933, a few years after the British High commissioner, Lord Plumer, laid the foundation stone in 1928. The five athletes won a
grant to travel and attend the Olympics.

The first leg of the train trip was to Lydda (al-Lid) close to Jaffa, then another
train took them to Haifa, from where they boarded a Greek ship towards Athens.
At each stage, a snapshot was included in the album. It is possible that the photographs were placed in the album following its purchase in Berlin, as most
images would be of the return journey, rather than its start, though the pictures are not organised starting from Berlin backwards. Several pictures were
taken on board, including one with the ship's Greek captain and others with
some of the passengers they befriended. Although, in one of the photographs,
we see the friends wearing *kūfiyya*, or the Arab headdress, we cannot be sure
that this reflects a nationalist sentiment, though certainly it is an indication
of identity. At the same time, the playfulness of some photographs in which
the friends appear wearing not only the kūfiyya, but even the *tarbush*, or the
Ottoman *fās*, could be seen as markers of class identity or acts of masquerade.

Upon arrival in Athens, the group visited its archaeological sites and took a
number of snapshots before sailing to the Croatian port of Dubrovnik where
they enjoyed a swim and the scenic port. They eventually arrived, one would
imagine by train, to Berlin where they attended a number of games including
handball, fuzzball and hockey. The tickets for the games were also included in
the album.

Looking at this album from the standpoint of today, one cannot ignore the
fact that it was simply an album of fun and leisure, something that nowadays
never seems to emerge in all the studies about Palestine before 1948, including the increasingly popular nostalgia among Palestinians about the 'beautiful
past'. This is an instance in which nothing can be found that indicates that
the Palestinians were fighting colonialism or making fabulous achievements.
Perhaps this is what makes this album so powerful if seen in the context of the
politics of the loss of the homeland, for it is an album that illustrates that life
in Palestine was rather normal, and the Palestinians were no different than any
other people in the world.

2   Conclusion

The question that will no doubt surface following such a quick description of
the albums relates to what is it that we can conclude from looking at these

FIGURE 5.13   *The friends at train station in Lydda during their*
return trip, 1936. Olympic Album,
George Mushabek
IMAGE COURTESY OF THE MUSHABEK FAMILY

albums together. To answer this, we need to return to the three observations
with which the essay started, namely, the observations about Palestine and the
Palestinians; about vernacular photography; and about photographic albums.
Concluding with these questions, I would suggest a few reflections that could
be a starting point for answers that I will need to further contemplate for
future studies.

Starting with the theme of albums, this chapter attempts to make it clear
that albums are rarely just collections of random pictures put together without
serious consideration for their order. Rather they constitute both intentional
visual narratives that recount an already envisioned narrative fashioned
by their compilers, and archives in which photographs that were deemed

180   NASSAR

FIGURES 5.14–16   *The friends onboard the Greek ship and visiting monuments in Greece.* Olympic Album, George Mushabek
IMAGE COURTESY OF THE MUSHABEK FAMILY

significant by the collector were preserved. The three albums under study illustrate these two points. For Jawharriyya, Luci, and Mushabek, their albums tell stories that are, in general, of private interest, and document the lives, or portions of them, of the individuals who assembled them. As such, they reflect both the single events depicted in each photograph, as well as visions that were intentionally offered to the viewer. This reflects not only certain issues about their authors and their aspirations, but about the society and the historical period in which they were produced as albums.

Similarly, vernacular photographs are significant in the study of the history of everyday life, as they capture people in settings less formal than the carefully planned professional studio portraits. They show people in moments of leisure that constitute part of their regular life, enabling social historians to unearth information about how life was at the time at which the photographs were captured.

As the photographs at hand are of Palestinian life, they provide us with immense amounts of information about ordinary middle-class life in Palestine before its destruction. They enable us to excavate lives that were marginalised by the dominant Palestinian national discourses of peasant hood and the land. Instead, they depict the life of the urban middle class. The very practice of collecting photographs in albums and the narratives those albums convey, affirm to us as viewers that life was, after all, normal in Palestine in many respects. People had 'normal' hopes and desires, conducting their lives not anticipating that their world was about to collapse. They provide us with the potential of a counter narrative that does not focus on violence but on normalcy, and opens up the possibility of exploring the variety of possible narratives about the history of Palestine, rather than just a single national discourse. At the same time, the albums and the photographs attest beyond doubt that, in the words of Maḥmūd Darwīsh, Palestinians were once 'there, and they remember'.[19]

Bibliography

Edwards, Elizabeth. *Raw Histories: Photographs, Anthropology and Museums*. Oxford: Berg., 2001.

Gallop, Jane. "Observation of a Mother." In *The Family Gaze*, edited by Marianne Hirsch, 67–84. Dartmouth: University Press of New England, 1999.

Hammarberg, Gitta. "The First Russian Women's Journals and the Construction of the Reader." In *Women in Russian Culture and Society, 1700–1825*, edited by Wendy Rosslyn and Alessandra Tosi, 83–104. New York: Palgrave McMillan, 2007.

---

19   The poem by Darwish is entitled "I am There," and the reference is to the verse in the poem that says: I come from there and remember. The translation of the poem is available at: https://www.asmalldoseoftoxicology.org/voices-through-walls/2018/3/6/poem-i-am-there-by-mahmoud-darwish (accessed on December 31, 2019).

Hirsch, Marianne. *Family Frames: Photography, Narrative, and Postmemory*. Cambridge: Harvard University Press, 1997.

Jawharriyyeh, Wasif. *The Storyteller of Jerusalem: The Life and Times of Wasif Jawharriyyeh*, edited by Salim Tamari and Issam Nassar. Northampton, MA: Interlink Publishing Group, 2014.

Musleh-Motut, Nawal. "From Palestine to the Canadian Diaspora: The Multiple Social Biographies of the Musleh Family's Photographic Archive." *Middle East Journal of Culture and Communication* 8 (2015): 307–326.

Nassar, Issam. "The Wasif Jawharriyyeh Collection: Illustrating Jerusalem during the First Half of the 20th Century". In *Ordinary Jerusalem, 1840–1940: Opening New Archives, Revisiting a Global City*, edited by Angelos Dalachanis and Vincent Lemire, 385–398. Leiden: Brill, 2018.

Rose, Gillian. *Doing Family Photography: The Domestic, The Public and The Politics of Sentiment*. Rematerialising Cultural Geography. Kent, UK: Ashgate, 2010.

Seikaly, Sherene. *Men of Capital: Scarcity and Economy in Mandate Palestine*. Stanford: Stanford University Press, 2016.

Toxipedia. "Poem "I Am There" by Mahmoud Darwish." Accessed December 31, 2019. https://www.asmalldoseoftoxicology.org/voices-through-walls/2018/3/6/poem-i-am-there-by-mahmoud-darwish.

Wildangel, René. "More than the Mufti: Other Arab-Palestinian Voices on Nazi Germany, 1933–1945, and Their Postwar Narrations." In *Arab Responses to Fascism and Nazism: Attraction and Repulsion*, edited by Israel Gershoni, 101–126. Austin: University of Texas Press, 2014.

PART 2

Points of Perspective: Photographers and Their Lens

∵

Resilient Resistance: Colonial Biblical, Archaeological and Ethnographical Imaginaries in the Work of Chalil Raad (Khalīl Raʻd), 1891–1948

Rona Sela

Chalil Raad[1] was one of the most important Arab photographers in the Middle East, beginning in the late nineteenth century, and one of the first – if not *the* first – active in Palestine (Fig. 6.1). Though born in Lebanon, Raad lived in Palestine for seven decades, was professionally active, mainly in it, for six, and created a significant and impressive oeuvre. He photographed the everyday life of the locals, mainly indigenous Palestinian urban and rural landscapes, social/family scenes, and portraits in the studio or in the public sphere, in a staged, semi-staged or documentary manner, for commercial and

---

1 I write Raad's personal name with a C (Chalil), although the correct transliteration is Khalīl, and his family name Raad, although the correct transliteration is Raʼd. I believe the name should be rendered according to the person's choice, and this is usually my policy with all languages Figs 6.1, 6.3, 6.5, 6.6, 6.8–10, 6.18. The information on Chalil Raad comes from the following sources: Yeshayahu Nir, *Beyerushlayim Ubeerets-Israel Be'kvot Tslamim Rishonim* (Tel Aviv: IDF Publishing House, 1986); Dan Kyram, "Hatslamim Harishonim Yeavodatam," *Ariel* 66–67 (1990): 153–4; Ellie Shiler, "Nofei Erets-Israel Be'inei Hatsalamim Harishonim," *Ariel* 66–67 (1989): 17–23; Ellie Shiler and Menahem Levin, "Albomay Hayedu'im Shel Khalil Raʼad," *Ariel* 68–70 (1990): 216–9; a biographical list 'obtained by Fouad C. Debbas from Raad's daughter (Ruth-R.S.). I received from Fouad in December 1988 in Paris' (National Library, Warman Collection, Raad File. All quotes by Ruth are from this letter); the author's talks with Debbas during 1999; Rona Sela, *Tsilum Befalastin/Erets-Israel Bishnot Hashloshim Vea'arba'im* (Tel Aviv: Hakibbutz Hameuchad Publishing House and Herzliya Museum, 2000), 163–176, https://www.academia.edu/36679969/In_the_Eyes_of_the_Beholder-_Aspects_of_Early _Palestinian_Photography; Badr Al-Hajj, "Khalil Raad – Jerusalem Photographer," *Jerusalem Quarterly* 11–12 (2001): 34–9; Issam Nassar, *Laqatat Mughayira: al-Taswir al-Futugrafi al-Mubakir fi Filastin* (Beirut and Ramallah: Kutub and Qattan Foundation, 2005); Rona Sela, *Chalil Raad – Tatslumim, 1891–1948* (Tel Aviv: Helena, 2010); a long correspondence with George Raad from 2005–2010; Salim Tamari, "The War Photography of Khalil Raad," in *Palestine Before 1948, Not Just Memory, Khalil Raad (1854–1957)*, ed. Vera Tamari (Beirut: Institute for Palestine Studies, 2013), 17–25; Vera Tamari, "Khalil Raad (1854–1957) – Palestine's Pioneer Photographer," in *Palestine Before 1948, Not Just Memory, Khalil Raad (1854–1957)*, ed. Vera Tamari (Beirut: Institute for Palestine Studies, 2013), 7–11; Institute for Palestine Studies (IPS), "Palestinian Photographers before 1948: Documenting Life in a Time of Change," *Palestinian Journeys*, accessed September 8, 2019.

FIGURE 6.1   *The store of Raad in Jaffa St Jerusalem*, 1930s.
PHOTOGRAPHER UNKNOWN

other purposes. He was also active in military and ethnographic photography and was apparently the first Arab and local archaeological photographer in Palestine.[2] Simultaneously, he travelled around the Middle East, giving expression to Arab life in a period of reorganisation and reform, the *Tanzimat* (the massive restructuring of the Ottoman Empire) and *al-Nahda* (awakening or renaissance), reflecting 'the afterimage of modernity.'[3]

By the turn of the century, other Arab photographers had also become active in major Palestinian cities, including figures such as photographers from the Bāsil and Buwarshī families[4] and Zakariyyā Abū Fahīla (1885–1951)[5] in

2   American Colony photographers also documented excavations in Palestine (Edna Barromi-Perlman, "Archaeology, Zionism, and Photography in Palestine. Analysis of the Use of Dimensions of People in Photographs," *Journal of Landscape Ecology* 10, no. 3 (2017): 49), though these were foreigners who had moved to Jerusalem and started to photograph archaeology long after Raad.

3   Stephen Sheehi, "The Nahḍa After-Image," *Third Text* 26, no. 4 (2012): 409.

4   Mitri Al-Raheb, "Karimeh Abbud: Almrah Khlf Al'dsa," in *Karimeh Abbud*, eds. Mitri Al-Raheb, Ahmad Marwat and Issam Nassar (Bethlehem: Diyar, 2011), 49.

5   Institute for Palestine Studies, "Palestinian Photographers before 1948."

Bethlehem, Nāṣir Sābā[6] in Nazareth and Dāwūd Sabūnjī and 'Isā Sawabīnī in Jaffa.[7] European and American photographers also began operating in Palestine and the wider region during the second half of the nineteenth century, linked to colonial interests and significantly shaping the way the land and its populations were presented and represented.[8] Armenians were also among the first photographers to work in Palestine, influencing the local scene through the unique contributions of, for instance, Patriarch Issay Garabedian, who established a workshop at St James Monastery in the 1850s, and his students Kevork,[9] Garabed Krikorian, J.H. Halladjian (in Jerusalem and Haifa), H. Mardikian and Josef Toumayan.[10]

In 2000, Raad's work was exhibited for the first time as part of a group show dedicated to the history of Palestinian photography,[11] followed by a 2010 solo exhibition accompanied by a monograph.[12] Chalil Raad had marketed his work extensively and left a comprehensive, well-catalogued archive.[13] These

---

6   He opened a photography store in 1897; Susan Slyomovics, "Edward Said's Nazareth," *Framework: The Journal of Cinema and Media* 50, nos. 1/2 (2009): 42.

7   Sabounji, a Christian, had been active in Beirut since 1863, moved to Jaffa in 1892 and was the first Arab photographer to operate there; Nir, *Beyerushlayim Ubeerets-Israel*, 99, 225. He was the brother of the photographers Louis and Jurji Sabounji; the latter had a studio in Beirut and was the 'first 'Arab' studio owner', see Stephen Sheehi, *The Arab Imago: A Social History of Portrait Photography, 1860–1910* (Princeton: Princeton University Press, 2016), 29. Issa Sawabini was active in Jaffa around 1912 and opened a studio in Ajami neighbourhood; *The Palestine Directory* 1920, 193.

8   Nir, *Beyerushlayim Ubeerets-Israel*; Nissan Perez, *Focus East, Early Photography in the Near East 1839–1885* (New York: Harry H. Abrams, Inc. Publishers, 1988); Kyram, "Hatslamim Harishonim Yeavodatam"; Shiller, "Nofei Erets-Israel Be'inei Hatsalamim Harishonim," 17–23; Kathleen Stewart Howe, *Revealing the Holy Land: The Photographic Exploration of Palestine* (Santa Barbara: Santa Barbara Museum of Art, 1997); Issam Nassar, "'Biblification' in the Service of Colonialism. Jerusalem in Nineteenth-century Photography," *Third Text* (2007): 317–326; Sela, *Tsilum Befalastin*, 19–23; Sela, *Khalil Raad*, 19–34; Andrea Merli, "A New Art in an Ancient Land: Palestine through the lens of early European Photographers," *Jerusalem Quarterly* 50 (2012): 23–36.

9   First name is unknown.

10   'J. Toumayan, Bab-el-Jjeddid [New Gate-R.S.] ... Artistic Photographer, Best Finished Photos of All Sizes and Styles, taken in Native Costumes'; *The Palestine Directory* 1920, 193. He had a store in Suliman Street in Jerusalem; *Sefer Hareshimot Lemishar Yet'asiyah, Sefer Haktovot*, 1936, 33.
      The Greek photographer Miltiades Savvidès, started working in Jerusalem at the end of the nineteenth century and later also in Ajami (Jaffa); *Palestine Directory* 1920, 193.

11   Sela, *Tsilum Befalastin*.

12   Sela, *Khalil Raad*.

13   Chalil Raad and John Krikorian, *1930 Catalogue of Lantern Slides and Views made by C. Raad & J. Krikorian of Sites, Scenes, Ceremonies, Costumes, etc. of Palestine & Syria Identical with Bible History, C. Raad & J. Krikorian Photographers. Jerusalem, Palestine* (Jerusalem: The

have enabled me to deepen study of various aspects of his work, including the subjects on which he focused, how he catalogued and captioned his images, how he promoted his work and, in particular, to shed light on the complexity faced by indigenous photographers during this vibrant period. This article aims to augment discussion around the dilemmas that Raad himself likely faced from the outset of his professional career, in view of his central role in the Palestinian community, the winds of modernity (*al-Nahda*), the Western colonialist tendencies in the region and subsequently the Zionist settlement and British occupation of Palestine.[14] Particular attention is paid here to examining Raad's response as a local Arab photographer to Biblical, Holy Land and archaeological/ethnographical 'imaginative geographies of Orientalism'[15] imposed by foreign and Zionist visual mediators.

From the nineteenth century onwards, the Palestinian presence in the region was concealed or misrepresented by colonialist representations and 'seizure of narratives',[16] a process of elimination from Westerner's and Zionist's consciousness. Furthermore, since 1930s, and especially since the *Nakba* (1948), Palestinian archives and material were seized or looted by Jewish and Israeli forces and individuals and deleted from the public sphere by the Israeli colonial regime of knowledge by additional means.[17] Other resources were lost or damaged and subsequent wars between Israel and Arab states and the Palestinians. While Palestinians are still fighting to regain their missing archives

---

Commercial Press, 1930; Fig. 6.8); Chalil Raad, *1933 Catalogue of Lantern Slides and Views made by C. Raad Photographer of Sites, Scenes, Ceremonies, Costumes, Etc. Etc., of Palestine & Syria Identical with Bible. History* (Jerusalem: Beyt-Ul-Makdes Press, 1933; Figs 6.9 and 6.10).

14   Sela, *Tsilum Befalastin*, 163–176; Rona Sela, "Historiya Metsulemet Shel Falastine," *Teoriya Ubikoret* 31 (2007): 302–10; Sela, *Khalil Raad*, 19–47.

15   Derek Gregory, "Emperors of the Gaze: Photographic Practices and Productions of Space in Egypt, 1839–1914," in *Picturing Place: Photography and the Geographical Imagination*, eds. Joan Schwartz and James Ryan (London: I.B. Tauris, 2003), 224.

16   Borrowed from Fekri Hassan, "Imperialist Appropriations of Egyptian Obelisks," in *Views of Ancient Egypt since Napoleon Bonaparte: Imperialism, Colonialism and Modern Appropriations*, ed. David Jeffreys (London: Cavendish, 2003), 19–68.

17   Walid Khalidi, *Before Their Diaspora, A Photographic History of the Palestinians 1876–1948* (Washington D.C.: Institute for Palestine Studies, 1991); Sela, *Tsilum Befalastin*, 24–37; Rona Sela. *Le'iyun Hatsibur – Tslumeu Falastinim Ba'rchiyonim Hatsva'yim Beisrael* (Tel Aviv: Helena and Minshar Gallery, 2009); Rona Sela, "Genealogy of Colonial Plunder and Erasure – Israel's Control over Palestinian Archives," *Social Semiotics* 28, no. 2 (2018): 201–29; Rona Sela, *Limu'ayanh al-Jamhur-al-falasṭiniwn fy al-A'rshifat al-'skariyyah al-I'sra'iliyyah* (Ramallah: Madar Center, 2018); Rona Sela, "'Imprisoned Photographs': The Looted Archive of Photo Rissas (Rassas) – Ibrahim and Chalil (Khalil) Rissas," *INTERMÉDIAL* 32 (2018).

FIGURE 6.2
*Chalil Raad and Annie
Muller in their Wedding
Day*, 1919.
PHOTOGRAPHER
UNKNOWN

and collect fragments from their past, fighting against 'archival absence' (evidence or materials)[18] and write their 'history without documents',[19] Raad's archive reveals the very destructiveness of colonialism. At the same time, it enables us to shed light on 'archival imaginaries ... archives both shadow and real, and conditions both intellectual and material'.[20]

18   Ali Behdad, *Camera Orientalis: Reflections on Photography of the Middle East* (Chicago: Chicago University Press, 2016).

19   Omnia El-Shakry, "'History without Documents': The Vexed Archives of Decolonization in the Middle East," *American Historical Review* 120, no. 3 (2015): 920–934.

20   Ibid., 934.

1   Biography

Chalil Raad was born in Lebanon in 1869.[21] After the death of his father, Anīs, Raad was sent to study in Jerusalem at a school managed by Bishop Gobat. There, he learnt the art of photography from the local Armenian photographer Garabed Krikorian, travelling in 1890 to study in Basel (following his high school teacher from Basel who came to Jerusalem to study Arabic for his doctoral dissertation) where he met his future wife, Annie Muller. Due to the difficulties of WWI, Muller moved to Jerusalem only in 1919, and the two married (Fig. 6.2). At first, the family lived in the upscale Talbiyya neighbourhood and became deeply involved in local community life; in 1941 (Fig. 6.3) they moved to the Greek Colony.

Raad began working independently in 1891, opening his own studio by 1895 (Fig. 6.4).[22] In 1899, he ran an advertisement in the Hebrew newspaper *Hahavatselet* to market his work also to the Jewish community: 'Let it now be known and announced that whoever seeks photographic pictures of all kinds, at the finest quality and for an affordable price, is welcome to contact me [...] ! Chalil Raad. My workshop is located outside the [old] city [of Jerusalem], near Hotel Howard,[23] at the bookbinder Rabbi Leib Kahana of Safed (Fig. 6.5)."[24] In the early 1910s, Raad was appointed Prussian Court Photographer, a post which gave him diplomatic immunity and most likely

---

21   In determining Raad's year of birth, I relied on Ruth Raad's records, according to which her father married in 1919 at age fifty, information that is consistent with George Raad's estimation that his father was born between 1865 and 1870 (emails from George to the author, November 10, 2005; November 17, 2008). Al-Hajj, "Khalil Raad – Jerusalem Photographer"; Tamari, "Khalil Raad (1854–1957)," 7–13; and Akram Zaatari (correspondence from September 1, 2017 and December 4, 2017) claim that Raad was born in 1854 and that his father died in 1860. However, according to Ruth, it is probable that his father was poisoned (the year is not indicated) and that his grandfather died in 1860.

22   'Raad, P. [probably photographer], Established 1895' (*Sefer Hareshimott*, 1936, 34). The studio was also listed in the *1920 Palestine Directory* (no editor, 193).

23   Opened in 1891, the hotel later changed its name to 'Du Park', and in 1907 to 'Fast' (David Kroyanker, *Rehḥov Yafo Beyerushalyim* (Jerusalem: Jerusalem Institute for Israeli Research and Keter Publishing House, 2005, 30, 158, 359).

24   No editor, *Hahavatselet*, July 24, 1899, 320 (translated from Hebrew). Raad placed an additional advertisement in another Hebrew newspaper, *Hashkafa*: 'I hereby present my workshop to the distinguished public, which does not offer the cheapest, but certainly does offer the best quality [...]. This I can guarantee, because the pictures will remain intact for a long time [...] Note well the name C. Raad. Every day I receive thank-you letters for work well done, particularly from people of European descent' (Translated from Hebrew, no editor, June 8, 1906, 7). I have not found yet advertisements by Raad in Arabic newspapers in Palestine.

FIGURE 6.3 *Raad Family*, 1932. From left to right: Chalil, George, Ruth and Annie
UNKNOWN PHOTOGRAPHER

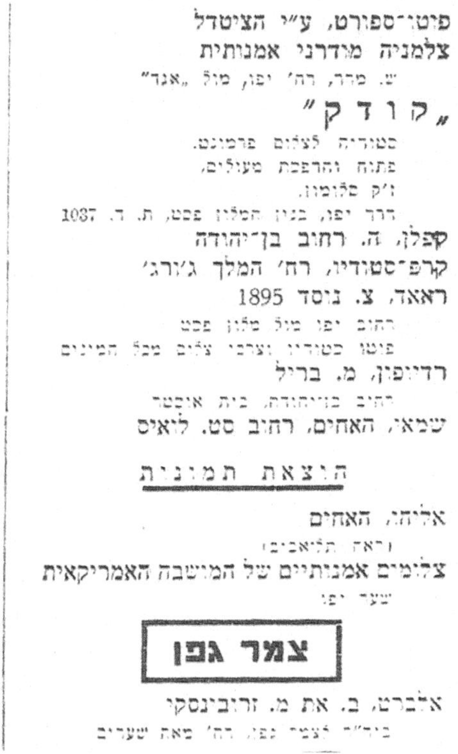

פיטו־ספורט, ע״י הציטדל

צלמניה מודרני אמנותית

"ש. מדר, רח' יפו, מול "אגד

„ ק ו ד ק "

סטודיה לצלים פרמיננט.

פתוח והרפבת מעולים.

וי'ק בלומון.

דרך יפו, בנין המלון פבט, ת. ד. 1037

ספלן, ה. רחוב בן־יהודה

קרפ־סטודיו, רח' המלך ג׳ורג׳

ראאד, צ. נוסד 1895

רחוב יפו מול מלון פבט

פיטו סטודיו ועדכי צלים מכל המינים

רדיופון, מ. בריל

רחוב בניהודה, בית אוקטר

שמאי, האחים, רחוב סט. ליאיס

הוצאת תמונית

אליהו, האחים

(ראה תל־אביב)

צלומים אמנותיים של המושבה האמריקאית

שער יפו

צמר גפן

אלברט, ב. את מ. זרובינסקי

בוי"ר לצמר גפו, רח' מאת שעריב

FIGURE 6.4
Raad, P. [probably photographer],
Established 1895' (*Sefer
Hareshimott*, 1936, 34)

enabled him to travel freely (Fig. 6.6).[25] The fact that he spoke Arabic, English, German and Turkish was instrumental in this regard. Raad also acted as an official Ottoman photographer, producing portraits of military officers preparing for battle[26] and other local facets of the war. Raad's partnership with the Jewish bookbinder probably ended sometimes in the early twentieth century.[27]

Raad's studio was located next to that of the Greek photographer Militad Savvidès, and in front of Krikorian's studio (Fig. 6.7), in what can be identified as the first Palestinian visual centre. Until WWI, Raad was in professional competition with Garabed Krikorian, a contest that transformed into collaboration in 1917 after Garabed's son, John, returned to Jerusalem from his studies (1913 or 1914) and married Raad's niece, Najla.[28] John Krikorian primarily photographed portraits in the studio, while Raad toured the region and documented landscapes, people and events.[29] Raad and Krikorian published a textual catalogue of their work in 1930,[30] most likely to garner interest from buyers worldwide (Fig. 6.8). The partnership appears to have ended by 1933, when Raad published a similar textual catalogue bearing only his name, (Figs 6.9 and 6.10),[31] which he used to sell images from the 1287 photographs of his Holy Land collection.[32] Raad was also active in the local community, including in philanthropy. On 12th December 1939, for example, he hosted in his studio a display of embroidered dresses sown by the Women's Club

---

25   His 1914 stationary carries the logo 'C. Raad, Kgl. [Royal] Preusischer Photograph' (Central Zionist Archive, KKL3/29, July 13, 1914).

26   These images are mentioned in Raad, *1933 Catalogue*, 35–6 and Sela, *Khalil Raad*, 244–35, and located in the Middle East Centre Archive in Oxford: https://brill.com/fileasset/downloads_products/31858_Guide.pdf (correspondence, January-March 2010).

27   In 1920 and 1921, he publicised his studio, at the same location without mentioning the rabbi's name: *Kol Yerushalayim Lishnat TRPA* (1921, a Hebrew almanac); *Sefer Shimushi, Sefer Yedi'ot, Sefer Adresa'ot* (Jerusalem: Levy, 1921); *The Palestine Directory* 1920, 193.

28   Who moved to Jerusalem from Lebanon with her mother Sarah and grandmother Saada.

29   Al-Hajj, "Khalil Raad – Jerusalem Photographer," 37–8. Ruth Raad wrote that her father also liked drawing, though hitherto, none of his drawings have been discovered. It is possible that he drew the logo stitched on the back of his photographs (Sela, *Khalil Raad*, 256).

30   Raad and Krikorian, *1930 Catalogue*. Perhaps earlier catalogues were also published.

31   Raad, *1933 Catalogue*. Comparison between the catalogue of 1930 (when Krikorian and Raad worked together) and the Catalogue of Raad from 1933, suggests that the images Krikorian photographed during their partnership (mainly portraits?) remained in Raad's possession and were distributed as Raad's images.

32   Al-Hajj mentions 1,230 photographs (Al-Hajj, "Khalil Raad – Jerusalem Photographer"). In the visual albums, the highest number is 1151. The photographs in the albums and textual lists are organised thematically. Raad did not date his images. Therefore, it is impossible to analyse his work chronologically.

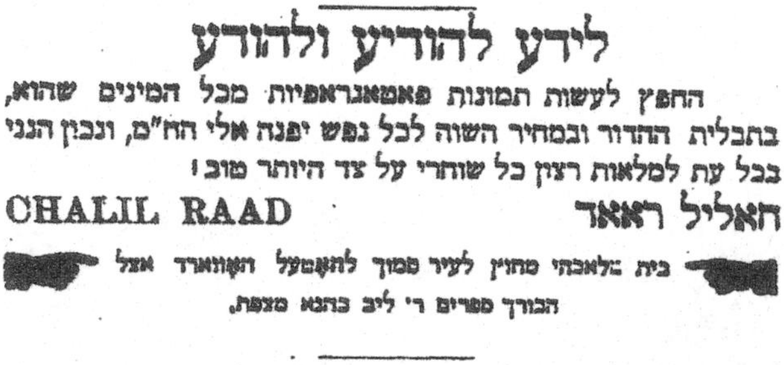

לידע להודיע ולהודע

החפץ לעשות תמונות פאטאגראפיית מכל המינים שהוא,
בתבלית ההדור ובמחיר השוה לכל נפש יפנה אלי הח"מ, ונכון הנני
בכל עת למלאות רצון כל שוחרי על צד היותר טוב!

CHALIL RAAD · חאליל ראאד

בית שלאבהי מחוץ לעיר סמוך להאטעל האווארד אצל
הבורך ספרים רי ליב כהנא מצפת.

FIGURE 6.5 'Let it now be known and announced that whoever seeks
photographic pictures of all kinds, at the finest quality
and for an affordable price, is welcome to contact me [...] !
Chalil Raad. My workshop is located outside the [old] city
[of Jerusalem], near Hotel Howard at the bookbinder Rabbi
Leib Kahana of Safed'. *Hahavatselet*, 24th July, 1899, 320
(translated from Hebrew)

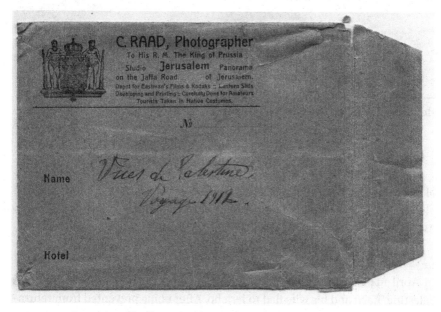

FIGURE 6.6 *An envelope (for film negative) with stamp of Prussian Court Photographer.*
COURTESY OF NATIONAL LIBRARY, JERUSALEM

FIGURE 6.7 *Jaffa Street, Jerusalem*, 1898–1914. On the right side Raad's and Savides' stores. On the left side, Krikorians' store, American Colony Photography Department
IMAGE COURTESY OF THE LIBRARY OF CONGRESS

of Ramallah, using the proceeds to buy clothes for schoolchildren and the blind. He also directed a photography club at the Young Men's Christian Association (YMCA).[33]

1.1 Chalil Raad's Archive

In April 1948, around one month before the end of the British Mandate in Palestine, Raad and his wife fled to Jericho. After being prevented from returning to their home (an ethnic cleansing strategy of the conquering forces), the couple were forced into exile in Lebanon. It was there that Raad died

---

33 *The Palestine Post*, December 12, 1939, 2; December 27, 1939 and December 19, 1936, 6. For information on the Photography Club, see *The Palestine Post*, October 5, 1938, 4.

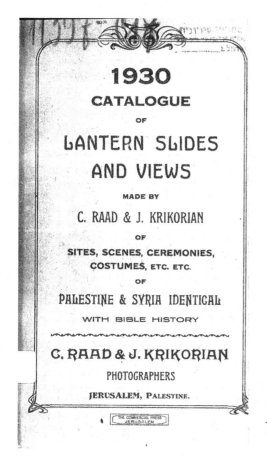

1930

CATALOGUE

OF

LANTERN SLIDES AND VIEWS

MADE BY

C. RAAD & J. KRIKORIAN

OF

SITES, SCENES, CEREMONIES, COSTUMES, ETC. ETC.

OF

PALESTINE & SYRIA IDENTICAL

WITH BIBLE HISTORY

C. RAAD & J. KRIKORIAN

PHOTOGRAPHERS

JERUSALEM, PALESTINE.

THE COMMERCIAL PRESS
JERUSALEM

FIGURE 6.8
Chalil Raad and John Krikorian, 1930.
*Catalogue of Lantern Slides and Views
made by C. Raad & J. Krikorian of
Sites, Scenes, Ceremonies, Costumes,
etc. of Palestine & Syria Identical
with Bible History, C. Raad &
J. Krikorian Photographers. Jerusalem,
Palestine* (Jerusalem: The Commercial
Press, 1930)

sometime between 1955 and 1957.[34] His studio was destroyed in the battles of 1948, with some of its contents looted by soldiers and civilians, others lost and some rescued by the family. In a partly destroyed area – 'abandoned' in Zionist-colonialist terminology that erases, camouflages or reinterprets evidence which contradicts the Israeli narrative – Zionist soldiers 'found' albums scattered on the floor of Chalil Raad's studio. 'Only the albums remained, because nobody took any interest in them, apart from a young company commander ... who was interested in the country's history. This is how this invaluable asset was saved.'[35] Another group of looted photographs by Raad,

---

34   George Raad dates his father's death to 1955, whereas both Ruth and Vera Tamari indicate that it was in 1957.

35   Shiler, '"Albomay Hayedu'im," 217–19; Sela, *Tsilum Befalastin*, 166; Sela, *Khalil Raad*, 16. Being an Israeli, I was able to see the albums, like other seized/looted images stored in

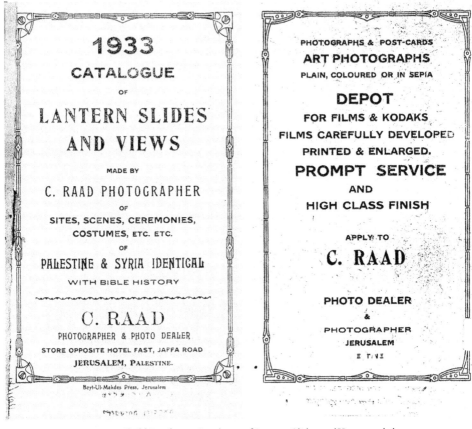

FIGURES 6.9 AND 6.10   Chalil Raad, *1933 Catalogue of Lantern Slides and Views made by*
C. Raad Photographer of Sites, Scenes, Ceremonies, Costumes, Etc. Etc., of Palestine
& Syria Identical with Bible History (Jerusalem: Beyt-Ul-Makdes Press, 1933)

together with photographs by the Rissās (Rassās) Studio and American Colony
Photographers, have lately been 'revealed' according to the Israeli newspaper
Haaretz.[36] They were 'rescued' from a burning photography store in Jerusalem
during the 1947–1949 War of 'Independence' by an Israeli commander named
Moshe Carmel. The looting is described in euphemistic terms as a 'rescue' from

---

Israeli archives, if they were open, or if I succeeded after a fight to open them, while
Palestinians face obstacles.

36   Nir Hasson, "Hundreds of Photos Found from When Israel's War of Independence Raged,"
Haaretz, December 9, 2018, https://www.haaretz.com/israel-news/premium.MAGAZINE
-hundreds-of-photos-found-from-when-the-1948-war-raged-1.6725444.

the flames, though in reality the photographs were stolen after the fire. The article in *Haaretz* declines to discuss why the photographs were not returned to their original owners and were instead 'donated' to an Israeli-Zionist institution, and why the archive of the institution catalogued the looters as the owners.[37]

The wartime pillage of Palestinian property by individuals was prohibited under international law,[38] but whether the pillaged items were given as gifts, sold to third parties or exchanged hands by other means, they were consistently used to glorify the looters in their social milieu, serving as 'trophies' or 'souvenirs' from the battlefield.[39] If they were sold or transferred to official state archives, they were managed, catalogued and interpreted according to a Zionist terminology, usually censored for many years, reflecting the newly established power hierarchy between looter and original owner, but most strongly the destruction of Palestinian culture.[40] When they remained in private hands – as have many archives pillaged by individuals for private gain – they were usually treated in a patronising or biased way, and their meaning is cleansed. Usually they are also closed to researchers, and thus erased from the public sphere. Raad's albums have not been subject to alteration by their Israeli owners and are preserved as Raad originally constructed them, organised according to subject. Among their contents, which also can be viewed in the textual catalogues,[41] is documentation of rural and urban areas in Palestine (landscapes, their inhabitants, familial scenes and documentation of everyday life with a focus on ethnographic aspects), Jerusalem and its surroundings as seen from various angles and aspects (religious, touristic, etc.), as well as archaeological excavations, maps and plans. A small portion of Raad's work is dedicated to Ottoman aspects of the First World War, Arab resistance to colonisation, cities and locations in the Middle East (such as Petra, Amman, Damascus and Sinai), and Jewish (pre-or Zionist) communities. Like the textual

---

37   Sela, "'Imprisoned Photographs'."
38   Ibid. I discuss separate seizure by state bodies (Sela, *Le'iyun Hatsibur*; Sela, "Genealogy of Colonial Plunder and Erasure"; Sela, *Limu'ayanh al-Jamhur-al-falasṭiniwn*) and looting by individuals, Sela, "'Imprisoned Photographs'."
39   Sela, "'Imprisoned Photographs'."
40   Sela, "Genealogy of Colonial Plunder and Erasure."
41   Raad's albums, which I found (and viewed) after long research and many obstacles, are identical with the textual catalogues and with the way Raad's negatives are numbered. Since the albums are not open (yet), I published the entire 1933 textual catalogue of Raad for the benefit of future research in Sela, *Khalil Raad*, 227–255 (I first published the catalogue's cover and main contents in Sela, *Tsilum Befalastin*, 167). Raad's negatives (3000 in number) are open for research at the IPS.

catalogues, the albums served as a visual index of the photographer's work and appear to have been displayed in the store for potential clients. Each is composed of a large number of black cardboard pages onto which four to six of Raad's original photographs relating to a specific subject matter are glued. The images are accompanied by text (hand-written or machine typed) inscribed by Raad himself (Fig. 6.11).

Raad's negative archive, stored in the darkroom of a different building on Jaffa Street, was saved from looting. The building was located in an area between Jordan and Israel that was considered a no-man's land from the years after the 1948 war up until 1967. Ruth Raad and her husband Robert asked for the assistance of an Italian friend of Raad's, who worked in the bookstore of Būlus Sa'id inside Jaffa Gate. Despite the difficulties, he managed to enter the no-man's land after the armistice.[42] Ruth Raad donated the collection of around 3,000 negatives to the Institute for Palestine Studies (IPS).[43]

2   The Holy Land in Nineteenth Century Colonialist Photography

Chalil Raad began his photographic work during the last decade of the nineteenth century in an environment shaped by modern Arab[44] and Euro-American forces. The new medium of photography, which emerged in 1839, was 'exported' to the Middle East by many foreign photographers, developing a colonialist photographic language. Expeditions that included government and military officials, academic researchers and scientists, writers, religious institutions, and commercial bodies were sent to explore the region, with participating photographers and illustrators translating imperialist aspirations and Western interests in the Near East into visual language. The French government, for example, equipped various institutions of information gathering and knowledge production with the new photographic technology 'to further the project of academic Orientalism,'[45] as exemplified by the work of Frédéric Goupil-Fesquet in Egypt. John Cramb, the Scottish official photographer to

42   Al-Hajj, "Khalil Raad – Jerusalem Photographer."
43   Correspondence with the IPS, February 13, 2010.
44   Zeynep Çelik, "Photographing Mundane Modernity," in *Camera Ottomana: Photography and Modernity in the Ottoman Empire, 1840–1914*, eds. Zeynep Çelik and Edhem Eldem (Istanbul: Koç University Press, 2015), 154–200. See also Sheehi, *The Arab Imago*, xxv–xxix.
45   Ali Behdad, 'Mediated Visions: Early Photography of the Middle East and Orientalist Network,' *History of Photography* 41, no.4 (2017), 365.

the Queen, was also commissioned by Glasgow publisher William Collins to make a series of views of Biblical sites in Jerusalem, while Maxime Du Camp and Auguste Salzmann were sponsored on a mission by the French Ministry of Public Education.[46] The new art form remained consistent with Orientalist-iconographic tastes, encompassing a variety of imagery and representation, including panoramic landscapes and monuments, exotic scenes and archetypes, staged studio portraits, archaeological sites, close-ups of archaeological remains, and Biblical and deserted landscapes.

Multiple studies have examined the work of foreign photographers in the Middle East, including their contributions to European and American colonial projects in the region, through the prism of Said's theory of Orientalism. Where some emphasise the 'imperialist lens'[47] through which 'the camera captures and ultimately re-presents the monuments of the Orient ... [and the] effacement of the native population',[48] others foreground 'imperialist appropriation',[49] with the images treated as 'mirrored photographs' of the 'imaginary or mental mould existing in the Westerner's mind'.[50] Similarly, Europeans have been described in related scholarship as 'emperors of the gaze' managing a 'scopic regime',[51] whereby photography was presented as a tool in the quest for knowledge. It framed the imperialistic perspective and served as 'a way to dominate the Orient',[52] while creating and assimilating the colonial gaze. In a period of rapid colonial expansion, early photography asserted human absence, depicting vast parts of the world as deserted, 'vacant spaces, empty cities and villages' or needing a *mission civilisatrice*.[53] The camera imbued Orientalism with scientific credibility and thereby functioned as a central pillar in the Orientalist framework. Mediating Western desires and fantasies, it gave photographers a set of conventions through which to structure Middle Eastern cultures for consumption by Western audiences.[54]

---

46   Ibid., 366, 374.
47   Keri Berg, "The Imperialist Lens: Du Camp, Salzmann and Early French Photography," *Early Popular Visual Culture* 6, no. 1 (April 2008).
48   Ibid., 11.
49   Fekri Hassan, "Imperialist Appropriations of Egyptian Obelisks.".
50   Perez, *Focus East*, 50.
51   Gregory, "Emperors of the Gaze," 224–25.
52   Berg, "The Imperialist Lens," 4.
53   Abigail Solomon-Godeau, "A Photographer in Jerusalem, 1855: Auguste Salzmann and his Times," in *Photography at the Dock*, ed. Abigail Solomon-Godeau (Minnesota: University of Minnesota Press, 1991), 159.
54   Behdad, *Camera Orientalis*. Behdad shows that Linda Nochlin was among the firsts to relate to the interpretation of Said's *Orientalism* in art, at the same time, discusses various researchers (mainly art-historians), criticised the use of Said's theory to apply equally to

802 The busy Port of Jaffa

803 Two old men of Emmaus playing games

804 Two women threshing with flail

805 Camel looking through the needle's eye

a 806 An Orange tree with Oranges

806 Wrapping Oranges

FIGURE 6.11 AND FIGURE 6.12 *Pages from Raad's Albums*

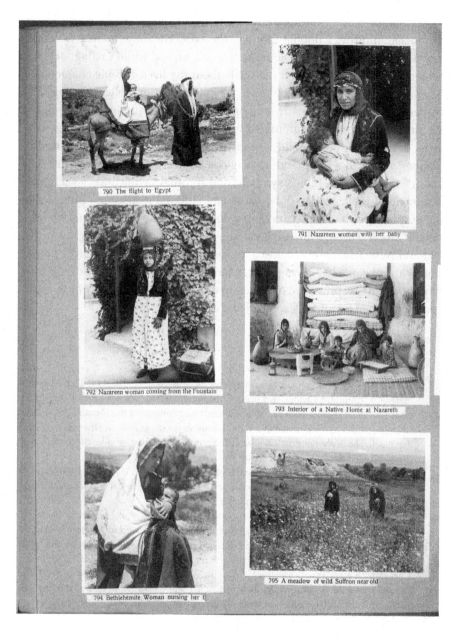

790 The flight to Egypt

791 Nazareen woman with her baby

792 Nazareen woman coming from the Fountain

793 Interior of a Native Home at Nazareth

794 Bethlehemite Woman nursing her b

795 A meadow of wild Suffron near old

Furthermore, and while focusing on the Holy Land through colonial lenses, the imagination was 'double framed'; the Westerner was framed as having 'the ability to draw the people he sees as he wishes' while casting locals 'as subjects that could teach him the truth about the lives of Bible characters'.[55] As many studies show, this resulted in a 'bibliolatry',[56] or biblical ideology. The (American) 'visual culture surrounding the Holy Land',[57] for instance, depicted the 'authentic' experience grounded in a national identification with the concepts of a chosen people and a promised land,[58] while (British) 'Crusading mania'[59] reflected a longstanding religious-biblical impulse toward the Holy Land.[60] Rooted in the Bible's 'symbolic and spiritual significance',[61] such work documented Biblical sites, holy places and Oriental landscapes, foregrounding purportedly abandoned and empty locations while wilfully ignoring local inhabitants.[62] Through focusing on subjects associated with events in the Old and New Testaments (landscapes, ruins, ancient places, Biblical names, sites with religious-historical significance), it provided visual 'proof' that the Biblical world was preserved or frozen in time, and that the reality of the Holy Land was one of an underdeveloped and exploitable world.

---

visual representation. Behdad, "Mediated Visions," 364–366. See also Michelle Woodward, "Between Orientalist Clichés and Images of Modernization," *History of Photography* 27, no. 4 (2003), 363; Zeynep Çelik, "Colonialism, Orientalism and the Canon," *Art Bulletin* 78 (1996): 202–205 and "vernacular Orientalism" as an opposition to Orientalism: Eitan Bar-Yosef, *The Holy Land in English Culture 1799–1917: Palestine and the Question of Orientalism* (Oxford: Oxford University Press, 2005), 88.

55   Daniel Martin Varisco, "Orientalism and Bibliolatry. Framing the Holy Land in Nineteenth Century Protestant Bible Customs Texts," in *Orientalism Revisited: Art, Land and Voyage*, ed. Ian Richard Netton (London: Routledge, 2013), 190.

56   Ibid.

57   John Davis, *The Landscape of Belief: Encountering the Holy Land in Nineteenth-Century American Art and Culture* (Princeton: Princeton University Press, 1996), 27. On the influence of the biblical paradigm on the US since eighteenth century, see also Mark Finney, 'Christian Zionism, the US and the Middle East: A Sketch and Brief Analysis,' in *The Bible, Zionism and Palestine: The Bible's Role in Conflict and Liberation in Israel-Palestine*, ed. Michael Sandford (Dunedin, New Zealand: Relegere Academic Press, 2016), 21–23.

58   Davis, *The Landscape of Belie*, 27–72.

59   Bar-Yosef, *The Holy Land in English Culture*, 246.

60   Ibid. Bar-Yosef and John Davis relate to visual/popular means.

61   Paolo Maggiolini, "Studies and Souvenirs of Palestine and Transjordan: the Revival of the Latin Patriarchate of Jerusalem and the Rediscovery of the Holy Land during the Nineteenth Century," in *Orientalism, Revisited Art, Land and Voyage*, ed. Ian Richard Netton (London: Routledge, 2013), 165–175.

62   Solomon-Godeau, "A Photographer in Jerusalem," 159.

Research confirms that only a small number of local people had in fact been photographed since the beginning of photography in Palestine.[63] Among the few examples are images by the French Bonfils family, who opened a studio in Beirut (active, 1867–1918).[64] The minority of local inhabitants who were photographed were often presented as undeveloped or as Biblical characters.[65] Images from the (same) Bonfils studio, for example, depict a Palestinian boy and girl in a wheat field described as 'Boaz Field, Biblical Scene'.[66] Configurations such as this were repeated across photobooks and illustrations. Similarly, photographs of individuals and sites were often 'adorned' by Biblical verses or references to Biblical events. With such images in high demand, this approach was also employed by foreign photographers living in Palestine, including American Colony photographers. The local Palestinian population was thus designated the function of preserving ancient Biblical life; they were not seen, but served as mere figments of a colonialist imagination.[67] In turn, the activities of the imperialist came to reflect 'layer upon layer of interests, official learning, institutional pressure that covered the Orient as a subject matter and as a territory during the late half of the nineteenth century'.[68]

Early twentieth century Zionist propaganda made similar use of the Biblical imagery developed by Orientalism in order to justify the return of a people to 'their ancient land'.[69] The visual infrastructure founded by Western photographers thereby fulfilled an important function in strengthening such Biblical imagery. Accordingly, Palestinians were instrumentalised in photography to preserve the Biblical era, presented as emblems of an ancient Jewish life,[70] with the resulting images legitimating a Zionist expulsion and erasure (from both land and imagination) of the Palestinian presence. For example, Ephraim

---

63   Ibid; Nir, *Beyerushlayim Ubeerets-Israel*,118; Nassar, *Photographing Jerusalem*, 36.

64   Woodward, "Between Orientalist Clichés," 363.

65   Yeshayahu Nir, "Reshit Hatsilum Berets-Israel," *Ariel* 66–67 (1989): 9–16.

66   Sometimes entitled as "Ruth and Boaz".

67   Dani Rabinowitz, *A'ntropologiya Yehafalasṭinim* (Ra'anana: Hamerkaz Leḥeker Hatarbut Ha'aravit, 1998).

68   Edward Said, Orientalism (New York: Vintage Books, 1994), 192.

69   Ilan Pappé, "The Bible in the Service of Zionism, 'We do not Believe in God, but He Nonetheless Promised us Palestine'," in *The Bible, Zionism and Palestine: The Bible's Role in Conflict and Liberation in Israel-Palestine*, ed. Michael Sandford (Dunedin, New Zealand: Relegere Academic Press, 2007), 7; Finney, "Christian Zionism," 21; Nur Masalha, *The Bible and Zionism: Invented Traditions, Archaeology and Post-Colonialism in Palestine* (London & New York: Zed Books, 2007). Avi Rubin gives three examples – from Egypt, India and the Zionist movement – to the way Orientalism was inherent by Eastern elites, to construct nationalism: Avi Rubin, "Hamizrah Davar Ehad Vehama'rav Davar Aher", *Jama'a* 7 (2001): 72–4.

70   Sela, *Tsilum Befalastin*, 19–23; Rabinowitz, *A'ntropologiya Yehafalasṭinim*, 35–36.

Moses Lilien, a Jewish illustrator and member of the Zionist movement who co-founded the Bezalel Art School together with artist Boris Schatz, photographed local Palestinians, Samaritans and members of Jewish communities for a Biblical illustrations series.[71] Lilien visited Palestine several times for the project between 1906 and 1918, while also publishing a number of photographs in the press. One such image of a Palestinian man, 'Young Man in a White Keffiyeh' (1906), was used to illustrate the figure of Joshua (1908),[72] while the photograph 'Arab Riding a Donkey' was used to depict Balaam (1906).[73] Similarly effective was the trend at the time of staging 'exotic' studio portraits of Westerners or local Jews, dressed up in Palestinian clothing with Oriental-looking objects in the background; scenes which catered to Eurocentric fantasies of an enchanted Orient.[74] As Zionist writers and visual-creators looked to Palestine and its inhabitants through a prism crystalised in European Orientalist culture, 'Zionist art came to the Orient equipped with acquired blindness ... and continued in this direction also after the authentic contact with him'.[75]

3   Photography in the Shadow of Conflict

3.1   'Customs, Characters'
Against this Western mode of imagination and knowledge production around the East and its attitude towards the local population, Raad devoted a considerable portion of his work to depicting the vibrant and productive lives of both rural and urban Palestinians (Figs 6.11, 6.12). His work captured sites and views around the country from a Palestinian perspective reflecting modernity's new social order while introducing 'a new style of representation'.[76] As an ethnographic photographer, he also devoted a major section of his work to

---

71   Micha Bar-Am, *Painting with Light: Photographic Aspects of the Work of Ephraim Mose Lilien* (Israel: Tel Aviv Museum of Art, 1991).

72   Ibid., 62–3. The image alluded also to figure of Theodor Herzl.

73   Ibid., 164–65. Lilien had contacts with Raad and may have been influenced by the latter. In a letter Lilien wrote to his wife (June 27, 1914) he told her that he was touring the country on a horse with a local guide and taking photographs to produce biblical illustrations. He then added that he would usually develop the plates after dinner with Raad, and by the time he washed them it was 11.00 p.m. and he would go to bed (Ruti Ofek, *E.M. Lilien Ha'man Hatsiyoni Harishon* (Tefen: The Open Museum, 1997), 160.

74   See, e.g. photos by Soskin in Sela, *Tsilum Befalastin*, 21–23.

75   Ariel Hirschfeld, "Qadima," in *To the East? To the East: Orientalism in the Arts in Israel*, eds. Yigal Zalmona and Tamar Manor-Fridman (Jerusalem: The Israel Museum, 1998), 14.

76   Woodward, "Between Orientalist Cliches," 373.

'Customs, Characters',[77] in which he dealt with a breadth of subjects, including education, professions, everyday family and communal life, culture, heritage and clothing (Figs 6.13 and 6.14).

Unlike the Orientalist 'figure studies' and 'types' that were staged by photographers to capture some 'hidden essence' of cultural mystique,[78] and colonialism's institutionalised 'scientific' classification of locals for purposes of domination,[79] Raad as an indigenous photographer established an autonomous gaze for his community (Figs 6.15 and 6.16).[80] Moreover, by contrast with his Palestinian colleagues who avoided photographing Zionist settlements, Raad sought to purposefully document and counter the Zionist colonisation process. Among his subjects were members of the Old Yishuv and the accelerating Zionist settlement of cities and rural locations.[81] When in 1914 Arthur Ruppin, director of the Palestine Office of the Zionist Organization, asked to buy hand-painted photographs for Zionist propaganda purposes, Raad avoided selling him such images.[82] Sections of his work were meanwhile devoted to documenting 'The Arab Struggle against Balfour Declaration Day',[83] the Nabī Mūsā procession (Fig. 6.17), the Palestinian demonstrations of 1928–9 and 1936–39 and Palestinian leaders such as Mufti Ḥājj Amīn al-Ḥusaynī.[84]

Researchers have thus asserted that 'Raad's work defies the obfuscating view of his Western counterparts, whose work, consciously or not, served the cause of

77   Raad, *1933 Catalogue*, 25; Sela, *Khalil Raad*, 239.

78   Gregory, "Emperors of the Gaze," 225.

79   Susan Slyomovics, "Visual Ethnography, Stereotypes and Photographing Algeria," in *Orientalism Revisited: Art, Land and Voyage*, ed. Ian Richard Netto (London: Routledge, 2013), 132–134.

80   These photographs were also published in Gustaf Dalman, *Arbeit und Sitte in Palästina* (Germany: Georg Olms Verlagsbuchhandlung, 1964). He also presented Palestinian heritage exhibitions in his store, showing traditional Palestinian dresses, as discussed above, and documented the Samaritans.

81   Documenting various Zionist settlements, he accompanied George Davis, who describes how the 'famous Jerusalemite photographer' went with him, at his expense, in order to 'take photos that both he and we would like to save from this trip' (George Davis, Rebuilding Palestine According to Prophecy [USA: The Million Testaments Campaigns,1935], 19).

82   July 13, 1914; Central Zionist Archive, KKL3/29.

83   Raad, *1933 Catalogue*, 39; printed in Sela, *Khalil Raad*, 246.

84   He also documented the British occupation and Turkish surrender in WWI (1917). These images are important as, until recently, it was believed that only the American Colony photographers had documented the event (Ellie Shiler, "75 Shanim Lekibush Yerushalim Bidei Habritim (1917–1992)," *Ariel* 88 (1992): 63–4). I am grateful to Rachel Lev, American Colony's archivist, who shared with me the information about the documentation of the surrender.

FIGURE 6.13   *Native children of Banias*, undated. Chalil Raad. No. 745 in Raad's albums/
textual catalogue

colonialism and led to the fall of Palestine in 1948'.[85] Moreover, his production
can be characterised as an individual and oppositional response to the complex realities of a time in which Western ideas, as well as the modern *Al-Nahda*
knowledge production, were reified.

3.2   *The Holy Land*

Analysis of Raad's work reveals a continuous, resilient dialogue (both visual
and textual) with the way the land was presented in the west. Raad's stationery
from 1914, for example, bears the description 'Photographer of historical places
in black, colour and sepia' and 'characters from the Land of the Bible'.[86] In 1920,
he likewise marketed his work by stressing the country's Biblical history, with
captions such as: 'A large Collection of Lantern photographs of Biblical and

85   Al-Hajj, "Khalil Raad – Jerusalem Photographer," 39. See also: Khalidi, *Before Their
Diaspora*; Elias Sanbar, *Les Palestiniens, la photographie d'une terre et de son people de 1839
à nos jours* (Paris: Hazan, 2004); Tamari, "Khalil Raad (1854–1957)," 7–13; Tamari, "The War
Photography of Khalil Raad."
86   Central Zionist archive, KKL3/29.

FIGURE 6.14   *Women of Ramallah embroidering*, undated. Chalil Raad. No. 285 in Raad's albums/textual catalogue

FIGURE 6.15   *Boy selling oranges,* undated. Chalil Raad. No. a269 in Raad's albums/textual catalogue

FIGURE 6.16   *Untitled*, undated (uncatalogued). Chalil Raad

FIGURE 6.17   *The Mufti leaving with the procession to Nabī Mūsā*, date unknown. Chalil Raad.
No. a230 in Raad's albums/textual catalogue

Historical Places in Palestine and Syria' (Fig. 6.18). In doing so, Raad established 'stylistic and expressive patterns that were different from those brought
by the European photographers but mimicked their familiar and institutional
versions [...] similar to photography in other 'colonial countries'.[87]

Raad photographed sites mentioned in the New Testament, including the
House of Simon the Tanner in Jaffa and the Inn of the Good Samaritan, as
well as places symbolically associated with Christianity, such as a carpentry
workshop in Nazareth, and girls from Bethlehem and Nazareth carrying babies
(see Fig. 6.12). Other locations of Christian religious-historical significance
regularly photographed by Raad included the Hall of the Last Supper and the
Via Dolorosa with its stations of the cross, all of which were common icons in
Western photography of the Holy Land. Moreover, Raad embellished some of
his photos with texts from the New Testament, situating his images in a given
religious-biblical context. For example, one photograph of a young Palestinian
shepherd is entitled, 'Bringing back the Lost Sheep', alluding to: 'rejoice with

---

87   Translated from Hebrew. Nir, "Beyerushlayim Ubeerets-Israel," 100.

FIGURE 6.18   *The Palestine Directory*, 1920.

me; I have found my lost sheep' (*Luke* 15:6).[88] Another image is named 'Camel Looking through the Eye of a Needle' (see Fig. 6.11 above), invoking the lines, 'It is easier for a camel to go through the eye of a needle, than for a rich man to enter into the kingdom of God' (*Matthew 19*: 24; KJV). Raad also photographed locations referred to in the Old Testament, including sites where Biblical figures lived or major events took place, such as a photograph of a Palestinian boy seated against the background of Zorah, with the caption 'Zorah, Samson's Home'; a Palestinian girl in a wheat field entitled 'Ruth the Gleaner' (Fig. 6.19); a photograph of Palestinian boys on the edge of a pit called, 'Joseph's Well, Dothan,' and 'Ahab's Well Near Jezreel'. The admiration garnered by such images was noted by Raad himself, as he claimed in a 1906 advertisement: 'Every day I receive thank-you letters [...] particularly from people of European descent'.

3.3   *Biblical Archaeology*

Research has repeatedly shown how archaeologists were among the first to rally to the colonialist cause as the discipline developed in direct relation to imperialism and colonialism.[89] Derek Gregory highlights how ruins in

---

88   See also Sela, *Tsilum Befalastin*, 167–68.
89   Berg, "The Imperialist Lens," 10. See also Barromi-Perlman, "Archaeology, Zionism, and Photography in Palestine"; Jane Lydon and Uzma Rizvi, *Handbook of Postcolonial Archaeology* (Walnut Creek, CA: Routledge, 2010); Paul Lane, "Possibilities for a postcolonial archaeology in sub-Saharan Africa: indigenous and usable past," *World Archaeology* 43, no. 1 (2011): 7–25; Albert Glock, "Archaeology as Cultural Survival: The Future of the Palestinian Past," *Journal of Palestine Studies* 23, no. 3 (1994): 70–84.

FIGURE 6.19   *Ruth the gleaner*, undated. Chalil Raad. No. 656 in Raad's albums/textual
                catalogue

Egypt were stripped of the culture of the village and 'ordered as geometries,
systematic arrangements of planes and surfaces that exposed the endur-
ing structure of an ancient civilization'.[90] Archaeology remains strongly
Eurocentric and thus, on a global scale, it privileges Western perspectives.[91] As
such, the archaeology of Palestine has been dominated by a so-called 'Biblical
archaeology'.[92] The monumental and archaeological imaginary focused mainly
on ancient places, virtually empty of human inhabitation, a vacant space. So
too, as research has underscored, archaeology was used as a cultural-nationalist
practice in the struggle to construct a Zionist identity that associated ancient
objects with national causes.[93] In fact, the science of archaeology in Palestine
functioned (and in many ways continues to function) as a domain in which

90   Gregory, "Emperors of the Gaze," 224.
91   Lane, "Possibilities for a postcolonial archaeology," 8.
92   Glock, "Archaeology as Cultural Survival," 71.
93   Nadia Abu El-Haj, "Producing (Arti) Facts: Archaeology and Power during the British
      Mandate of Palestine," *Israel Studies* 7, no. 2 (2002): 33; Glock, "Archaeology as Cultural
      Survival," 71.

a colonial-cultural imagination is given form.[94] Historically, it enjoyed the status of a scientific practice, with the camera perceived as a positivist tool that created accurate, objective depictions of the world, 'serving as epistemic markers'.[95]

Raad accompanied many Western archaeological excavations, sometimes as an official employee and sometimes documenting them out of his own personal interest in archaeology and Biblical sites, and probably was influenced by these Western scholars.[96] As early as June 1902, Raad accompanied Peters and Thiersch in their exploration of the painted tombs in Maresha (in the Beit Guvrin area), photographing the Hellenistic frescoes. 'Under many difficulties, [he] obtained such excellent results',[97] despite the fact that there was not enough air inside the caves to ventilate the smoke created by the magnesium flashlight, making the air too dense to breathe after a shot or two.[98] David Jacobson argues that the importance of Raad's work in documenting the paintings from the third century BC lay in the fact that they were executed on soft limestone walls and were in danger of deterioration.[99] Furthermore, having joined the Badè Expedition at Tall Al- Nasaba in 1927[100] and the Haverford expedition in the spring of 1928, his participation in Eliyahu Grant's expedition reflected his motivation to explore important Biblical sites, such as the ancient Beth Shemesh (Figs 6.20, 6.21).[101] Grant emphasised the British Mandate government's support for scientists and explorers eager to '[discover] the ancient

94   El-Haj, "Reflections on Archaeology and Israeli Settler-Nationhood," *Radical History Review* 86: 149–163.

95   Nadia Abu El-Haj, *Facts on the Ground: Archaeological Practice and Territorial Self-Fashioning in Israeli Society* (Chicago: University of Chicago Press, 2001), 2.

96   The textual catalogue indicates which excavation he accompanied.

97   John Peters and Hermann Thiersch, *Painted Tombs in the Necropolis of Marissa (Marêshah)* (London: Palestine Exploration Fund, 1905), xvii.

98   Ibid, 3.

99   David Jacobson, *The Hellenistic Paintings of Marisa, Palestine Exploration Fund* (London: Maney, 2007).

100   Raad also joined the Badè expedition excavating in Mispah (1926–35). He was not the official photographer of the excavations in Tell Al-Nasbeh (Chester Charlton McCown, *Tell En-Nasbeh Excavated under the Direction of The Late William Frederic Badè. Volume I, Archaeological and Historical Results* (Berkeley: Palestine Institute of Pacific School of Religion and the American Schools of Oriental Research, 1947), xi).

101   Raad indicated that the excavations were led by Grant (1928–1933); Raad, *1933 Catalogue*, 21; Sela, *Khalil Raad*, 237). See also, Elihu Grant, *Beth-Shemesh (Palestine). Progress of the Haverford Archaeological Expedition* (Haverford, PA: Biblical and Kindred Studies, 1929), 9. British archaeologist Duncan Mackenzie excavated there earlier (1911–12) for the Palestine Exploration Fund (PEF).

FIGURE 6.20   *Old Canaanite wall at Beith-Shems and women carrying baskets of debris,*
c. 1928–1933. Chalil Raad. Excavation conducted by Dr. Grant, 1928–1933,
No. a148 in Raad's albums/textual catalogue

FIGURE 6.21   *Washing and cleaning potshards* c. 1928–1933. Chalil Raad. Excavation
conducted by Dr. Grant, 1928–1933, No. a144 in Raad's albums/textual
catalogue)

Canaan'.[102] In this spirit, he also documented the remains of ancient Jewish settlements, such as the 'Excavations at Bethel of Jewish Period'; 'Excavations of Samaria at Jewish Period'; 'Tomb of Absalom'; and 'Rachel's Tomb'.[103] Glock argues that although Albright succeeded at Bayt Mirsim in developing new typological frameworks, the biblical connections remained, 'illuminating' the general historical background.[104] Raad also joined archaeological excavation expeditions to Mispah, Ashkelon, Jerusalem, al-Khalīl (Hebron, directed by Dr Madre), Tall Balāta and Nāblus (conducted in 1913–14 or 1926–27 by the Sellin expedition), Bayt-Mirsim (1926–32);[105] Beit She'an;[106] Megiddo (Majīdū);[107] Samaria (Harvard University, Fig. 6.22);[108] Bethel (1934); Mispah; and Ashkelon, as well as expeditions elsewhere in the Middle East. The names of the archaeological sites in Raad's catalogues are often written in Hebrew transliteration. The heritage and memory of the colonised land were expropriated from the indigenous population to be replaced with 'true heritage' and simulated into

---

102   Grant, *Beth Shemesh (Palestine)*, 13.
103   All quotes referring to Raad's work are from Raad, *1933 Catalogue*, 3–55; Sela, *Khalil Raad*, 227–254. Particularly interesting is Photograph 326c, called 'Jewish Settlement at the Foot of Mount Gilboa Overlooking Gideon's Spring', connecting the Jewish past and present. The settlement is Kibbutz Ein Harod. Established in 1921, Raad probably photographed it not long afterwards, since it used to be located next to the spring, right below Mount Gilboa, as suggested in Raad's caption and seen in the photograph. A few years later, it moved to a nearby hill.
104   Glock, "Archaeology as Cultural Survival," 73.
105   William Albright, *The Excavation of Tell Beit Mirsim, Vol. II. The Bronze Age* (New Haven, CT: American Schools of Oriental Research, 1938).
106   Apparently by an expedition of the Pennsylvania Museum (1921–33) headed by Clarence Fisher, Alan Rowe and Gerald Fitzgerald. Although multiple photos are included in the book, it is not noted whether they have been taken by Raad. Gerald Fitzgerald, *Beth-Shean Excavations 1921–1923* (Philadelphia: The University Press, 1931).
107   Raad does not indicate in the visual albums which archaeological expedition he accompanied (by Gottlieb Schumacher in 1903–5, or by the Oriental Institute of the University of Chicago in 1925), as opposed to other cases where this information is provided. The albums do not include enough photos from these excavations to identify the expedition.
108   Raad, *1933 Catalogue*, 54; Sela, *Khalil Raad*, 254. Samaria was also excavated by two expeditions: the Harvard expedition (1908–10) and the Crowfoot expedition (1931–35). The findings of the first were published in a two-volume book that included detailed notes, photos, documents, illustrations, logs and information about the photographs, their development, cataloguing, etc. George Andrew Reisner, Stanley Clarence Fisher, and David Gordon Lyon, *Harvard Excavation at Samaria 1908–1910*, 1st volume (Cambridge, MA: Harvard University Press, 1924), 45. Despite this richness of detail, the photographer/s is/are not mentioned by name.

Western culture.[109] This practice is reminiscent of the activities of French archaeologists in Tunisia for example, who portrayed themselves not only as 'protectors', but also excavators of heritage and history – that is, as creators of memory, fulfilling a fantasy of a lost world.[110]

While recording these excavations, their discoveries and the work of foreign archaeologists in order to expand the visual database about sites, Raad also documented vast numbers of Palestinian labourers (both men and women) at work, digging (see Fig. 6.20 above) or cleaning articles (see Fig. 6.21 above). Glock demonstrates how during the Mandate, 'Palestinian employees greatly outnumbered the others ... by and large they served as guardians at sites around the country, museum guards and attendants, messengers, and cleaners. Only a fraction of the seventy-three Palestinians employed by the department held higher positions',[111] yet none of them was documented by Raad. Often, in fact, workers were occasionally used to model relations of height or size with artifacts that were central in the image,[112] with formal aspects employed in the service of constructing colonialist knowledge. For instance, Raad's images of the remains of the crusader church in Samaria with figures standing alongside (see Fig. 6.22 below) recalls the photographs and photographic strategies of the Bonfils in Samaria. Like his Western colleagues, Raad adopted some iconographic and thematic aspects in depicting archaeological and architectonic sites, ornaments and remains (such as the house of Martha and Mary and Capernaum) and photographed close-ups of structures with ornamental elements, indicating his dialogue with their work.

---

109   Yehoshua Ben-Arieh, "Hamosadot Hazarim Learchiologya Velehakirat Erets-Israel Bitkufat Hamandat: Helek B," *Cathedra: For the History of Eretz Israel and Its Yishuv* 93 (1999): 136.

110   Annie E. Coombes, *Reinventing Africa: Museums, Material Culture and Popular Imagination in Late Victorian and Edwardian England* (New Haven, CT: Yale University Press, 1995), 193.

111   Glock, "Archaeology as Cultural Survival," 75. Although most of them were connected to the western/British production of knowledge in their education or occupation before and during the Mandate, many focused on Palestinian cultural traditions (folklore, architecture and the social context of the village house). Ibid., 72–79.

Sarah Irving discusses the role of Yusif Khazin and Yusif Kanaan in PEF excavations that were employed in managing professional scientific work before and in the early British Mandate (Sarah Irving, "A Tale of Two Yusifs: Recovering Arab Agency in PEF Excavations 1890–1924," *Palestine Exploration Quarterly* 149, no. 3 (2017): 223–236.

112   Barromi-Perlman, "Archaeology, Zionism, and Photography in Palestine," 49–51.

FIGURE 6.22   *Ruins of an old crusader in Samaria.* Chalil Raad. Excavation conducted by
                Prof. Sellin, 1913–1914 or 1926–1927, No. 317 in Raad's albums/textual catalogue

4   Resilient Resistance

Research has illuminated how indigenous photography constituted an oppositional locus or resistant iconography, characterised by the invention of a local
practice which produced its own hybrid vocabulary. The Istanbul-based Sébah
commercial photography studio, for instance, adapted several conventional
European clichés, such as photographs of occupational types, to suit their
'self-visions' as 'modernising', while at the same time (especially with regard
to community portraits), emphasising order and modernity within indigenous
historical structures. This practice indicated a perspective that did not fit com-
fortably into the Orientalist mode.[113] In parallel, the construction of a modern
middle-class subjectivity resulted in Iranian photography of the time being
characterised by representation of lower class 'types' – in essence, a domestic
Orientalist practice which mapped aspects of Western civilisational discourse
onto Iranian social structures.[114] Stephen Sheehi, who discusses early Arab
and especially Lebanese imago, shows too that the adoption of foreign practices and technologies was not a passive act but 'an ideological act by which
non-Western subjects claimed ownership of modernity'.[115] In this regard, Avi
Rubin shows that Orientalism was inherent in Ottoman discourse generated by
the local population as a vehicle for inner criticism and change mobilisation.[116]
Louise Bethlehem advocates reading beyond the narrow dialectics of 'oppression versus liberation'[117] as 'incomplete forms of resistance' or 'limited forms
of emulation'.[118] Through developing a flexible, dual approach that sheds light
on new sites of identity formation and protest,[119] hybridity may in this case
be recast as subversion[120] or a mode of camouflage.[121] In other words, it can
be argued that deceptive, multifaceted and sometimes contradictory features

---

113   Woodward, "Between Orientalist Clichés," 371–373. See also: Çelik, "Photographing
       Mundane Modernity"
114   Behdad, *Camera Orientalis*, 126.
115   Stephen Sheehi, "A Social History of Early Arab Photography or a Prolegomenon to an
       Archaeology of the Lebanese Imago of the Lebanese Imago," International Journal of
       Middle East Studies. 39 (2007): 178.
116   Rubin, "Hamizrah Davar Ehad Vehama'rav Davar Aher", 78.
117   Louise Bethlehem, "Likra't hibridiyut aheret," *Teoriya Ubiḳoret* 29 (2016): 193–204.
118   Ibid., 202.
119   Lila Abu-Lughod, "The Romance of Resistance: Tracing Transformations of Power through
       Bedouin Women," *American Anthropologist* 17, no. 1 (1990): 41–55.
120   David Jefferess, *Postcolonial Resistance: Culture, Liberation and Transformation* (Toronto:
       University of Toronto Press, Scholarly Publishing Division, 2008).
121   Homi K. Bhabha, "Of Mimicry and Man: The Ambivalence of Colonial Discourse,"
       October 28, *Discipleship: A Special Issue on Psychoanalysis* (1984): 125–133.

form part of an obfuscation mechanism, a mask designed to wrap resistance. Accordingly, Raad's assimilation of one language into another may be read as a form of 'symbolic opposition'.[122] Rather than a binary, unidirectional process of liberation from Western patterns in favour of developing an independent indigenous culture, what unfolds is an alternative interactive process 'in order to improve the model's fit to the local country and 'culture''. In other words, the process is not static, but dynamic, multi-layered and replete with contradictions that stem from a colonial context.

This article evolves from and elaborates on extensive research into the power mechanisms of visual colonialism that contribute to an erasure of indigenous cultures. Most specifically, it examines how the work of Palestinian photographer Chalil Raad responds to and counters the destructiveness of colonialism.[123] As with other photographers and creators in the region, Raad's resistance was shaped in relation to the fictional Orientalist lens, while at the same time developing a unique autonomous gaze. On a reductive 'purist' or 'binary' level, it becomes clear that the language of Western colonialist photography has been internalised, 'inherent' and normalised in the local photographer's work. At the same time, Raad enabled the return of the voices of those who were silenced by colonialism. This article, however, proposes refocusing attention away from the indigenous practitioner's subjugation to colonial discourse toward the various strategies of resilient resistance that he or she may employ – among them appropriation, deconstruction, disruption, cross-referencing and reassembly. It thereby seeks to reformulate these practices through a wider lens that does not coalesce into mere oppositionality but highlights such a problematisation and seeks to address the complex relations at play. In a world of dualism and dialogue, this research shifts (together with Raad) between poles of representation and meaning. Raad's work may be difficult to wholly comprehend without discussing how Palestine's visual history has been (and is) written over more than a century of national conflict and in the service of conflicting political causes, be they Western, Zionist or Palestinian. This text articulates the struggle – which is still raging – for the image of the conflict, that is powerfully bound with its historical roots and against the colonial erasure of Palestinian historiography.

---

122   James Scott, *The Moral Economy of the Peasant: Rebellion and Subsistence in Southeast Asia* (New Haven, CT: Yale University Press, 1976), 84.

123   See also Sheehi, "A Social History of Early Arab Photography," 179.

In doing so, it considers (among other concerns) whether Raad in fact photographed archaeology as an anti-colonial or indigenous practice,[124] and how his work was 'shaped by indigenous knowledges'[125] that structured the decolonisation processes. Did he seek to challenge colonialist archaeology through a multi-faceted approach in order to construct an alternate conception of the past to that forged by Western archaeology?[126] It may be that Raad's work teaches us about other decolonised or different options of representation, interpretation and resistance that should be rethought. In the shadow of ongoing colonialism and oppression in Israel/Palestine, in the midst of an intractable conflict, and in view of the continued struggle against erasure, and for its visual aspects, its overt and covert layers and its competing political and ideological justifications and rationalisations, such questions remain open.

Acknowledgments

This research and article could not have been completed without the generous assistance of George Raad, Chalil Raad's son (R.I.P.) and his family. I am also grateful for their permission to publish his father's photographs and their family photographs.

Bibliography

Abu El-Haj, Nadia. *Facts on the Ground: Archaeological Practice and Territorial Self-Fashioning in Israeli Society.* Chicago: University of Chicago Press, 2001.

Abu El-Haj, Nadia. "Producing (Arti) Facts: Archaeology and Power During the British Mandate of Palestine." *Israel Studies* 7, no. 2 (Summer 2002): 33–61.

Abu El-Haj, Nadia. "Reflections on Archaeology and Israeli Settler-Nationhood." *Radical History Review* 86: 149–163.

Abu-Lughod, Lila. "The Romance of Resistance: Tracing Transformations of Power through Bedouin Women." *American Anthropologist* 17, no. 1 (1990): 41–55.

---

124 Sonya Atalay, "Indigenous Archaeology as Decolonizing Practice," *The American Indian Quarterly* 30 (2006): 280–310; Lane, "Possibilities for a postcolonial archaeology."

125 C. Smith and H.M. Wobst, "The Next Step: An Archaeology for Social Justice," in *Indigenous Archaeologies: Decolonizing Theory and Practice*, eds. C. Smith and H.M. Wobst (London: Routledge, 2005), 394.

126 Bruce Trigger, "The History of African Archaeology in World Perspective," in *A History of African Archaeology*, eds. Peter Robertshaw and Bruce Trigger (London: James Currey, 1990), 309–19.

Albright, William. *The Excavation of Tell Beit Mirsim, Vol. II. The Bronze Age*. New Haven, CT: American Schools of Oriental Research, 1938.

Al-Hajj, Badr. "Khalil Raad – Jerusalem Photographer." *Jerusalem Quarterly* 11–12 (2001): 34–39.

Al-Raheb, Mitri. "Karimeh Abbud: Almrah Khlf Al'dsa." ("The Woman behind the Lens"). In *Karimeh Abbud*, edited by Mitri Al-Raheb, Ahmad Marwat and Issam Nassar, 32–59. Bethlehem: Diyar, 2011.

Atalay, Sonya. "Indigenous Archaeology as Decolonizing Practice." *The American Indian Quarterly* 30 (2006): 280–310.

Bar-Am, Micha. *Painting with Light: Photographic Aspects of the Work of Ephraim Mose Lilien*. Israel: Tel Aviv Museum of Art, 1991.

Barromi-Perlman, Edna. "Archeology, Zionism, and Photography in Palestine. Analysis of the Use of Dimensions of People in Photographs." *Journal of Landscape Ecology* 10, no. 3 (2017): 49–57.

Bar-Yosef, Eitan. *The Holy Land in English Culture 1799–1917: Palestine and the Question of Orientalism*. Oxford: Oxford University Press, 2005.

Behdad, Ali. *Camera Orientalis: Reflections on Photography of the Middle East*. Chicago: University of Chicago Press, 2016.

Behdad, Ali. "Mediated Visions: Early Photography of the Middle East and Orientalist Network." *History of Photography* 41, no. 4 (2017): 362–375.

Ben-Arieh, Yehoshua. "Hamosadot Hazarim Learchiologya Velehakirat Erets-Israel Bitkufat Hamandat: Helek B." ("Non-Jewish Institutions and the Research of Palestine during the British Mandate Period: Part Two"). *Cathedra: For the History of Eretz Israel and Its Yishuv* (1999): 111–142.

Berg, Keri. "The Imperialist Lens: Du Camp, Salzmann and Early French Photography." *Early Popular Visual Culture* 6, no. 1 (April 2008): 1–17.

Bethlehem, Louise. "Likra't hibridiyut aheret." ("Towards a different hybridity"). *Teoriya Ubikoret (Theory & Criticism)* 29 (2016): 193–204.

Bhabha, Homi. K. "Of Mimicry and Man: The Ambivalence of Colonial Discourse." *October* 28, *Discipleship: A Special Issue on Psychoanalysis* (1984): 125–133.

Çelik, Zeynep. "Colonialism, Orientalism and the Canon." *Art Bulletin* 78 (1996): 202–205.

Çelik, Zeynep. "Photographing Mundane Modernity." In *Camera Ottomana: Photography and Modernity in the Ottoman Empire, 1840–1914*, edited by Zeynep Çelik and Edhem Eldem, 154–200. Istanbul: Koç University Press, 2015.

Coombes, Annie E. *Reinventing Africa: Museums, Material Culture and Popular Imagination in Late Victorian and Edwardian England*. New Haven, CT: Yale University Press, 1995.

Dalman, Gustaf. *Arbeit und Sitte in Palästina*. Germany: Georg Olms Verlagsbuchhandlung, 1964.

Davis, George. *Rebuilding Palestine According to Prophecy*. Philadelphia, PA: The Million Testaments Campaigns, 1935.

Davis, John. *The Landscape of Belief: Encountering the Holy Land in Nineteenth-Century American Art and Culture*. Princeton: Princeton University Press, 1996.

El-Shakry, Omnia. ""History without Documents": The Vexed Archives of Decolonization in the Middle East." *American Historical Review* 120, no. 3 (June 2015): 920–934.

Finney, Mark. "Christian Zionism, the US and the Middle East: A Sketch and Brief Analysis." In *The Bible, Zionism and Palestine: The Bible's Role in Conflict and Liberation in Israel-Palestine*, edited by Michael Sandford, 20–31. Dunedin, New Zealand: Relegere Academic Press, 2016.

Fitzgerald, Gerald. *Beth-Shean Excavations 1921–1923*. Philadelphia: The University Press, 1931.

Glock, Albert. "Archaeology as Cultural Survival: The Future of the Palestinian Past." *Journal of Palestine Studies* 23, no. 3 (Spring 1994): 70–84.

Grant, Elihu. *Beth Shemesh (Palestine). Progress of the Haverford Archaeological Expedition*. Haverford, PA: Biblical and Kindred Studies, 1929.

Gregory, Derek. "Emperors of the Gaze: Photographic Practices and Productions of Space in Egypt, 1839–1914." In *Picturing Place: Photography and the Geographical Imagination*, edited by Joan Schwartz and James Ryan, 195–225. London: I.B. Tauris, 2003.

Hahavatselet, July 24, 1899.

Hashkafa, 1906.

Hassan, Fekri. "Imperialist Appropriations of Egyptian Obelisks." In *Views of Ancient Egypt since Napoleon Bonaparte: Imperialism, Colonialism and Modern Appropriations*, edited by David Jeffreys, 19–68. London: Cavendish, 2003.

Hasson, Nir. "Hundreds of Photos Found from When Israel's War of Independence Raged." *Haaretz*, December 9, 2018. https://www.haaretz.com/israel-news/premium .MAGAZINE-hundreds-of-photos-found-from-when-the-1948-war-raged-1.6725444.

Hirschfeld, Ariel. "Qadima." In *To the East? To the East: Orientalism in the Arts in Israel*, edited by Yigal Zalmona and Tamar Manor-Fridman, 11–31. Jerusalem: The Israel Museum, 1998.

Institute for Palestine Studies (IPS). "Palestinian Photographers before 1948: Documenting Life in a Time of Change." *Palestinian Journeys*. Accessed September 8, 2019. https://www.paljourneys.org/en/timeline/highlight/10522/palestinian-photo graphers-1948.

Irving, Sarah. "A Tale of Two Yusifs: Recovering Arab Agency in PEF Excavations 1890–1924." *Palestine Exploration Quarterly* 149, no. 3 (2017): 223–236.

Jacobson, David. *The Hellenistic Paintings of Marisa (Palestine Exploration Fund)*. London: Maney, 2007.

James, Ryan R. and Joan M. Schwartz, eds. *Picturing Place: Photography and the Geographical Imagination*. London: I.B. Tauris, 2003.

Jefferess, David. *Postcolonial Resistance: Culture, Liberation and Transformation.* Toronto: University of Toronto Press, Scholarly Publishing Division, 2008.

Khalidi, Walid. *Before Their Diaspora, A Photographic History of the Palestinians 1876–1948.* Washington D.C.: Institute for Palestine Studies, 1991.

Kol Yerushalayim Lishnat TRPA. 1921, a Hebrew almanac.

Kroyanker, David. *Reḥḥov Yafo Beyerushalyim. (Jaffa Street in Jerusalem).* Jerusalem: Jerusalem Institute for Israeli Research and Keter Publishing House, 2005.

Kyram, Dan. "Hatslamim Harishonim Veavodatam." ("The First Photographers and Their Work"). *Ariel* 66–67, *Tsilume Erets-Israel Harishonim, Masa' Be'kvot Tslamim Rishonim. (Early Photographs of Palestine: In the Footsteps of the First Photographers)* (1990): 24–159.

Lane, Paul. "Possibilities for a postcolonial archaeology in sub-Saharan Africa: indigenous and usable past." *World Archaeology* 43, no. 1 (March 2011): 7–25.

Lydon, Jane and Uzma Rizvi. *Handbook of Postcolonial Archaeology.* Walnut Creek, CA: Routledge, 2010.

Macmillan and Co. *Guide to Palestine and Egypt.* London: Macmillan, 1903.

Maggiolini, Paolo. "Studies and Souvenirs of Palestine and Transjordan: The Revival of the Latin Patriarchate of Jerusalem and the Rediscovery of the Holy Land during the Nineteenth Century." In *Orientalism, Revisited Art, Land and Voyage,* edited by Ian Richard Netton, 165–175. London: Routledge, 2013.

Masalha, Nur. *The Bible and Zionism: Invented Traditions, Archaeology and Post-Colonialism in Palestine.* London & New York: Zed Books, 2007.

McCown, Chester Charlton. *Tell En-Nasbeh Excavated Under the Direction of The Late William Frederic Badè. Volume I, Archaeological and Historical Results.* Berkeley, CA: Palestine Institute of Pacific School of Religion and the American Schools of Oriental Research, 1947.

Merli, Andrea. "A New Art in an Ancient Land: Palestine through the lens of early European Photographers." *Jerusalem Quarterly* 50 (2012): 23–36.

Nassar, Issam. *Laqatat Mughayira: al-Taswir al-Futugrafi al-Mubakir fi Filastin. (Different Snapshots: Palestine in Early Photography).* Beirut and Ramallah: Kutub and Qattan Foundation, 2005.

Nassar, Issam. "'Biblification' in the Service of Colonialism. Jerusalem in Nineteenth-century Photography." *Third Text* (2007): 317–26.

Nir, Yeshayahu. *Beyerushlayim Ubeerets-Israel Be'kvot Tslamim Rishonim. (In Jerusalem and the Land of Israel, In the Footsteps of Early Photographers).* Tel Aviv: IDF Publishing House, 1986.

Nir, Yeshayahu. "Reshit Hatsilum Berets-Israel." ("Early Photography in Eretz-Israel"). *Ariel* 66–67, *Tsilume Erets-Israel Harishonim, Masa' Be'kvot Tslamim Rishonim. (Early Photographs of Palestine: In the Footsteps of the First Photographers)* (1989): 9–16.

Ofek, Ruti. *E.M. Lilien – Ha'man Hatsiyoni Harishon (E.M. Lilien – the first Zionist artist).* Tefen: The Open Museum, 1997.

Onne, Eyal. *Photographic Heritage of the Holy Land 1839–1914.* Manchester: Manchester Polytechnic Institute of Advanced Studies, 1980.

The Palestine Directory, 1920.

Pappé, Ilan. "The Bible in the Service of Zionism, 'We do not Believe in God, but He Nonetheless Promised us Palestine'." In *The Bible, Zionism and Palestine: The Bible's Role in Conflict and Liberation in Israel-Palestine,* edited by Michael Sandford, 205–217. Dunedin, New Zealand: Relegere Academic Press, 2007.

Perez, Nissan N. *Focus East, Early Photography in the Near East 1839–1885.* New York: Harry H. Abrams, 1988.

Peters, John and Hermann Thiersch. *Painted Tombs in the Necropolis of Marissa (Marêshah).* London: Palestine Exploration Fund, 1905.

Raad, Chalil. *1933 Catalogue of Lantern Slides and Views made by C. Raad Photographer of Sites, Scenes, Ceremonies, Costumes, Etc. Etc., of Palestine & Syria Identical with Bible. History.* Jerusalem: Beyt-Ul-Makdes Press, 1933.

Raad, Chalil and John Krikorian. *1930 Catalogue of Lantern Slides and Views made by C. Raad & J. Krikorian of Sites, Scenes, Ceremonies, Costumes, etc. of Palestine & Syria Identical with Bible History, C. Raad & J. Krikorian Photographers.* Jerusalem: The Commercial Press, 1930.

Rabinowitz, Dani. *A'ntropologiya Vehafalastinim. (Anthropology and the Palestinians).* Ra'anana: Hamerkaz Leheker Hatarbut Ha'aravit (The Center for the Arab Society Research), 1998.

Reisner, George Andrew, Stanley Clarence Fisher and David Gordon Lyon. *Harvard Excavation at Samaria 1908–1910.* 1st Volume. Cambridge, MA: Harvard Press, 1924.

Rubin. Avi. "Hamizrah Davar Ehad Vehama'rav Davar Aher" (The East One Thing, and the West Another One?"). *Jama'a* 7 (2001): 54–81.

Said, Edward. *Orientalism.* New York: Vintage Books, 1994.

Sanbar, Elias. *Les Palestiniens, la photographie d'une terre et de son people de 1839 à nos jours.* Paris: Hazan, 2004.

Scott, James. *The Moral Economy of the Peasant: Rebellion and Subsistence in Southeast Asia.* New Haven, CT: Yale University Press, 1976.

Sefer Hareshimot Lemishar Vet'asiyah, Sefer Haktovot (The Book of Commercial and Industry, Address Book), 1936.

Sefer Shimushi, Sefer Yedi'ot, Sefer Adresa'ot (Useful Book, Information Book, Address Book). Jerusalem: Levy, 1921.

Sela, Rona. *Tsilum Befalastin/Erets-Israel Bishnot Hashloshim Vea'arba'im. (Photography in Palestine in the 1930s & 1940s).* Tel Aviv: Hakibuts Hameuchad Publishing House and Herzliya Museum, 2000. For the English translation of the chapter on Palestinian photography, 163–176, see: https://www.academia.edu/36679969/In_the_Eyes_of _the_Beholder_-Aspects_of_Early_Palestinian_Photography. Accessed 30 July, 2018.

Sela, Rona. "Historiya Metsulemet Shel Falastine." ("Photographed History of Palestine"). *Teoriya Ubikoret* (*Theory & Criticism*) 31 (2007): 302–310.

Sela, Rona. *Le'iyun Hatsibur – Tslumeu Falastinim Ba'rchiyonim Hatsva'yim Beisrael.* (*Made Public – Palestinian Photographs in Military Archives in Israel*). Tel Aviv: Helena and Minshar Gallery, 2009.

Sela, Rona. *Khalil Raad – Tslumim, 1891–1948.* (*Chalil Raad Photographs, 1891–1948*). Tel Aviv: Helena, 2010.

Sela, Rona. *Limu'ayanh al-Jamhur al-falastiniun fi al-a'rshifat al-'askariyya al-Isra'iliyya.* (*Made Public – Palestinians in Military Archives in Israel*). Ramallah: Madar Center, 2018.

Sela, Rona. "Genealogy of Colonial Plunder and Erasure – Israel's Control over Palestinian Archives." *Social Semiotics* 28, no. 2 (2018): 201–229.

Sela, Rona. ""Imprisoned Photographs": The Looted Archive of Photo Rissas (Rassas) – Ibrahim and Chalil (Khalil) Rissas." *INTERMÉDIAL* 32 (Autumn 2018).

Sheehi, Stephen. "A Social History of Early Arab Photography or a Prolegomenon to an Archaeology of the Lebanese Imago of the Lebanese Imago." *International Journal of Middle East Studies* 39 (2007): 177–208.

Sheehi, Stephen. "The Nahḍa After-Image." *Third Text* 26, no. 4 (2012): 401–414.

Sheehi, Stephen. *The Arab Imago: A Social History of Portrait Photography, 1860–1910.* Princeton: Princeton University Press, 2016.

Shiler, Ellie. "Nofei Erets-Israel Be'inei Hatsalamim Harishonim." ("The First Photographers and Their Work"). *Ariel* 66–67, *Tsilume Erets-Israel Harishonim, Masa' Be'kvot Tslamim Rishonim* (*Early Photographs of Palestine: In the Footsteps of the First Photographers*) (1989): 17–23.

Shiler, Ellie and Menahem Levin. "Albomay Hayedu'im Shel Khalil Ra'ad." ("The Known Albums of Chalil Raad"). *Ariel* 68–70 (1990): 216–19.

Slyomovics, Susan. "Edward Said's Nazareth." *Framework: The Journal of Cinema and Media* 50, nos. 1/2 (2009): 9–45.

Smith, Claire and Hans Martin Wobst. "The Next Step: An Archaeology for Social Justice." In *Indigenous Archaeologies: Decolonizing Theory and Practice*, edited by C. Smith and H.M. Wobst, 392–394. London: Routledge, 2005.

Solomon-Godeau, Abigail. "A Photographer in Jerusalem, 1855: Auguste Salzmann and his Times." In *Photography at the Dock*, edited by Abigail Solomon-Godeau, 150–168. Minnesota: University of Minnesota Press, 1991.

Stewart Howe, Kathleen. *Revealing the Holy Land: The Photographic Exploration of Palestine.* Santa Barbara: Santa Barbara Museum of Art, 1997.

Tamari, Salim. "The War Photography of Khalil Raad." In *Palestine Before 1948, Not Just Memory, Khalil Raad (1854–1957)* (*Filastin qabl 1948: laysat mujarrad dhakira: Khalil Ra'd (1854–1957)*), edited by Vera Tamari, 17–25. Beirut: Institute for Palestine Studies, 2013.

Tamari, Vera. "Khalil Raad (1854–1957) – Palestine's Pioneer Photographer." In *Palestine Before 1948, Not Just Memory, Khalil Raad (1854–1957)* (*Filastin qabl 1948: laysat mujarrad dhakira: Khalil Ra'd (1854–1957)*), edited by Vera Tamari, 7–11. Beirut: Institute for Palestine Studies, 2013.

The Palestine Post. December 19, 1936, October 5, 1938; December 12, 1939; December 27, 1939.

Trigger, Bruce. "The History of African Archaeology in World Perspective." In *A History of African Archaeology*, edited by Peter Robertshaw and Bruce Trigger, 309–319. London: James Currey, 1990.

Varisco, Daniel Martin. "Orientalism and Bibliolatry. Framing the Holy Land in Nineteenth Century Protestant Bible Customs Texts." In *Orientalism Revisited: Art, Land and Voyage*, edited by Ian Richard Netton, 187–204. London: Routledge, 2013.

Woodward, Michelle. "Between Orientalist Clichés and Images of Modernization." *History of Photography* 27, no. 4 (2003): 363–374.

CHAPTER 7

Open Roads: John D. Whiting, *Diary in Photos*, 1934–1939

Rachel Lev

Over centuries, Western artists and media have created a potent visual archive of the Middle East that is largely made up of clichés of violence, chaos, and Orientalist tropes of exoticism. Contemporary photographers and cultural workers are crafting new mechanisms for memorialising history through photography as they and their fellow citizens experience it, effectively creating an archive where they belong.[1]

∴

Set in 1930s Palestine, Lebanon, Syria, Jordan, Egypt and Turkey, John D. Whiting's *Diary in Photos* series (1934–1939) offers a rare example of a visual genre intertwined with major events, daily life, family relations and personal emotive observations, sketching a rich ethnographic portrait of private and public life in Mandate Palestine and neighbouring cultures during the 1930s. In its entirety, this corpus offers the reader a rare cultural panorama of the region in the period before 1948.

The underlying assumption of this work is the existence of a reciprocal relationship between the photographer and the photographic subject and between the photographer and the landscape. By looking at the corpus in its entirety, rather than extracting sections dealing with discrete narratives, we encounter a cartographic rendering of people, places and events Whiting encountered during his trips and exploration of the Middle East and his life as a member of the American Colony in Jerusalem. We can begin to understand the complex position that Whiting held, despite the sometimes critical interpretations that contemporary readings bring to the archive.

---

1 Michelle L. Woodward, "Creating Memory and History," *Photographies* 2, no. 1 (2009): 21-35.1 0.1080/17540760802696930.

© RACHEL LEV, 2021 | DOI:10.1163/9789004437944_008

FIGURE 7.1 *John D. Whiting* [left], *Ḥusayn Salīm Afandī al-Ḥusaynī (Hussein Selim Effendi al-Husseini)* [Mayor of Jerusalem] *and Ismāʿīl Bay al-Ḥusaynī (Ismail Bey al-Husseini)* [Director of Education], c. 1908. From *Members and Activities of the American Colony*, c. 1890–1906. Photograph album. Photographer Unknown. Visual Materials from the papers of John D. Whiting
PRINTS & PHOTOGRAPHS DIVISION, LIBRARY OF CONGRESS, WASHINGTON, D.C.

Can we relate to the *Diary in Photos* as an autonomous corpus, in which the creator documented the Middle East in a manner that reflects the multiple identities of the subjects depicted against a constantly changing backdrop? Did his ethnographic knowledge, personality, biography and status within the American Colony in Jerusalem influence his attitude toward the various individuals, communities and places with which he interacted? Is this influence expressed across the body of the work or in specific series? Are we, as interpreters, able to read the *Diary in Photos* in its entirety?

John D. Whiting (1882–1951) a man of broad talents and interests, was a Jerusalem-born and a member of the American Colony in Jerusalem, an American Christian community established in Jerusalem in 1881 by small group of Americans from Chicago, Ill. Whiting worked as a personal tour guide, curator, collector, ethnographer, geographer, writer, photographer, amateur botanist and Deputy Consul of United States of America in Jerusalem. While creating the *Diary in Photos*, Whiting crossed Palestine and the Middle East hundreds of times, met with dozens of people, dined with kings, guided archaeological expeditions and slept in Bedouin tents. He toured capital cities and isolated settlements, teeming markets and sacred sites. He researched local cultures and published articles on natural science and ethnography in *National Geographic*.[2] He also served as a consultant for British Mandate officials in Palestine since 1917 and participated in the British Mandate's social and political processes, as a professional, with his family and the American Colony collective.

The *Diary in Photos* series consists of five parchment-bound volumes 24 cm in height and 15 cm in width, each with between 100 and 250 photographs, in 9 × 9 cm sepia tone prints. The photographs are mounted on cardboard, with two photographs arranged vertically on each page and four photographs per double spread. In all, the diaries consist of over 900 photographs that Whiting had selected out of some 2,800 images taken with his personal Rolleiflex camera from 1934 to 1939.

This period is particularly poignant, coinciding with both 'The Great Revolt' (by Palestinians against the British, in protest against continued Zionist immigration, 1936–39) and the Fifth Aliyah (the fifth wave of Zionist immigration from Europe, 1929–1939).

Exploration of the Holy Land as an aspect of faith was etched into the identity of the American Colony in Jerusalem from its founding by Horatio and Anna Spafford in 1881. Travel and studies of the Holy Land continued to mark

---

2 John D. Whiting's articles were published in *National Geographic* between 1913 and 1940. See the full list at the end of the bibliography.

FIGURE 7.2   *Studio Portrait of John D. Whiting*, c. 1905–1910. From *Portraits of the Vester*
             and Whiting Families and the American Colony, 1905–1913. Photograph album.
             Photographer unknown. Visual Materials from the Papers of John D. Whiting
             PRINTS & PHOTOGRAPHS DIVISION, LIBRARY OF CONGRESS,
             WASHINGTON, D.C.

the congregation's identity as younger members adopted exploration-related
professions, which included archaeology, land surveying, tour guiding, photography, botany, ethnography, and hosting. The latter – hosting – exposed
them to like-minded explorers and artists who would often stay for pro-
longed periods as their guests. Similarly, the work of the American Colony
Photo Department (ACPD), a collective of fifteen known photographers of
Palestinian, American, Indian and Swedish origins, involved extensive travels
to remote places in well-planned photographic expeditions.[3]

The late nineteenth century saw the establishment of state-sponsored religious research institutes in Jerusalem, whose new inhabitants' knowledge and
aspirations complemented those of the Colony. To name just a few, the French

3   Rachel Lev, "Photography and Genius Loci: Hol Lars (Lewis) Larson's photograph 'Kaiserin
    Augusta Victoria Stiftung on Olivet' (1910–1914)." In *Tracing the Jerusalem Code, Volume III*,
    ed. Ragnhild J. Zorgati, Anna Bohlin, 2021.

FIGURE 7.3 Typical *Diary in Photos* album page.
Above: Trip to Trans-Jordan with four Anglo-Catholic Sisters, 1937.
Sketching in Kasr Kharani
Below: Trip to Trans-Jordan with four Anglo-Catholic Sisters, 1937.
Sketching in Kasr Kharani
Note: In most cases, the *Diary in Photos* image captions presented
here are quotations of captions written by Whiting as a supplement
to his *Diary*.
From *Diary in Photos*, Volume II, 1936–1937.
Visual Materials from the Papers of John D. Whiting
PRINTS AND PHOTOGRAPHS DIVISION, LIBRARY OF CONGRESS,
WASHINGTON, D.C.

École Biblique et Archéologique Française, founded in 1890, followed by the American School of Oriental Research (today the W.F. Albright Institute of Archaeological Research), founded in 1900, and the Deutsches Evangelisches Institut für Altertumswissenschaft des Heiligen Lands, founded in 1902. The new inhabitants of these institutions established close ties with members of the American Colony that harboured similar interests. These encounters proved formative and led guests and hosts into fruitful exchanges and common ventures. For Whiting, and other younger generations of the Colony, it was a further schooling. Lars E. Lind recalls in his memoir:

> Archaeology seemed to spur on the study of theology. A majority of the annual students from the colleges of Europe were theological graduates; Palestine Archaeology was in fact inseparable from Bible research. The Colony was a host to the great majority of American students and the young men of the Colony, thanks to their intimate knowledge of

FIGURE 7.4 *Group portrait of the Vester and Whiting Families at the American Colony, 1924.*
With John D. Whiting (third from left up, wearing dark suit). ACPD photographers.
Glass Negative. From American Colony Members and Associates, 1880s–1930s.
Glass Negative Collection
AMERICAN COLONY ARCHIVE JERUSALEM

the land and the Arabic language, became the guides and interpreters of the annual excursions.[4]

The *Diary in Photos* is a personal account maintained over a span of six years with a range of contrasting, seemingly unrelated themes: historical events, as well as journeys with unusual personalities; wild nature alongside the rich culture of Bedouin tribes; historical sites and royal wedding ceremonies; a turtle laying eggs in the American Colony gardens and stormy demonstrations in the streets of Jerusalem following the publication of the 1939 White Paper, as well as intimate family gatherings and official encounters. As in real life, Whiting's photographic diaries intertwine major events, daily life, family relations, and personal emotive observations.

The progression of photographs follows a chronicle of written diaries that span the years 1905 to 1941[5] but do not cover the entire period. Possibly, some of the diaries were lost. Whiting was a diligent, concise writer. In an abbreviated style, not unlike today's Twitter, he documents his daily schedules and lists his trips on the diary's first pages.

> Drove to Laila's house and then to pigeon cave via Ras Beirut.
> In Dog river and saw the inscriptions. Sunday, October 27 [1907][6]

He writes in order to record dates, locations, weather, people with whom he travels or interacts, historical sites, and major interests. At times, he expands his abbreviated descriptions and uses the data later in carefully written ethnographic and geographic articles. One example is his description of the Samaritan Passover ceremony on Mt. Gerizim (Jarizīm) near Shechem (Nablus) on April 1, 1916, which Whiting published as a limited edition album in Sweden[7] in 1917 and as an article in *National Geographic* in January 1920,[8]

---

4 Lind, "Jerusalem Before Zionism and the American (Swedish) Colony," 209.

5 John D. Whiting, *Diaries*, John D. Whiting Papers, Manuscript Division, Library of Congress, Washington D.C., Box 1, 1905–1918; Box 2, 1934–1935; Box 3, 1938–1941. See also: *Finding Aid to John D. Whiting Papers*: https://hdl.loc.gov/loc.mss/eadmss.ms008123.

6 Ibid., Box 1, 1905–1918.

7 John D. Whiting and Lewis Larsson, *Samaritanernas päskfest I ord och bild* (*Passover Celebrations of the Samaritans in Words and Pictures*), Limited edition, no. 159 of 300, intro. Sven Anders Hedin and Selma Lagerlöf (Stockholm: Albert Bonniers Forlag, 1917); Rare Books Collection, American Colony Archive, Jerusalem.

8 See Yazan Kopty's discussion of John D. Whiting's article, "The Last Israelitish [Israelite] Blood Sacrifice" in this volume.

a   b   c   d

FIGURE 7.5 Typical *Diary in Photos* album pages (from left to right)
a. Tortoise laying eggs / Jewish Protest to White Paper, 1939.
b. Jewish Protest to White Paper, 1939.
c. Iris Trip to Syria. Kasr el Banat / Bedouin woman and boy digging Kimme, 1939.
d. Iris Trip to Syria, Camel calf just born, 1939.
Diary in Photos, Volume V, 1939. Visual Materials from the Papers of John D. Whiting
PRINTS AND PHOTOGRAPHS DIVISION, LIBRARY OF CONGRESS, WASHINGTON, D.C.

both with Hol Lars (Lewis) Larsson's photographic rendering of the event.[9] In the ethnographic articles Whiting published in *National Geographic* from 1913 to 1940, he links description and interpretation of the present cultures and the biblical ethos. One article, 'Bedouins in the Bible Lands',[10] documents a disappearing culture that was replete with charm and depth. Most of his articles are illustrated with the work of the ACPD photographers taken during well planned photographic expeditions.

Between 1934 and 1939, his written diaries follow his visual diaries closely and serve to complement them. While adding the captions to the photographs in the diaries, Whiting often refers to the written diaries.

Whiting served two terms as Deputy Consul of the United States of America from 1908 to 1915, specialising in agriculture and geography. During this period, he published numerous consular reports on issues of commerce and labour,

---

9   John D. Whiting, "The Last Israelitish [Israelite] Blood Sacrifice: How the Vanishing Samaritans Celebrate the Passover on Sacred Mount Gerizim," *National Geographic Magazine* XXXVII (January 1920): 1–46, https://archive.org/details/lastisraelitishboowhit/page/42/mode/2up.
10   John D. Whiting, "Bedouin Life in Bible Lands. The Nomads of the 'House of Hair' Offer Unstinted Hospitality to an American," *National Geographic Magazine*, LXXI (January 1937): 58–83.

1603.

FIGURE 7.6   To Syria with the Bowens, 10th–20th December. Lebanon
reforesters at work, 1937. From John D. Whiting's *Diary in Photos*,
Volume II, 1936–1937. Photograph album. Visual Materials from
the Papers of John D. Whiting
PRINTS & PHOTOGRAPHS DIVISION, LIBRARY OF CONGRESS,
WASHINGTON, D.C.

archaeology and, presciently, animal welfare.[11] His 19th July, 1909 report is
titled 'Railroads in Far East, Description of the Damascus Mecca Line'.[12] During
the First World War, he joined the Red Crescent emergency medical service.
Along with other Colony members, he initiated several projects for the welfare
of Jerusalem residents, including a day centre for women and children, a soup
kitchen and military hospitals in Jerusalem. In 1918,[13] he began working for
the British Secret Intelligence Service, updating geopolitical maps and serving

---

11   John D. Whiting. *Consular and Trade Reports*, 1909–1915. John D. Whiting Papers,
     Manuscript Division, Library of Congress, Washington D.C., Box 16, 1909–1915.
12   Ibid.
13   See Karène Sanchez Summerer Norig Neveu chapter in this volume related to Jaussen's
     information-gathering for the French during the same period.

FIGURE 7.7   Staff of the American Consulate, Jerusalem, 1910–1914. With William Coffin,
Consul General of United States of America, John D. Whiting (second from
left, leaning against the wall), Deputy Consul, the *qawās* (consular guards) and
others. Photographer unknown. From *Early Photographs of the American Colony,
1870–1925*, Photograph album.
AMERICAN COLONY ARCHIVE JERUSALEM

as an interpreter in Arabic.[14] At the same time, Whiting collaborated with
architect Charles Robert Ashbee (1862–1942), the civic advisor of the City of
Jerusalem,[15] and the Pro-Jerusalem Council, a multicultural decision-making
body, founded by Sir Ronald Storrs to prepare restoration plans for Jerusalem
and its surrounding neighbourhoods. Whiting and the other American Colony
members developed close relationships with the British Mandate's government's leaders who would often dine and stay the American Colony.

14   John D. Whiting, handwritten note describing his work for the British Secret Intelligence
       Service in 1918. American Colony Archive, Jerusalem. The note compares John D. Whiting's
       role in the map division of the British Secret Intelligence Service to that of Aaron
       Aaronsohn (1876–1919), who did similar work in northern Palestine. The note appears to
       be a personal statement of John D. Whiting, but it is not signed.

15   *Jerusalem, 1920–1922, Being the Records of the Pro-Jerusalem Council During the First Two
       Years of the Civil Administration*, by Ashbee, C.R. (Charles Robert Ashbee, 1863–1942),
       https://archive.org/details/jerusalem192019200ashbuoft.

The scope of the corpus precludes extensive analysis within the confined context of a chapter, but there are several interlinking themes that help to frame it. First, it gives us some insights into the cultural complexity of identity in the British Mandate period to which Whiting's albums correspond. Second, the albums reveal how Whiting's position facilitated international exchanges. Third, it shows how Whiting's genre of photographic diaries affects our reading of them.

1   Identity and the Complexity of Belonging

Whiting was part of the American Colony Photo Department from its founding in 1896 until its dispersal in 1934. Yet, these diaries express his own personal viewpoint, not that of the collective. His statement is as an individual photographer and is simultaneously investigative, documentary, and particular. It reflects his own life, the reality of the Middle East, its permanent and temporary residents, the political transformations of his time and the region's natural and cultural landscapes.

Whiting was born in Jerusalem in 1882, one year after his parents John and Mary Whiting and his sister Ruth immigrated to Palestine from Chicago, along with the founders of the American Colony community, Horatio Gates Spafford and Anna T. Spafford. The original community of seventeen Americans and two British aspired to witness a spiritual awakening and hoped to witness the lost glory of Jerusalem restored. They settled on a high hill inside the Muslim Quarter of Jerusalem's Old City, between Herod's Gate and Damascus Gate. Members lived an ascetic lifestyle and purified themselves in anticipation of the messianic event by doing good works for others.

In 1896, when Whiting was fourteen, the American Colony expanded and absorbed a new group of some 120 men, women, and children, seventy-seven of whom were Swedes with a similar messianic, millenarian identity. Unexpectedly, several of the younger generation expanded the boundaries of the sect from religious messianism to a secular ethic that sanctified the everyday acts, and became active participants in Jerusalem's commercial and cultural life as well as in the dramatic changes that affected the region. Others awakened from their idealistic dream only to be shattered by the harsh reality of communal life in Jerusalem, which led them to abandon the collective.

Whiting came of age at a time when Jerusalem was inundated with Americans and Europeans making pilgrimage, research or leisure tours to the Holy Land. Many stayed at the American Colony guest house and participated in the commune's internal social dynamic. Leading Christian archaeological research institutions were established near the Colony in the Sheikh Jarrah neighbourhood. Some became close collaborators with the Colony and were assisted by Whiting's extensive knowledge of the Land and its archaeology.

Like other members of the Colony, Whiting spoke fluent Arabic. While still a young adult he travelled extensively in the Jerusalem environs and beyond. The people he met during these journeys became friends for life, were they locals or foreigners who temporarily resided in the Holy Land. He had great admiration for the leaders of the Bedouin tribes and their customs, making repeated visits to their tents, attending their ceremonies and exploring their culture. He visited them alone as well as with his family and community or with guests whom he escorted on guided tours. A few of his Arab friends who studied in the first integrated school in Jerusalem established by the Colony became leaders in Jerusalem and Mandate Palestine.[16]

2   To Petra and Syria with Sir Edgar Horne, 1935

A good example of the complex space which the American Colony in Jerusalem,[17] and indeed Whiting himself, occupied was in April 1935, when Whiting accompanied Sir Edgar Horne, politician and chairman of British Prudential Insurance Company, on a fourteen-day tour of the entire Middle East. Whiting orchestrated the trip for Horne and his entourage, including flights and meetings with Haj Amin Husseini (1897–1974), the Grand Mufti of Jerusalem. The journey began in Cairo and passed through Jerusalem. The group continued to the newly built (1932) water-activated power station at Naharayīm, which was partially sponsored by the Prudential Company on land purchased from Amīr ʿAbdallāh. There, the group met with Zionist engineer Pinchas Rutenberg, who had envisioned the project and brought it to completion. From Naharayīm, the delegation went on to visit Tiberias and Beirut.[18]

---

16   Lars E. Lind, "Jerusalem Before Zionism and the 'American' (Swedish) Colony," Lars E. Lind Papers (1979), Manuscript Division, Library of Congress, Washington D.C., Box 2, 244.

17   'American Colony in Jerusalem' relates to the historical name of the community active in Jerusalem between 1881 and 1948. The American Colony Hotel, established early in the 1950s is owned today by descendants of the historical community.

18   John D. Whiting, *Diary in Photos* Vol. I, part 2, 1935. "To Petra with Sir Edgar Horne; Edgar Horne in Syria; Visual materials from the papers of John D. Whiting, Prints and Photographs Division, Library of Congress, Washington, D.C., https://www.loc.gov/resource/ppmsca.17161/?sp=2&st=gallery (Images 51–63 in the full-page digital album version).

The photographed series of the journey with Horne consists of 26 photographic prints and begins on a page that displays the final image from Whiting's previous tour, a flock of storks against a cloudy sky. Under this photograph, Whiting placed a snapshot taken from the interior of Sir Edgar Horne's room in the Shepherd Hotel in Cairo. The lens looked out onto the hotel garden surrounded by trees, fountains, gazebos and seating areas. In contrast to the schema of thematic albums, Whiting juxtaposes subtle visual transitions when shifting narratives, with the landscape often becoming the binding element between the stories. The series ends with Sir Edgar in silhouette in Nāqūra, leaning on a rock, gazing towards the Mediterranean, holding a branch in one hand and a cup of tea in the other. Whiting's photographs rarely include close-ups. In the thumbnail compilation of photographs, the landscape is a dominant feature. For the most part of this series, the individual subject, sometimes unidentifiable, is seen in miniature against an open landscape, whether natural, archaeological or urban. Whiting amalgamates his subjects within the landscapes of the Levant as a contextual element. This he applies to photographs of Sir Edgar and his entourage as well as to photographs of a Domari girl and her brother as she dances before guests on the road to Jerash.

On 8th April, Whiting photographed Horne and a member of the entourage, Mr Lever, at the airport with an Imperial Airways airplane seen at background. They took off and flew over the Gulf of Suez, while Whiting photographed from the air the mountainous landscape of the Gulf, the city of Suez (Suwās) and Fort Tawfīq port. In his diary on that day, Whiting wrote:

> We reached Abuassi airport, where a three-engine Imperial Airways airplane awaiting us. Took seats after being weighted etc. Started at 8.11 and left around 8.13. [...] At 8:30 flying at 4500 ft. 10:15 bumpy 5000 ft. up. 10:15 Gulf of Arabia sight. [...] 10.55 over Petra Valley, 6500 ft. up. [...] 11:40 landed on Fjord (?). [The flight] was bumpy all the time after first recorded. Sir Edgar [Horne] slept and read a lot, said he was scared [...] Reached Cook camp by 3:30 p.m. Beer and tea and then took Mr. Lever to the Crusader castle and down Wad [valley] Syngh [near Petra].[...] Captain Loraine piloted plane helped by Mr. Coster.[19]

On 13th April, Horne picked up Whiting at the American Colony store at Jaffa Gate. They visited Bethesda pool in the Muslim Quarter of the Old City of

---

19   John D. Whiting, *Diaries*, John D. Whiting Papers, Manuscript Division, Library of Congress, Washington D.C., Box 2, 1934–1935.

a   c

b   d

FIGURE 7.8 Trip to Petra and Syria with Sir Edgar Horne and Mr Lever, 1935
          Note: The four photograph compilations illustrating the highlighted series is a
          partial selection from the complete album series. Please follow the footnotes links
          to see the full album pages series.
          a. Sir Edgar and Mr Lever. Tomb of the Urn, Petra, 1935.
          b. Sir Edgar at El Khazna, Petra, 1935.
          c. Mr Lever on top of the Crusader Castle, Petra, 1935.
          d. Sir Edgar [Horne] in the siq, Petra, 1935.
          From John D. Whiting, *Diary in Photos*, Volume I, Part II, 1935. Photograph album.
          Visual Materials from the Papers of John D. Whiting
          PRINTS AND PHOTOGRAPHS DIVISION, LIBRARY OF CONGRESS,
          WASHINGTON, D.C.

Jerusalem and the Temple Mount area. On the morning of April 17th, Whiting with Horne met with the Grand Mufti for a long interview. Earlier that week, Whiting accompanied Mr Lever and Mr Muelford to a meeting with the Grand Mufti, who asked the Prudential officials for a loan of 100,000 pounds for the purchase of land and the construction of a building in Jaffa.[20] In the afternoon, Whiting escorted Horne to Bethlehem and Solomon's Pools. They ended their day over tea at the King David Hotel, a central meeting point for the British Mandate officials. On 19th April, Horne and Whiting travelled through Transjordan to Syria. They visited the Temple of Artemis in Jerash and the Nahārayīm power station, where Rutenberg explained the workings of the station to Sir Edgar. In his diary on that day, Whiting wrote:

> First thing in the morning found Mr. Joshua Gordon in Hotel trying to telephone us. [...] Mr. Asherwood and Mr. Lever saw him almost at once and made arrangements for visits to Zionist activities [...]. I had a long time alone with Mr. Joshua [Yehoshua] Gordon [Zionist, coordinator between Zionists and British authorities] [...] and was able to tell him about Col. Layton and then brought up questions if I would be wanted in the party. He wanted me to go along. I drove to the German settlements and then to Rutenberg [Nahārayīm power station]. Found both brothers and wife of [Avraham]. After lunch together looked over words and departed. It seems Prudential lent Rutenberg lot of money but it was quickly repaid to Mr. Lever's consternation. We drove through Tiberias on to Nazareth. [...][21]

The interior shot of the Nahārayīm power station resembles a dramatic scene from Fritz Lang's 1927 futuristic film 'Metropolis', with engineer Pinchas Rutenberg explaining the power station workings to Sir Edgar Horne. Rutenberg's brother Avraham stands beside them with his wife, looking towards the camera, while Pinchas Rutenberg and Horne focus on the explanations. The exterior shot, taken against the massive concrete dam in Nahārayīm, shows the British gentlemen involved in a dialogue at the front, Rutenberg and his brother talking to each other on the right side, while Whiting, who had handed the camera to someone else, is seen standing behind them all, in contemplation, his hands behind his back. These two images manifest the evolving

---

20 A perusal of his 1935 diaries reveals that Whiting visits the Mufti several times both with guests and in private. He also calls the Mufti to discuss the loan request with him.

21 John D. Whiting, *Diaries*, John D. Whiting Papers, Manuscript Division, Library of Congress, Washington D.C., Box 2, 1934–1935.

tensions between the British powers and the Zionists as well as between the Zionists and the American Colony. The diminished scale of the human figure against the dominance of the context, a distinct feature of Whiting photography, is evident here too.

Photographs of the journey show the entourage visiting sites and historical monuments. At times, Bedouins or Domaris penetrate the photograph's frame. The group is seen sitting together in Jerash, conducting a lively intimate conversation against the monumental archaeological landscape. At other times, Horne appears alone against a vast natural backdrop, as in Nāqūra, northern Palestine. Even when Whiting photographs the group in Jerusalem against the Prudential offices in the background, his subjects seem distant and disconnected. This is a group of wealthy tourists with a clear economic interest, which lays an anchor in Palestine during Mandate rule. In the local consciousness, Whiting is considered a well-informed tour guide, and thus his services are procured to escort the respected delegation. He escorts them on their visits to the Mufti and apparently also serves as their translator.

Whiting hesitated visiting the Zionist project. The tension between him and Rutenberg is an indirect manifestation of the rising strains between British

FIGURE 7.9 AND FIGURE 7.10 Trip to Petra and Syria with Sir Edgar Horne and Mr Lever, 1935. Left: Mr Rutenberg (younger) explains to Sir Edgar the workings, 1935.
Trip to Petra and Syria with Sir Edgar Horne and Mr Lever, 1935. Right: The party outside the electrical station, 1935. From John D. Whiting, *Diary in Photos*, Volume I, Part II, 1935. Photograph album. Visual Materials from the Papers of John D. Whiting
PRINTS AND PHOTOGRAPHS DIVISION, LIBRARY OF CONGRESS, WASHINGTON, D.C.

authorities, Palestinians and Zionists.[22] Whiting was known for his work with
the British Secret Intelligence Service and was a close ally of Palestinians
and the Mandate officials, and thus, Rutenberg might have considered him as
persona non grata. Yehoshua Gordon, the coordinator between the Zionists
and the British Mandate authorities, convinced Whiting to join the tour despite
his hesitations.

In 1935, Whiting's political position was located at the juncture between the
Palestinians, represented by his close ties with the Mufti Ḥājj Amīn al- Ḥusaynī,
and the British authorities. The identity of the American Colony as a neutral
entity throughout the Ottoman rule and in the early twentieth century enabled
its members to develop close ties with Palestinians, who frequented the Colony
premises and institutions and developed friendly relationships with its members. The violent struggles however, between Palestinians and Zionist changed
the political map and skewed the location of the American Colony's identity in
relationship to British. Aside from the encounter at Nahārayīm and Whiting's
long conversation with Yehoshua Gordon, this series documents the visit of
the Prudential president and delegation as a potential business-oriented tour.

Mary Roberts and Jocelyn Hackforth-Jones[23] attempt to contrast the term
'stereotypical stasis' with cultural processes when iconographic conventions
cross borders between East and West. They claim that multiple cultural identities have mutual influence, and their implications must be studied. The
Orientalist practice modifies its central position in defining the exotic 'other' to
transpositions of ideas from one disciplinary field to another.[24] These researchers cite Fred Bohar, who examines the term 'period value'. This term asserts
that photographic content is accessible to the viewer long after it is created,
in a manner different than the accessibility of conventional academic textual
knowledge. We must study, claim Robert and Hackforth-Jones, what is defined
as 'the connected world of empires' to discover intercultural connections that
were ignored when the focus is concentrated solely on the parameters of imperialist European cultures.[25]

The movement between Orientalist tropes and the connected histories
that 'period value' yields, shows the complexities of relating to indigenous
cultures that cannot be ignored. Entirely compressing such complex bodies
of work into Orientalist paradigms forces the reader to adopt this viewpoint

---

22   Ibid.
23   Jocelyn Hackforth-Jones and Mary Roberts, "Introduction: Visualizing Culture across
        the Edges of Empires," in *Edges of Empire: Orientalism and Visual Culture*, eds. Jocelyn
        Hackforth-Jones and Mary Robert (Oxford: Blackwell Publishing, 2005), 2.
24   Ibid., 15.
25   Ibid., 17.

as the dominant history while ignoring the 'period value' encoded in the photographs. Multi-faceted narratives are the only accounts capable of contradicting erroneous stereotypes and collective interpretations. This act of 'writing and interpretation becomes a true mission, capable of recharging the collective memory with components that were deleted from it because they were read incorrectly'.[26]

By contrast, should academic research choose to examine photographs from an aesthetic or exotic viewpoint alone, the photographs lose parts of their historical narrative. At its heart, they encode the identities of individuals and groups and the complex relationships among these identities. Micklewright asserts that in the past thirty years, the term 'Orientalist' has been used broadly, without critical reflection. The individuals who collect, preserve, display and print such collections must adopt the interpretive potential contained in this fluid diversity of identities, instead of compressing it into the grey category of Orientalism.[27]

3   Wedding of Emir Talal (Amīr Ṭalāl), 1934

Volume I of the *Diary in Photos* includes six photographs from the grandiose wedding of Amīr Ṭalāl in Amman.[28] A complementary set of fifteen photographs of the wedding ceremony taken by Whiting on the same day constitutes part of Whiting's thematic photographic series titled 'Bedouins in Jordan and Other Locations'. Here, Whiting focuses on the Bedouins depicted during the wedding festivity customs.[29]

> Sorenson, David [Whiting], Jock [Vester], and myself rode in the car to Amman. We arrived in the afternoon and discovered that the wedding procession had already begun. This was the wedding of Emir Talal, the son of Emir Abdullah. The procession began at the Parliament building

---

26   Woodward, "Creating Memory and History," 27.

27   Nancy Micklewright, "Orientalism and Photography," in *The Poetics and Politics of Place: Ottoman Istanbul and British Orientalism*, eds. Zeynep Inankur, Reina Lewis, and Mary Roberts (Seattle, WA: University of Washington Press, 2011), 106.

28   John D. Whiting, *Diary in Photos*, Vol. I, 1934–1935, "Wedding of Emir Talal," 26–27 Nov. 1945. Visual materials from the papers of John D. Whiting. Library of Congress, Washington, D.C., https://www.loc.gov/resource/ppmsca.17161/?sp=1&st=gallery (Pages 35–38 in the full-page digital album version).

29   John D. Whiting, *Bedouins in Jordan and Other Locations*, 1934–1935, https://www.loc.gov/pictures/item/2007682814/ (Pages 29–37 in the full-page digital album version).

and continued to the palace. Bedouins on horses, with swords. The *mah-mal* [bridal tent] from Damascus was mounted on a large camel and escorted by two Circassian [guards], each bearing an Arab flag. Several Bedouins wore armour on their backs. Sorenson and I ran after the group to the palace and took good photographs.[30]

One of these photographs (Fig. 7.11), shows Amīr 'Abdallāh standing on the palace entrance steps, with Bedouin and Circassian representatives on his left and a group of British Mandate representatives in uniforms on his right, all gazing at the camera. The current group of photographs includes a scene of the procession accompanying the bride who rides in the traditional *mahmal* tent mounted on a camel. They lead the bride towards the palace, her escorts alongside. Next, we see a parade of Bedouin knights on horseback, wearing plated armour, with round metal shields hung across their backs and swords in hand. Another photograph shows preparation of the feast for the 'tribes' outside the palace. The high commissioner is hosted at the king's table at noon and Palestinian dignitaries attend the evening reception. A close-up of the king's noble horse is excluded by Whiting when editing the *Diary in Photos*, but appears as part of the same event in the thematic album *Bedouins in Jordan and Other Locations*.[31]

The relationship between Whiting and King 'Abdallāh of Transjordan is evident in ACPD photographs beginning in 1921, when Whiting met Abdullah and other dignitaries at a ceremony held at Augusta Victoria, then the British Civil Administration headquarters. At the ceremony, Abdullah accepted the offer of Winston Churchill, Herbert Samuel, and T.E. Lawrence to rule Eastern Transjordan under British Mandate authority. This event was photographed in detail by the ACPD photographers as depicted in the *World War I and the British Mandate in Palestine, 1917–1926*, photograph album. A second encounter between Mandate leaders and Abdullah took place in April of that year near Amman, and was documented by Colony photographer Lewis (Hol Lars) Larsson. Whiting participated in the event and hobnobbed with Emir 'Abdallāh, T.E. Lawrence, and other Mandate dignitaries.[32]

---

30   John D. Whiting, *Diaries*, John D. Whiting Papers, Manuscript Division, Library of Congress, Washington D.C., Box 2, 1934–1935.

31   John D. Whiting, *Bedouins in Jordan and Other Locations, 1934–1935*. Photograph Album. Visual Materials from the Papers of John. D. Whiting, Prints and Photographs Division, Library of Congress, Washington, D.C.

32   Hol Lars (Lewis) Larsson, ACPD photographers, *Meetings of British, Arab, and Bedouin Officials in Amman, Jordan, April 1921*, photograph album, https://www.loc.gov/item/2007675257/.

a

c

b

d

FIGURE 7.11   Wedding of Emir Talal (Amīr Ṭalāl), Amman, November 26 & 27, 1934.
a. Emir Abdullah (with Shaykh Mutgal el Fiez) watching the procession
passing palace, 1934.
b. Bedouin Warriors in medieval armour, 1934.
c. Returning from the Palace. 'The *mahmal*', 1934.
d. Emir Abdulla's Horse, 1934.
From John D. Whiting, *Diary in Photos*, Volume I, 1934. Photograph album.
From John D. Whiting, Bedouins in Jordan and Other Locations, 1934–1935.
Photograph album. Visual Materials of the Papers of John D. Whiting
PRINTS AND PHOTOGRAPHS DIVISION, LIBRARY OF CONGRESS,
WASHINGTON, D.C.

FIGURE 7.12   Bedouin and Circassian Leaders, Amman, April 17, 1921. With T.E. Lawrence (third from right in grey suit and hat) and John D. Whiting (sixth from right), posing with an airplane and pilot at Amman Jordan. From Meetings of British, Arab and Bedouin officials, Amman, Jordan, 1921. Photograph album. Hol Lars (Lewis) Larsson, ACPD. Visual Materials from the Papers of John D. Whiting
PRINTS & PHOTOGRAPHS DIVISION, LIBRARY OF CONGRESS, WASHINGTON, D.C.

4   Bedu Camp at Deir El-Belah (Dayr Al-Balaḥ), 1934

Given Whiting's tenure as Deputy Consul and his position in British Mandate society, one of the series in the 1934 volume of the photographic diaries that has particular resonance represents an event that took place in September when Whiting escorted Ely E. Palmer (1887–1977), the newly appointed Consul General of the United States of America in Jerusalem and his wife on a three-day trip to southern Palestine, at the invitation of ʿĀrif al-ʿĀrif. They were joined by Whiting's wife Grace, their son Wilson, Anna Grace Vester Lind (daughter of Bertha Vester, Grace's sister) as well as Mrs. Rolston and Whiting's dog Barak. Whiting and his party stayed at ʿĀrif al-ʿĀrif's Bedouin camp and watched camel and horseraces in Gaza. ʿĀrif al-ʿĀrif prepared a Bedouin tent for the men and a new British tent for the women. He sent a cook and a waiter to provide his guests with the city-style dishes to which they were accustomed. Riding on camels and horses, they travelled back and forth from Gaza to the camp in Dayr al-Balah.[33]

ʿĀrif al-ʿĀrif (1892–1973) was a Palestinian journalist, politician, writer, and historian who studied in Istanbul and worked as a journalist and translator for the Foreign Office. During the First World War, he served as an officer of the Ottoman Empire, was captured on the Caucasus front, and sent to a prison camp in Siberia. While in prison, he edited a handwritten newspaper and translated the writings of Ernst Heinrich Haeckel (1834–1919; German zoologist, naturalist, philosopher, physician, and artist) into Turkish. After the Russian Revolution, ʿĀrif al-ʿĀrif returned to Palestine, where he became a political activist and editor of the Syrian newspaper *Sūriyya al-Janūbiyya*, the first Arabic nationalist newspaper published in Jerusalem.[34]

ʿĀrif al-ʿĀrif took part in the Nabi Musa festival of 1920, which led to mass riots during which he was arrested. After he was released, he fled to Syria with Ḥājj Amīn al-Ḥusaynī (1895–1974), the Grand Mufti of Jerusalem. Later he advised the Palestinians against violence, and encouraged them to adopt 'the quiet, courage and discipline of their opponents'.[35] In Damascus, he became Consul of the Syrian Congress, founded the Palestinian Arab Society and became its general secretary. After the French invaded Syria in 1920, he fled to Transjordan, returned to Jerusalem, and became district officer of Beersheba and later of Gaza. After 1948, he became Ramallah's district officer and director of the Palestine Archaeological Museum, now the Rockefeller Museum.

The photographic series of this journey depicts the small group of guests and hosts in a quiet, relaxed atmosphere at the Gaza seashore.[36] Whiting's selective compilation of eight photographs depicts the narrative elements carefully. He first presents the party watching the Gaza races, without showing us the races, and on the same page exposes the setting of the camp, with a tree and camels kneeling at front. The locals are presented next, with one of

33 John D. Whiting, *Diaries in Photos* Vol. I, 1934–1935, "Bedu [Bedouin] Camp at Deir el-Belah [Dier al-Balah,]" (29 Sept.–1 Oct. 1934), in *Visual Materials from the Papers of John D. Whiting*, 29–32, Prints and Photographs Division, Library of Congress, Washington, D.C. https://www.loc.gov/resource/ppmsca.17161/?st=gallery (follow images 25–28 in the full-page digital version).

34 Bernard Wasserstein, "'Clipping the Claws of Colonisers': Arab Officials in the Government of Palestine, 1917–1948," *Middle Eastern Studies* 13, no. 2 (1977): 171–194.

35 Ibid.

36 John D. Whiting, *Diaries in Photos*, Vol. I, 1934–1935, "Bedu [Bedouin] Camp at Deir el-Belah [Dier al-Balah.]" (29 Sept.–1 Oct. 1935 https://www.loc.gov/item/2007675295/ (follow images 25–28 in the full-page digital version).

a

c

b

d

FIGURE 7.13   Bedu Camp at Dayr al-Balaḥ. Invitation of ʿĀrif Bay, Sept. 29–Oct.1, 1934
a. Watching the Gaza races.
b. The camp near Deir el Belah, 1934.
c. Lunch in Bedouin tent. Grace [Whiting], Mr. Palmer, Mrs. Palmer, ʿĀrif Bay
and the Sheikh
d. The party on the sands
From John D. Whiting, *Diary in Photos*, Volume I, 1934. Photograph album.
Visual Materials from the Papers of John D. Whiting
PRINTS AND PHOTOGRAPHS DIVISION, LIBRARY OF CONGRESS,
WASHINGTON, D.C.

the hosts, and a 'Gypsy' (Domari[37]) belly dancer entertains the guests, while a musician plays for her. Interior tents scenes follow with the amusing image of Consul Palmer on his knees shaving in front of a hand mirror and, in another tent, the party sitting together after lunch enjoying conversation with ʿĀrif al-ʿĀrif. The next image takes us outside again to show ʿĀrif al-ʿĀrif's 'ladies' tent, and the series concludes in a magnificent scene of Bedouin hosts with guests in swimming costumes, posing for Whiting's camera behind a row of kneeling camels, against the sea of Gaza.

Whiting's lens is as light as his pen. In his scenes, not one personality appears more important than any other. ʿĀrif al-ʿĀrif plays the gracious host. He enables the guests to set aside their usual formal diplomatic manners and indulge in each other's company, enjoying the atmosphere, sea, sand dunes, races, music and local dancing. This scene is a climactic encounter between ʿĀrif al-ʿĀrif, Ely E. Palmer, John D. Whiting and his family, Bedouins, and the sheikh of Dayr al-Balah. Whiting knew each of the personalities, and he made the connections between Palmer and his wife and ʿĀrif al-ʿĀrif, thus offering an informal setting for diplomatic relationships.

The setting seems to enable the guests to free themselves from the social conventions that characterised European and American diplomacy. Likely, the encounter supported the development of emotive and intellectual sharing between the guests and their hosts, under Whiting's and ʿĀrif al-ʿĀrif orchestration. Based on this series and other series in the *Diary in Photos* corpus, Whiting and ʿĀrif al-ʿĀrif apparently had a close friendship nourished by their common interests.

Palmer arrived in Palestine on 11th March, 1934, on board the steamer *Excalibur*. The Tel Aviv municipality held a formal reception in his honour at Beit Ha'am (a cultural meeting place). Before commencing the voyage, Palmer had met with representatives of the Jewish community at the Pennsylvania Hotel in New York. Community leaders expressed the hope that he would enjoy his new position and contribute to transforming Palestine into a joyful, fruitful (Zionist) land. On his part, Ely Palmer declared diplomatically that he took a broad view of his appointment in Jerusalem and that he was interested not only in 'friends', but also in foreigners. In contrast, it seems that Whiting

---

37   The Doms are a people related to the Romani of Europe. Sometimes they are referred to as 'Gypsies' or 'Middle Eastern Gypsies' in English, and *'Nawar'* in Arabic. In Palestine, they specialised in two particular trades, metalwork and entertainment. See Yaron Matras, "Two Domari Legends About the Origins of the Doms," *Romani Studies*, 5th series (10, 2000): 53–79.

organised the meeting in Dayr el-Belah in order to promote diplomatic relations between Palmer and ʿArif al-ʿArif.

5   To Palmyra with Cromwell Party, 15th–19th April, 1938

Perhaps one of the more curious themes of Whiting's visual diaries is the series of 24 photographs documenting the visit of tobacco heiress Doris Duke Cromwell (1912–1993) in Damascus and Palmyra. After her wedding in 1935 to James Cromwell, the couple began a well-planned honeymoon trip around the world. During the trip, Doris gained an appreciation of the rich Islamic artistic and architectural tradition and began to collect Persian and Middle Eastern and Islamic art for her home in Florida. While the couple were in Hawaii, Doris decided to use these artifacts to decorate her planned mansion in Honolulu instead. Arthur Upham Pope (1881–1969), was an American expert on Persian art and culture and a professor of philosophy and aesthetics who aided the Cromwells in organising the excursion. In March 1938, Doris travelled to Iran and the Middle East for six weeks to purchase Islamic art works for her home in Hawaii, which she named *Shangri La*. The journey began in Alexandria and the Cromwells visited also Cairo, Luxor, Lydda (Lod), Damascus, Palmyra, Aleppo, Baalbek, Haran, Baghdad, Tehran, Mashad, Isfahan and Istanbul.[38] Upham Pope booked the Cromwells and their party a private KLM plane for the journey and introduced them to merchants and consultants who appraised their selected items. The Cromwell visited Damascus twice, once in March and second in April and in both events Whiting was present. His written diaries recall both meetings but his visual diaries recall only the April Meeting with the Cromwells in Damascus and Palmyra.

The first meeting with the Cromwells and their party took place in Damascus between 15th and 17th March, 1938 and the second between April 14 and 19 1938. Whiting is called by Georges Asfār of the prominent Damascus-based antiquities firm of Asfār & Sārkīs (Georges 'Geo' Asfār and Jean Sārkīs) with whom Vester & Co., the American Colony Store in Jerusalem, had commercial relations, to bring over a rare rug for Cromwells and to consult Asfār and Sārkīs in managing the purchase process. The Cromwells arrived in Damascus on 16th March and Whiting guided them on their first tour of the area. The Cromwell party continued to visit bazaars and markets and Whiting writes that 'it was

38   John D. Whiting, *Diary in Photos*, Vol. III, 1938. To Palmyra with Cromwell party, April 15–19, 1938.Visual materials from the papers of John D. Whiting Library of Congress, Washington D.C., https://www.loc.gov/resource/ppmsca.17413/?sp=2&st=gallery (Follow full-page digital album version, image 42–52).

hard to keep track of them'. On 17th March, Whiting meets the Cromwells and joins them with Asfār and Sārkīs in search for additional artifacts.[39]

A month later, On 15th April, 1938, 4:30 a.m. Whiting left the American Colony for Damascus to continue to advise the Cromwells on their purchases of artifacts and as their interpreter of the events in Palmyra. On his way to Damascus, he took a few photos which he titled 'Pipe-line near Afūla [North East Palestine] on fire at dawn' and displayed these as the opening images of this series, to memorialise events in Palestine in contrast to Damascus. With Whiting as consultant, Doris purchased dozens of items worth hundreds of thousands of dollars.[40] Following their visit in Damascus, the Cromwells travelled to Palmyra on their private KLM plane, escorted by Whiting. At Palmyra, they were received by Asfar and Sarkis as well as local dignitaries including Emir Fawas, leaders of Bedouin and Domari tribes and of the French regime and were hosted by the mayor of Palmyra for lunch. They then attended an impressive, staged performance of camel, horse, and donkey races, and a 'Gypsy' (Domari) wedding. Residents of Palmyra, local Bedouins, and French officers of the Desert Patrol were also present and captured in Whiting's camera.

---

39   John D. Whiting, *Diaries*, John D. Whiting Papers, Manuscript Division, Library of Congress, Washington D.C., Box 3, 1938–1941. Whiting's 1938 diary consists of detailed descriptions of the Cromwells artifacts purchase process. Whiting writes in his diary: March 17 Thursday – Damascus; Cromwell. Ran out to see the reed flute maker and then to glass works and settled acts and chose few pieces and designed some Jordan water bottles in Ammonite shape. Met Geo [Asfar] and party [the Cromwells] at Asfar store at 10. We took them out in search of upholstering Persian shawl designs. It early became evident that they wanted to go alone. We left them and after a time they (Mr. and Mrs. Cromwell and Ruth) returned to Asfar and asked to see pearl inlaid furniture. We took them to the old bazaars and found what they were trying to buy from them. He had asked them fabulous prices. We had asked them to dinner but they refused, but now he turned to Geo and said they would like to have dinner. We at once sent Sammy to start the dinner. It was a hectic afternoon but finally we gained their confidence. Toward evening I bought two bureaus for them for 5.30 pounds and they were delighted. They bought a little statue, door knockers, ivory cat etc. We had a sumptuous dinner lasting from 10 to about 12 midnight sitting on ground around tray.

40   One of Duke's stunning purchases in 1938 was a traditional Damascus painted wood-paneled room that she later modified for one of the rooms in Shangri La. This is the famous traditional 1830 Damascus wood-paneled room. https://www.hisour.com/damascus-room-shangri-la-museum-of-islamic-art-culture-design-49582/. Duke maintained commercial relations with Asfar and Sarkis in the years following her 1938 visit. Doris Duke Papers, Doris Duke Charitable Foundation Historical Archives, David M. Rubenstein Rare Book & Manuscript Library, Duke University.

a

c

b

d

FIGURE 7.14   To Palmyra with Cromwell Party, April 15–19, 1938
a. Reception party at Palmyra aerodrome, 1938.
b. Desert Patrol riding standing atop camels, 1938.
c. The camel chariot race driven by black riders in gazell[e]-skin suits, 1938.
d. A Bedouin wedding staged by Gypsies. Accompanying the bride on the
mahmal, 1938.
From John D. Whiting, *Diary in Photos*, Volume III, 1938. Photograph album.
Visual Materials from the Papers of John D. Whiting
PRINTS AND PHOTOGRAPHS DIVISION LIBRARY OF CONGRESS,
WASHINGTON, D.C.

At 11:30 a.m. we were in the air. We flew over Damascus and the mosque, and then through the desert to Palmyra. [...] The gardens of Damascus a mosaic, saw the lake for the first time, then the endless, rolling desert. [... We flew] parallel to it, and then to south of Tombs valley. Circled Arab castle and landed at 12:30. Emir Fawaz met us with three negro slaves dressed in purple. We drove to the mayor's home for lunch [...] After lunch – donkey, camel and chariot races. The women could not leave the tents and were sent to the hotel. After supper of roast lamb in open, went to Captain's attractive home, Gypsy dance.[41] April 18, 1938.

The photographs of the impressive Desert Patrol who ride camels while standing, dressed in long white robes and ʿabāya, displays the power of the Palmyra Bedouin community. The photograph of women and children of the city of Palmyra who watched the special demonstration is no less impressive.[42]

A month earlier, Whiting noted in his dairy that while in Damascus to meet the Cromwells, Amīr Fahāmī called and informed him 'that there was to be a big festivity in the desert of Palmyra on the 16, 17, 18 [of April.] We are expecting the Cromwells back on the 15th [of April, writes Whiting] so that will just fit in with our desire to give them a special good time'.[43]

Throughout her lifetime, Doris Duke Cromwell collected over 4,500 items of Islamic art, and eventually established an institution for the preservation of Islamic art that is still active today.[44] Her home in Hawaii today is the Shangri La Museum for Islamic Art, Design & Culture.

Asfār and Sārkīs are not identified in the photographic series, but based on the detailed descriptions in Whiting's written diaries, and on photographs taken by Duke, we can imagine their Damascus shop and the elite group of expert dealers that marketed art and antiquities as well as their marketing strategies. Asfār's business acumen and the commercial relations between him and Whiting, on behalf of the American Colony Stores, is apparent but also unexpected. While Whiting waited for Asfār in vain in his store to join in the

41   John D. Whiting, *Diaries*, John D. Whiting Papers, Manuscript Division, Library of Congress, Washington D.C., Box 3, 1938–1941.

42   John D. Whiting, *Diary in Photos*, Vol. III, 1938, "To Palmyra with Cromwell party," 15–19 April 1938; "City women watching the races," LC-DIG-ppmsca-17414-00088 (Digital file from original on page 48, no. 1769). https://www.loc.gov/resource/ppmsca.17414/?sp=88.

43   John D. Whiting, *Diaries*, John D. Whiting Papers, Manuscript Division, Library of Congress, Washington D.C., Box 3, 1938–1941.

44   The Shangri La Museum for Islamic Art and Design website displays Islamic Art that was purchased by Doris Duke in Damascus in 1938, as well as the invoices of purchases. https://collection.shangrilahawaii.org/collections/32672/artwork-on-view/objects.

FIGURE 7.15   City Women [and Children] Watching the Races. To Palmyra
with Cromwell Party, April 15–19, 1938. From John D. Whiting,
Diary in Photos, Volume III, 1938. Photograph album. Visual
Materials from the Papers of John D. Whiting
PRINTS AND PHOTOGRAPHS DIVISION, LIBRARY OF
CONGRESS, WASHINGTON, D.C.

sale of a rug he brought over from Jerusalem, Asfār visited Mrs. Cromwell in her
hotel room and sold her the rug for $39,000.

In his written diary, Whiting describes the fascinating negotiations during which Mrs Cromwell purchased the artifacts from Asfār and Sārkīs and
other Damascene merchants and bazaars. The purchase processes included
generous hosting in the home of Asfār's partner, Sārkīs, who prepared a feast
for lunch: baklawa with meat, stuffed chicken and pastries filled with cream
and pistachios. An evening dinner was 'sumptuous', with both hosts and their
guests sitting for hours around a tray.[45]

---

45   The *Diary in Photos* series constitutes a selection of approximately 900 photographs from
approximately 2,800 photographs taken by Whiting from 1934 and 1949. It is unfortunate
that the rejected images are not available for research online.

From the moment the group boarded the plane in Palmyra, Whiting documented the series of outdoor events.[46] In his lens, he captured city women and children watching the races, and the camel chariot race driven by a black man wearing gazelle-skin costumes. He documented the Bedouin camel riders waiting for the signal to mount their saddles and the Desert Patrol in their white uniforms, riding on camels while standing and holding the reigns. The ostentatious display continued with Palmyra 'Gypsies' staging a wedding. First, the bride was raised onto her *mahmal* tent on camelback accompanied by dancing. The bride was then 'kidnapped' in a staged raid. The 'kidnappers' were caught and the bride was returned to the tent by the Desert Patrol, to the accompaniment of drums and revelry. At the end of the demonstration, a French general awarded prizes to the participants. The particularities of such staged 'kidnapping' on the one hand plays into Orientalist tropes, but in reading the performativity of such an event, and Whiting's diary notes taken in Palmyra, as well as viewing a short home movie taken by the Cromwells[47] we begin to understand the cultural meaning that underlines the ceremony.

Whiting writes that the event was 'a mock GHAZU,' (a staged *ghazū*,)[48] a performative raid that developed from pre-Islamic tribal traditions where tribesmen raided caravans, looted, kidnapped and engaged in slave trade, except during two months of the year that were known as the 'Forbidden Months' or the 'Holy Months.' During these months, the tribes could not launch raids 'for safety of the travellers and trade and survival of the Arab desert's economy.'[49]

---

46 John D. Whiting, *Diaries*, John D. Whiting Papers, Manuscript Division, Library of Congress, Washington D.C., Box 3, 1938–1941.

47 Follow link to the rare footage titled 'Travels in the Middle East 1938' at the Doris Duke Charitable Foundation Historical Archives, David M. Rubenstein Rare Book and Manuscript Library, Duke University. (Minute 17.06 to minute 18.15). https://exhibits. library.duke.edu/exhibits/show/dorisduke/movie.

48 John D. Whiting, *Diaries*, John D. Whiting Papers, Manuscript Division, Library of Congress, Washington D.C., Box 3, 1938–1941.
    Diary notes were taken during 'a mock GHAZU,' e.g., staged launched (GHAZU) raids. The staged GHAZU continued all night with constructing the bridal tent [*mahmal,*] dancing 'Gypsies' accompanying the bride and depositing her on the tent:
    [...] During the joyful event, 'regular bedu' came rushing on their camels firing their rifles and stole the bride, loading her on a camel behind an Arab. The tent [*mahmal*] was pulled down and dust thrown in the air. The camel corps now arrived from a distance and rescued the bride and brought her back, with the raiders handcuffed.

49 Frederic P. Issace. 2003. "Indigenous People Under the Rule of Islam. Part II: The Rise and Spread of the Message (Ghazu) raid". http://members.oktiv.net/fpi/IPUROI/ 16PART2Ghazzu%20Raid.html.

FIGURE 7.16   To Palmyra with Cromwell party, April 15–19, 1938. A traditional
'mock (*ghazū*)' raid. The bride alights from the camel, 1938.
From John D. Whiting, *Diary in Photos*, Volume III, 1938.
Photograph album. Visual Materials from the Papers of
John D. Whiting
PRINTS AND PHOTOGRAPHS DIVISION, LIBRARY OF
CONGRESS, WASHINGTON, D.C.

The performativity of the Bedouins and 'Gypsies', entertainment being one
of the predominant industries of the Domari, in the presence of local and
international dignitaries shows that the ceremony was likely practised with
regularity to memorialise the importance of safe desert commerce, an event
that gestures toward a local understanding of cultural diplomacy with the
extension of an invitation to the Cromwells during their purchasing expedition.

The setting shows once again the complex space which Whiting inhabited.
Given his expert role, facilitating the purchase of artifacts for the Cromwell
collection, and his initiative to invite the Cromwells to watch the performance, shows that Whiting understood the Western market for the Orient,
in both cultural and mercantile terms. He was also in a position to facilitate

this within local social networks including the Damascene merchants, the 'regular' Bedouins of Palmyra, the 'Gypsies', the Camel Corps Bedouins and the French regime.

With this in mind, we must place Whiting as a conduit within a broader nexus of modern relations. He was involved in both international and regional networks of art and antiquities sales as well as diplomatic relations. He was also active in regional and local networks of cultural exploration, while facilitating the meeting of meaning-making between cultural consumers and producers, outlined in the introduction to this volume, within a global context. The meeting of the local, the regional and the global as exemplified by the Cromwell's visit shows a complex confluence of actors that range from Amīr Fahāmī, the urban firm of Asfār & Sārkīs, The American Colony Stores, Whiting himself included; to scholarly international networks, such as Upham Pope; and the Bedouin and Domari performers, whose indigenous knowledge and traditions highlight at least some agency with the proffering of performative cultural production; and, of course, to the Cromwells, whose consumption of culture was shaped by local and global forces. Notwithstanding the power dynamics Whiting shows us – the Bedouin and Domari performers, for instance, are not named in his diary, unlike Western and urban Middle Eastern actors – implicit in this complicated network of actors is the underscoring of local and regional urban-rural divides. This also highlights the importance of contextualising period value as outlined in the previous section.

We might also view the articles Whiting published abroad, both for National Geographic in the US, his consular reports and publications in Sweden, as well as his commercial relations with international clientele as a co-manager of Vester & Co., American Colony Stores as continuities of his specific understanding of the market for Palestine abroad and the facilitations of local relationships with the west.

The presence of the British Mandate government and increasing tensions between Zionists and Palestinians permeate the photographic diaries, and we may easily apply imperialistic paradigms to the selected examples. Yet analysis of the series shows at the same time an unusual panorama of local cultural and natural phenomenon that is permeated by extensive regional systems of mutual cultural influences. For example, Doris Duke Cromwell's search for Islamic art in the region unfolds patterns of commercial relationships that stretch beyond the Syrian merchants to regional and international networks of dealers and consultants, while local communities joined forces to secure the deal.

Doris Duke Cromwell's fascinating story of her early Islamic art purchasing tour is inspiring, but at the same time it challenges the ethics involved in transferring art objects from their places of origin to Western countries, using an extensive local and international commercial network to support the deals and acquisition of cultural artifacts. The UNESCO Convention Concerning the Protection of the World Cultural and Natural Heritage[50] aims to preserve cultural treasures in their places of origin. With the perspective of time, specifically in the light of today's destruction of cultural heritage treasures in Palmyra and Syria, Doris Duke Cromwell's shopping trip for local Islamic art and Duke's efforts to preserve Islamic culture may be judged differently.[51]

6   Conclusion: 'Meta-Archives' as Alternative Histories

By recording his trips, and through a careful editorial process, Whiting managed to create an inter-related personal, cultural, and spatial matrix in time. Studying a visual diary is very different experience to examining topical photograph albums which, according to Nancy Micklewright,[52] involves viewing a collection of photographs 'that was mediated by some kind of a selection process'. Thus, examining a compilation from the point of view of its assembly is a crucial aspect of working with a photographic series. The visual diary presents us with additional challenges. It appears to be a compilation that was arranged chronologically, yet it preserves encoded data that can only be traced through visually migrating back and forth from the detail to the entire corpus.

Modern commentators face additional moral questions. Many historical remnants were lost, including those of the members of the photography collective who left the Colony in the early 1930s and settled elsewhere in Jerusalem. The large collection of photographs and negatives belonging to Lewis (Hol Lars) Larsson, the chief photographer of the ACPD, disappeared in 1947 from his home on Jerusalem's Nablus Road after it was bombed. A collection of seven thousand negatives belonging to brothers Jamāl and Najīb Albīnā, who joined the ACPD after World War I and pursued their own work later on, also disappeared from storage in the corner of Julian's Way and Mamilla Road in

---

50   The Unesco Convention for Preservation of Cultural Heritage https://whc.unesco.org/en/conventiontext/ displays the full convention in several languages.

51   Doris Duke Papers, Doris Duke Charitable Foundation Historical Archives, David M. Rubenstein Rare Book and Manuscript Library, Duke University.

52   Nancy Micklewright, "Alternative Histories of Photography in the Ottoman Middle East," in *Photography's Orientalism: New Essays in Colonial Representation*, eds. Ali Behdad and Luke Gartlan (Los Angeles: Getty Research Institute, 2013), 75–92.

Jerusalem after they were forced to leave.[53] Significant section of photographic collections created by the renowned Palestinian photographer Khalīl Raʿad as well as the work of Ḥannā Ṣāfiyya were also lost.

Local researchers Mustafa Kabha and Guy Raz,[54] Rona Sela,[55] and Gish Amit[56] expose parallel creative processes that have served the ideological policies of nascent Zionism. In expression of that policy, access to photographic remains that were confiscated or appropriated has been blocked for many years, due to the fear that the data they contained would be used to contradict the dominant ideology.

In contrast, pre-1948 Christian research institutions in Palestine preserve large bodies of unprocessed photographic oeuvre as can be seen in the work of Karène Sanchez Summerer and Norig Neveu in this volume. The slow exposure of these materials presents us with additional challenge. While political conflicts present a physical threat to photography, an ideological threat is rooted in the interpretability of photographic remnants that were preserved and are accessible to us, such as Whiting's *Diaries in Photos* or the photograph collection of the École Biblique, in a manner that will enable us to extract the 'parallel alternative histories' trapped within the genres.[57]

Travel and exploration reflect continuous relationships between the photographer and the subject, and the photographer and the landscape. Through exploration of these relationships a complex visual historiographic record is written. In the manner that it is edited, a thematic photographic album often erases parts of history and reorganises other parts. According to David Bate, this editing process represents an ideological apparatus through which the editor reprograms existing memory, not in the way it was, but in the way he wishes others to remember it.[58] In essence, Bate claims, this is an iconoclastic argument, because the range of images in an album differ from those recorded in the human memory. Similarly, Bate also asserts that the growth of museums and cultural institutions envelops within it the trend of redesigning

---

53   Iris Albina, "Souvenir from Gethsemane: Portrait of the Albina Brothers," *Jerusalem Quarterly* 60 (2014): 59.

54   Mustafa Kahba and Guy Raz, *Memory of Place: A Photographic History of Wadi Ara, 1903–2008* (Jerusalem: The Umm El-Fahem Art Gallery, 2008).

55   Rona Sela, *For Public Review: Photographs of Palestinians in Military Archives in Israel* (Tel Aviv: Helena Publishing, 2009).

56   Amit Gish, *Ex Libris: The History of Appropriation, Preservation, and Theft in the National Library of Jerusalem* (Jerusalem: Van Leer Institute, 2014).

57   See Karène Sanchez Summerer and Norig Neveu's chapter in this volume, "The Dominicans Photographic Collection in Jerusalem."

58   David Bate, "The Memory of Photography," *Photographies* 3, no. 2 (September 2010): 250.

human memory by erasing elements that were rejected from the cultural sphere by institutions of the dominant regime. Bate[59] refers also to Foucault's iconoclastic argument in 'Film and Popular Memory'[60] and compares a photographic corpus to 'image banks' that can potentially suppress personal memory and often replaces it.

Exploring the *Diary in Photos* reveals an unfamiliar reality that escaped the editing process – a Middle East that is unfettered by borders and populated by permanent and changing, mutually influential heterogeneous groups, as well as dominating foreign political forces. The historical memory of the Zionist-Palestinian conflict is present in Whiting's work, but it does not become dominant, due to the swift transitions which are the inherent nature of the genre. Examining Whiting work solely through the Orientalist paradigms ignores the richness of its cultural diversity and the memory of an open-borders Middle East.

The *Diary in Photos* series maintains a rather fluid 'meta-form' that absorbed complex visual memories through the day-by-day visual documentation. It resembles therefore a motion picture: its singular frames cannot exist without relating them to the sequence. Modern interpretation must therefore decipher it and release the broad range of 'parallel alternative histories' trapped in its entirety. An index of Whiting's 1934 and 1935 trips emphasises the cultural jigsaw captured in the entire work.[61] The genre's perspective fits well within the photographic work created by other Christian explorers in Jerusalem, but remained unexplored for generations. It was created as Whiting's personal memory apparatus, but at the same time it maintains a matrix of popular cultural memory 'which existed but had no way for expressing itself'.[62]

We must aim to develop reflective, critical visual tools that will enable us release the 'meta forms' that are trapped in confined bodies of work, rather than extracting components in an attempt to justify dominant ideologies or Orientalist paradigms. This will enable a new reading, and even if such readings are only partial, they have the power to gradually create a 'meta-archive' that can potentially inspire a sense of belonging and identity of younger generations in the region.

---

59   Ibid., 251.

60   Michel Foucault, "Film and Popular Memory," Reprinted in *Foucault Live* (New York: Semiotexte, 1989).

61   Rachel Lev, Index of photographic series presented in *Diary in Photos* vol. I, 1934–1935, Parts I and II. (September 2020) https://drive.google.com/drive/folders/19IYnTPU-6F1h KtJfwpo8Kgh5CfM7qKzU?usp=sharing.

62   Bate, "The Memory of Photography," 250–251.

Bibliography

Archival Sources

A   John D. Whiting, *Diaries in Photos*

Whiting, John D. *Diary in Photos* vol. I, 1934–1935. Visual materials from the papers of John D. Whiting. Library of Congress, Washington D.C. https://www.loc.gov/item/2007675295/.

Whiting, John D. *Diary in Photos* vol. II, 1936–1937. Visual materials from the papers of John D. Whiting. Library of Congress, Washington D.C. https://www.loc.gov/item/2007675297/.

Whiting, John D. *Diary in Photos* vol. III, 1938. Visual materials from the papers of John D. Whiting Library of Congress, Washington D.C. https://www.loc.gov/item/2007675285/.

Whiting, John D. *Diary in Photos* vol. IV, 1938. Visual materials from the papers of John D. Whiting. Library of Congress, Washington D.C. https://www.loc.gov/item/2007675264/.

Whiting, John D. *Diary in Photos* vol. V, 1939. Visual materials from the papers of John D. Whiting. Library of Congress, Washington, D.C. https://www.loc.gov/item/2007675290/.

B   John D. Whiting, Written Diaries

Whiting, John D. *Diaries*. John D. Whiting Papers. Manuscript Division, Library of Congress, Washington D.C. Box 1, 1905–1918; Box 2, 1934–1935; Box 3, 1938–1941. (Typed transcript of John D. Whiting Diaries. American Colony Archive Collections, Jerusalem. Restricted Access.).

C   John D. Whiting, Consular Reports

Whiting, John D. *Consular Reports, 1909–1915*. John D. Whiting Papers. Manuscript Division, Library of Congress, Washington D.C., Box 16, 1909–1915.

D   John D. Whiting, National Geographic Articles, 1913–1940

Library of Congress, Washington, D.C. LC Call number: G1.N27.

Copies of NGM issues with Whiting articles are also found in the Manuscript Division John D. Whiting Papers along with correspondence related to the articles.

Whiting, John D. "From Jerusalem to Aleppo." *National Geographic Magazine* XXIV (January 1913): 71–113.

Whiting, John D. "Jerusalem's Locust Plague." *National Geographic Magazine* XXVIII (December 1915): 511–550.

Whiting, John D. "The Last Israelitish [Israelite] Blood Sacrifice: How the Vanishing Samaritans Celebrate the Passover on Sacred Mount Gerizim." *National Geographic*

Magazine XXXVII (January 1920): 1–46. https://archive.org/details/lastisraelitish boowhit/page/42/mode/2up.

Whiting, John D. "Among the Bethlehem Shepherds: A Visit to the Valley Which David Probably Recalled When He Wrote the Twenty -third Psalm." *National Geographic Magazine* L (December 1926): 729–753.

Whiting, John D. "Bethlehem and the Christmas Story." *National Geographic Magazine* LVI (December 1929): 699–736.

Whiting, John D. "Petra, Ancient Caravan Stronghold." *National Geographic Magazine* LXVII (February 1935): 129–165.

Whiting, John D. "Bedouin Life in Bible Lands. the Nomads of the 'House of Hair' Offer Unstinted Hospitality to an American." *National Geographic Magazine* LXXI (January 1937): 58–83.

Whiting, John D. "Where Early Christians Lived in Cones of Rock: A Journey in Cappadocia in Turkey." *National Geographic Magazine* LXXVI, no. 6 (December 1939): 763–802.

Whiting, John D. "Canoeing down the River Jordan." *National Geographic Magazine* LXXVIII (December 1940): 781–808.

Secondary Sources

Ariel, Yaakov and Ruth Kark. "Messianism, Holiness, Charisma, and Community: The American-Swedish Colony in Jerusalem, 1881–1933." *Church History* 65, no. 4 (1996): 641–657.

Barthes, Roland. *Camera Lucida*. New York: Hill and Wang, 1981.

Bate, David. "The Memory of Photography." *Photographies* 3, no. 2 (2010): 243–257.

El-Hajj, Badr. "Khalil Raad, Jerusalem Photographer." *Journal of Palestine Studies* 11–12 (2001): 34–39.

Foucault, Michel. "Film and Popular Memory." Reprinted in *Foucault Live*. New York: Semiotext(e), 1989.

Freud, Sigmund. "The 'Mystic Writing-pad'." Reprinted in *On Metapsychology: The Theory of Psychoanalysis: Beyond the Pleasure Principle, Ego and the Id and Other Works*, edited by Albert Dickson, 427–433. Harmondsworth: Penguin, 1984.

Gish, Amit. *Eks libris: historyah shel gezel, shimur ye-nikus ba-Sifriyah ha-le'umit bi-Yerushalayim* (Ex Libris: The History of Appropriation, Preservation, and Theft in the National Library of Jerusalem). Jerusalem: Van Leer Institute, 2014.

Hackforth-Jones, Jocelyn and Mary Roberts. "Introduction: Visualising Culture across the Edges of Empires." In *Edges of Empire: Orientalism and Visual Culture*, edited by Jocelyn Hackforth-Jones and Mary Roberts, 1–19. Oxford: Blackwell Publishing, 2005.

Kabha, Mustafa and Guy Raz. *Memory of Place: A Photographic History of Wadi Ara, 1903–2008*. Jerusalem: The Umm el-Fahem Art Gallery, 2008.

Kracauer, Siegfried. *History: The Last Things before the Last.* Translated by Paul Oskar Kristellar. Princeton: Wiener, 1994.

Le Goff, Jacques. *History and Memory.* Translated by Steven Rendall and Elizabeth Claman. New York: Columbia University Press, 1992.

Lind, E. Lars. "Jerusalem Before Zionism and the American (Swedish) Colony." Lars E. Lind Papers. Box 2. Manuscript Division, Library of Congress, Washington D.C. (1979).

Micklewright, Nancy. "Alternative Histories of Photography in the Ottoman Middle East." In *Photography's Orientalism: New Essays in Colonial Representation*, edited by Ali Behdad and Luke Gartlan, 75–92. Los Angeles: Getty Research Institute, 2013.

Mickelwright, Nancy. "Orientalism and Photography." In *The Poetics and Politics of Place: Ottoman Istanbul and British Orientalism*, edited by Zeynep Inankur, Reina Lewis and Mary Roberts, 99–110. Seattle, WA: University of Washington Press, 2011.

Micklewright, Nancy. "Personal, Public, and Political (Re) Constructions: Photographs and Consumption." In *Consumption Studies and the History of the Ottoman Empire*, edited by Donald Quataert, 261–86. Binghamton: SUNY Press, 2000.

Nassar, Issam. "The Wasif Jawharieh Photographic Collection." *Journal of Palestine Studies* 11–12 (2001): 39–43.

Nir, Yeshayahu. *The Bible and the Image: The History of Photography in the Holy Land 1839–1899.* Philadelphia: University of Pennsylvania Press, 1986.

Onne, Eyal. *The Photographic Heritage of the Holy Land, 1839–1914.* Manchester: Manchester Polytechnic, 1980.

Raz, Guy. "Fifty years to Helmar Lerski's Death: A Pioneer of Modern Photography in Palestine," (In Hebrew) *Haaretz*, September 27, 2006. http://www.haaretz.co.il/literature/1.1140718.

Raz, Guy. "The Photographer is the Mirror-Image of His Landscape." (In Hebrew) Avi Chai website (2011). http://www.bac.org.il/hbrha/article/hatzlm-hava-tbnyt -nvph-mvldtv.

Said, Edward. *Orientalism.* New York: Vintage Books, 1979.

Sela, Rona. *In the Eyes of the Beholder – Aspects of Early Palestinian Photography.* Translated from the Hebrew under the title *Photography in Palestine/The Land of Israel in the 1930s–40s.* Herzlia: Hakibbutz Hameu'had and Herzliya Museum of Art, 2000.

Sela, Rona. *Photography in Palestine/The Land of Israel in the 1930s–40s.* (In Hebrew) Hertzlia: Hakibbutz Hameu'had and Herzliya Museum of Art, 2000. http://www .ronasela.com/he/details.asp?listid=39.

Sela, Rona. "For Public Review: Photographs of Palestinians in Military Archives in Israel." (In Hebrew) Tel Aviv: Helena Publishing, 2009.

Sela, Rona. "Land of Mirrors." (In Hebrew) *Haaretz*, July 22, 2011. http://www.haaretz. co.il/misc/1.1181774.

Sela, Rona. *Ḥalil Ra'ad: tatslumim 1891–1948.* Tel Aviv: Helena Publishing, 2013.

Tveit, Odd Karsten. *Anna's House, the American Colony in Jerusalem.* Translated by Peter Scott-Hansen. Nicosia: Rimal Publication, 2011.

Wasserstein, Bernard. "'Clipping the Claws of Colonisers': Arab Officials in the Government of Palestine, 1917–1948." *Middle Eastern Studies* 13, no 2 (1977): 171–194.

Whiting, John D. and Lewis Larsson. *Samaritanernas päskfest I ord och bild.* (*Passover Celebrations of the Samaritans in Words and Pictures*). With introductions by Sven Anders Hedin and Selma Lagerlöf. Limited edition, no. 159 of 300. Stockholm: Albert Bonniers Forlag. Rare Books Collection, American Colony Archive, Jerusalem, 1917.

Woodward, Michelle L. "Between Orientalist Clichés and Images of Modernization: Photographic Practice in the Late Ottoman Era." *History of Photography* 27, no. 4 (2003): 363–74.

Woodward, Michelle L. "Creating Memory and History." *Photographies* 2, no. 1 (2009): 21–35.

Documenting the Social: Frank Scholten Taxonomising Identity in British Mandate Palestine

Sary Zananiri

Frank Scholten, a Dutchman and photographer, travelled to Palestine in 1921, staying a little over two years. The wealth of photographs he produced provides us with a particular insight into the vast changes the country was experiencing in the aftermath of World War I and the fall of the Ottoman Empire. His documentary style of photography, and his project to produce an illustrated Bible, demonstrates a complicated confluence of religious narrative and modern scientific methodologies, as well as post-Ottoman and European approaches to social organisation. Both the Scholten Collection[1] and the man himself are significantly understudied. In attempting to understand Scholten's unique approach to photography, attention must be paid to his background as well as the social and political context of early British Mandate Palestine to fully grasp the taxonomies he employed.

Scholten, much like the complicated body of photographs he left behind, defies typical categorisations given the ways he approached the imaging of Palestine. Scholten's lens gives us a rare insight into Palestine society from elites to villagers. He captures ethno-confessional diversity as well as the significant shifts taking place in the early 1920s. The many contradictions that he and his work embody, makes for a very particular lens through which to view the social histories of the establishment of the British Mandate in Palestine, showing a collision of more typical readings dealing with the Biblical past against the modern life which such imaging typically effaces.

In attempting to map Scholten's photographic outputs and methodology, we need to take into account the complexity of the milieu with which he was associated in Europe, the cultural contexts into which he was born and lived

---

1 The Frank Scholten Collection was closed to the public for many years. It is currently in the process of being digitised, catalogued and made publicly available for the first time. Given the collection's transitional period, where references are made to boxes, they are from the older pre-catalogue system that will soon be defunct. Image references are from the new incoming system.

as well as the complicated set of materials he both collected and produced in his study of Palestine.

This complexity beckons several questions. How did Scholten's background as a member of the Dutch elite, a Catholic convert and a homosexual colour his approach to understanding the diversity of Palestine from an ethno-confessional and class perspective? What role did contemporary networks of scholarship play in shaping his complex approach to Palestine? And, most importantly, what can the collision of modern[2] scholarly approaches and Biblical narrative in his photographs tell us about the effects of the enormous social changes on the many communities in Palestine?

This chapter will first discuss Scholten's background before considering the scholarly methodologies and contexts with which he was engaged and implicated. It will then consider and compare the social context in both Palestine and Europe, leading to an examination of selected works from the Scholten Collection.

1   Frank Scholten

Frank Scholten, who was born in 1881 and died in 1942, lived through a period of transition that bridged two worlds. His class background and education cemented his elite status within Dutch society, but we can suppose, from his familial rifts,[3] his homosexuality and its related legal transgressions,[4] he was also an outsider.

Coming from a well-to-do family with links to the Dutch aristocracy,[5] the commercial necessities of photographic practice can be seen as playing little part in guiding Scholten's lens, making him free of the commercial demands

---

2 Modern here is defined as the product of industrialisation, in cultural terms and in line with the sociological definition proffered by Anthony Giddens, *The Consequences of Modernity* (Cambridge: Polity Press, 1991): 1–21.

3 For instance, he left home shortly after his father's death and, later, a series of exchanges between Scholten and his step-mother in the wake of the stock market crash in 1929 show the turbulence of familial relations, see Teresa Lidia Kwiecień, "Frank Scholten", *Depth of Field* 40 (December 2008). https://depthoffield.universiteitleiden.nl/2540f05en/. Accessed February 22, 2020.

4 Theo van der Meer, *Jonkheer mr. Jacob Anton Schorer (1866–1957): Een biografie van homoseksualiteit* (Amsterdam: Schorer Boeken, 2007), 159–63.

5 His father, grandfather and great-grandfather had been among the top officials of the Dutch investment bank Nachenius Tjeenk and his mother was a 'jonkvrouw', an honorific title denoting nobility. See van der Meer, *Jonkheer mr. Jacob Anton Schorer (1866–1957)*, 162 and Kwiecień, "Frank Scholten."

of the photographic market that most professional photographers dealt with. Estimates of the Scholten Collection that is currently being catalogued sit around twelve thousand printed photographs and fourteen thousand negatives alongside a significant body of images, ephemera and books that he collected as well as his postcard correspondence, mostly with his friend Geertje Pooyar. The photographs taken by Scholten appear to start from the late World War I period in The Netherlands, to images of his travels through Germany, Italy and Greece in 1920 to the more than two years he spent in Palestine from 1921 to 23,[6] which comprise the bulk of the collection. There are also smaller collections of images from France, the UK and other parts of Europe, presumably taken when he later returned to Europe.

When Scholten died in 1942 from later complications related to a car accident, he left this array of material to the Netherlands Institute for the Near East (NINO). Alongside this was his library, a collection of 'found images' including photographs, postcards, prints and images clipped from books, and other assorted ephemera. These found images were annotated and generally pasted to boards in line with contemporary practices of archiving photographs of art historical subjects. He also left notes towards a 16-volume set of photo books titled 'Palestine Illustrated'[7] only two of which were published (though in four language editions), and a sum of money to continue the production of his unpublished work, for which he left behind some notes and arrangements of images.

As a photographer, Scholten took a documentary approach, and one that was, at least in Palestine, high in output. The photographic collections he left behind show a diverse array of local subjects and geographies including cities, towns, villages, the countryside and the desert. In his time in Palestine, he travelled the country extensively, as well as trips to Lebanon, Syria and Jordan. He

---

6   Kwiecień, "Frank Scholten".

7   For details of Scholten's various editions see: François Scholten, *La Palestine Illustrée: Tableau Complet de la Terre Sainte par la Photographie, Évoquant les Souvenirs de la Bible, du Talmud et du Coran, et se rapportant au passé comme au présent, Vol I La porte d'entrée – Jaffa Vol II. Jaffa la Belle* (Paris: Jean Budry & Co., 1929). German: Frank Scholten, *Palästina – Bibel, Talmud, Koran. Eine vollständige Darstellung aller Textstellen in eigenen künstlerischen Aufnahmen aus Gegenwart und Vergangenheit des Heiligen Landes. Bd. I: DIE EINGANGSPFORTE. JAFFA. Mit 449 Abbildungen in Kupfertiefdruck, Bd. II: JAFFA, DIE SCHÖNE. Mit 371 Abbildungen in Kupfertiefdruck* (Stuttgart: Hoffmann, 1930). English: Frank Scholten and G. Robinson Lees, eds., *Palestine Illustrated including References to Passages Illustrated in the Bible, the Talmud and the Koran, Vol.1 Gate of Entrance, Vol.2 Jaffa the Beautiful* (London: Green Longmans, 1931) and Dutch: Frank Scholten, *Palestina: Bijbel, Talmud, Koran. Een volledige illustratie van alle teksten door middel van eigen artistieke foto's uit het heden en verleden van het Heilige Land De toegangspoort Jaffa* (Leiden: Sijthoff, 1935).

FIGURE 8.1   *Untitled*, 1921–23. Frank Scholten. Jaffa Port. Digitised negative. Frank Scholten.
UBL_NINO_F_Scholten_Jaffa_o6_oo48, Frank Scholten Collection
IMAGE COURTESY OF NINO AND UBL

photographed people, archaeology, sites of religious significance, urban street-
scapes and rural villages, domestic interiors, social and religious events, the
new colonial networks that the incoming British Mandate brought with it, and
the early days of Tel Aviv, still in its infancy in the early 1920s.

Scholten's background was in many ways fundamental to the lens through
which he viewed Palestine. Born to a wealthy Protestant family, Scholten
converted to Catholicism before travelling to Palestine,[8] though evidence of
exactly when the conversion took place has yet to be found.

In the Netherlands, the social system of pillarisation[9] broke society into
confessional and political spheres having wide ranging consequences from the
provision of health and educational structures to which media outlets communities engaged with. Scholten's conversion perhaps points the particular

---

8   In a postcard to his friend Geertje dated 16th January, 1920 Scholten talks of attending
     confession and taking communion at St Peters in Rome. I would like to thank Lara van der
     Hammen for her translation of some of the postcards. Frank Scholten Collection, Box E2.
9   Harry Post, *Pillarization: An analysis of Dutch and Belgian society* (Aldershot [etc.]:
     Avebury, 1989).

sensitivity towards similar structures of Ottoman Millet system, which had been reshaped significantly during the Empire's nineteenth century Tanzimat Reforms, that were still very much in place, though beginning to morph, at the beginning of the British Mandate.

After growing up in Amsterdam, he received a liberal education in Berlin around the turn of the twentieth century.[10] In this time spent between his native Netherlands and Berlin's bohemian milieu, Scholten was brought into contact with the social and political world of the early homosexual emancipation movement. He is known to have stayed in Berlin with the famous German sexologist Magnus Hirschfeld.[11] Berlin had become a place known for its sexual openness.[12] Scholten also frequented the working-class area of De Pijp in Amsterdam, the setting for Jacob Israël de Haan's openly gay novel *Pijpelijntjes* (1904),[13] which was similarly colourful.

In 1920, he left The Netherlands amidst legal charges related to his activities that involved soliciting young military men on trains and at Amsterdam's Central station (Fig. 8.14). He was subsequently charged with two years jail in absentia.[14] In its first year, his travels took him to Italy, Greece, Germany and Switzerland. Within his collected images we see works of art from antiquity, the Renaissance and modern works, which reflect his wide art historical interests and support the idea of an anachronistic Grand Tour of sorts. A number of smaller photo albums from this period underscore his documentary style, showing a mixture of street scenes with portraits of people he encountered.[15]

The second part of his journey, continuing onwards to Palestine, might be seen as more in line with ideas of a pilgrimage, perhaps with a redemptive tone given his legal predicaments at home. He had a significant library of six

---

10   Kwiecień, "Frank Scholten".

11   Van der Meer, *Jonkheer mr. Jacob Anton Schorer (1866–1957)*, 215.

12   Robert Deam Tobin quotes an aristocratic client of British sexologist Havelock Ellis who had travelled extensively suggesting that Berlin was "more extensive, freer and easier than anywhere else in the Orient or Occident", which makes an interesting point of comparison to someone like Scholten. R. Deam Tobin, *Peripheral Desires: The German Discovery of Sex* (Philadelphia: University of Pennsylvania Press, 2015), 1.

13   J. Haan and W. Simons, *Pijpelijntjes* (Amsterdam: Van Cleef, 1904).

14   Jos van Waterschoot, Bert Sliggers, and Marita Mathijsen, *Onder De Toonbank: Pornografie En Erotica in De Nederlanden* (Amsterdam: Uitgeverij van Oorschot, 2018), 172–173.

15   Of the 12 boxes of photographs, photographic albums and negatives produced by Scholten, only two in the UBL collection deals with European images, although another two have recently been found in the NINO (The Netherlands Institute for Near East) stores which contain mixture of photographs Scholten took in Europe and postcards he collected. These will be amalgamated with the broader collection at UBL.

thousand books with him in Palestine,[16] from which we can suppose that he had planned his photographic project in advance.

Both Scholten as a figure and the material he left behind, raise important questions about his singular view of Palestine. Given his employment of complicated taxonomies, how did he approach the imaging of Palestine? How did his identity and his milieu, scholarly or otherwise, influence these taxonomies? By what means did he relate Biblical narrative to the modern life he encountered and imaged in Palestine?

2 Modern Scholarship and Scholten's Taxonomies

One might be tempted to ascribe the term amateur to Scholten's photographic practice, given his lack of commercial investment more typical of 'Holy Land' genres of photography. Despite this, it is perhaps more fitting to see him as harking back to earlier modes of being, such as the aristocratic scholar-gentleman of the Enlightenment or the devotee of classical antiquity, given his time in Italy and Greece and some of the materials he had collected. In this regard, the scholarly overtones of the collection make for an interesting foil to those of the École biblique discussed by Karène Sanchez Summerer and Norig Neveu in their chapter on the Dominican photo library.[17]

In this light, we might look to art historical methodologies of the day to contextualise Scholten's practice. Much of found images – those images he collected – are pasted to cardboard, reference their source and a Biblical quotation relevant to the image, place or event depicted, and were left in various states of preparation.

Though the collection is currently being catalogued by the photography department in special collection at Leiden University Library (UBL), the methodology is typical of art historical approaches of the late nineteenth century and early twentieth century, in which source images were pasted to board, carefully labelled, taxonomised and organised into folders.

Through the current cataloguing project, it has become evident that much of the collected images were in a process of being sorted. Several categories emerge. The first are those images that have been pasted to card, with a

---

16   Kwiecień, "Frank Scholten".
17   Several postcards from Scholten to his friend Geertje Pooyar in Volendam mention social and professional interactions with the Dominicans during his time in Palestine. While it is hard to gauge the extent of relations from a series of postcards, it would seem that Scholten's pedagogical approach may have reflected the Dominicans' approach to presenting photography as a kind of evidence. Frank Scholten Collection, Box E2.

reference to their source be it a book or an individual and a Biblical quote (which is sometimes also appended with a particular translation of the Bible). The second category is unpasted, and just a clipping, with either a Bible quotation, a reference to its source or both. The third category is other images that have been clipped from various locations that are not appended at all. This third category of material typically consists of smaller images that are of a less interesting quality. It would seem that as Scholten was collecting and processing these found images he either never completed the process or disregarded the third category as rejects.

A good point of comparison, both culturally and chronologically, might be the German Kunsthistorisches Institut in Florenz (KHI) established in 1897, which consists of a photographic archive of Italian artworks that range from antiquity to the modern era, taxonomised by material, era and location. The KHI Collection both parallels the period which Scholten was producing his own archive, as well as providing an insight into Northern European approaches to the Mediterranean. The KHI Collection comprises of photographs of artworks that were pasted onto card, which were then appended with the title of the artwork depicted in the photograph, the date the photograph was taken, the name of the photographer as well as other relevant information about the artwork. These 'plates' were then taxonomised by geography and period of the artwork depicted, then stored in boxes, forming the core of the KHI archive.

In a postcard dated 3rd May, 1922, written from Jerusalem to his friend Geertje in the Netherlands, Scholten wrote 'These days I'm preparing to leave again; gluing pics, writing letters and making visits'.[18] It is unclear whether this postcard is in reference to the found images he was collecting or the photographs he was producing, that exist as loose photographs, photographs pasted to card and photographs pasted into albums. Another postcard to Geertje sent 5th May, 1922 states 'I am very busy these days with gifts for my family. Photographs (24 pieces each) for my grandmother in Amsterdam, for my mother, for my three aunts, for my uncle and for my two sisters. So much family!' This would perhaps indicate working on his own photographs, rather than found images, and may explain some of the more eclectic albums in the collection, such as the series he titled *Choses Intéressante* ('Interesting Things').

Within Scholten's photographic corpus, there is a numbering system that occurs within sections of his loose photographs pasted to card and the albums (though not seemingly the unpasted loose images). Punctuating the loose images pasted to card are other cards without photographs that have numbers applied to them with some sort of letter transfer technique (Fig. 8.2). This

---

18   Postcard to Geertje, Frank Scholten Legacy collection, Frank Scholten Collection, Box A2.

FIGURE 8.2   Cardboard divider with letter transfers. UBL_NINO_F_Scholten_Fotos_
Doos_07_0285. Frank Scholten Collection
IMAGE COURTESY OF NINO AND UBL

would hint that at some stage there an order to the collection that appears to correlate to several ledgers, but sadly with the multiple moves of the collection, this order appears to have been lost and would constitute a very significant project to reinstate.

Among the textual references he made on the found images and cards to which they were pasted, and indeed in the books he published, were references to different translations of the Bible from the Vulgate by Glaire and Vigouroux in French to Martini's La Sacra Bibbia in Italian to the Greiner Bibel in German. This textual approach to the Bible also shows scholarly engagement with the theological, particularly textual criticism and 'the quest for the historical Jesus',[19] which had been a growing field in the late nineteenth and early twentieth century.

Alongside these references were many more references to interpretive texts dealing with the Bible, Biblical history and the history of Palestine. Many of

---

19   Albert Schweitzer's book of the same name, published in German in 1910, capitalised on this interest and attempted to study the various historical approaches to the life of Jesus. See Albert Schweitzer, trans. W. Montgomery, *The Quest for the Historical Jesus: A Critical Study of its Progress from Reimarus to Wrede* (London: Adam and Charles Black, 1911): 21.

these were also illustrated, giving him a good knowledge of the visual vocabularies used to depict Palestine and the 'Holy Land in Western authored photos'.

Scholten's methodology of taxonomisation was likely developed during
time spent in Berlin, both during his studies and afterwards. Such methodologies show a nuanced understanding of scholarly, art historical methodologies
and at least a working, if not broader, knowledge of theological debate, particularly around textual criticism and Biblical history.

Within the German context, Scholten spent with Magnus Hirschfeld, the
German physician, sexologist and founder of the Humanitarian Scientific
Committee, an organisation dedicated to advocating for the rights of sexual
minorities. In 1910, Scholten was staying with Hirschfeld, likely through introduction by the early gay rights activist Jacob Schorer, who founded of the Dutch
chapter of the Humanitarian Scientific Committee.[20] At that time, Hirschfeld
had just published *Die Transvestiten*,[21] one of the early studies on transvestites
and cross-dressing. Contemporary critiques of the work notwithstanding, it was
a significant landmark that for the first time attempted to taxonomise gender
and sexuality in the emergent science of sexology.[22] The milieu which Scholten
inhabited in Europe, points towards an engagement with the cutting-edge academic research methodologies of the day, that focused on the categorisation
and taxonomisation of identity. It is possible that Scholten derived the ethnographic taxonomies that he employed in his published volumes partially from
Hirschfeld's own explorations of sexual and gender taxonomy.

We see the complexities of confessional, ethnic, class and cultural demarca-
tions that show the early Mandate as a period in which the cosmopolitanism
of Ottoman legacies was overlayed with an incoming European milieu, both
Jewish and Christian (Fig 8.3). Through the course of the Mandate period,
nationalist narratives would come to solidify nationalist projects culturally,
politically and physically, and indeed cement the newly created national borders, as it did elsewhere in the former empire,[23] effectively undermining the
complexity of ethnic, national, confessional and class dimensions that had

---

20   Van der Meer, *Jonkheer mr. Jacob Anton Schorer (1866–1957)*, 171–176.

21   Magnus Hirschfeld, *The Transvestites*, trans. M.A. Lombardi cited in text; Magnus
       Hirschfeld, "Die intersexuelle Konstitution Zwischenstufen": 23 cited in: Darryl B. Hill,
       "Sexuality and Gender in Hirschfeld's Die Transvestiten: A Case of the "Elusive Evidence
       of the Ordinary", *Journal of the History of Sexuality* 14, no. 3 (2005): 316–332; https://www
       .jstor.org/stable/3704656, accessed February 22, 2020.

22   Hill, "Sexuality and Gender in Hirschfeld's Die Transvestiten", 316.

23   Prescient examples in the north of the former Ottoman Empire are the Armenian geno-
       cide or the so-called 'population exchanges' between Greece and Turkey in considering
       the broader context and effects of rising nationalism, both of which were roughly con-
       temporaneous to Scholten's period of travel.

FIGURE 8.3 *Untitled*, 1921–23. Frank Scholten. A ship arriving in the Port of Jaffa. Digitised negative. UBL_NINO_F_Scholten_Jaffa_16_0008, Frank Scholten Collection
IMAGE COURTESY OF NINO AND UBL

developed through the late Ottoman period and into the opening years of the British Mandate.

The amorphous political and cultural possibilities posed for Palestinians by the ailing Ottoman Empire in the early twentieth century and during World War I gave rise to significant political debates within indigenous communities.[24] Firstly, in whether to support the Ottomans or the Allies during the war and secondly, with respect to Zionist immigration and the British support for it. Alongside, and linked to such political debate, was the context of the *Nahda* (the 'awakening' or 'Arab Renaissance'), the cultural renewal that underpinned Arab nationalism and occurred slightly later in Palestine's smaller cities than larger centres like Beirut or Cairo. With the beginning of the British Mandate there were new certainties in terms of peace and post war redevelopment, but also new uncertainties with regards to Zionism and its support by the British that coloured the period. While Palestinian nationalism had certainly

---

24 For a good summary of some of these debates, see Ihsan Salih Turjman and Salim Tamari, *Year of the locust: A Soldier's Diary and the Erasure of Palestine's Ottoman Past* (Berkley: University of California Press, 2015).

pre-dated the British Mandate,[25] as had Zionism,[26] the cultural structures the British Mandate created would exacerbate and cement difference, particularly through language policy,[27] strongly honing identity formation processes into categories of 'Arab' and 'Jew' and effectively erasing the complex and intricate cultural identifications (and their legislated support structure) of the Ottoman era.

Given the political and cultural context of the 1910s and 20s, we see much of this tumult playing out in the Scholten collection, particularly in the inventory of ethno-confessional taxonomies Scholten employed.

A brief inventory of the taxonomies Scholten employed in the captioning of his photographs includes Greek-Orthodox, Catholic, Melkite, Protestant, Muslim and Jewish Palestinians; German, Russian, Spanish, Hungarian, Romanian, Moroccan, Iranian, Bukharan and other Arab Jewish communities; British, French, German, Greek, Russian and Italian Europeans, as well as Americans, and also Egyptians, Sudanese, Indians and Nepalese reflective of the incoming colonial administration and its networks. Scholten also attends to class divides within many of these cultural and confessional taxonomic designations that, within the rubric of Ottoman social structures, also indicates an understanding of urban-rural divides.

3   Modern Forces: Taxonomy and Transnational Social Contexts

3.1   *From Pillar to Millet*

While we can deduce, from the scholarly networks he inhabited, how Scholten was engaged and influenced by a number of disciplines and the methodologies which they produced, another way of framing his work and practice is through the ways he connected the social contexts within which he functioned on a macro level. These social frameworks demonstrate transnational connections, whether through systems of social formation, contexts surrounding issues of language or the vocabularies of visual culture. These macro level social systems

---

25   See, for instance, the hostility towards Zionism in the Arabic press before the First World War. Emanuel Beška, *From Ambivalence to Hostility: The Arabic Newspaper Filasṭīn And Zionism, 1911–1914* (Slovak Academic Press: Bratislava, 2016).

26   The First Zionist Congress was held in August 1897 which established what would become the World Zionist Organization.

27   This can be seen in the support of Hebrew as part of British language policy in Palestine despite its initial marginality during the period of revival. See for instance Andrea L. Stanton, "'This Is Jerusalem Calling': State Radio in Mandate Palestine", *Journal of Palestine Studies* 47, no 2 (2018): 13–14.

can be seen as operating in tandem with scholarly discourses in his output, but separating them in framing Scholten's output gives us an insight into the broader social and historical forces that were formative in shaping his world view.

The context of *Verzuiling*, literally 'compartmentalisation' in Dutch, but known as *pillarisation* in English, was a key concept for understanding the social formations of Dutch society from the late nineteenth century until the 1960s.[28] Dutch pillarisation created four primary socio-political groupings: a Catholic, Protestant, liberal and socialist pillars.[29]

For Scholten, growing up in the last decades of the nineteenth century, he would have witnessed the establishment and growing influence of Abraham Kuyper's Anti-Revolutionary Party (ARP), a neo-Calvinist organisation that would eventually see Kuyper as Prime Minister from 1901–05.[30] Kuyper was instrumental in the formalisation of pillarisation.

There are several scholarly interpretations behind the rise of the pillarisation. Firstly, pillarisation as a means of 'emancipation' within the context of class politics in socialist pillar, the 'kleyne luden' (small people) of the middle- and working-class Protestant pillar, and the subordination of Catholics by the Protestant kingdom, each of which sat against the liberal pillar, drawn primarily from the upper classes. Secondly, as a confessional safeguarding around the processes of secularisation with the rise of modern forces in the nineteenth century. Thirdly, as a means of cementing the status of elites internally within each pillar. And finally, given emergence of pillars from the mid nineteenth century set against the backdrop of industrialisation and technological innovation, there is an argument that the apparatus of modernity enabled the opportunity, for the first time, to organise larger scale networks of supra-local organisations.[31] Without delving into the debates beyond the scope of this paper, it is clear that modernity had a significant role in codifying pillarisation in the Netherlands, and with it, the population itself.

While it is important to stress that agreement on the universal totality of pillarisation in compartmentalising Dutch communities is divided on how intensely its effects were felt and experienced, suffice it to say the system certainly mediated much of historical social life from media like newspapers and magazines to social and leisure associations, education including

---

28   James D. Bratt, *Abraham Kuyper: Modern Calvinist, Christian Democrat.* 2nd Impression (Grand Rapids, Michigan: Eerdmans Library of Religious Biography, 2013): 343.

29   Staf Hellemans, "Pillarization ('Verzuiling'). On Organized 'Self-Contained Worlds' in the Modern World", *The American Sociologist*, 51 (2020): 125.

30   James D. Bratt, *Abraham Kuyper*, xxiii–xxviii.

31   Hellemans, *Pillarization*, 130.

universities, welfare and philanthropic endeavours, and even unions and other professional associations.

In this regard, Scholten's conversion to Catholicism probably also negotiated a distinct social shift personally. Certainly the correspondence between him and his friend Geertje who lived in Volendam gives a significant sense of the extensive Catholic networks through which Scholten operated in Palestine, from social contact with the Dominicans of École biblique to patronising institutions like Notre Dame to his links indigenous Catholic communities across class boundaries.

One of the more significant considerations that elements of Scholten's background, his arrival in Palestine and the social shifts his conversion may have engendered, is comparison to the complexities of Ottoman communalism. The Millet system that had been in place since the Ottoman conquest of Constantinople in 1453, but had undergone significant reforms in the second half of the nineteenth century,[32] paralleling the emergence of pillarisation in the The Netherlands.

In 1856, Sulṭān ʿAbd al-Majīd I affirmed the equal status of Muslim and non-Muslim Ottoman subjects alike. This constituted a significant shift in policy from the protected, but subordinate status of *dhimmi* with the *jizya*, extra taxes payed by members of such millets.[33] Alongside this, a number of new millets, or pillars as they might have been identified by the Dutch Scholten, were added through the course of the nineteenth century, mainly in reference to specific denominations of Christianity. Nonetheless, the shift in status from dhimmi to citizen had a broader political utility in the administration of the Empire, particularly in addressing the developing political affinities that derived from the intervention and protection of smaller non-Muslim communities by the European powers.[34]

The nature of the broader context of shifting political regimes in early Mandate Palestine would create 'minorities' (within a Western nation state framework) from communities that had historically been millets within the Ottoman Imperial framework,[35] adding yet more complexity to ways we must

---

32   Karen Barkey and George Gavrilis, "The Ottoman Millet System: Non-Territorial Autonomy and its Contemporary Legacy", *Ethnopolitics* 15, no. 1 (2016): 24–42.

33   Heather Sharkey, "History Rhymes? Late Ottoman Millets and Post-Ottoman Minorities in the Middle East", *International Journal of Middle East Studies* 50, no. 4 (2018): 760–761.

34   For more information on such cultural diplomacy and its effects on Christian communities, see Karène Sanchez Summerer and Sary Zananiri, eds., *European Cultural Diplomacy and Arab Christians in Palestine, 1918–1948. Between Contention and Connection* (London: Palgrave Macmillan, 2021).

35   Sharkey, *History Rhymes?*, 760–764.

understand early 1920s Palestine. This however underscores the emerging shifts of identity formation processes in the period.

There is no direct evidence of how Scholten understood either the Millet system or pillarisation. However, as the various taxonomies outlined at the end of the previous section of this chapter attest, Scholten was very attentive to the complicated social context of post-Ottoman Palestine in his various designations. This demonstrates at least a perception of communitarian difference. The context of pillarisation and, in Scholten's case, its transgression, may partially explain, in combination with his scholarly engagements, his complex use of taxonomies within the complex communal nature of recently post-Ottoman Palestine.

3.2   Transnational and Transcommunal Concerns

The significant collection of found images that Scholten collected, shows an interest in Biblical narrative, the classical world, Renaissance art and architecture, religious art, Orientalist imaging as well as the works of photographers, illustrators and printmakers vested in the depiction of Palestine and the Biblical. In piecing together the relationship of these found images and the photographs Scholten took during his years in Palestine, we can see an attempt to frame the complex social life he found in Palestine. The materials he collected range in production date from the 1850s to the late 1930s and deal with significantly longer chronology in the artworks they depict, from the ancient to the modern. While the range of images largely deal with Palestine, the Bible or Biblical history, sometimes in oblique ways, certain themes can be detected that link seemingly disparate areas of Scholten's interests. One such theme is repeated collections of the Biblical figure of David, from image reproductions of Michelangelo's masterpiece[36] to Arnold Zadikow's[37] modernist rendition to clippings from religious books and illustrated bibles, including several that show David's relationship to Jonathan (Fig. 8.17).[38]

This Biblical material and images of Palestine sits alongside other, much smaller, categories such as satirical cartoons commenting on Dutch politics of the day, socialist posters and other assorted political materials. Such material may have been of personal political interest, but also reflect interest in other

---

36   Along with many other artists of the Renaissance, Michelangelo's married classical Greco-Roman sculptural aesthetics with Christian narrative.

37   Arnold Zadikow was a German-Jewish modernist sculpturer. Incidentally, he is also known to have produced Magnus Hirschfeld's headstone.

38   The ambiguities of the relationship between David and Jonathan, the son of Saul, were often used to justify homosexual relations theologically. Interestingly, Oscar Wilde quoted this as part of his defence during his infamous trial for homosexuality. See https://www .famous-trials.com/wilde/327-home, accessed February 22, 2020.

pillars within the Dutch social system. However, when read in combination Scholten's proximity to the Humanitarian Scientific Committee and his 'queering' of religious imagery – point to at least some consideration of questions of social justice, both temporal and spiritual. A complex picture of Scholten's perspective begins to emerge around the rubrics of religion, sexuality and art history, particularly when intersected with broader social context. Borrowing from various scholarly disciplines, the taxonomical principles he applies to his photography in Palestine attempts to synthesise something that approaches an anthropological study from images of a diversity of people to religious events, like Nabī Mūsā, which was itself undergoing rapid changes from a religious to a nationalist festival in this period (Figs. 8.4 and 8.5).[39]

After his return to Europe, Scholten held his only exhibition, *Palestine in Transition* in London's Brook Street Gallery from 25th to 29th February, 1924. It was organised under the auspices of the Anglo-Palestinian Club,[40] a Zionist organisation that had been founded two years earlier.[41] It would seem that Scholten viewed his exhibition more as an opportunity for progressing his career or Catholic interests, rather than a position of political partisanship given attitudes relayed in his postcards to Geertje. On the 25th July, 1922, in the aftermath of the British White Paper[42] Scholten wrote 'Arrived in Jerusalem yesterday evening, to avoid that Jewish Feast in Tel Aviv. I did not want to toast (champagne) to the health of the Jews, and on their possession of the H. Land. That is why I dodged it'.[43]

Confessional concerns seem to be at the core of Scholten's aims for the exhibition: 'They object to those Catholic texts, but I am not moved to put them in a Protestant way. I'd prefer not exhibit'.[44] What it does underscore, however, is the development of a Zionist cultural diplomacy, particularly in the UK where it served to capitalise on Zionist-Protestant affinities and the political gains made with the Balfour Declaration, just seven years earlier. The exhibition comprised of around 2,000 photographs. Sadly, either no catalogue was

---

39   Awad Halaby, "Islamic Ritual and Palestinian Nationalism: al-Hajj Amin and the Prophet Moses Festival in Jerusalem, 1921 to 1936," in *Jerusalem Interrupted: Modernity and Colonial Transformation 1917-Present*, ed. Lena Jayyusi (Northampton, MA: Interlink Publishing: 2013), 139–152.

40   *The British Journal of Photography*, February 29, 1924, 130.

41   William Rubinstein and Michael Jolles, *The Palgrave Dictionary of Anglo-Jewish* History (London: Palgrave MacMillan UK, 2011), 69.

42   The White Paper was written by the then Secretary of the State for the Colonies, Winston Churchill and released on 3rd June, 1922.

43   Postcard to Geertje, 25th July, 1922, Frank Scholten Collection, Box E2.

44   Postcard to Geertje 16th February, 1924, Frank Scholten Collection, Box E2.

FIGURES 8.4 AND 8.5   *Jour Nabī Mūsā* and *Untitled* (also Nabī Mūsā), 1921–23. Frank
Scholten, UBL_NINO_F_Scholten_Fotos_Doos_02_0071
and UBL_NINO_F_Scholten_Fotos_Doos_02_0072. Frank
Scholten Collection

IMAGES COURTESY OF NINO AND UBL

produced or it has been lost.[45] The exhibition, however, received positive reviews from the British press, both Jewish and non-Jewish, for showing the nature of modernity in the ancient 'Holy Land'.[46]

3.3   *Towards the Biblical Moderne*

By the time Scholten had arrived in Palestine a Western scholarly culture had developed. A number of permanent institutes had been established such as École Biblique et Archéologique Française de Jérusalem (1890), the American School of Oriental Study (1900) and British School of Archaeology in Jerusalem (1919). These archaeological institutions by their very nature were, of course, more vested in the ancient past – often in Biblical terms – rather than the present moment, but each were attempting to employ new scholarly methodologies, including the use of photography, in dealing with archaeology in Palestine.

The institutionalisation and reassessment of biblification, both in Scholten's corpus and elsewhere, and the attempt to reconcile Biblical interest with that of modern, scientific methodology, is what we might term the *Biblical Moderne*.[47] The Biblical Moderne represents a rupture in biblified representation that either consciously or unconsciously attempted to build on, correct and legitimise previous generations of imaging by reconciling them with modern scholarly approaches, a concept that looms large in the methodological approaches that Scholten employed in his work.

On the one hand, Scholten is clearly cognisant of his Christian, and specifically Catholic, positioning given the majority of the titles he referenced.[48] His attempts to mediate a position denotes a somewhat liberal and inclusive subject position that we can presume was drawn from the formative cultural context he had inhabited in Europe. On the other hand, he also adopts a problematic assumption of scholarly objectivity under the auspices of the *scientific*, which can be seen in the centring of Christianity in the quotation of Christian,

---

45   I tried to trace a catalogue at the British Library and National Arts Library. While I found numerous catalogues from the Brook Street Gallery in the same period, it appears that one was not published for what was only a one-week exhibition.

46   There were a number of reviews of the exhibition, these include *The British Journal of Photography*, February 29, 1924; "Life in Palestine"; *Times* (London, England) 26 Feb. 1924, 5; *The Times Digital Archive*. Web. 28 Sept. 2018; *The Universe The Catholic Newspaper*, February 29th, 1924.

47   I would like to thank Stephen Sheehi for suggesting this useful term in feedback on this chapter during the conference that led to this publication.

48   A full inventory has yet to be made, but the titles he references and the sources of found images indicate that he had a significant library on the topics of Palestine, biblical history and theology.

Muslim and Jewish scriptures in his two published volumes, the notation of his found images and the notes towards the other 14 volumes.

Published in four different language editions[49] (French, German, English and only the first volume of two in Dutch), the images maintain uniformity across each imprint, but the emphasis on quotations shift slightly in each language. It is worth noting that the differences between the various language editions often paralleled the relationships of those language speakers to the communities he was photographing in Palestine. This could show a nuanced understanding of colonial geo-politics in each of the language markets he addressed or may simply be marketing machinery to different groups of European-language speakers. In either case, the catering to a particular language market with slightly more sources from their respective tongues belies the colonial relations and cultural affinities that had developed in the Ottoman era and into the British Mandate.

Though it has to be said they are only very slight differences, the French edition (1929), for example, has extra quotations for Catholic, Armenian and Sephardic communities; the German (1930) emphasis on German Templars, Protestants and Ashkenazis; the English (1931) a similar focus to the German, but with a few more evangelical references. The Dutch edition, of which only one volume was published, is slightly harder to compare, but does reference a number of Dutch works on Christianity that the others do not.[50]

The fact that the images remain uniform across all four language editions,[51] hints that either he regarded the image as having a universal value or that he regarded the images – as informal and intimate as they often are – as a form of ethnographic data collection for his project for which text was regarded as secondary evidence. If this is the case, it would constitute an interesting inversion of biblified imaging practices, in which the primacy of Biblical text was typically used to read the 'Holy Land'. Instead, we could position Scholten as prioritising the primacy of the image over the quotations to which he had ascribed them. This again hints at a certain focus on modern scientific methodologies influenced by the taxonomies above, but also at the same time reinforces the sanctity of the land, still positioning it within some rubric of biblification. The reconciliation of the Biblical and scientific is perhaps where we might place Scholten's work within the trope of the Biblical Moderne.

---

49   It seems a Spanish edition was also proposed, but never produced, see postcard to Geertje 13th May, 1931, Frank Scholten Collection, Box E2.

50   Sary Zananiri, "Frank Scholten: Landschap in het Brits Mandaat Palestina", *Fotografisch Geheugen* 96 (December 2018).

51   There is however a printing error in one edition, where the pages are out of sequence, however the images were clearly marked with the same numbers as the other editions.

4   Modernity, Orientalism and Biblification: Applying Taxonomies
       to Scholten in Palestine

The process of remediating Palestine and Palestinians in photography for
western circulation networks, as many chapters of this volume attest, was primarily focused on the use of the Biblical to interpret what might otherwise
have been seen as a 'foreign' world. The familiarity of the Biblical, both as a
textual narrative and, by the early 1920s, as a familiar imaging trope, relied on
bridging a gap between the western consumer of such images and the otherness of the so-called 'Orient' through the construction of a Western Biblical
imaginary. Biblification, as Issam Nassar terms it, actively highlighted the
Biblical narrative, remediating modern Palestine to an ancient past in a process
that excised (Palestinian) modernity.[52] In many ways, this is a stark contrast
to Scholten's approach, which, as the title of his 1924 exhibition *Palestine in
Transition* implied, depicted a place undergoing rapid changes brought about
by modernity.

4.1   *Class and Urban-Rural Divides*
Western photographers producing work for a Western audience had predominantly concerned themselves with the Biblical, while local photographers
focused on a mixture of production for local consumption, be it through the
commissioning of studio portraits, *carte de visite*,[53] documenting events for the
state, religious authorities, the media and academia, as well as similar biblified production as their western counterparts for a similar western market.[54]
Scholten is a rarity in terms of visiting photographers, in that he photographed

---

52   For a more detailed discussion and definition of biblification see: Issam Nassar,
      "'Biblification' in the Service of Colonialism: Jerusalem in Nineteenth-century
      Photography", *Third Text* 20, no. 374 (2006): 317–326; Issam Nassar, "Colonization by
      Imagination", in *City of Collision*, eds. P. Misselwitz, T. Rieniets, Z. Efrat, R. Khamaisi and
      R. Nasrallah (Basel: Birkhäuser, 2006); Issam Nassar, *European Portrayals of Jerusalem:
      Religious Fascinations and Colonialist Imaginations* (Lewiston, NY: Edwin Mellen Press,
      2006).
53   A useful chapter that frames the social and ideological implications of studio portraiture
      and specifically the phenomenon of the *carte de visite* in the Arab World until 1910 is
      Stephen Sheehi's chapter, "The Carte de Visite: The Sociability of New Men and Women",
      in his book *The Arab Imago: A Social History of Portrait Photography 1860–1910* (Princeton:
      Princeton University Press, 2016), 53–74.
54   For instance, see the photographic outputs of Khalīl Ra'ad from his photographs of World
      War I commissioned by the Ottomans, Salim Tamari, "The War Photography of Khalil
      Raad: Ottoman Modernity and the Biblical Gaze", *Jerusalem Quarterly* 52 (2013): 25–37, to
      works that specifically focus on the biblical see images from his catalogue in chapter 6 of
      this volume.

portraits of local people, both elites as well as those from more humble back-grounds, making the collection of specific importance to garnering an overview of the rapid shifts taking place in the early 1920s.

To contextualise the importance of Scholten's corpus, we might turn our attention to the British Mandate's various urban planning policies, as Nadi Abusaada has written in his chapter. Jerusalem, as many other cities, was chang-ing rapidly, even with the early urban planning schemes developed by William McLean and Charles Ashbee, which progressively removed the nineteenth and early twentieth century urban growth abutting the Old City Walls in Jerusalem to quite physically separate the Old City, with its all its religious connotations, from its suburban surroundings.[55] This demonstrates a very physical iteration biblification of the Old City and its environs, prosecuted within romanticism of the British Arts and Crafts movement of which Ashbee was an adherent. On the other hand, the taxonomies employed by British planners paid little atten-tion to Palestinian villages on the urban peripheries that grew into some of the most well-built sections of the new city. As Rana Barakat points out, they were regarded as rural and hence outside of British taxonomies of either ancient or modern,[56] but were also disregarded within demographic studies of the city,[57] showing the erasure of semi-rural Palestinian communities on the urban periphery, even on a bureaucratic level by ignoring the category altogether.

Based on looking at Scholten's corpus broadly, it would be fair to say that the majority of photographs he took were documentary in nature. They are gener-ally not staged when in public space. Although he certainly made portraits of people, even in these posed contexts they tend towards the casual snapshot, rather than the more formal language and conventions of studio photography. It is important to conceive of Scholten's photographic practice as one which purveys a relative *naturalism*, if not one which frames a particularised per-spective, but there are indeed still limitations to how we might contextualise Scholten's interactions.

In an article in the Dutch press dated April, 1934, Scholten described how he managed relations, particularly with rural communities. This ranged from pleasantries and platitudes, to an incident where Scholten worked with his chauffeur to get a photograph of a shepherd. His chauffeur suggested that if a shepherd didn't have his photograph taken, a war with Mussolini in Italy might

55   Roberto Mazza, *Jerusalem from the Ottomans to the British* (London: I.B. Tauris, 2009).
56   Rana Barakat, "Urban planning, colonialism and the Pro-Jerusalem Society," *Jerusalem Quarterly* 65 (Spring 2017): 32.
57   Rana Barakat, "The Jerusalem Fellah: Popular Politics in Mandate-Era Palestine," *Journal of Palestine Studies* vol. 46, no. 1 (Autumn 2016): 9.

FIGURE 8.6 *Untitled*, 1921–23. Frank Scholten. A shepherd playing the flute. UBL_NINO_F
_Scholten_Fotos_Doos_16_0821, Frank Scholten Collection
IMAGE COURTESY OF NINO

break out.[58] While it is easy to admire the breadth and depth of Scholten's corpus, it would be a romanticisation to assume his class background created equal footings between himself and many of his photographic subjects.

Scholten's village landscapes, particularly Yazūr, on Jaffa's periphery, give us a case study in some of the tensions between the Biblical and the modern. In *Figs. 8.7* and *8.8*, women and children are gathered in rural costume in the village of Yazūr, just 6 km east of central Jaffa and near the site of today's Ben Gurion Airport. A rustic prickly pear hedge, trees and a crowd of women and children conjure up the image's biblified settings of its photographic forebears. Were it a film of the 1920s, it would not be difficult to imagine Jesus' imminent arrival. Indeed, reading it as filmic speaks to its fundamentally modern quality.

---

58   [Author unknown] "Een Nederlander in Nieuw-Palestina" van Houten's Eigen Tijdschrift
      (April 1934) cut from a magazine and pasted into a notebook of press clippings collected
      by Scholten on his projects, Scholten collection. With thanks to Maartje Alders for bring-
      ing this article to my attention. Frank Scholten Collection, Box marked 'Jan van Duren'.

FIGURES 8.7 AND 8.8   *Yazur*, 1921–23. Frank Scholten, UBL_NINO_F_Scholten
_Fotos_Doos_04_0403 and UBL_NINO_F_Scholten_Fotos_
Doos_04_0025. Frank Scholten Collection
IMAGES COURTESY OF NINO AND UBL

It seems composed, yet a blurred figure walks through the scene, indicating a spontaneous shot.

Fig. 8.8 speaks to personal dynamics. The three women at the front, despite modesty in front of the camera, look directly into the lens, the one in the front clearly smiling, despite the shadow across her face. There is a sense of familiarity, even friendship. This naturalistic, documentary approach makes us reassess *Fig. 8.7*. What could have been a staged biblified cliché is indeed a spontaneous documentation of the rural scene, albeit the same subject matter that more biblified photography would privilege.[59] And yet, within biblification as an imaging convention, such a reading seems difficult to avoid given the weight of previous photographic production.

To help contextualise the social dimensions of such a scene, we might turn our attention to some of the scholarly endeavours of the period. One particular scholar of note was Tawfīq Kanaʿān (Canaan,) a medical doctor and anthropologist. While serving in his medical capacity, Kanaʿān conducted much of his field research into Palestinian folklore and also developed a collection of folk amulets, now housed at the Birzeit Museum. Kanaʿān published widely, particularly in the *Journal of Palestinian Oriental Society*. In the early 1920s, he published a number of scholarly studies that dealt with folk beliefs, for instance *Haunted Springs and Water Demons in Palestine* (1920)[60] and *Folklore of the Seasons in Palestine* (1923),[61] but continued his writing well into the 1930s.

The work of Kanaʿān makes an interesting foil for considering class relations in early Mandate Palestine, particularly in the division between middle classes and rural working communities. As a member of the professional class, he was one of a circle of intellectuals who were very much engaged increasingly in modern transnational scholarly practices. His research interests, however, were very much in rural communities and folklore, a culture that was increasingly affected by processes of urbanisation as Stephen Sheehi shows in his chapter. Kanaʿān's ethnographic work was actively documenting the vanishing rural folklore and practice for posterity, underscoring the vastly different lived experience of modernity that class delineated in Palestine.

---

59   It is also a typology that came to be reproduced constantly in cinema in the next few years
      as the first Hollywood biblical epics gained currency through the 1920s. See Sary Zananiri,
      "From Still to Moving Image: Shifting Representation of Jerusalem and Palestinians in the
      Western Biblical Imaginary", *Jerusalem Quarterly* 67 (2016): 64–81.

60   Tawfiq Canaan, "Haunted Springs and Water Demons in Palestine", *Journal of Palestinian
      Oriental Society*, vol. I (1920–21): 153–170.

61   Tawfiq Canaan, "Folklore of the Seasons in Palestine", *Journal of Palestinian Oriental
      Society*, vol. X (1923).

FIGURE 8.9 *Untitled*, 1921–23. Frank Scholten. A village house decorated with patterns similar
to cross stitch. UBL_NINO_F_Scholten_Fotos_Doos_16_0820. Frank Scholten
Collection
IMAGE COURTESY OF NINO AND UBL

The role of photography, and biblified photographic production, has been
extensively explored as a by-product of colonial relations and the Western
Biblical imaginary,[62] but the formative moment of the early years of the British
Mandate saw a significant shift in demography. The incoming European communities (both Jewish and otherwise) and the urban expansion of cities like
Jerusalem[63] and Jaffa to encompass what were historically Palestinian villages on the urban peripheries into their suburban sprawl, breached, in the
physicality of architectural form, the historical distance between urban and
rural communities.

This tension between the Biblical and the modern (and perhaps implicitly
between the rural and the urban) took on new dimensions in the making of
colonial claims. As outlined in the introduction to this volume, Orientalism,
like biblification, eschewed the modern, but through a different operation.

---

62   Nassar, "'Biblification' in the Service of Colonialism"; Nassar, "Colonization by
     Imagination,"; Nassar, "European Portrayals of Jerusalem".
63   Barakat, "The Jerusalem Fellah," 9–12.

FIGURE 8.10   *Tel Aviv*, 1921–23. Frank Scholten, UBL_NINO_F_Scholten_Fotos_
Doos_17_0186, Frank Scholten Collection
IMAGE COURTESY OF NINO AND UBL

Where biblification relies on the interpretation of the image through a process of familiarisation (that is to say, making the image legible through Biblical
narrative), Orientalism is a system that relies on demarcating otherness by
the positioning of the 'Orient' and inhabitants *against* modernity. In very
similar ways to biblification, the production, consumption and circulation
of Orientalist photographs overlapped with similar demographics to biblified cultural materials: the Western photographic market. But here again, the
context of class in both the production and consumption of photography, is
important to note.

4.2   *Oriental Bodies*

A photo of a Jewish couple, marked by Scholten as having been taken in Tel
Aviv, elaborates on the ways in which Ottoman communalism was morphing
(Fig. 8.10). The woman on the left appears in numerous Scholten photographs
ranging from her work as nurse in Jewish quarantine stations through to social-
ising with a predominantly male Zionist social circle. Annotations from other
photographs of the couple in the same outfits suggests they had just become
engaged. From her head wear and the date of the photograph (1921–23),

it would seem a safe presumption that she was a Third Aliyah migrant. The context of anti-Jewish pogroms in Eastern Europe as World War I ended, in combination with the restriction of Jewish migration to the US and Western Europe[64] led a new generation of Jewish migrants to Palestine in the years after the First World War. This photo is particularly telling in terms of the porous social attitudes. She is wearing a *thawb*, a traditional cross-stitched Palestinian dress, combined with an Eastern European headscarf.

Indigenous photographers in Palestine also took part in similar activities, some offering traditional clothing as 'dress ups' for studio portraits to both tourists and the local population. While the motivations that led Palestinians and foreigners alike to be photographed in such costume may have differences and overlaps as Issam Nassar writes in his chapter of this volume (Figs. 5.6 and 5.7), assumptions can be made of both groupings in laying claim to indigeneity. Implicitly, a particular relationship between class and modernity emerges, that gives us a sense of the transnational entanglements constructed by a performance of class.

Very significant questions of cultural appropriation aside, Fig. 8.10 of the woman wearing a *thawb* is not simply an Ashkenazi testing of whether they want to embody some sort of Palestinian Oriental positioning. It is, in a sense, embodying two completely different subject positions within the same Jewish body, asking whether that body fits within rubrics of 'Palestinian-ness' within identity formation processes so endemic to the period. The *thawb* itself appears to be made from a mixture of patterns not related to a particular locality or region, though the v-shaped design does on some level reference a typology based in Ramallah designs.[65] While the *thawb* points on one level to an assimilationist attitude, it also denotes the popularisation of the *thawb* as a marker of identity, and perhaps a marker of 'authenticity', as we look to the *thawb* from Bethlehem worn by the girl discussed in Kopty's chapter at the American Colony (Fig. 9.5).

In this regard, as an image, this underscores amorphous identities that would become actively formalised in the years after this photo was made. The 'honeymoon' context of a new relationship aside, the act of donning the *thawb* may appear to be a simple gesture of trying new clothing, which certainly has antecedents in Palestinian studio photography, but it belies the complex positioning of Jewish identity within a framework that is at one and the same time part of Europe and also removed from it. This duality is one that had significant

---

64   Immigration Restriction Act of 1921 in USA and the Alien Act of 1905 in Britain both had
      significant impacts on Jewish possibilities for emigration from Eastern Europe.
65   I would like to thank Wafa Ghnaim from *Tatreez and Tea* for this useful information.

impacts for Jews in Europe. As Grossmann points out, the uneasy positioning of a spectrum of Jewishness in Europe, from ancient and Oriental to modern and European, was not without its consequences in ways the Ashkenazi communities were remediated in photography from Palestine to the West. She notes that Theodor Harburger criticised Karl Gröber's photo book of Palestine in a review, saying that only images of religious Oriental Jews at the Wailing Wall were published in it rather than those images of the Zionist 'new Jew'.[66]

In looking more broadly at the growing rubrics of orientalisation, the question of class becomes key if we consider Palestine as being the central node in which a series of transnational networks converge. For the Jewish middle classes of Central Europe, the renewal of Jewish culture during the Weimar Republic termed by Michael Brenner as a renaissance saw a particular shift in German perceptions of Jewishness in the rising context of Zionism.[67]

Jewish communities in 1920s Germany were increasingly seen as part of pluralist vision of cosmopolitan culture[68] and, within the rubric of Zionism, a vanguard of German culture in the so-called 'Holy Land', a trope which would have been familiar to someone like Frank Scholten who had been educated in Berlin.

On the other hand, the development of Jewish identity in the Yishuv and the rise of National Socialism in the 1930s required a certain orientalisation of Jewishness to accommodate Zionist ideology.[69] Zionism required this orientalisation as a means of recouping an 'ancient Jewish past' which would come to be embodied in Jewish Arabs such as Yemenite metal workers, deployed as Zionist cultural diplomacy,[70] but at the same moment Zionism also embodied that which was fundamentally modern, particularly the narrative of bringing of technology and progress to Palestine.[71]

The mercantile Palestinian middle classes would also be photographed by Scholten both directly, like the portrait of ʿĪsā al-ʿĪsā with his child[72] (Fig. 8.11)

66   Rebekka Grossmann, "Negotiating Presences: Palestine and the Weimar German Gaze", *Jewish Social Studies* 23, no. 2 (2018): 145.

67   Michael Brenner, *The Renaissance of Jewish Culture in Weimar Germany* (New Haven, CT: Yale University Press 1998).

68   Grossmann, "Negotiating Presences: Palestine and the Weimar German Gaze", 138.

69   Ibid., 160–161.

70   Nisa Ari, "Competition in the Cultural Sector: Handicrafts and the Rise of the Trade Fair in British Mandate Palestine", in *European Cultural Diplomacy and Arab Christians in Palestine, 1918–1948. Between Contention and Connection*, eds. Karène Sanchez Summerer and Sary Zananiri (London: Palgrave MacMillan, 2021), 231.

71   Grossmann, "Negotiating Presences: Palestine and the Weimar German Gaze", 150.

72   Scholten, *Palestine Illustrated*, vol. 1, 67, image 128.

FIGURE 8.11   *Untitled*, 1921–23. Frank Scholten. Portrait of ʿĪsā al-ʿĪsā and son
                 Raja. UBL_NINO_F_Scholten_Fotos_Doos_07_0407, Frank Scholten
                 Collection
                 IMAGE COURTESY OF NINO AND UBL

or young men enjoying their fast cars (Fig. 8.12) or indirectly, like the lavish interior of a Christian, upper middle-class Palestinian home in Jaffa.[73]

Images of these middle classes differ greatly from the rural and working-class Palestinians who were so often portrayed as embodying the spirit of the Biblical vestige of ancient times. The embodied experience of modernity necessitates consideration of the class connotations of what it meant to live a 'modern' lifestyle. Images such as these point to an Eastern Mediterranean vernacular of modernity, one which was still denoted by the wearing of a *tarbush* or the use of pointed arches in architecture, despite essentially containing the same furniture and accoutrements an equivalent household in the West might.[74]

---

73   Scholten, *Palestine Illustrated*, vol. 2, 67, image 141.
74   Seikaly, *Men of Capital: Scarcity and Economy in Mandate Palestine* (Stanford: Stanford
      University Press, 2016): 36–41; Keith David Watenpaugh, *Being Modern in the Middle East:*

FIGURE 8.12   *Untitled*, 1921–23. Frank Scholten. UBL_NINO_F_Scholten_Fotos_
                Doos_17_0215, Frank Scholten Collection
                IMAGE COURTESY OF NINO AND UBL

Taken in conjunction with the series of images about Palestinian industry,
particularly the lumber, soap and orange exports that Scholten imaged,[75] we
see a world which is connected through commerce and, within a few years of
Scholten's time in Palestine, would establish important multinational financial
institutions like the Arab Bank (founded 1930) and later Intra Bank (founded
1951, but with antecedents in the Mandate period) by Yusif Baydas, son of the
Nahda literary figure Khalīl Baydas. This 'orientalised' iteration of modernity
at once shows the results of participation in international trade and commerce, but also the cultural fractures between urban and rural life, the growing
middle class and, implicitly, the continuities of the pre-war legacies of the
Tanzimat Reforms.

    As Keith Watenpaugh outlines in the first chapter of his book *Being Modern
in the Middle East*, the ethnically and confessionally diverse middle classes
of the late Ottoman period was small, but disproportionately influential. Its

---

Revolution, Nationalism, Colonialism, and the Arab Middle Class (Princeton: Princeton
University Press, 2012), chapter 1.

75   Scholten, *Palestine Illustrated*, vol. 2, images 118–129 and 231–259.

relationships to technology, liquid financial assets and its privileged relationship to education[76] had come about through confessionally-specific
affiliations that tethered communities to various European states through
various modes of cultural diplomacy, for example in the arena of education.
This shows yet another layer to the multiplicity of networks embedded in early
Mandate Palestine.

The fact that Scholten referred slightly differently to each of the ethnic
and confessionally diverse communities of Palestine in the different language
versions of the first volume of his books once again underscores these colonial relationships. But it also points to his nuanced understanding of broader
geo-political relationships enabled by European cultural diplomacy, in which
those communities are related back to his Western readership through
such affiliations.

4.3   Taxonomising a Colonial Landscape

Scholten's photographic collection shows us a world in which British colonial
rule brought new populations into the already diverse post-Ottoman landscape. He shows us British soldiers, from Tommies to Gurkhas, but also French
and American troops. The upsurge in Eastern European anti-Semitism in the
early 1920s would bring new and significantly larger migrations of European
Jews as part of the Third Aliyah. By the early 1920s, several generations of
modern, mercantile, middle class and globally connected Palestinians[77] had
engaged with the world well beyond the former Ottoman empire's borders,
taking part in international discussions about nationalist aspirations with
former compatriots who were now neighbours in Syria, Lebanon and Egypt
and very much engaged with the European powers who had established and
cemented their presences in nineteenth century Palestine.

This deft conjuring of landscapes further afield is perhaps most visible in
images of the incoming South Asian communities Scholten photographed.
Gurkha regiments had been part of the British army since the early nineteenth century. By World War I, they comprised eleven regiments, each
greatly expanded with extra battalions, numbering a total of 200,000 men.[78]
The Gurkhas were involved in General Allenby's campaign in Palestine and

76   Watenpaugh, *Being Modern in the Middle East*, 26–27.
77   For instance, in the mother of pearl trade, which saw Palestinian trading communi-
      ties developed in Paris, Manchester, Kiev, Port-au-Prince and Manila see Jacob Norris,
      "Exporting the Holy Land: Artisans and Merchant Migrants in Ottoman-Era Bethlehem",
      Mashriq & Mahjar 1, no. 2 (2013).
78   Alan Axelrod and Michael Dubowe, *Mercenaries: A Guide to Private Armies and Private
      Military Companies* (Thousand Oaks, CA: CQ Press, 2014), 70.

FIGURE 8.13   *Untitled*, 1921–23. Frank Scholten. Gurkhas in Jerusalem leaving for Nabī Mūsā.
UBL_NINO_F_Scholten_Fotos_Doos_02_0074, Frank Scholten Collection
IMAGE COURTESY OF NINO AND UBL

W.T. Massey describes the loss of South Asian lives euphemistically in terms of 'sacrifice' in the British capture of Jerusalem.[79] The proliferation of images showing South Asian participations in the Nabi Musa festival give us a sense of other complex encounters, which require considerable further research at a later stage.

The changing nature of Nabī Mūsā from a religious festival to a nationalist expression exemplified by the riots of 1920 raises quite a series of questions: how did South Asian troops participating in Nabī Mūsā relate to shifts in local politics in Palestine? Did they view the growth of Palestinian nationalism through the lens of Indian politics, particularly the Lucknow Pact between the Indian National Congress and the Muslim League in 1916 and the civil unrest of the early 1920s? Did this create transnational anti-colonial solidarities or were the Gurkhas simply regarded by Palestinians as just another arm of the British

79   See William Thomas Massey, *How Jerusalem Was Won Being the Record of Allenby's Campaign in Palestine* (1919), Ebook available via https://www.gutenberg.org/cache/epub/10098/pg10098.html, accessed October 18, 2019.

FIGURE 8.14   *Zweedsche matrozen*, 1918–19. Frank Scholten. 'Swedish sailors' at Amsterdam
Centraal Station. Part of his album 'Amsterdam'. UBL_NINO_F_Scholten_
Netherlands_Amsterdam_010, Frank Scholten Collection
IMAGE COURTESY OF NINO AND UBL

occupation of Palestine? Sadly, these questions of colonial mobility and their
impacts must be left for further research.

4.4   A Queer Lens?

What the images of the Gurkhas and other troops show is how the apparatus of the Great War, and its aftermath, facilitated colonial mobility. Scant
evidence exists of Scholten's relationships in Palestine beyond photographic
records and brief notations in postcards. However, inferring from legal records
in the Netherlands, which document his sexual encounters with military men
at Amsterdam Centraal Station,[80] we might propose that the proliferation
of various populations of troops in Palestine also provided opportunities for

---

80   Van der Meer, *Jonkheer mr. Jacob Anton Schorer (1866–1957)*, 159.

homosocial interactions, which cut across class divides. This thesis is certainly supported by the amount of images of military men and homosocial spaces in his Palestinian photographs. The images of Nissan Huts at the British military base in Sarafand, one of the most significant bases in Palestine, certainly seem to be anomalous within more typical readings of Palestine amongst Western photographers, even amongst the plethora of soldiers' albums from World War I and the years afterwards.

The time that Scholten spent in Palestine, therefore, can be seen as a period of post-Ottoman entrenchment of the British, very much a world that was undergoing radical shifts and changes in relation to demography, administration and culture, but also one in which Ottoman imperial mobility across the Eastern Mediterranean was changing to a globalised framework of British colonial mobility and newly formed borders framed new cultural identifications.

We can infer from repeated images of people in the photographic collection, that Scholten had a wide circle of friends and acquaintances in Palestine. Certainly, from his published works, we can also gather his nuanced understanding of post-Ottoman communal structures. Apart from a biographical article by Teresa Kwiecień[81] and another short study by me,[82] there are but a few secondary sources on Scholten, generally in studies of other personalities such Jacob Israël de Haan,[83] Jacob Schorer[84] or more general studies of Dutch histories of sexuality that deal with the years in Europe preceding his time in Palestine. Consideration of these studies paints a strong queer subtext to the collection.

Homosexual relations had been decriminalised across the Ottoman Empire in 1858 as part of the Tanzimat Reforms, although they would be recriminalised by the British first with anti-Sodomy legislation in 1927 and then the banning homosexual relations in 1936.[85] Analysis of court records from the 1930s and 40s, during the period in which homosexuality had been recriminalised, certainly point to cross-communal homosexual relations as not uncommon.[86]

---

81   Kwiecień, "Frank Scholten".

82   Zananiri, "Frank Scholten: landschap in het Brits Mandaat Palestina".

83   Ludy Giebels, produced a number of works on De Haan, which have mentions of Scholten, including a photo he had taken of De Haan in Jericho. Likewise, Scholten is mentioned in J. Fontijn, *Onrust: Het leven van Jacob Israël de Haan, 1881–1924* (Amsterdam: De Bezige Bij, 2015).

84   Van der Meer, *Jonkheer mr. Jacob Anton Schorer (1866–1957)*.

85   Orna Alyagon Darr, "Narratives of 'Sodomy' and 'Unnatural Offences' in the Courts of Mandate Palestine (1918–1948)," published online by Cambridge University Press (2017): 241–242.

86   Orna Alyagon Darr, *Plausible Crime Stories* (Cambridge: Cambridge University Press, 2019): 31–32.

FIGURE 8.15 AND 8.16   *Untitled* [marked Sarafand], 1921–23. Frank Scholten. Nissan huts
used as soldiers' barracks at the British Military Base in Sarafand.
UBL_NINO_F_Scholten_Fotos_Doos_16_1005 and UBL_NINO_F
_Scholten_Fotos_Doos_16_1009, Frank Scholten Collection
IMAGES COURTESY OF NINO AND UBL

Given the gaps in legal records for the early 1920s, we can but infer the social situation from later prosecutions and hope that further research on the topic through other documents like memoirs will be undertaken in the future.

In the arena of sexual diversity during the early 1920s two points stand out. Firstly, that legal (and, at least to some degree, social) attitudes to homosexuality were subjected to similarly changing forces and codification as the other arenas of society. Secondly, that the queer networks within the complicated ethno-confessional context of the period, at least to some degree cut across communal divides, as the relationship between de Haan and his partner ʿAdīl Aweidah attest.

The queer subtext to much of the Scholten collection taken at a surface level, may appear to contradict the history of Orientalist and biblified imaging. However, the repeated images of David in Scholten's found images, for instance, cut across different eras, art styles, mediums and artists in a comparative mode. While this underscores a scholarly comparison on an art historical level, it also speaks to modes of transnational and transcultural comparison that attempt to come to grips with the differing treatment of the Biblical figure through a queer lens across time, culture and geography, effectively threading across otherwise disparate categories.

In many ways, however, these queer subtexts uphold Scholten's gestures towards modernity. This, taken with intellectual milieu in which Scholten mixed, the influence of scholarly methodologies and the new theories of sexuality he was exposed to, we can begin to understand the complexity of Scholten's project in Palestine.

Taken in conjunction with his conversion to Catholicism and the art historical materials present in his collected images, we might infer an engagement with André Rafflovich's *Uranism et Unisexualité* of 1896. A liberal Catholic, Rafflovich argued that same-sex desire had given rise to much of Western high culture, making *inverts* (a historical British term of the period for homosexuals) the ideal priest. Invoking Platonic ideals, he argued that occasional homosexual lapses were sins, but not grievous errors.[87]

While biblification and orientalisation, both in Europe and the Arab World, were used to delineate the limitations of civility, the authority of classicism, with its implications of rationality would, as per Rafflovich, buttress colonial notions of 'Western Civilisation' and hence colonial power dynamics. In the Scholten collection, their conflation with biblification and its latent

---

87   For more information see Frederick S. Roden, "Queer Christian: The Catholic Homosexual Apologia and Gay/Lesbian Practice", *International Journal of Sexuality and Gender Studies* 6, no. 4 (2001): 252.

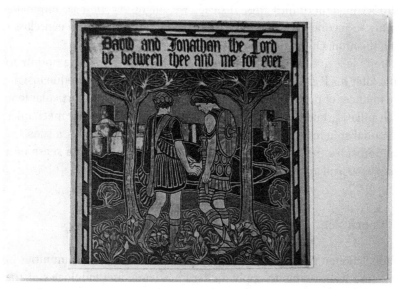

FIGURE 8.17 *David and Jonathan*, 1891. George Heywood Sumner, published in
'The Studio', 1891. From the 'found images' collection, Frank Scholten
Collection, Box A8
IMAGE COURTESY OF NINO

FIGURE 8.18 *Untitled* [French soldiers in Jerusalem], 1921–23. Frank Scholten. UBL_
NINO_F_Scholten_Fotos_Doos_17_0216, Frank Scholten Collection
IMAGE COURTESY OF NINO AND UBL

homoeroticism undermines this. Instead, we might see him as implicitly attempting to reconcile or create a complicated confluence between classicism, biblification, Orientalism and modernity.

Scholten's lens and what might be termed a 'pilgrimage of redemption' to Palestine after his legal troubles in the Netherlands, gives us a unique insight into the nuances of post-Ottoman communalism from the very particular lens of Dutch pillarisation. This sensitive understanding of the social mechanics of communal spheres in combination with a queer lens gives us a sense of cultural porosities that the early Mandate engendered, but also a sense of a modern sexological approach that underpins his attitude.

5   Conclusion

The Frank Scholten Collection, through its complex study of communities in Palestine and its attempts to apply modern academic methodologies of the day, stands testament to a period of significant cultural and social reorganisation, both in Palestine and Europe. What Scholten's methodology and the collection he left behind show is a world in which modernity was fundamental to creating descriptive taxonomies, a process of ordering the world through scholarly engagement.

While the lack of detailed textual information beyond postcard correspondence and image annotations hinders a complete picture of Scholten's corpus, the picture that does emerges from the Scholten collection is a complex one. From the photographic and found image annotations, we can see he drew on a diversity of scholarly fields from early medicalised and theological theories of sexuality, Western art historical methodologies, Palestinian and Biblical history, and theological enquiries into text. On a photographic level, we see evidence that he was acutely aware of the different ethno-confessional affiliations in local communities and within his publications we see an understanding of how those communities had affinities with the Western powers active in the region. However, on a personal level we can but make inferences from the Scholten collection on the ways he might have drawn, perceived or experienced parallels between different social systems of organisation, like Dutch pillarisation and the Ottoman Millet system, both products of their respective nineteenth century modern social policies.

This complicated matrix of taxonomies generated by Scholten engages carefully with histories of biblified and Orientalist imaging of the 'Holy Land'. His lens illustrates how biblification and Orientalism were produced by modernity, but also how the three interacted, producing an intimate portrait of the establishment of the British Mandate and early Mandate society. This interaction gives us a useful framework for analysing the shifting ethnic, confessional and class diversity of Palestine during the establishment of the British Mandate period in demarcating communities. But more importantly, it serves our understanding of the shifting contexts of modernity that demonstrates the production of the framework of the Biblical Moderne in the portrayal of local communities.

This is further complicated by the queerness of Scholten's lens. Liberal Catholic thought around homosexuality may have been an attractive factor in his conversion, but the social dynamics around sexuality, and implicitly class, is evident in the repeated images of handsome men, particularly in the military, as well as homosocial spaces like male dorm rooms and workplaces. These images hint at the ways Scholten may have operated socially in terms of liaisons with other men, but also the ways in which his homosexuality may also have transgressed communal boundaries and contributed to his understanding of the different 'compartments' in social systems like pillarisation or the Ottoman millet.

Scholten shows us a version of Palestinian society that connects to the world through many networks, but also a context of complexity that gave rise to significantly less nuanced identities as the nationalist aspirations of the period progressed, most embodied by the disastrous consequences of British colonial rule.

Bibliography

Primary Sources

The Frank Scholten Collection, Netherlands Institute for the Near East, Leiden University Library.

Secondary Sources

Ari, Nisa. "Competition in the Cultural Sector: Handicrafts and the Rise of the Trade Fair in British Mandate Palestine." In *European Cultural Diplomacy and Arab Christians in Palestine, 1918–1948. Between Contention and Connection*, edited by Karène Sanchez Summerer and Sary Zananiri. London: Palgrave MacMillan, 2020.

Axelrod, Alan and Michael Dubowe. *Mercenaries: A Guide to Private Armies and Private Military Companies*. Thousand Oaks, CA: CQ Press, 2014.

Barakat, Rana. "The Jerusalem Fellah: Popular Politics in Mandate-Era Palestine." *Journal of Palestine Studies* 46, no. 1 (2016): 7–19.

Barakat, Rana. "Urban planning, colonialism and the Pro-Jerusalem Society." *Journal of Palestine Studies* 65, no. 1 (2016): 22–34.

Barkey, Karen and Gavrilis, George. "The Ottoman Millet System: Non-Territorial Autonomy and its Contemporary Legacy", *Ethnopolitics* 15, no. 1 (2016): 24–42.

Beška, Emanuel *From Ambivalence to Hostility: The Arabic Newspaper Filasṭīn And Zionism, 1911–1914.* Slovak Academic Press: Bratislava, 2016.

Bratt, James D. *Abraham Kuyper: Modern Calvinist, Christian Democrat.* 2nd Impression. Grand Rapids, Mich.: Eerdmans, 2013.

Brenner, Michael. *The Renaissance of Jewish Culture in Weimar* Germany. New Haven, CT: Yale University Press, 1998.

Canaan, Tawfik. "Haunted Springs and Water Demons in Palestine." *Journal of Palestinian Oriental Society* vol. 1 (1920–21): 153–170.

Canaan, Tawfik. "Folklore of the Seasons in Palestine." *Journal of Palestinian Oriental Society* vol. 3, no. 1 (1923): 21–35.

Darr, Orna Alyagon. "Narratives of 'Sodomy' and 'Unnatural Offences' in the Courts of Mandate Palestine (1918–1948)." *Law and History Review* 35, no.1 (2017): 235–260.

Darr, Orna Alyagon. *Plausible Crime Stories.* Cambridge: Cambridge University Press, 2019.

Deam Tobin, Robert. *Peripheral Desires: The German Discovery of Sex.* Philadelphia: University of Pennsylvania , 2015.

"Een Nederlander in Nieuw-Palestina", *van Houten's Eigen Tijdschrift.* April 1934.

Fontijn, J. *Onrust: Het leven van Jacob Israël de Haan, 1881–1924.* Amsterdam: De Bezige Bij, 2015.

Giddens, Anthony. *The Consequences of Modernity.* Cambridge: Polity Press, 1991.

Grossmann, Rebekka. "Negotiating Presences: Palestine and the Weimar German Gaze." *Jewish Social Studies* 23, no. 2 (2018): 137–172.

Grossmann, Rebekka. "Image Transfer and Visual Friction: Staging Palestine in the National Socialist Spectacle." *The Leo Baeck Institute Yearbook* 64, no. 1 (2019):19–45.

Haan, Jacob Israel de and W. Simons. *Pijpelijntjes.* Amsterdam: Van Cleef, 1904.

Halaby, Awad. "Islamic Ritual and Palestinian Nationalism: al-Hajj Amin and the Prophet Moses Festival in Jerusalem, 1921 to 1936." In *Jerusalem Interrupted: Modernity and Colonial Transformation 1917-Present,* edited by Lena Jayyusi, 139–152. Northampton, MA: Interlink Publishing: 2013.

Hellemans, Staf. "Pillarization ('Verzuiling'). On Organized 'Self-Contained Worlds' in the Modern World", *The American Sociologist* 51 (2020): 125.

Hill, Darryl B. "Sexuality and Gender in Hirschfeld's Die Transvestiten: A Case of the 'Elusive Evidence of the Ordinary'." *Journal of the History of Sexuality* 14, no. 3 (2005): 316–332.

Jayyusi, Lena. ed. *Jerusalem Interrupted: Modernity and Colonial Transformation 1917-Present.* Northampton, MA: Interlink Publishing: 2013.

Kwiecień, Teresa Lidia. "Frank Scholten." *Depth of Field* 40 (December 2008), Article No.: 5. https://depthoffield.universiteitleiden.nl/2540f05en/.

"Life in Palestine." *Times* (London, England) 26 Feb. 1924. *The Times Digital Archive.* Web.

Linder, Douglas O. "The Trials of Oscar Wilde: An Account." *Famous Trials* https:// www.famous-trials.com/wilde/327-home. Accessed February 22, 2020.

Massey, William Thomas. *How Jerusalem Was Won Being the Record of Allenby's Campaign in Palestine* (2003). Available online via http://www.gutenberg.org/ cache/epub/10098/pg10098-images.html.

Mazza, Roberto. *Jerusalem from the Ottomans to the British.* London: I.B. Tauris, 2009.

Meer, T. van der. *Jonkheer mr. Jacob Anton Schorer (1866–1957) Een biografie van homoseksualiteit.* Amsterdam: Schorer Boeken, 2007.

Nasser, Issam. "'Biblification' in the Service of Colonialism: Jerusalem in Nineteenth-century Photography." *Third Text* 20, no. 374 (2006): 317–326.

Nassar, Issam. "Colonization by Imagination." In *City of Collision,* edited by P. Misselwitz, T. Rieniets, Z. Efrat, R. Khamaisi and R. Nasrallah, 222–226. Basel: Birkhäuser, 2006.

Nassar, Issam. "European Portrayals of Jerusalem: Religious Fascinations and Colonialist Imaginations." Lewiston, NY: Edwin Mellen Press, 2006.

Norris, Jacob "Exporting the Holy Land: Artisans and Merchant Migrants in Ottoman-Era Bethlehem", *Mashriq & Mahjar* 1, no. 2 (2013).

Phoning Photos by Wire: 5 Minutes to Send and 28 Minutes to Develop a Picture, Current Opinion (1913–1925); New York vol. LXXVII, (Jul-Dec 1924): 88.

Post, H. *Pillarization: An analysis of Dutch and Belgian society.* Aldershot [etc.]: Avebury, 1989.

Roden, Frederick. "Queer Christian: The Catholic Homosexual Apologia and Gay/ Lesbian Practice." *International Journal of Sexuality and Gender Studies* 6, no. 4 (Oct. 2001): 251–265.

Rubinstein, William., and Jolles, Michael A. *The Palgrave Dictionary of Anglo-Jewish History.* London: Palgrave MacMillan UK, 2011.

Sanchez Summerer, Karène and Zananiri, Sary., eds., *European Cultural Diplomacy and Arab Christians in Palestine, 1918–1948. Between Contention and Connection.* London: Palgrave Macmillan, 2020.

Scholten, François. *La Palestine Illustrée: Tableau Complet de la Terre Sainte par la Photographie, Évoquant les Souvenirs de la Bible, du Talmud et du Coran, et se Rapportant au Passé comme au présent, Vol I La porte d'entrée – Jaffa Vol II. Jaffa la Belle.* Paris: Jean Budry & Co., 1929.

Scholten, Frank. *Palästina – Bibel, Talmud, Koran. Eine vollständige Darstellung aller Textstellen in eigenen künstlerischen Aufnahmen aus Gegenwart und Vergangenheit des Heiligen Landes. Bd. I: DIE EINGANGSPFORTE. JAFFA. Mit 449 Abbildungen in*

Kupfertiefdruck, Bd. II: JAFFA, DIE SCHÖNE. Mit 371 Abbildungen in Kupfertiefdruck. Stuttgart: Hoffmann, 1930.

Scholten, Frank and G. Robinson Lees, eds. *Palestine Illustrated including References to Passages Illustrated in the Bible, the Talmud and the Koran, Vol. 1 Gate of Entrance, Vol. 2 Jaffa the Beautiful.* London: Green Longmans, 1931.

Scholten, Frank. *Palestina: Bijbel, Talmud, Koran. Een volledige illustratie van alle teksten door middel van eigen artistieke foto's uit het heden en verleden van het Heilige Land De toegangspoort Jaffa.* Leiden: Sijthoff, 1935.

Schweitzer, Albert., trans. W. Montgomery, *The Quest for the Historical Jesus: A Critical Study of its Progress from Reimarus to Wrede.* London: Adam and Charles Black, 1911.

Seikaly, *Men of Capital: Scarcity and Economy in Mandate Palestine.* Stanford: Stanford University Press, 2016.

Sharkey, Heather "History Rhymes? Late Ottoman Millets and Post-Ottoman Minorities in the Middle East", *International Journal of Middle East Studies* 50, no. 4 (2018): 760–764.

Sheehi, Stephen. *The Arab Imago: A Social History of Portrait Photography 1860–1910.* Princeton: Princeton University Press, 2016.

Stanton, Andrea L., "'This Is Jerusalem Calling': State Radio in Mandate Palestine", *Jerusalem Quarterly* 50, no. 2 (2012): 6–22.

Tamari, Salim. "The War Photography of Khalil Raad: Ottoman Modernity and the Biblical Gaze." *Jerusalem Quarterly* 52 (2013): 25–37.

The British Journal of Photography, February 29, 1924.

The Universe The Catholic Newspaper, February 29, 1924.

Turjman, Ihsan Salih, and Salim Tamari, *Year of the locust: a soldier's diary and the erasure of Palestine's Ottoman past.* Berkley: University of California Press, 2015.

Watenpaugh, Keith David. *Being Modern in the Middle East: Revolution, Nationalism, Colonialism, and the Arab Middle Class.* Princeton: Princeton University Press, 2012.

Waterschoot, Jos van, Bert Sliggers and Marita Mathijsen. *Onder De Toonbank: Pornografie En Erotica in De Nederlanden.* Amsterdam: Uitgeverij van Oorschot, 2018.

Wilde, Oscar. https://www.famous-trials.com/wilde/327-home.

Zananiri, Sary. "From Still to Moving Image: Shifting Representation of Jerusalem and Palestinians in the Western Biblical Imaginary." *Jerusalem Quarterly* 67 (2016): 64–81.

Zananiri, Sary. "Frank Scholten: landschap in het Brits Mandaat Palestina." *Fotografische Geheugen* (December 2018).

PART 3

After Effects: Methodologies, Approaches and Reconceptualising Photography

∴

CHAPTER 9

Edward Keith-Roach's Favourite Things: Indigenising National Geographic's Images of Mandatory Palestine

Yazan Kopty

My research on *National Geographic Magazine*'s 110-year coverage of Palestine began with an article in the January 1920 issue titled 'The Last Israelitish Blood Sacrifice: How the Vanishing Samaritans Celebrate Passover on Sacred Mount Gerizim' by John D. Whiting.[1] I came across the article while looking for photographs of Nablus and its environs to supplement the trove of family photographs that I had found at my grandparents' house that were taken in the first half of the twentieth century. I had dozens of images of private spaces, of family members posing, of celebrations and visits, and wanted to situate those domestic and familial scenes within the larger geographic, cultural and socio-political contexts. The first photograph in Whiting's article is of a stretch of road on the lower slopes of Mount Gerizim (Jarizīm), perched just above the southwestern corner of Nablus with Mount Ebal ('Aybāl) rising in the distance. Even though I had never been there or seen any photographs of that particular spot, I knew exactly where it was within the imagined geography that I had constructed from my family's stories and photographs.

While the main text of Whiting's article meandered through the history of the Nablus region and of the Samaritan community in particular, the accompanying photographs sped ahead to the Passover rituals that would be described later in the text. In the backgrounds of these photographs, I scanned the faces of the non-Samaritan onlookers – Muslim and Christian visitors from Nablus and the surrounding villages, including my family's ancestral village of Rafīdiyyā – for anyone who resembled the ancestors I knew from our family photographs. I had heard that as neighbours and friends of the small Samaritan community, my family attended the festival every year, and even though I did not find any definitive matches in the photographs, I imagined them into those moments nonetheless.

---

1 The article is advertised on the cover of the issue as "The Last Blood Sacrifice, a Samaritan Rite in Palestine".

© YAZAN KOPTY, 2021 | DOI:10.1163/9789004437944_010

Whiting and the editors' objective with the article was to weave together geographic descriptions, historical narratives, Biblical references and first-person travelogue to transport, inform and entertain their readers in 1920, while mine was to insert my family memories and stories into it decades later and to extract from it images, descriptions, and the lived knowledge that I was missing. I continued this work by identifying and collecting every article published in *National Geographic Magazine* about historic Palestine and began excavating them in a similar way.

Through this process, I began to notice recurring tones and tropes in the magazine's coverage of Palestine and Palestinians that made me wonder who were the writers, photographers and editors that represented Palestine to the magazine's readership, and what perspectives, prejudices, knowledge and opinions they brought to that work? These questions led me to the National Geographic Society archives where I began searching the feature files associated with each published work including background research, editorial notes and correspondences. During the course of my research, I was given access to the photographic archives of the Society which contain both the images published in the magazine and a much larger collection of images that were never published. It was my encounters *with* and *between* these two sets of images that shifted my project and its questions away from the makers of the magazine to those represented in its pages. My project *Imagining the Holy* became my attempt at creating a methodology to reframe National Geographic's images of Palestine from the perspective of the photographs' subjects, and to activate them as sites of indigenous knowledge, memory and power.

1   The Magazine

By the time that *National Geographic Magazine* began its coverage of Palestine in 1909, the publication had already begun to shift from its initial incarnation as a scholarly journal of the National Geographic Society towards the popular scientific-educational publication that it has been ever since. The Society was founded in January 1888 as a scientific institution modelled after geographical societies in Europe and the Americas, such as the Royal Geographic Society in London and the American Geographical Society in New York. As Tamar Rothenberg notes in her study of the first six decades of *National Geographic Magazine*, these geographical societies 'existed as centres of geographical information, broadly construed to include commercial, botanical, geological and anthropological angles, among others, with emphasis on knowledge about and derived from exploration'.[2] In October 1888, the Society published the first issue of its magazine with an announcement asserting its mission 'to increase and diffuse geographic knowledge', and explaining the *raison d'être* of its magazine as 'one of the means of accomplishing these purposes'.[3] During its first decade, the Society's focus on professional and academic geography was evident in the makeup of its membership and the magazine's list of featured writers, both of which included a core of scientifically trained geographers. By the turn of the century though, the magazine had evolved into a more accessible, friendly and visual publication, and with it, the Society's membership began to boom.

In their seminal work on the magazine's influence on American culture, Catherine Lutz and Jane Collins examine the surge in the magazine's popularity within the wider context of mass circulation magazines at the turn of the century and the ways that it successfully positioned itself on the border between science and pleasure.[4] The membership numbers alone testify to this success: from 1,300 members in 1898 to 2,300 in 1903; from 3,400 to 11,000 in 1905 alone; and by 1912, over 100,000 due-paying members.[5] Internally, the rise in the magazine's prominence and popularity coincided with the beginning of the half-century-long tenure of its most formative editor, Gilbert H. Grosvenor (1899 to 1954);[6] externally, it was driven by the Spanish-American War of 1898 and national interest in the American takeover of Spain's colonial possessions of Cuba, Puerto Rico and the Philippines, and annexation of the islands of Hawaii. As John Hyde, the magazine's first editor, remarked in the June 1899 issue, 'It is doubtful if the study of any branch of human knowledge ever before received so sudden and powerful a stimulus as the events of the past year have given to the study of geography'.[7] *National Geographic Magazine* was eager and perfectly poised to meet this demand.

While many of the places the magazine covered were new to American readers – including the United States' new colonial possessions – Palestine was both *familiar to* and *cherished by* its mostly white and Protestant readership, at

---

2 Tamar Y. Rothenberg, *Presenting America's World: Strategies of Innocence in National Geographic Magazine, 1888–1945* (Hampshire: Ashgate Publishing Limited, 2007), 26.

3 "Announcement," *National Geographic Magazine* 1, no. 1 (October 1888): i.

4 Catherine A. Lutz and Jane L. Collins, *Reading National Geographic* (Chicago: The University of Chicago Press, 1993).

5 Julie A. Tuason, "The Ideology of Empire in National Geographic Magazine's Coverage of the Philippines, 1898–1908," *Geographical Review* 89, no. 1 (Jan 1999): 38.

6 Lutz, *Reading National Geographic*, 20–24.

7 John Hyde, "The National Geographic Society," *National Geographic Magazine* 10, no. 6 (June 1899): 222.

least in its Biblified form, imagined and represented in literature, art, Passion Plays and nativity scenes well before the invention of photography. This inherited Biblical lens through which the magazine's writers, photographers, editors and readers viewed Palestine created a foundational tension between what was in contemporary Palestine and what they were hoping to find there.

2   The Present-Day Inhabitants of the Land

The first mention of Palestine in the pages of *National Geographic Magazine* is in a December 1909 feature by Franklin E. Hoskins titled 'The Route Over Which Moses Led The Children of Israel Out of Egypt'. In his introduction, he recounts:

> A few years ago a young woman about to visit the Holy Land called on an old lady friend who loved her Bible and read it frequently from beginning to end, and told her that she soon hoped to see Jerusalem, Bethlehem, Galilee and all the places associated with the life of Christ. The old lady put down her work, removed her silver-rimmed spectacles, and exclaimed: "Well now! I knew that all those places were in the Bible, but I never thought of their being on the earth!"[8]

Hoskins, a Presbyterian missionary based in Beirut, quickly assures his readers that indeed 'the Desert of the Exodus has an actual existence upon the face of the earth, and that the route of the Exodus is being mapped and studied and photographed by enthusiastic scholars and travellers'.[9] In Hoskins' account of his forty-day journey across Sinai to 'earthly Jerusalem', the mandate of the Society vis-a-vis geographic knowledge and the stories from his Bible are presented as inseparable and mutually reinforcing. Indeed, the purpose of his account is to prove the veracity of the Book of Exodus through his geographical observations of 'the almost changeless Peninsula of Sinai'.[10] In the decades that followed, several other magazine contributors wrote features that echoed the goal of Hoskins' 1909 piece: to use the contemporary people and places of Palestine to illustrate and prove the Bible.

---

8   Franklin E. Hoskins, "The Route Over Which Moses Led the Children of Israel Out of Egypt," *National Geographic Magazine* 20, no. 12 (December 1909): 1011.
9   Ibid.
10   Ibid., 1038.

This approach to Palestine places *National Geographic Magazine*'s early coverage within the vast and abundant genre of 'Holy Land' travelogues written by Europeans and North Americans from the mid-nineteenth and early twentieth centuries. Alexander Schölch describes this literary landscape as part of a religious-cultural 'opening up' of Palestine that accompanied European economic and political penetration of the region beginning around 1831. Schölch discusses not only the records written by 'missionaries, pilgrims, and 'Palestine explorers', but also writings by national associations with religious and Biblical-archaeological interests in Palestine that had 'confessional, scientific, and political orientations and which had their own publications'.[11] While *National Geographic Magazine* was not one of these pilgrim-tourist travelogues or Holy Land-focused journals, its coverage of Palestine overlapped with both while reaching a much larger and broader audience than either in the United States. Like these works, the first decade of Palestine coverage portrayed contemporary Palestine primarily as a land of Biblical ruins and residues, and viewed everything in sight through a religious lens in an effort to marry a Euro-American Protestant imaginary to actual places and populations.[12]

Issam Nassar explains this 'biblification' of Palestine in his discussion of nineteenth century photography of Jerusalem and draws links between the photographic practices that were part of this genre of Holy Land exploration and European colonial expansion.[13] He argues that these practices which included emptying landscapes of people, a focus on sites featured in the Bible, the mislabelling and misrepresenting of people and places, and the posing of native people as Bible characters, as contributing 'to the shaping in the European mind of an image of Palestine as a dream land ... 'waiting to be reclaimed both spiritually and physically".[14] British and Zionist colonisation of Palestine and the ongoing erasure and subjugation of Palestinians as necessities of those projects cannot be understood without examining this genre of literature and photography which helped inspire and fuel both projects.

---

11   Alexander Schölch, *Palestine in Transformation, 1856–1882,* trans. M.C. Gerrity and W.C. Young (Washington, D.C.: Institute for Palestine Studies, 1993), 60.

12   Sometimes quite literally as evidenced by the titles of two features written by John D. Whiting in March 1914 "Village Life in the Holy Land: A description of the life of the present-day inhabitants of Palestine, showing how, in many cases, their customs are the same as in Bible times" and in December 1915 "Jerusalem's Locust Plague: Being a Description of the Recent Locust Influx into Palestine, and Comparing Same with Ancient Locust Invasions as Narrated in the Old World's History Book, the Bible."

13   Issam Nassar, "'Biblification' in the Service of Colonialism: Jerusalem in Nineteenth-century Photography," *Third Text* 20, nos. 3/4 (2006): 317–326.

14   Nassar, "'Biblification' in the Service of Colonialism," 326.

In the case of *National Geographic Magazine's* coverage, the impulse to 'biblify' Palestine was at times at odds with the magazine's ethnographic interests. An early example of this tension can be seen in the March 1914 issue in an article by John D. Whiting titled 'Village Life in the Holy Land: A description of the life of the present-day inhabitants of Palestine, showing how, in many cases, their customs are the same as in Bible times'.[15] Here, instead of erasing or minimising the native people of Palestine, they are brought to the forefront of Whiting's storytelling, but with the intention of using them as Biblical reenactors rather than protagonists in their own right. In a section titled 'The Land, Not the People, Conserves the Old Customs', Whiting asserts that 'One cannot become even tolerably acquainted with Palestine without perceiving that it is the *land* that has preserved the ancient customs. Its present-day-inhabitants, who have nothing in common with the modern Jews who crowd Jerusalem, are still perpetuating the life of Abraham and the customs and ways of the people who lived here at the time of Christ'.[16] In order to explain how these mostly Arab and mostly Muslim people fit into the static Biblical framework that he and his readers have in mind, Whiting offers this theory which at once fetishises villagers as symbols of Biblical continuity while disinheriting Palestinians at the same time: they look and live like the people of the Bible, but they are not the descendants of those people.

In a companion piece published in the January 1937 issue titled 'Bedouin Life in Bible Lands: The Nomads of the 'Houses of Hair' Offer Unstinted Hospitality to an American',[17] Whiting similarly punctuates his account of Bedouin life in Palestine with Biblical references in an effort to dress his descriptions of their contemporary cultures as illustrations of the Bible. Unlike the way he frames the *fallāhīn* (villagers) in his first story, here Whiting calls back to Bible-era Bedouins as direct ancestors of his subjects and even uses examples of contemporary social and material culture to explain Biblical episodes and details.

In both cases, Whiting's commentary proffers many of the ambiguities relating to the portrayal of Palestinian indigeneity in the Western Biblical imaginary during interwar years.[18] In the middle of the two decades that separated his village and Bedouin stories, Whiting wrote to Dr. Franklin L. Fisher, the magazine's Chief of the Illustrations Division, in 1928: 'I have planned to

---

15   John D. Whiting, "Village Life in the Holy Land," *National Geographic Magazine* 25, no. 3 (March 1914): 249–314.

16   Whiting, "Village Life in the Holy Land," 251–253.

17   John D. Whiting, "Bedouin Life in Bible Lands," *National Geographic Magazine* 71, no. 1 (January 1937): 58–83.

18   Sary Zananiri "From Still to Moving Images: Shifting Representation of Jerusalem and Palestinians in the Western Biblical Imaginary," *Jerusalem Quarterly* 67 (2016): 73–74.

write 'Bedouin Life in the Holy Land' as a sort of mate to 'Village Life' that you long ago used. Other stories such as 'City Life', 'The Fishermen of Galilee', 'The Talisman' etc. have suggested themselves'.[19] It is unclear why an urban life story never materialised, but it would have offered an interesting case study in regard to biblification, the way it ascribes/undermines Palestinian indigeneity, and the class dimensions that both entail.

The question of Palestinian indigeneity would remain unresolved in the magazine for many decades to come, informed and complicated by its dependence on Biblical archetypes to drive its Palestine storytelling. As recently as June 1992, in an aptly named article titled 'Who are the Palestinians?', Tad Szulc asserts that, 'The ancestors of today's Palestinians appeared along the south-eastern Mediterranean coast more than five millennia ago and settled down to a life of fishing, farming, and herding. But they also endured wars with Israelites; domination from Assyrians, Chaldeans, Persians, and Romans; and eventually 400 years of rule by the Ottoman Turks'.[20] On the same page as this statement is a caption for a photograph from inside the Ibrahimi Mosque that explains, 'Jews and Arabs share a common ancestor at Hebron's Tomb of the Patriarchs (right), where Judaism's first families – Abraham and son Isaac, their wives Sara and Rebecca – are said to be buried. Abraham fathered another son, Ishmael, from whom Arabs claim descent. Nearly all Palestinians are Arab, and most are Muslim'. A few pages later, Szulc mentions King David and his battles with the Philistines, who he says are 'among the forefathers of the Palestinians'.[21] These assertions are made matter-of-factly without an indication of complexity or controversy, or any attempt to reconcile them. The only consistent logic between the three origin stories is that they are anchored in Biblical hagiography, rather than historiography. The inability of the article to coherently answer the question it poses in its title is both the result, and another example, of the magazine's century of biblified coverage and the limitations of this framework.

Even today, contemporary Palestine is rarely mentioned in the magazine or any of National Geographic's content without at least a nod to its Biblical past, often in juxtaposition to the political realities of modern-day Palestine/Israel, as though the mythologised history recounted in the Bible is essential to understanding its contemporary condition.[22]

---

19   J.D.W. to F.L.F., 3 July 1928, NGS Library and Archives.

20   Tad Szulc, "Who are the Palestinians?" *National Geographic Magazine* 181, no. 6 (June 1992): 92.

21   Ibid., 102.

22   Interestingly, while Palestine cannot be mentioned without evoking the Bible, sites and events of Biblical interest can be mentioned without Palestine, such as the 2017–2019

3   The Reconquest of the Holy Land

National Geographic Magazine's second decade of coverage of Palestine coincided with the beginning of the British Mandate, adding an explicit promotion of colonialism to its Bible-tethered storytelling. In Charles W. Whitehair's October 1918 article 'An Old Jewel in the Proper Setting: An Eyewitness's Account of the Reconquest of the Holy Land by Twentieth Century Crusaders',[23] readers are given a front-row seat to the British military conquest and occupation of Ottoman Palestine. Whitehair, who apparently travelled to Palestine at the invitation of General Allenby,[24] plays the role of embedded war correspondent while using his account to justify and celebrate the beginning of British colonial rule in the 'Holy Land'. It is clear in the article that he is not only an eye-witness to this acceleration of the British colonial project in Palestine, but an active agent in its propaganda. He praises the British generals, disparages the Turks and Germans, claims that the local population has been freed from tyranny, and that the land has been rescued from misuse and is promised to the Jewish people. Whitehair ends by stating that 'Palestine today is beginning a new chapter of her history, which is entirely due to the courageous and wise administration of her British liberators'.[25] This statement exemplifies how *National Geographic Magazine* would go on to portray the next two decades of British colonialism as a force of modernisation, economic progress and religious redemption. Over the course of the Mandate period, Zionist colonisation would come to share credit for this trifecta of progress in the magazine's coverage until the end of British rule when the mantle is passed to the State of Israel as the embattled, pioneer nation making the dessert bloom. Unlike the biblified lens applied uniquely to Palestine, the magazine's support for British colonialism was not a unique instance of pro-imperialist coverage.

The Spanish-American War was a watershed moment in the history of the magazine, both in terms of rapidly expanding its readership and in marking the beginning of several decades of pro-imperial coverage. As Julie A. Tuason

---

Tomb of Christ exhibition at the National Geographic Museum in Washington D.C. which did not mention Palestine/Palestinians (or Israel/Israelis) in any of the text-based or audio-visual information about Jerusalem and the renovation of the Church of the Holy Sepulchre, including explanations about the indigenous *sabt en-nour* (Saturday of Fire) ceremony celebrated by Palestinian Christians.

23   Charles Whitehair, "An Old Jewel in the Proper Setting: An Eyewitness's Account of the Reconquest of the Holy Land by Twentieth Century Crusaders," *National Geographic Magazine* 34, no. 4 (October 1918): 325–344.

24   "The Red Cross in Palestine," *The Red Cross Magazine* 14 (1919): 60.

25   Whitehair, "An Old Jewel in the Proper Setting: An Eyewitness's Account of the Reconquest of the Holy Land by Twentieth Century Crusaders," 344.

explains in her examination of the magazine's coverage of the Philippines between 1898 and 1908, *National Geographic Magazine*'s status as a reputable scientific publication allowed it to 'effectively proffer an essentially imperialist agenda under the guise of scientific progress'.[26] Whether it was American imperialism in the Philippines or British colonialism in Palestine, the magazine's outlook on Anglo-American colonial projects was the same.

In the context of the unfolding colonial project that would result in the ethnic cleansing of Palestine,[27] Whiting's reference to Palestinians as 'the present-day inhabitants of the land' takes on an even more sinister tone. The dislocation of Palestinians from their history by *National Geographic Magazine* and others in order to satisfy the logic of Palestine as Bible Land should be understood as foundational – not exceptional or incidental – to the success of British and Zionist subjugation and displacement of Palestinians.

Most often, the magazine's support for the British colonial project in Palestine manifested itself in the tone and scope of its coverage rather than praise for specific policies or actions. Yet a closer look reveals a symbiotic relationship between the magazine and the British colonial administration. This relationship is most evident in two features that were written by Major Edward Keith-Roach while he served in the colonial administration, the first in December 1927 when he was the Deputy District Commissioner of Jerusalem and the second in April 1934 when he was the District Commissioner of Northern Palestine. The 1927 article titled 'The Pageant of Jerusalem: The Capital of the Land of Three Great Faiths Is Still the Holy City for Christian, Moslem, and Jew',[28] is of particular interest as it was written by Keith-Roach and illustrated mostly with photographs taken by the magazine's most famous staff photographer at the time, Maynard Owen Williams.

In her chapter about Williams and his 30 years as *National Geographic Magazine*'s chief foreign correspondent, Rothenberg notes that if 'someone were looking for a representative figure to embody the physiognomic and cultural essence of 'National Geographic land' in the early-to-mid twentieth century, Maynard Owen Williams would be a prime candidate'.[29] She describes him precisely: 'White, Anglo-Saxon, Protestant, big and athletic, well-educated

26   Tuason, "The Ideology of Empire," 50.

27   See Ilan Pappe, *The Ethnic Cleansing of Palestine* (London: Oneworld Publications, 2006) and Nur Masalha, *The Palestine Nakba: Decolonising History, Narrating the Subaltern, Reclaiming Memory* (London and New York: Zed Books, 2012).

28   Edward Keith-Roach, "The Pageant of Jerusalem: The Capital of the Land of Three Great Faiths Is Still the Holy City for Christian, Moslem, and Jew," *National Geographic Magazine* 52, no. 6 (1927): 635–681.

29   Rothenberg, *Presenting America's World*, 99.

and bespectacled, friendly and affable'. Before joining the magazine as one of its first staff correspondents, Williams worked as a missionary teacher in Beirut and Hangchow and as a foreign correspondent for the *Christian Herald*. His most famous assignment for *National Geographic Magazine* was his coverage of the Citroën-Haardt Trans-Asiatic Expedition from Beirut to Beijing in 1931. With some proficiency in Arabic and years of experience in the Levant, he contributed text and photographs to ten of the 26 features that included coverage of Palestine between 1919 and 1952. Despite frequent disagreements with the editorial staff of the magazine, Williams believed in the potential of *National Geographic Magazine* to foster international brotherhood, and his role as a mediator between the magazine's readers and the beauty of the world and its peoples. In this way, Rothenberg notes, Williams' work not only supported, but also embodied 'the *Geographic's* apolitical pretensions and humanist pronouncements'[30] even as the magazine was implicitly and explicitly supporting imperialism, capitalist penetration and Euro-American supremacy at home and abroad.

In her review of Edward Keith-Roach's memoirs *Pasha of Jerusalem: Memoirs of a District Commissioner under the British Mandate*, Jane Power describes Keith-Roach as 'an almost stereotypical British district administrator: decent and conscientious; concerned for the natives and interested in their customs and surroundings, but liable to misinterpret them; secure in western cultural superiority; willing to improvise a solution to any problem'.[31] One of twelve children of a Gloucester vicar, Keith-Roach went to India as a young man and started his career at the Mercantile Bank at the height of the British Raj. While serving in the British-officered Egyptian Army during World War I, Keith-Roach was stationed in Sudan where he learned Arabic and served as District Commissioner of Eastern Darfur. In 1919, he joined the colonial military administration in Palestine where he remained until 1943 as part of the Mandate civil administration, earning him the nickname 'Pasha of Jerusalem' by Reuters for what they saw as his even-handed dealings with both Jews and Arabs in Palestine. The fact that this nickname was given by Reuters and not by the indigenous or immigrant communities in Palestine is important to note, as is the fact that he styled himself as such in the title of his memoir. Keith-Roach's confidence in his intimate and authoritative knowledge of Palestine is not only apparent in the two Palestine features he wrote for *National Geographic*

---

30   Ibid., 103.

31   Jane Power, Review of *Pasha of Jerusalem: Memoirs of a District Commissioner Under the British Mandate*, by Edward Keith-Roach and Paul Eedle, *Middle East Studies Association Bulletin* 32, no. 2 (1998), 270–271.

Magazine,[32] but also the two travel handbooks he edited with Harry Luke, *The Handbook of Palestine* (1922)[33] and *The Handbook of Palestine and Trans-Jordan* (1930).[34] In all of these texts, Keith-Roach displays no qualms in speaking for and about Palestine and its people, like a benevolent pasha describing the subjects and territory under his rule.

Keith-Roach's relationship with National Geographic began in the early 1920s when he met Gilbert Grosvenor at a luncheon in Washington D.C. Grosvenor, a high-society figure and known Anglophile, was fascinated by Keith-Roach's stories from his postings and would later publish the first of Keith-Roach's contributions to the magazine in January 1924 about his time in Darfur titled 'Adventures Among the 'Lost Tribes of Islam' in Eastern Darfur: A Personal Narrative of Exploring, Mapping, and Setting Up a Government in the Anglo-Egyptian Sudan Borderland'. In addition to his seemingly friendly relationship with Grosvenor, it is clear from his letters to and from Williams that the men shared a close professional relationship while working on the December 1927 issue and that Keith-Roach had a significant influence over Williams' experience in Palestine and the subsequent coverage that came out of it.

Firstly, Keith-Roach facilitated Williams' shooting trips around Palestine by supplying assistants and most probably transportation and introductions.[35] This offers some insight into the access that Williams had, how he might have been received by the subjects of his photographs, and the circumstances and power dynamics of his interactions with them. Secondly, it is also clear that Keith-Roach was very sensitive to his official position as Deputy District Commissioner and saw his article as both a potential liability and an opportunity to increase his influence. In a correction to one of the captions written by Williams, he says, 'The great thing in describing a man of importance in no circumstances, should you draw attention to either his bigotry, his conservatism or anything which may detract from the dignity of his own religious thought. For example, Rabbi Kuk only shows half his decoration, as he does not like to

---

32 His second feature on Palestine titled "Changing Palestine" was published in April 1934 when he was District Commissioner of Northern Palestine.

33 Harry Charles Luke and Edward Keith-Roach, *The Handbook of Palestine* (London: MacMillan, 1922).

34 Harry Charles Luke and Edward Keith-Roach, *The Handbook of Palestine and Trans-Jordan* (London: MacMillan, 1930). Salim Tamari notes that the 1922 handbook was written primarily as a military manual, but that it also targeted civilian visitors to Palestine. See Salim Tamari, "Shifting Ottoman Conceptions of Palestine, Part 1: Filistin Risalesi and the two Jamals," *Jerusalem Quarterly* 47 (2011): 33.

35 M.O.W. to E.K.-R., 12 September 1927, NGS Library and Archives.

be seen wearing the cross. Rabbi Meier does not. There is however, no necessity or need to draw the public's attention to this idiosyncrasy.'[36] While on the one hand, he worried about offending individuals of high rank, he also saw the opportunity to use his article to boost his own reputation and promote it as a form of soft diplomacy between his office and those same individuals and important institutions in Palestine.

After the completion of the article, Keith-Roach requested that 27 copies of the December 1927 issue be shipped to him in order to be gifted to high-ranking members of Jerusalem's social, political, and religious elites.[37] In another letter the following month, Keith-Roach even suggested that the Society prepare bound copies that could be presented to the President of the United States, His Majesty the King, the Secretary of State for the Colonies and the High Commissioner.[38] Keith-Roach's eagerness to promote his feature among the most important and powerful and the Society's eagerness to do the same indicate both a proximity to power and an aspiration for greater prestige and influence. Besides this elite list of recipients, the greater influence that Keith-Roach and Williams had was on *National Geographic Magazine*'s readership which reached over a million members by the end of 1927.

The final article is structured as a grand walking tour of Jerusalem beginning outside the walls of the Old City near the citadel where women from the surrounding villages were selling their agricultural produce in the morning and ending at the Damascus Gate where the 'Last Post' can be heard being played from the police camp on Mount Scopus as night falls. Little effort is spent to explain or justify British rule or the author's position vis-a-vis the places and people he describes. Instead, the benevolence of the colonial regime is suggested in the fanfare of multi-ethnic, multi-religious coexistence and the seamless mingling of ancient and modern. Jerusalem, 'where eras jostle one another as races do'.[39] This vision of and for Jerusalem echoes that of the Pro-Jerusalem Society in its paternalistic and charitable tone towards the improvement of public works while simultaneously fetishising and codifying the supposedly authentic and ancient. Keith-Roach's approach is less didactic though as he revels in the exciting sensory experience of walking through Jerusalem, sharing his detailed knowledge of each trade, place, dress, and

---

36   E.K.-R. to M.O.W., 12 August 1927, NGS Library and Archives.
37   E.K.-R. to M.O.W., 20 August 1927, NGS Library and Archives.
38   E.K.-R. to M.O.W., September 1927, NGS Library and Archives.
39   Keith-Roach, "The Pageant of Jerusalem: The Capital of the Land of Three Great Faiths Is Still the Holy City for Christian, Moslem, and Jew," 641.

scene. Interspersed between Keith-Roach's beautiful and energetic descriptions are photographs mostly by the American Colony Photographers, Khalīl Ra'ad and, of course, Williams.

As a reminder of the intimate relationship between photography and colonialism, the story opens with an aerial photograph of Jerusalem taken by the British Air Ministry; a grid system is noted along the top and left margins with corresponding coordinates in the caption that mark Jerusalem's most important sites. The American Colony and Ra'ad photographs come from each studio's respective commercial catalogues of Holy Land photographs, including semi-posed, naturalistic scenes and vistas of daily life. Williams photographs, on the other hand, are mostly posed portraits, the type of character studies that he was most known for and which marked both his and *National Geographic Magazine*'s style. Exactly as Keith-Roach emphasises Jerusalem's diversity in his text, Williams' portraits include a representative sample of every religion, ethnicity and rank of Jerusalem's inhabitants.

While Keith-Roach notes in the article that all roads in Palestine lead to Jerusalem, his descriptions detach it from the rest of the country save the list of specialised agricultural produce brought from different parts of Palestine to be sold in Jerusalem: 'luscious oranges from Jaffa, grapes from Hebron, apricots from Bethlehem and Beit Jala, nectarines and peaches from near-by villages, bananas from Jericho, and enormous watermelons from the coast near Caesarea'.[40] And, while the ethnic and religious makeup of Jerusalem was indeed unique to Palestine at that time, there is no indication of what the rest of the country looked like or how Jerusalem was linked to it, either geographically, economically, culturally or politically. In Keith-Roach's telling, Britain's colonial power (and all the violence and subjugation that it entailed) gets subsumed by the city's internationalism as if the British are just one of the many groups of people who roam the narrow and ancient alleyways of the Holy City rather than being the ones who forcibly rule it. As Keith-Roach writes in his last letter to Gilbert H. Grosvenor about his 1927 piece: 'Jerusalem, belonging as it were not only to Palestine but to the whole world, one cannot but be sincerely grateful for the manner in which you have been able to put these photographic records before your readers, and I hope that my article may not prove unworthy of its distinguished place'.[41] Keith-Roach rightly emphasised the importance of the magazine's photographs in driving its popular appeal and storytelling power, in this instance working in tandem with his text to

---

40   Ibid., 637.
41   E.K.-R. to G.G., November 1927, NGS Library and Archives.

de-emphasise Jerusalem's Arab Palestinian character and popularise its image as a timeless, global and *ownable* place.

In this feature, in particular, the published images closely reflect the perspective and narrative of Keith-Roach's text; this was not always the case in *National Geographic Magazine*, and even when it was, images could be (and often were) viewed on their own. Examining the magazine's published photographs this way becomes even more interesting when encountering them within National Geographic's larger photographic archive which includes not only the photographs that were printed in the magazine, but the millions that were not.

4   **Edward Keith-Roach's Favourite Things**

There are over 12 million objects in the photographic archive of the National Geographic Society. The archive itself began as the editorial archive of *National Geographic Magazine* and the majority of the photographs it contains are images that were collected or commissioned by the magazine. Most were never published. Today, the archive remains among the foremost records of natural and human history, containing images from every corner, terrain, depth and altitude of the world, as well as many from beyond our planet. The archive holds a vast collection of images from Mandatory Palestine, including 3,000 black-and-white prints and almost 200 autochrome plates. The majority of these images were taken by magazine staff or commissioned photographers, but the collection also includes many photographs taken by amateur and professional photographers who gifted, sent samples, or sold their photographs to National Geographic. The largest share of the collection are images made by Maynard Owen Williams.

The black-and-white photographs are gelatine silver prints, dry-mounted on linen boards, with a typed caption pasted on the back, and at least two stamped dates indicating when the photograph was received by the archive and when it was indexed. In the case of Williams' photographs, the majority were received in 1927 with detailed captions that include a mixture of personal anecdotal narratives, explanations of local customs and details, and general information about locations, events and subjects. In very few cases, and only with individuals of religious, political or social importance, subjects are identified by name. Although thousands of people are represented in the images which cover a wide range of subjects, themes and geographies, only one perspective is seen and heard: that of Williams through his camera and his captions.

FIGURE 9.1   'Zerin, formally Jezreel, city of Ahab and Jezebel, looks off past Little Hermon to
Nazareth and its well, here seen, is not far from the road, but it is seldom visited
by travelers. The costume of the women is unusually colorful but I could not get
them to pose for color plates. In the background are the Galilean hills west of
Nazareth. Palestine.' Unpublished photograph and caption by Maynard Owen
Williams, 1927
IMAGE COURTESY OF NATIONAL GEOGRAPHIC SOCIETY LIBRARY
AND ARCHIVES

As I began exploring the collection through Williams' eyes and eavesdropping
on his one-sided conversations with the magazine editors and staff who were
the primary audience for his captions, I found it difficult to engage with the
photographs beyond the frames and frameworks that he had set. This was partially due to the sheer number and high aesthetic quality of the images, and
the detailed and immersive captions that accompanied them. There was so
much to engage with that was authored by Williams, that I felt trapped in a
Palestine that could only be viewed through his eyes. Within that space, the
most I could do was critique what he chose to photograph and write (in particular, the biblification of people and places, as well as frequent examples
of misogynistic, racist and racialised language); mine his images and texts
for details that I wanted to explore further; and corroborate or challenge the
information that he presented. Unexpectedly, it was the presence of Edward

FIGURE 9.2 'Photograph of Abdel Kader Shihabi, Official Calligrapher to the Government of
Palestine, and the finest calligrapher in this part of the world. Among Moslems,
calligraphy is the highest form of art and the best work commands prices for
which very fair painters would gladly do a portrait or a landscape. In this view
are shown some famous samples of calligraphy, some of them very old and many
of them very valuable. ($200 to $700). Jerusalem.' Unpublished photograph and
caption by Maynard Owen Williams, 1927. A portrait of Shihabi posing alone in
his studio was published with Keith-Roach's December 1927 article
IMAGE COURTESY OF NATIONAL GEOGRAPHIC SOCIETY LIBRARY
AND ARCHIVES

Keith-Roach in a few of Williams' unpublished photographs that helped
me traverse his frames and frameworks and encounter the images in a different way.

Edward Keith-Roach is present in five sets of images taken by Williams. He
appears first as a subject in two sets of photographs, one with his Arabian pony
and another with his wife in their 'Bean Twelve' car. He is present again in
relation to another photographed subject, Keith-Roach's personal *qawās* (body
guard/ceremonial armed guard) who posed for portraits on the grounds of
Government House in a military-style uniform and outside of the American
Colony in local dress. And in two other instances where Keith-Roach's desires
and opinions are recorded in Williams' captions: the first, a pair of images
of a traffic policeman outside the Jaffa Gate in which Williams notes that

FIGURE 9.3 'Governor Keith-Roach's personal *qawās* wearing a head scarf and camel hair crown, outside the American Colony at Jerusalem, Palestine.' Unpublished photograph and caption by Maynard Owen Williams, 1927
IMAGE COURTESY OF NATIONAL GEOGRAPHIC SOCIETY LIBRARY AND ARCHIVES

Keith-Roach is 'very desirous' of a photograph of him and that he would like a photograph included with his story, and second, in series of portraits of a young woman taken at the American Colony as Williams notes: 'A young Christian Arab girl, whom Governor Keith-Roach thinks the prettiest girl in Palestine, wearing the Bethlehem costume'.

These series of photographs were mixed between the hundreds of other photographs taken by Williams in Palestine between 1926–1927, disconnected from Keith-Roach's published article. Indeed, before I read the captions that mentioned Keith-Roach, I had not connected the creation of this larger body of photographs to Williams' travels through Palestine for that particular feature – the same series of trips that Keith-Roach helped facilitate and influence. Even without Keith-Roach's assistance or direction, Williams' travels across Palestine would involve vastly unequal interactions between the American photographer and his local subjects. Connecting Keith-Roach to the rest of Williams' photographs further emphasises and exemplifies the intense concentration of power that is both documented and maintained in the National Geographic archives.

Understanding these connections also transformed my encounter with the photographs that were published in the 1927 issue. Whereas in the magazine, the photographs of Jerusalem had helped isolate and detach it from the rest of Palestine (geographically, culturally, politically, etc.), in the archive they were easily placed back into the larger collection that they were pulled from and re-encountered within the whole. Prompted by Keith-Roach's spectre, I could see more clearly how images could be reimagined through their placement, presentation and reception, regardless of their geneses.

In *Civil Imagination: A Political Ontology of Photography* Ariella Azoulay offers a useful framework that distinguishes between 'the photographed event' and the 'event of photography'.[42] *The photographed event* – the policeman directing traffic in the road, the *qawās* posing for his portrait, the young woman posing in Bethlehem dress – is distinct from the *event of photography*, encounter(s) with the photograph itself. Azoulay argues that even the knowledge that a photograph exists, extends the *event of photography* around it as the viewer or potential viewer encounters it in person or in their imagination. Furthermore, while the political circumstances and power relations that led to *the photographed event* are fixed and frozen (and documented in the image),

---

42   Ariella Azoulay, *Civil Imagination: A Political Ontology of Photography*, trans. L. Bethlehem (London: Verso, 2012).

the political circumstances and power relations around the photograph and encounters with it are not.

In the case of Williams' photographs taken in Mandate Palestine in collaboration with Keith-Roach, the *photographed events* were determined by a complicated power landscape that included technological, economic, cultural and political dimensions. This is true of all of Williams' photographs, but for those images that were eventually published as part of the feature authored by Keith-Roach, they were also used to fortify and expand that same power landscape by extending the *event of photography* into every living room in which the December 1927 issue was read. For the majority of Williams' images which were not published, the *event of photography* remained dormant while access to the photographs and the knowledge of their very existence was suspended to all but a few people, until I had my own encounters with the images.

Take for example the photographs of the Jaffa Gate policeman. It is clear from Williams' unpublished captions that he took the photograph at Keith-Roach's request. The published caption says: 'THE TRAFFIC POLICEMAN OUTSIDE THE JAFFA GATE: Common sense rather than mere regulations is needed for the complex task of directing the movements of animals, people, and machines in the throbbing life of Jerusalem'.[43] Encountering the same image in the archive offers a slightly different interpretation, one focused on why the image was captured (at Keith-Roach's behest), rather than what it might illustrate. In the archive, the viewer can only guess why Keith-Roach was interested in this image and might arrive at a different reading, perhaps one about Palestinian modernity that is separate from an ancient-modern dichotomy or a suggestion of colonial improvement.

The portraits of the young woman in Bethlehem dress is another example. The published caption that accompanies her black-and-white photograph in Keith-Roach's article says, 'A CHRISTIAN GIRL OF JERUSALEM IN BETHLEHEM COSTUME: The coin-spangled, high tarboosh, which denotes the married woman, usually is hidden under the spotless veil'.[44] A few pages later in Williams' photo-essay which follows the Keith-Roach article, the autochrome of the same young woman is captioned as, 'MANY AMERICAN VISITORS TO JERUSALEM WILL RECOGNIZE THIS GIRL: A young Christian student in a handicrafts class at the American Colony is here wearing the Bethlehem

---

43   Keith-Roach, "Pageant of Jerusalem," 649.
44   Keith-Roach, "Pageant of Jerusalem," 643.

FIGURE 9.4 'Major Keith-Roach is very desirous of a picture of the Jaffa Gate traffic cop.
I show him here amid such traffic as passes. The view is north up Jaffa Road from
near the walls of the Citadel. Jerusalem, Palestine.' Unpublished photograph and
caption by Maynard Owen Williams, 1927. A closer view of this policeman
taken from a different angle was published with Keith-Roach's December 1927
article
IMAGE COURTESY OF NATIONAL GEOGRAPHIC SOCIETY LIBRARY
AND ARCHIVES

costume'.[45] From these published images and captions, the magazine's readers
would have no idea about Keith-Roach's desiring gaze, which also may have
influenced Williams' decision to take the photograph in the first place.

The portraits of this young woman match a series of unpublished portraits of another young woman at the American Colony wearing an identical
outfit. In the captions of the second woman's images, there is no mention
of Keith-Roach, but she is referred to as a servant working at the American
Colony. From close analysis of both series of photographs, it appears that the
two young women are wearing the same exact dress and headdress, suggesting that this was a costume that both chose, or were asked, to pose in. Widad
Kawar, the world's foremost expert in Palestinian textiles and dress, has identified the outfit as a low-quality Bethlehem-style dress and headpiece that would

---

45   Maynard Owen Williams, "Color Records from the Changing Life of the Holy Land,"
National Geographic Magazine 52, no. 6 (1927): 696.

FIGURE 9.5 'A young Christian Arab girl, whom Governor Keith-Roach thinks the prettiest
girl in Palestine, wearing the Bethlehem costume. Jerusalem.' Unpublished
photograph and caption by Maynard Owen Williams, 1927 A similar portrait
of this young woman was published in black-and-white with Keith-Roach's
December 1927 article and another in colour in Williams' companion
photo-essay of autochromes from Jerusalem in the same issue
IMAGE COURTESY OF NATIONAL GEOGRAPHIC SOCIETY LIBRARY
AND ARCHIVES

have been produced for the tourist market[46] rather than worn by Palestinian women as their personal attire.[47]

This analysis widens the gap even further between what these images actually capture and what was presented by the magazine and perceived by its readers. For example, the *shaṭwa* which the published caption calls a 'high *ṭarbush*' is correctly explained as a headdress worn by married women from the Bethlehem region, yet if this outfit was a costume worn only for the photograph, the marital status of these women may be different than what is suggested. Similarly, the published caption mentions that American visitors to Jerusalem would recognise the young woman, indicating that she was a fixture at the American Colony; could she also have been a servant like the other woman who was photographed in the same outfit, and not, or not only, a handicraft student as is indicated in the magazine? Would identifying her as a servant instead of a student take away from the photograph's charm or perceived authenticity to the magazine's readers? Were the power relations between this young woman and the Americans (the residents of the Colony and Williams) sanitised for the sake of cheerfulness? How did these possible misrepresentations affect the way that the images were viewed by readers of the magazine?

From the captions describing the photographs that include Keith-Roach's wife and car, we also learn that the couple lived at the American Colony during that period while they awaited the completion of their residence. Keith-Roach would have therefore been in close proximity to this young woman on a daily basis. What did the everyday interactions between a female Palestinian student/servant and a desiring male British colonial administrator of high rank look like? The possibilities become more sinister with one of the photographs from the series where the young woman is photographed without her headdress or embroidered outfit in what appears to be a kind of t-shirt. Whether her outfit and uncovered head is representative of what the young woman normally wore or whether she was asked to pose with her head uncovered in a type of undergarment, is difficult to tell, but it raises many more questions about the encounter between photographer and subject that is captured in this series of photographs.

Without encountering the same images in multiple locations, in multiple ways, and with a range of associated information, I would not have been able to increase and complicate my understanding of the *photographed*

---

46   It is noteworthy that the American Colony ran their own Holy Land souvenir shops in Jerusalem and abroad.

47   Interviews with Widad Kawar during the course of *Imagining the Holy* project 2018–2020.

event, or separate it from the *events of photography* and the possibilities that each encounter with the image offered/offers. In my initial encounters with Williams' published photographs, it was difficult for me to recognise and exercise the agency I had in viewing those images. They were presented as fully and authoritatively explained with the full weight of National Geographic and colonial narratives about Palestine behind them. The only option I could see was to react to how they were presented: to counter-argue, debunk, and qualify. While these types of critiques are important, they felt bounded and insufficient.

Unlike the published images that were codified in the magazine, the unpublished images felt more open to new interpretations and purposes. If the captions were just conversations between Williams and magazine staff, I could eavesdrop, but also ignore them if I wanted to, or complicate them with other information that I could piece together. Even the composition of the photographs – something that seemed fixed by Williams for all eternity – appeared more fluid as I pieced together images taken in series, a few disparate moments stitched back together into a longer encounter with new angles, new interruptions and new possibilities. Among those unpublished images, I finally understood the full agency I had as Azoulay's *event of photography* was extended to include my encounters with each photograph.

In the end, what I wanted to hear and amplify was the perspective of the subject. Already during both the *photographed event* and the *event of photography*, the photographer and his perspective dominated, especially when the *event of photography* occurred in the pages of *National Geographic Magazine* with an entire text written with the perceived legitimacy of someone like Keith-Roach. Without any accompanying record of the subject's perspective or experience – and with very little information about them to help reconstruct it – it seemed like an impossible task at best and a project of fiction-making at worst.

5   Indigenising the Images: A Methodology

In 2018, I began a collaboration with the National Geographic Society Library and Archives to activate my research with the Society's collection of Palestine photographs and develop a methodology to re-examine images from the perspectives of the subjects represented. The project, named *Imagining the Holy*, was designed as a community-based project meant to connect the images in the archive with the descendants of the people, places and moments captured in them, while also creating new spaces for critical discussion of how Palestine and Palestinians are imagined and represented.

My primary goals as Lead Researcher were twofold: first to facilitate access to these images which have not circulated before and which presently can only be viewed in person in Washington D.C.; and second, to create a process by which new layers of indigenous knowledge and narratives from Palestinians are attached to the images, opening them up to new and future meanings.

Many questions arose in the process of designing and launching the project. These can be divided into three primary sets of questions. Those that pertain to ideas of decolonisation and theoretical questions around how the project was conceived; those that consider the transformation of power and agency; and those that relate to the practical aspects of such a project and the possibilities and limitations that they create.

In a theoretical sense, and fundamentally, can we conceive of this as a project of decolonisation? Afterall, my central critique of *National Geographic Magazine*'s coverage of Palestine is that it directly and indirectly supported colonial projects that disenfranchised the same Palestinians whose images it was taking and selling. Yet, after returning to my understanding of a photograph as a document of an encounter between a photographer and a subject, and after examining the conditions and regimes that the images are held under and were being made accessible to me, the term 'decolonisation' fell short.

The images of Mandate Palestine in the National Geographic collection were taken during and within that period of colonialism. This is marked permanently in the construction of the images and in the relations that shaped the encounter between photographer and subject which the photographs document. They are images *of* colonialism, in addition to being images that were colonised and/or used to further colonial projects. Furthermore, trying to decolonise an image that captures a colonial moment felt like we would be limiting our work to the frame set by the photographer and the coloniality of that moment. Instead, I wanted to repurpose these fixed frames as a border to imagine beyond them, rather than be restricted inside them. As Elizabeth Edwards explains, the 'Frame, in the way it contains and constrains, heightens and produces a fracture which makes us intensely aware of what lies beyond. Thus there is a dialectic between boundary and endlessness; framed, constrained, edged yet uncontainable. It is the tension between the boundary of the photograph and the openness of its contexts which is at the root of its historical uncontainability in terms of meaning'.[48]

Another set of questions followed: how can images of Palestine and of Palestinians be decolonised when the colonisation of Palestine and of

---

48   Elizabeth Edwards, "Photography and the Performance of History," *Kronos* no. 27 (2001): 17.

Palestinians is ongoing? Even if the colonial potential of these images is less potent today than it was when they were made and circulated, the effects that they had are still evident and accumulating. As Stephen Sheehi notes in this very volume, 'Decolonisation of photography then is not magical undoing. It is not an ahistorical process or a reading through nationalist frameworks that sees indigenous photography as 'speaking back' to power'.[49]

My answer to these questions was to position the project as work of indigenisation rather than decolonisation. To indigenise images means to *make connections to* and *take ownership of* the people and places from which we come. It means working to connect each body and each place to itself and its descendants, image by image, rather than trying to symbolically remove the colonial from what is – at least in part – permanently colonial. It also means shifting our focus from the photographers to their subjects. The information provided by Widad Kawar about the woman in the Bethlehem dress is one such example.

With this shift in focus, a shift of power followed. This renegotiation demanded an additive process rather than a subtractive one. As such, our method to indigenise evolved to include three parts. Firstly, to recall and emphasise the subjectivity of the photographer as it manifests in image and text. The unpublished captions were the key to this process, revealing thoughts, actions, and agendas that shaped the making of the photographs, but reside silently or subtly within them.

Secondly, to create space within and around the photograph dedicated to holding the subjectivity of the photograph's subject. This began as a theoretical space by simply asking what the subject of the photograph might include in their own captions; it became materialised over the course of the project as it transformed into an active site for research and conversation, and eventually into a proposed metadata field assigned to collect possible answers. Even when this space remains unfilled, the act of holding space is essential to the redistribution of power.

Thirdly, to fill this space with the voices and spirits of the photographs' subjects, if not by themselves, then with the knowledge and experiences that those connected to them have inherited. With this final part of the process, the subject was no longer only represented in image alone, but with a similar presence and potential to speak as the photographer.

In this way, the project to indigenise these images not only illuminates the colonial power dynamics frozen in them, it fortifies the images against being

---

49   See Stephen Sheehi's chapter in this volume, "Decolonising the Photography of Palestine: Searching for a Method in a Plate of Hummus".

used to further ongoing colonisation by drowning out their colonial potential rather than trying to remove what is colonial but intrinsic to them.

The last set of questions we had to address involved the more practical elements of the project, but also questions that had to do with its fundamental purpose and spirit. Mostly importantly: who specifically would speak on behalf of the subjects since, as is the case for most of the photographs from the Mandate period, they could not speak for themselves? This led to another question: was a single new description enough to represent the perspective and experiences of the subject? A hierarchy of ideal participants emerged: the descendants of and/or those who knew the subjects first hand; community elders from the same places and communities who were familiar with the contexts and details around the subjects' lives and time period; academics and cultural heritage experts with specialised knowledge about the various tangible and intangible parts of the subjects' lives and experiences captured in the photographs; field researchers based in Palestine/Israel and around the world in the Diaspora who could help extend our research into communities of Palestinians all over the world. Once this list was established, the answer to the second question became clear: we needed as many new layers of description from as many ideal participants to even *begin* to approximate the voices and lived experiences of the subjects. In this way, we aimed to create a community of witnesses to speak near them, rather than for them.

In order to connect the thousands of images from the archive with these participants, we built an online digital research platform to host research copies of each image along with the photographer's captions and any archival metadata mentioned on the back of the photographs. Through this platform, participants anywhere in the world could view the collection, add new descriptions to the images, and read the descriptions added by other participants. The platform was built in consultation with the archive team at the National Geographic Society to ensure that the data collected through the platform could be migrated to the archive and its content management system in order to link each new description with its corresponding photograph.

In addition to the digital research platform, an Instagram account, https://@imaginingtheholy, was created for the project in order to share previously uncirculated images and to solicit new leads for our research. The popularity and ease of accessibility of this platform allowed us to introduce the project to a larger, younger and more diverse audience including recreational viewers and more active contributors who have used their own personal and professional networks to help us connect pieces and find new threads to follow. This platform has become indispensable for one of the most important contributions we are making through the project: giving names to the nameless subjects in the photographs. These leads have helped us connect to many descendants of

FIGURE 9.6   Hilweh Abu Tayr, born in the village of Umm Tuba in the Jerusalem District
and raised in Bethlehem, identified by her grandson, Rauf Malki. 'Moslem
woman wearing the fine costume seen on the day of the Nabī Mūsā
procession, Jerusalem, Palestine.' Unpublished photograph and caption by
Maynard Owen Williams, 1927. Another portrait of Abu Tayr was published
with Keith-Roach's December 1927 article and three other images in colour
of her and her mother were published in Williams' companion photo-essay
of autochromes from Jerusalem in the same issue

IMAGE COURTESY OF NATIONAL GEOGRAPHIC SOCIETY LIBRARY
AND ARCHIVES

subjects and to add the most important information to the photographs in our quest to listen for and amplify the voices and spirits of the subjects. It has been the clearest and most effective way to transform the power-dynamics in and around the image: placing the name of the subject directly beside the name of the photographer and transforming his subject from an anonymous model or Biblical stand-in to a person with a body, a name and a story. Maynard Owen Williams' photograph of a Moslem woman in Jerusalem becomes a photo-graph of Hilweh Abu Tayr taken in Jerusalem by Maynard Owen Williams. The photograph is transformed from being a work authored by the photographer to a document of an encounter between a photographer and a subject that resulted in the making of a photograph.

6   Conclusion

My encounters with the photographs in the National Geographic Society's archives transformed my understanding and relationship with the stories that *National Geographic Magazine* has published about Palestine and Palestinians over the past century. My initial interest in the writers, photographers and edi-tors was driven by an inability to imagine the images in the magazine separate from the voices and narratives that asserted sole authority over them. My pro-ject *Imagining the Holy* became an attempt to reimagine the images from the position and perspective of their subjects. In the course of piloting a method-ology that would allow me to do this, a few things became apparent.

Firstly, the indigenisation of photographs, which involves both a shift in focus and in power, also involves a shift in temporal boundaries. Whereby the voices and narratives ascribed to them by the writers, photographer and editors locked the images near the time of their making, our methodology cre-ated a way for voices and narratives to be newly and continually introduced. Indeed, *Imagining the Holy* ended up being an opening and a beginning, rather than a project that can or should be completed. As such, the project is ongoing and has transformed National Geographic's Palestine collection into a site of active conversation, reflection and negotiation.

Secondly, in a similar vein, our methodology to indigenise photographs could also be applied to photographs of Palestine and Palestinians held in other collections, as well as to photographs of other regions and peoples in National Geographic's collection. While colonial circumstances differ across geography and history, the process of elevating and centring indigenous subjectivities where they are missing, silenced or erased, can and should be replicated. This process does not aim to excise the non-indigenous from images (which as

I argue above, is not possible), but rather, it aims to complicate and redistribute power in order to reduce the colonial potential of the images and activate them as sites for indigenous knowledge, memory and power.

Thirdly, in the process of designing and implementing the project, it became clear that we were not only connecting Palestinians to images of ourselves and our homeland – and vice versa – but that by organising and participating in a community-based method, we were also connecting to each other. As Sheehi notes, 'The photograph is a social space, a collective process, a cultural and geographic articulation and a social object. As such, all are available for re-appropriation by the colonised in order to emancipate the subjects of the photograph, the *verum factum* and truth value of their experience, and the visibility of facts that are disavowed, permitting us as liberated subjects to create the opportunity for new social relations'.[50]

In the face of the ruptures and separation caused and exasperated by our colonial history, we could use photographs as a site of reconnection. As Edward Said wrote, 'All of us speak of *awdah*, 'return,' but do we mean that literally, or do we mean 'we must restore ourselves to ourselves'?... But is there any place that fits us, together with our accumulated memories and experiences?'[51] *Imagining the Holy* asks whether photographs of our ancestors, of ourselves, and of our homeland can be such a place.

Bibliography

Correspondence and Editorial Files Sources

National Geographic Society Library and Archives, National Geographic Society, Washington D.C.

Secondary Sources

"Announcement." *National Geographic Magazine* 1, no. 1 (October 1888): i–ii.

Azoulay, Ariella. *Civil Imagination: A Political Ontology of Photography*. Translated by Louise Bethlehem. London: Verso, 2012.

Edwards, Elizabeth. "Photography and the Performance of History." *Kronos* no. 27 (November 2001): 15–29.

Hartman, Saidiya. "Venus in Two Acts." *Small Axe* 26, 12, no. 2 (June 2008): 1–14.

Hoskins, Franklin E. "The Route Over Which Moses Led The Children of Israel Out of Egypt." *National Geographic Magazine* 20, no. 12 (December 1909): 1011–1038.

---

50   See Stephen Sheehi's chapter in this volume.

51   Edward Said, *After the Last Sky: Palestinian Lives* (New York: Pantheon Books, 1986): 33.

Hyde, John. "The National Geographic Society." *National Geographic Magazine* 10, no. 6 (June 1899): 220–223.

Keith-Roach, Edward. "The Pageant of Jerusalem: The Capital of the Land of Three Great Faiths Is Still the Holy City for Christian, Moslem, and Jew." *National Geographic Magazine* 52, no. 6 (December 1927): 635–681.

Keith-Roach, Edward and Luke, Harry Charles. *The Handbook of Palestine*, London: MacMillan, 1922.

Keith-Roach, Edward and Luke, Harry Charles. *The Handbook of Palestine and Trans-Jordan*, London: MacMillan, 1930.

Lutz, Catherine A. and Jane L. Collins. *Reading National Geographic.* Chicago: The University of Chicago Press, 1993.

Masalha, Nur. *The Palestine Nakba: Decolonising History, Narrating the Subaltern, Reclaiming Memory.* London and New York: Zed Books, 2012.

Nassar, Issam. "'Biblification' in the Service of Colonialism: Jerusalem in Nineteenth-century Photography." *Third Text* 20, nos. 3/4 (2006): 317–326.

Pappe, Ilan. *The Ethnic Cleansing of Palestine.* London: Oneworld Publications, 2006.

Power, Jane. "Review of *Pasha of Jerusalem: Memoirs of a District Commissioner Under the British Mandate,*" by Edward Keith-Roach and Paul Eedle, *Middle East Studies Association Bulletin* 32, no. 2 (1998), 270–271.

Rothenberg, Tamar Y. *Presenting America's World: Strategies of Innocence in National Geographic Magazine, 1888–1945.* Hampshire: Ashgate Publishing Limited, 2007.

Rossi, Roberto "The Almoner Altar and the 'Pasha of Jerusalem" *Museum of the Order of St John Blog.* http://museumstjohn.org.uk/almoner-altar-pasha-jerusalem/. Accessed December 3, 2019.

Said, Edward. *After the Last Sky: Palestinian Lives.* New York: Pantheon Books, 1986.

Schölch, Alexander. *Palestine in Transformation, 1856–1882.* Translated by M.C. Gerrity and W.C. Young. Washington, D.C.: Institute for Palestine Studies, 1993.

Sheehi, Stephen. "Decolonising the Photography of Palestine: Searching for a Method in a Plate of Hummus", 346–365. In: Sanchez Summerer, Karène and Sary Zananiri, *Imaging and Imagining Palestine: Photography, Modernity and the Biblical Lens.* Leiden/Boston: Brill, 2021.

Szulc, Tad. "Who are the Palestinians?" *National Geographic Magazine* 181, no. 6 (1992): 84–113.

Tamari, Salim. "Shifting Ottoman Conceptions of Palestine, Part 1: Filistin Risalesi and the two Jamals." *Jerusalem Quarterly* 47 (2011): 33.

"The Red Cross in Palestine." *The Red Cross Magazine,* January 1919.

Tuason, Julie A. "The Ideology of Empire in National Geographic Magazine's Coverage of the Philippines, 1898–1908." *Geographical Review* 89, no. 1 (Jan 1999): 34–53.

Whitehair, Charles. "An Old Jewel in the Proper Setting: An Eyewitness's Account of the Reconquest of the Holy Land by Twentieth Century Crusaders." *National Geographic Magazine* 34, no. 4 (October 1918): 325–344.

Whiting, John D. "Bedouin Life in Bible Lands," *National Geographic Magazine* 71, no. 1 (January 1937): 58–83.

Whiting, John D. "Village Life in the Holy Land." *National Geographic Magazine* 25, no. 3 (March 1914): 249–314.

Whiting, John D. "The Last Israelitish Blood Sacrifice." *National Geographic Magazine* 37, no. 1 (January 1920): 1–46.

Williams, Maynard Owen. "Color Records from the Changing Life of the Holy Land." *National Geographic Magazine* 52, no. 6 (December 1927): 682–707.

Zananiri, Sary. "From Still to Moving Images: Shifting Representation of Jerusalem and Palestinians in the Western Biblical Imaginary" *Jerusalem Quarterly* 67 (2016): 73–74.

Decolonising the Photography of Palestine: Searching for a Method in a Plate of Hummus

Stephen Sheehi

Kafr Qasim[1]
No commemoration, no flowers, no remembrance
No poetic verse humanizing the murdered. Not one line.
No shred from the shirt soaked in blood
Remains from our innocent brothers.
No one thing except shame.
Their ghosts continue to circle
Unearthing the graves in the ruins of Kafr Qasim.

SAMIH QASIM

∴

I begin this chapter with Samih Qasim's poem to Kafr Qasim, a village where the Israeli military massacred 48 Palestinians (23 of whom were children). In teaching us 'how to read a massacre', Rana Barakat forces us to remember that the structural and intentional violence of settler colonialism, in this case Zionism, must never decentre those narratives, presence and material realities of the indigenous population – the very selves targeted for elimination.[2] Let us keep this axiom, then, in mind when we consider militant methodologies to re-centre, witness and validate indigenous presence in settler-colonial photography. To start this exploration, I would like to start this inquiry then

---

1 Samih Qasim, "Kafr Qassim" (poem in Arabic) in Abdelwahab Elmessiri, *The Palestinian Wedding: A Bilingual Anthology of Contemporary Palestinian Poetry* (Washington, D.C.: Three Continents Press, 1982); my translation. Kafr Qasim was a village where Israeli Border Police, massacred 48 Palestinian-Israeli civilians (over half children under 17 and a pregnant women) on the eve of Israel's invasion of the Sinai in 1956. All victims were Israeli-Palestinian citizens.

2 Rana Barakat, "How to Read a Massacre in Palestine: Indigenous History as a Methodology of Liberation" (unpublished draft copy, 2019).

FIGURE 10.1   *'Turkish Official Teases Starving Armenian Children'*, 1915. (Featured in
Donald Bloxham)

with the familiar, to some, yet scandalous photograph. Indeed, a photograph
from the time of the British Mandate of Palestine. In some ways, it is not unrelated. It is likely that those familiar with the ongoing saga to recognise the
Armenian Genocide know this now infamous image, putatively of a 'Turkish
Official Taunting Armenians with Bread', also known as 'Famished Armenian
Children'. The image is found in Armin Wegnar's well-known photographs documenting the genocide, many of which he and fellow German officers took
while deployed in Ottoman Syria during World War I. Subsequently, the photograph was the cover-image of Donald Bloxham's 2010 *Great Game of Genocide*.[3]
The image is, however, not of starving and taunted Armenians but it is, in fact,
a staged French image used for funding raising to alleviate the Great Famine
in Lebanon during the same period. Rather than being identified as a scholarly error or a misidentified image, the photograph was deemed a 'forgery' by

---

3 Donald Bloxham, *The Great Game of Genocide: Imperialism, Nationalism, and the Destruction
   of the Ottoman Armenians* (Oxford: Oxford University Press, 2005).

Genocide-deniers. As such, it was used as one more piece of evidence that Armenians continue to be the liars and forgers, truly the 'seditious millet'.[4]

This controversy returns us to the perennial, if not banal, questions of photography's documentary 'validity', its constructedness, and its artifice in contrast to its 'truth-value'. Lacan reminds, however, that:

> *Méconnaissance* is not ignorance. [It] represents a certain organization of affirmations and negations, to which the subject is attached. Hence it cannot be conceived without correlate knowledge (*connaissance*)... [Therefore], behind one's misrecognition, there must surely be a kind of knowledge of what there is to misrecognize.[5]

But these questions seem to me to be a deflection from another issue that underscores the compulsion to forgery or the *méconnaissance* of the weak. This photographic *méconnaissance* of the colonised, of the genocided, happens when the photograph represents so fully and cogently one's own selfhood and material reality that are otherwise been denied by hegemonic power and its ability to control knowledge and *image* production.

Therefore, the question of forgery (locked in orbit with *méconnaissance*) raises not only the question of validity or truth of the photograph. More importantly, forgery raises the question of *right* to truth, the right to the social relations and *material realities* photography represents: the right to the *surplus truth-value of* the photograph (as value accumulated through the political economy of representation and image-circulation).

Let us move to an equally controversial image. An image that is 'real' but contested, indeed, legally contested. On 30th September 2000, two days after Ariel Sharon's provocative visit to the Ḥarām al-Sharīf, Muhammad Durrah, a 12-year-old boy, was shot dead in the arms of his father in Gaza by the Israeli army. He was shot in front of Talal Abu Rahma's camera, filming video footage for France 2 news. Captured in less than minute of video, Durrah's death was reduced to a series of photographic stills that circulated throughout Palestine, the Arab world and the globe. The image has become iconic. Despite the power of this image, or perhaps because of the power of this image, Israel retracted its initial admission of guilt to later deny the validity of the claims that Durrah

---

4   Vahakn Dadrian, "The Armenian Question and the Wartime Fate of the Armenians as Documented by the Officials of the Ottoman Empire's World War I Allies: Germany and Austria-Hungary," *International Journal of Middle East Studies* vol. 34, no. 1 (2002): 59–85.

5   Jacques Lacan, *The Seminar Book I: Freud's Papers on Technique 1953–54*, trans. John Forrester (New York: Norton, 1988), 167 (my translation tweak).

FIGURE 10.2   *Mohammed al-Durrah Mural.* Santa Fe, NM, by artist Remy.
IMAGE COURTESY OF ALEX DE VOSE

was killed by Israeli forces and contest the validity of the images. Charles Enderline, France 2's Israel Bureau chief, became embroiled in several legal battles around defamation of his character and the validity of his reporting of the incident.

Rather than serve as evidence for the violence that afflicts Palestinian civilians under occupation, the iconic image emerged as a point of contention, transformed in the international arena (and French courts) from an indictment of Israeli occupation to proof, or at least innuendo, of the deceitfulness of Palestinians. The alchemy of politics and power converted the photographic evidence of a murdered 12-year-old into a document that allegedly demonstrates artifice, deflection, manipulation and the sedition of the victim.

Melanie Phillips, a British commentator, has made a career off the 'controversy' that she played a large part in creating.[6] But even more so, Phillips mobilised the virility and ubiquity of the visual evidence of the Israeli murder of Durrah to allege that the image itself resulted in the true loss of many lives (meaning Jewish and Israeli-Jewish lives). Phillips' activism around the death image of Durrah makes us think of who has the right to determine the veracity of an image, the force and currency of an image. Nick Mirzeoff speaks of 'right

---

6   Melanie Phillips, "Faking a Killing," *Standpoint*, June 27, 2008, found at https://standpoint mag.co.uk/faking-a-killing-july/?page=0%2C0%2C0%2C0%2C0%2C0%2C0%2C0%2C0%2C0%2C0%2C0%2 C0%2C2.

to look' as a constituent tension within the history of modern visuality that comes into being through the claims and counterclaims between the coloniser and colonised.[7]

I recalibrate Nick Mirzeoff's formulation 'right to look' to a formulation of the right to the 'surplus truth value' of photography. Let me be clear that I am not talking about the right to representation. Indeed, a current trend in photography studies is to move away from focusing exclusively on the photographs of Orientalist photographers to try to locate indigenous histories of photography and/or the hidden role of indigenous assistants (often women as readily as men) of Western expatriate photographers. I am not referring to local histories and personal accounts, often very important accounts in themselves, being told through autogenerated photographs.[8]

Let us understand that the practice of photography is an *extractive process*, especially when it is in the hands of the coloniser, the imperialist or the Zionist settler. Even if the photographer seeks to 'humanise' the indigenous subject, this gesture of magnanimity originates from an economy of images, representations, commodity exchange, subjectivities, epistemology. Therefore, such knowledge-production is structured to extract all forms of wealth and value (whether subjective, aesthetic, historical or material) from the colonised and transfer it to the coloniser along with its *title* (that it creates from this process). Therefore, I am stating that the photograph-forged through this colonial subjective, political and epistemological economy must understood as property. This does not only include the photographic object, the processes and labour around its production and dissemination. The photographic index itself is property, whose surplus-value the coloniser has usurped as part of the colonising enterprise. When this right to the surplus truth-value of photography is managed in such a way that it excludes, when it is used to further *disavowal*, and when it perpetuates the interests of power, violence and denial, forgery rightfully becomes 'a weapon of the weak', who themselves seize the right to all surplus-value extracted from colonial people and lands in an on-going struggle with coloniality.

I am not arguing to assert the right to claim a forgery or a falsehood as real. Rather, I am arguing the *right to claim the representation of violence is real* and

7   Nicholas Mirzeoff, *The Right to Look: A Counterhistory of Visuality* (Durham, NC: Duke University Press, 2011).

8   See, for example, Naseeb Shaheen, *A Pictorial History of Ramallah* (Beirut: Arab Institute for Research and Publishing, 1992); Walid Khalidi, *Before Their Diaspora: A Photographic History of the Palestinians 1876–1948* (Washington D.C.: Institute for Palestine Studies, 1984); and Badr el-Hage, *Shweir and Its Hills: A Photographic Record*, trans. Sabah Ghandour (Beirut: Kutub, 2013).

that social conditions that make that representation are true. I am arguing the *right to claim the photograph because it is founded on a visual economy that is extractive*. Indeed, in thinking about our positionality and relationality to photography, this recalibration of the surplus value of photography should force researchers as well to consider the possible extractive nature of their research especially when handling, dominating, hording or claiming ownership over photographs that are given value because their content emerges from some social relationship with the colonised; in this case, Palestine and the Palestinians.[9]

Ariella Azoulay reminds us that, for a Palestinian, 'going to Israeli archives is not an option, because under the imperial regime of the archive he was deprived of the archives that existed in Palestine'.[10] Indeed, the Israeli archive 'houses' – or perhaps, better, confines under its naturalised policy of indefinite administration detention – not only purloined documents, images and artifacts, but suppressed facts and narratives that evince their historical claims, their narratives and stories of Zionist violence and dispossession.[11] Yet, still, the Israel archive is a contrived space predicated precisely on the control, management and erasure of Palestinians, collectively and individually. The Israeli archive is a place of dispossession and prohibition for the Palestinian, but also detainment and suppression. Coming up with strategies to resist and think through the histories delimited and demarcated by the settler society becomes even more complicated when we also remember that photography itself is deeply imbricated with colonialism and coloniality. That is, '[p]hotography was imperial from the very beginning', as Azoulay reminds us. The 'negation of people's right to actively participate in (let alone give consent to) being photographed is not part of the ontology of photography, but is the outcome of the extractive principle on which photography was first institutionalized'.[12] When one reconsiders the place of the archive and the 'nature of photography' then we understand the importance of why Rana Barakat asks us to centre and amplify Palestinian stories, narratives, and objects of knowledge – not

---

9   For another example of the decolonial method that allows us to seize the image and relocate it within centered Palestinian-Arab existence, material realities, and histories, see "The Palestinian Spectator and Emancipating History" in Issam Nassar, Stephen Sheehi, and Salim Tamari, *Camera Palestina: Photography and Displaced Histories of Palestine* (Berkeley: University of California Press, forthcoming).

10   Ariella Azoulay, *Potential History: Unlearning Imperialism* (New York: Verso, 2019), 163.

11   I am referring to the research of Israel's New Historians, who could enter the state archives to access documents pertaining to the 1948 Nakba when they were declassified. The most noteworthy of these works is the Ilan Pappé, *The Ethnic Cleansing of Palestine* (London and New York: Oneworld, 2006).

12   Azoulay, *Potential History*, 143.

settler-colonial places, spaces, and narratives – as elemental to 'writing/ righting' the history of Palestine.[13]

When we think about photography in the context of colonialism, in particular, we realise how the social relations that mediate the relationships around photography are further convoluted by the relationship of colonised peoples to visual regimes, social configurations and political formations that themselves are embroiled with the introduction of racial capitalism, colonialism, and modernity.[14] Photography then is always contaminated and a site of contention for the colonised to make claims. Photography is not only a locus of the production of meaning, but a locus for the production of knowledge for the colonised as much as the coloniser.

To be clear, when the right of photography, or the right to the truth-value of photography, is denied, when the right of the victim is denied by the victimiser, the weak have a right to emancipate the image, to tactically excavate 'truth-value'. The manifest of the image may, in fact, obfuscate this 'truth-value'. Therefore, the colonised may seek a method and practice to conjure indigenous knowledge through associations with other facts in order to represent the truth of the material conditions the image represents. *This is the beginning of the decolonisation of photography*. Methodologies of decolonisation do not dismiss the facticity of the photograph in a gesture towards radical relativism. In no way, do decolonial methodologies invent 'alternative facts', frequent among right-wing, ethno-nationalist, and fascist movements. Rather, they exorcise, in Alloula's words, the hegemony of colonial epistemology. They validate and centre the experiences, stories, knowledge and realities of indigenous people. They centre history and analysis on facts that have been displaced, shattered, buried (sometimes literally) and dismissed. Decolonial method understands that if truth is suppressed or pushed to the margins, it is because truth-value is mediated by power, force and conscription. Decolonial methodology, as Linda Tuhiwai Smith methodically shows us, truth is produced; truth is constructed through the production of knowledge, but also on the elevation of experience and affect; facts are discursive, collective and *social* products, while still being empirical.[15] Facts are empirical and relational, standing tension, complimentary and in relation to other facts. It is not coincidental that Edward Said in

---

13   Rana Barakat, "Writing/Righting Palestine Studies: Settler Colonialism, Indigenous Sovereignty and Resisting the Ghost(s) of History," *Settler Colonial Studies* 8, no. 3 (2018): 349–363.

14   See Stephen Sheehi, "The Nahda After-Image, or All Photography Expresses Social Relations," *Third Text* 26, no. 4 (2012): 401–414.

15   Linda Tuhiwai Smith, *Decolonizing Methodologies: Research and Indigenous Peoples* (New York: Zed Books, 2013).

Orientalism frequently looks to Giambattista Vico to unravel how discourses are produced through the constitution and arrangement of facts.[16] Facts are related to empirical and material realities, realities that we create through social forces and power structures; realities constructed through the dialectics of the powerful and social formations, those who they attempt to control, co-opt, and/or resist-through a number ideological and material means – knowledge production.

In this regard, I have argued elsewhere that photography is an example of Vico's *verum factum*.[17] The means of knowledge production is in the hands of the powerful. In the form of the photograph, it can constitute a visual archive that determines the parameters by which we define all that is seen.[18] Therefore, understanding the photograph as being a *verum factum* is not to say that just because we say something is true, it is true. But it is for us to wrestle control of the means of knowledge production by conjuring the latent and manifest content of photography, by connecting it to other facts, to material realities, in order to emancipate its meaning. Indeed, Katherine McKittrick entices us to believe the 'truthful lies' put forth by the archive that tell us of the violence until black people are born free. This impulse to 'trust the lies' is not to agree to their truth, but to produce a form of knowledge that serves to evince what black people know to be *the facts*; namely they are free despite all the social lies that perpetuates and naturalises violence against them.[19]

The correlation between the black experience in the United States and that of Palestinians in Palestine under Zionist hegemony should not be lost on us, despite the profound differences. Indeed, Saidiyah Hartman illustrates what I am alluding to when we think of seizing images, 'trusting the lie' in order to give witness to the *facts*. Hartman's handling of a number of photographs of anonymous black girls from the decades around the turn of the twentieth century tease out both the racial violence encoded in the images, but also lived experiences and social formations, indeed evidence of revolutionary and rebellious black lives, that escape the confines of a white supremist syntax of photographic representation.[20]

---

16   Edward Said, *Orientalism* (New York: Knopf, 1978).

17   For a theoretical development and demonstration of my theory of the *verum factum* of the photograph, see Chapter Four: "Writing Photography", in Sheehi, *Arab Imago*.

18   For a critique of the archive and photography's imperial and imperious relationship to it, see Azoulay, *Potential History*.

19   Katherine McKittrick, "Mathematics Black Life," *The Black Scholar* 44, no. 2 (2014): 21 and 20, respectively.

20   Saidiya Hartman, *Wayward Lives, Beautiful Experiments: Intimate Histories of Social Upheaval* (New York: Norton, 2019).

Speaking more to the images at hand, we are confident that, while the Armenian photograph is a 'fake', the facts it communicates are true: the Armenians were exterminated by the Ottoman government through deprivation. Even if the murder of Muhammad Durrah was staged as the most heinous and cynical critics suggest, the image stands as absolute and unequivocal evidence for the cruel realities of an illegal and brutal occupation and its effects on Palestinian children and their families.

1   What Is the Decolonisation of Photography

The decolonisation of photography is not magical undoing. It is not an ahistorical process or a reading through nationalist frameworks that sees indigenous photography as 'speaking back' to power. In the Middle East, at least, decolonisation of photography should not seek an 'epistemic reconstruction', in the words of South American thinker Aníbal Quijano.[21] Conjuring pre-Oedipal fragments of selfhood or awaking dormant histories are not the same as hoping to resurrect arcane or dead practices, fetishising them as authentic culture.

The process of decolonisation should not be confused with a recovery of a lost, destroyed or displaced self. It is the acknowledgement of lost selfhoods that are only knowable through their displacements and uncanny fragments, which themselves come to us through the filter of selfhood that is our own, but also doubled subjectivity as W.E.B. De Bois, Frantz Fanon, Abdelkebir al-Khatibi have observed. But, this is not its sole end. Decolonisation is the fleshing out, remembering, conjuring and an accounting of the ways in which extraction took place, but also continues to unfold, often with the complicity and conscription of indigenous bourgeoisie, politicians, oligarchs, and social formations. It is this process of decolonisation, along subjective, gender and class lines that authenticates, produces and centres indigenous, but not parochial, knowledge and conscientiousness.

If colonial modernity is a system of knowledge-production not simply empirical reality, as Santiago Castro-Gomez suggests, it is unlinkable from a colonial/modern/capitalist matrix of Middle Eastern subjectivities, practices, (and their subaltern negatives) through which the *necropolitics* of the colony and postcolony are naturalised.[22] Decolonisation therefore entails

---

21   Aníbal Quijano, "Coloniality and Modernity/Rationality," *Cultural Studies* 21, nos. 2–3 (2007): 176.

22   Santiago Castro-Gómez, "The Missing Chapter of Empire: Postmodern Re-organization of Coloniality and Post-Fordist Capitalism," *Cultural Studies* 21, nos. 2–3 (2007): 428–48.

then a seizure of means of knowledge production, among them photography, and thereby the seizure of the rights to photography and photographic representation. The seizure does not involve an adoption of an archive that lends credibility to a dominant, indigenous elite history of the Middle East; that is, using the photographic archive as evidence for the Middle East's belle époque, how women were liberated, how men were literate, went to the beach and drank whisky and loved democracy. The work of Fouad Debbas, Badr el-Hage, Michel Fani, for example, are a claim to nostalgia and absence, not a claim to the rights of looking or the claim to the rights of photography's truth value.[23]

For all their talk about discovering the 'lost heritage' of Middle East photography, the photograph, for them, is used to shore up nationalist and class nostalgia and displace the violence that operates within the latent content of the image. This nostalgic approach to photography creates the 'alt-history' or 'alt-heritage' and only instrumentalises photography as a means of justifying and naturalising one particular class world view and ideological hegemony.

I use the language of 'seizing' or appropriation because it allows us to be empowered, agile and militant with our methodology. In seizing photography, we seize 'expatriate, Orientalist, and state imagery' as readily as reaching to indigenous or 'vernacular' photography. Native photography itself is not understood as a resistance to imperialism or Orientalism, but is indicted in forms of power, class assertion and social formations. Therefore, it constitutes an object, indeed a site of contention, that itself needs to be seized, rehabilitated and repurposed. Decolonisation therefore entails a seizure of means of knowledge production, among them photography, and thereby the seizure of the rights to photography and photographic representation. The photograph is a social space, a collective process, a cultural and geographic articulation and a social object. As such, all are available for re-appropriation by the colonised in order to emancipate the subjects of the photograph, the *verum factum* and truth value of their experience, and the visibility of facts that are disavowed, permitting us as liberated subjects to create the opportunity for new social relations.

---

23   Fouad Debbas, *Beirut: Our Memory; A Guided Tour Illustrated with Picture Postcards*, 2nd ed. (Beirut: Naufal, 1986); Michel Fani, *Liban 1848–1914: L'atelier photographique de Ghazir* (Paris: Éditions de l'Escalier, 1995); Khalidi, *Before the Diaspora*; and Badr el-Hage, *Saudi Arabia: Caught in Time 1861–1939* (London: Garnet, 1997).

2   **Search for a Method**

Seizing the rights to photography demands a decolonial method that contains
a number of different techniques of radical appropriation. It is an understanding of photography as a multivalent practice, that involves a number of
indexical, empirical, ideological and representational fields that can be weap-
onised, converted into a plane of contention in order to seize the means of
ideological, economic or knowledge production.

What I hope to offer is not a grand and new method, but an organising
method. In many ways, this method dovetails with recent scholars in North
America such as Ali Behdad, Jennifer Bajorek and Hanna Feldman to 'unmoor'
or 'unfix' the image from the Orientalist lens, without necessarily understanding the collusion between Orientalist, colonialist and indigenous social
formations.[24] Likewise, Yazan Kopty, in this very volume, offers and practices
a method by which images are repatriated and re-indigenised despite their
extractive and exploitative origins with *National Geographic*. Furthermore, a
broad naming, corralling and rerouting of techniques that reappropriate and
reposition the colonial subject's relationality to the image has been practiced
by scholars, photographers and artists in the postcolony for decades. Malek
Alloula, for example, started this project when he announced a desire to 'force
the postcard to reveal what it holds back (the ideology of colonialism) and to
expose what is repressed in it (the sexual phantasm)'[25] His ground-breaking
book is explicitly referred to as an 'exorcism'.[26] Approaching the photograph
as an image-screen, as *verum factum*, is one such technique. Transfiguring the
photograph into a space to emancipate the colonised spectator within us (to riff
on Rancière), who has been denied the rights of visibility, who has been denied
to right to the truth value of photography.[27] How then is decolonising photography to be done? Since the surface of the photograph as an image-screen
is a locus of mediation of social relations (of power and resistance), Freud
and his approach to dream-work provide us with one technique for this

---

24   See Jennifer Bajorek, *Unfixed: Photography and Decolonial Imagination in West Africa*
        (Durham, NC: Duke University Press, 2020); Ali Behdad, *Camera Orientalis: Reflections on
        Photography of the Middle East* (Chicago: University of Chicago Press, 2016); and Hanna
        Feldman, *From a Nation Torn: Decolonizing Art and Representation in France, 1945–1962*
        (Durham, NC: Duke University Press, 2014).
25   Malek Alloula, *The Colonial Harem* (Minneapolis: University of Minnesota Press, 1985), 4.
26   Alloula, 5.
27   Jacques Rancière, *Politics of Aesthetics: Distribution of the Sensible*, translated by Gabriel
        Rockhill (London: Continuum, 2004).

decolonising methodology, allowing us to seize the image-screen as a composite of manifest and the latent content of positive, negative and displaced images.

In the manifest, we explore the indexical, the representational, the compositional, the aesthetic qualities of the photograph, all which communicate particular meanings within a dominant discourse. The manifest is read through the dominant ideology (and reproduces it) within particular social and political contexts. We may extend Marx's formulations of the essential components of economic formations to photography, found in 'Introduction to a Critique of Political Economy', where visual, like economic formations, are based on a series: production, distribution, exchange and consumption, where 'every form of production creates its own legal relations, forms of government, etc'.[28]

The latent is, however, all that makes the manifest legible and that which the manifest may displace. It is the alterity of the image, the denied, the displaced and the repressed. One searches for the latent in a number of ways, and the latent is multitude, but that does not mean everything goes. Like Freud's method, one maps the manifest through its narration and its index, and the latent through a process of association, historical inquiry, representational genealogy, *deep space* of discourses that make manifest intelligible and exploring the image's effect and affect.[29] To illustrate the method, I reach to an image that lays at the junction between the Genocide and the Occupation of Palestine, two issues bound by the denial of suffering and violence.

3   Palestine in a Plate of Hummus

Elia Kahvedjian (1910–1999) was born in Urfa and, by age five, was a refugee of the Armenian genocide. He lost five brothers, three sisters, mother, father, all uncles, aunts and grandparents, all save a sister who he found 18 years later. During the death march, his mother sold him to Kurds, where he was renamed 'Abdū and worked as a blacksmith's apprentice. When blacksmith's new wife didn't want him, Elia was 'thrown into the streets' and became a beggar, where, allegedly, he was almost kidnapped and murdered by cannibals in a tale right out of 1001 nights (given food, he was taken to cave, where he slipped and fell upon human skulls, as he escaped, the kidnapper threw a sword and injured

---

28   Karl Marx, "Introduction to a Critique of Political Economy," in *The German Ideology* (Amherst, NY: Prometheus, 1988), 5.

29   Sigmund Freud, *The Interpretation of Dreams. The Standard Edition of the Complete Psychological Works of Sigmund Freud*, IV and V (1900); James Strachey, trans. and ed. (London: Hogarth Press, 1953).

his leg where he carried a scar). By age 11, the American Near East Relief Foundation saved him along with thousands of Armenian orphans and relocated him to an orphanage in Nazareth, where he learned photography. He moved to Jerusalem and started to work for Hanania Brothers studio, eventually buying and renaming it 'Elia Photo Service'.[30]

Elia Photo Service was successful, partially due his relationship with the Jerusalem Order of Freemasons and its tight connections with British authorities, what his son, the current owner, referred to as 'help from above'. Elsewhere, his son states that Elia worked with the British Army and Air Force, developing and printing their pictures.[31] This is likely considering the existence of a small number of Kahvedjian's aerial photographs. The common rumour that I found in my own conversations with Jerusalemites was that Kahvedjian was British 'spy'. Perhaps coincidentally, his son relates that in 1948, a British officer told Kahvedjian to gather his things on the eve of the Nakba and leave his store on Jaffa Street.[32]

Kahvedjian's photographs differ from that of the American Colony and Khalīl Ra'ad. The former portrays Palestine as unaffected by British occupation and Zionist settlement. They idealise or exoticise Palestinians, largely naturalise British presence, and, to a lesser extent, document Zionist life in Palestine: images are, for example, of the wheat harvest, veiled women, fortune tellers, Domaris, coffee sellers, porters with blurred 'modern' men in background and sign which seems to be in Hebrew and Arabic; there are architectural photographs such as that of Damascus gate that diminish the presence of military offices whose blurry figures blend in with 'natives' in Arab garb. Images such as that of a shabby Jewish sous seller (clearly a member of the non-Ashkenazi Old Yishuv), the legendary Hurva Synagogue in Jewish Quarter, Dizengoff Square in Tel Aviv, a Purim parade, the entrance to Rosh Hanikra kibbutz, the Kapulsky coffee wagon (which would become an Israeli chain) and the Zeppelin over Jerusalem all are popular images among Israelis.[33]

---

30   This information was relayed first hand to me by Kevork Kahvedjian at Elia Photo in Jerusalem. Some of the biographical information can also be found in Kevork Kahvedjian, *Jerusalem Through My Father's Eyes* (Jerusalem: Elia Photo Service, 1998).

31   For an example, see "Aerial View of Jerusalem 1936," Kahvedjian, *Jerusalem Through My Father's Eyes*, 59.

32   Allen Williams, "Dom Photographs in the Collection of Elia Kahvedjian," in *Kuri: Journal of the Dom Research Center* vol. 1, no. 10 (2004), found at http://www.domresearch center.com/journal/110/elia110.html, last accessed Feb. 2, 2020; and Nir Hasson, "The Finest Photographs of Early 20th Century Palestine, Shuttered in Controversy," *Haaretz*, Feb. 5, 2012, http://www.haaretz.com/print-edition/features/the-finest-photographs-of -early-20th-century-palestine-shuttered-in-controversy-1.411086, last accessed Feb. 2, 2020.

33   Many of these images can be found in Kahvedjian, *Jerusalem Through My Father's Eyes*.

There are, however, among this collection a small handful of quotidian images, with movement and a documentary quality. One of the most popular photographs sold in Elia Photo Services is the image of men 'eating hummus' (1935). The image depicts workers in the winter in Jerusalem's Old City, eating hummus at an outdoor hummus kiosk. Indeed, the image can be read a number of ways. It is contemporary and even pushes back on many of the character types and idealised images of Kahvedjian's commercial practice.

On the one hand, what we can call the manifest level, the photograph can easily be romanticised, representing a space where the tribulations of Zionist colonisation and British rule in Palestine are absent. It can be seen as a sort of free-space of pure enjoyment, comradery and social interaction, which has yet to become saturated by the colonisation process or the vagaries of British rule.

The comments and analysis of the image, more often, concentrate on the centrality of hummus as a universal identification with these men, not as Palestinians, but as guys, like you, me and Israelis, who just cannot help but love hummus.

The impulse to displace the Palestinian experience, and indeed presence, in photography is captured in an interview precisely about this image by an Australian filmmaker, Trevor Graham. Graham started a blog, titled 'Make Hummus Not War'. In 2011 published an interview on his blog with Elia's son, Kevork Kahvedjian, who subsequently has passed away. Graham's project tracing Palestinian, Lebanese and Israeli competing claims to hummus eventually became a film by the same name.[34] Graham asks Elia's son what he thinks about the 'hummus controversy' where Israelis claim the dish as their own. The studio owner replies, hummus 'is so delicious, that everybody tries to claim it for themselves. It's okay. As long as it's delicious, I don't care. I don't mind'.[35] Kahvedjian clarifies his priorities, saying 'the situation here is hard for everyone, although I can tell you that the Armenians are positively neutral people. We are a family of photographers, and that's what interests us'.[36]

Kahvedjian's answer and the interviewer's questions – and certainly the commercial popularity of the trope of substituting hummus for contention – employs a critical psychological defensive mechanism; that of disavowal.

---

34   Trevor Graham, *Make Hummus Not War* (Australia, 2012), 1:17 mins.

35   Trevor Graham's 2011 interview with Kevork Kahvedjian is reproduced on his blog, *Make Hummus Not War*, found at http://www.makehummusnotwar.com/characters_14.html, last accessed Feb. 2, 2020.

36   "Elia Photo Service in Jerusalem," ClaudiaExpat, June 2012, found at https://www .expatclic.com/elia-photo-service-in-jerusalem/?lang=en, last accessed Feb. 3, 2020.

FIGURE 10.3   *Eating Hummus*, 1935. Elia Kahvedjian. Elia Studio Jerusalem

Disavowal (for Freud, or 'foreclosure' for Lacan – *Verwerfung-forclusion-repudiation*)[37] allows one to 'repudiate' discordant reality that threatens the self-image and ego-coherence. Disavowal splits off the part of reality from the self that causes dissonance and discomfort invoked by reality.

The obsession with hummus serves as a culinary universal that assumedly connects people and temporalities, but also it repudiates historical and social realities. Kahvedjian's disavowal of the historical and contemporary realities of Palestine protects the assumed 'neutrality' of the Armenian community within the Palestine-Israel conflict. It contains an annihilation anxiety passed down through the transgenerational transmission of the trauma of genocide and insisting the 'neutrality' of the Palestinian-Armenian community: let's ignore – that is, *disavow* – history. Let's repudiate the asymmetries of present realities. It's hard for everyone. Hummus is so delicious and photography is apolitical and what really 'interests us'.

But on a larger scale, the fixation of this indexical surface invokes a nostalgic identification with the act of simple eating, eating hummus *en pleine* air, on rustic tables, tin plates, with simple bread while the compactness of the image and the overflowing figures highlight the apolitical act of the universal

37   Jacques Lacan, *The Seminar. Book III. The Psychoses, 1955–56*, trans. Russell Grigg (New York: Norton, 1993).

sociability of eating. Everybody loves hummus. It defends the coherence of liberal narratives that assert 'make hummus not war', which is the name of the blogger's site.

The reading of 'eating hummus' and the rapture of hummus deflects from and denies the political and historical realities and imperatives of 1930s Palestine. Indeed, we do not have to 'care' about the claim that hummus can be 'Israeli' without being Palestinian because it is 'so delicious'. The retreat into the shared commonalities of our humanity, coupled still with the anonymity of the photograph's subjects, converts the image into a validation of the hummus-loving spectator *not* the Palestinian as a national, political and class subject. The official title, in fact, is 'Eating Hummus': a title with no subject.

To arrive at the latent, we start at this manifest, the all-male space broken by the variety of ages, the smile of the boy in the background acknowledging the photographic event while, at the same time, the three men are lost in the ecstasy of extending their bread into their dishes and the central figure is almost performative in his hummus rapture. There is no sense of 'traditional men' doing 'traditional' work, both terms that can only be ambiguous and clarified with stereotyped answers and images. The photograph is, however, unambiguously an image of men who work; modern workers. It is an infrequent image of 'real' Palestinian labourers, very likely carbing up in the morning for their long day's work in a cold, damp Jerusalem winter.

This reading is the beginning of latent analysis, which should not be confused with speculation. The analysis of the latent allows us to identify and root analysis in material and historical realities (in and out of the frame) that saturates an image and burst through the orientalised, commodifying lens. This liberation of an image allows it to be read as document and/or enunciation of the quotidian life of modern Palestinian labour. But what is outside this image of workers and kept at bay by the fetishised delights of hummus? The labour in this image is likely an effect of the historical moment, labour that was essential to the economic transformations and jostling of the 1930s. The origins of urban labour lay in the dispossession of Palestinian peasantry during the 1920s and 1930s, who were removed from lands after they were sold by absentee landlords to the Jewish National Fund. Others were subject to increased rents and ravaged by two decades of over-taxation. Yet more were adversely affected by the transformation of the Palestinian economy with the opening of Palestine's market to cheaper imported goods by the British.

The disenfranchisement and increased landlessness of the Palestinian peasantry led to the migration of rural Palestinian communities to urban areas, at the same time that the British declared a minimum wage for Palestinians less than that minimum wage required for Jewish labour.[38] As a result, the construction boom sparked by large scale Zionist construction projects and the Mandate government – a boom that contrasted the agricultural downturn – was often facilitated by cheap Palestinian labour until the Great Revolt of 1936.[39] To look at these labourers in 1935, we understand their origins and their material conditions. Moreover, we understand the history, the present and the direction of this image, not frozen in hummus rapture, but within their contemporary social relations that will make for a revolt.

These workers became the fighters of that popular uprising against Zionist colonisation and British rule. The Great Revolt of 1936–1939, in fact, started with a widespread and comprehensive national strike. The strike was largely organised and initiated by Palestinian labour, whose up-swell of pressure forced the Palestinian elite to sign on (and later usurp). Therefore, perhaps the more accurate title of this photograph should not be 'Eating Hummus, 1935' but 'Palestinians on the Eve of the Great Revolt'.

Bibliography

Alloula, Malek. *The Colonial Harem*. Minneapolis: University of Minnesota Press, 1985.

Azoulay, Ariella Aisha. *Potential History: Unlearning Imperialism*. New York: Verso, 2019.

Barakat, Rana. "The Jerusalem Fellah: Popular Politics in Mandate-Era Palestine." *Journal of Palestine Studies* VLVI, no. 1 (2016): 7–19.

---

38   Zachary Lockman clearly shows that the British worked to suppress the wages of Palestinian workers and peasantry and keep them always subordinate to and below mandated minimum wages for Jewish settlers. See Zachary Lockman, *Comrades and Enemies: Arab and Jewish Workers in Palestine, 1906–1948* (Berkeley: University of California Press, 1997); for example, 101–102. For a recent and very thorough examination of the process by which Zionist 'development' caused Palestinian peasantry to become dispossessed, see Charles Anderson, "The British Mandate and the crisis of Palestinian Landlessness, 1929–1936", *Middle Eastern Studies*, 54, no. 2 (2018), 171–215.

39   For a more extension discussion of the Great Revolt, see Rana Barakat, "The Jerusalem Fellah: Popular Politics in Mandate-Era Palestine," *Journal of Palestine Studies*, VLVI, no. 1 (2016); Matthew Kraig Kelly, "The Revolt of 1936: A Revision," *Journal of Palestine Studies*, VLIV, no. 2 (2015): 28–42; Julie Peteet, *Gender in Crisis: Women and the Palestinian Resistance Movement* (New York: Columbia University Press, 1991), 33–66; Ellen Fleischmann, *The Nation and Its "New" Women: The Palestinian Women's Movement 1920–1948* (Berkeley: University of California, 2003); and Ted Swedenburg, *Memories of Revolt: The 1936–1939 Rebellion and the Palestinian National Past* (Fayetteville: University of Arkansas, 2003).

Barakat, Rana. "Writing/Righting Palestine Studies: Settler Colonialism, Indigenous Sovereignty and Resisting the Ghost(s) of History." *Settler Colonial Studies* 8, no. 3 (2018): 349–363.

Bloxham, Donald. *The Great Game of Genocide: Imperialism, Nationalism, and the Destruction of the Ottoman Armenians.* Oxford: Oxford University Press, 2005.

Castro-Gómez, Santiago. "The Missing Chapter of Empire: Postmodern Re-organization of Coloniality and Post-Fordist Capitalism." *Cultural Studies* 21, nos. 2–3 (2007): 428–448.

Dadrian, Vahakn. "The Armenian Question and the Wartime Fate of the Armenians as Documented by the Officials of the Ottoman Empire's World War I Allies: Germany and Austria-Hungary." *International Journal of Middle East Studies* 34, no. 1 (2002): 59–85.

Debbas, Fouad. *Beirut: Our Memory; A Guided Tour Illustrated with Picture Postcards.* 2nd ed. Beirut: Naufal, 1986.

El-Hage, Badr. *Saudi Arabia: Caught in Time 1861–1939.* London: Garnet, 1997.

El-Hage, Badr. *Shweir and Its Hills: A Photographic Record.* Translated by Sabah Ghandour. Beirut: Kutub, 2013.

"Elia Photo Service in Jerusalem." ClaudiaExpat, June 2012. Found at https://www.expatclic.com/elia-photo-service-in-jerusalem/?lang=en. Last accessed Feb. 3, 2020.

Elmessiri, Abdelwahab. *The Palestinian Wedding: A Bilingual Anthology of Contemporary Palestinian Poetry.* Washington, D.C.: Three Continents Press, 1982.

Fani, Michel. *Liban 1848–1914: L'atelier photographique de Ghazir.* Paris: Éditions de l'Escalier, 1995.

Fleischmann, Ellen. *The Nation and Its "New" Women: The Palestinian Women's Movement 1920–1948.* Berkeley: University of California, 2003.

Graham, Trevor. Make Hummus Not War (Australia, 2012). Film and blog. Trevor Graham's 2011 interview with Kevork Kahvedjian is reproduced on his blog, found at http://www.makehummusnotwar.com/characters_14.html. Last accessed Feb. 2, 2020.

Hartman, Saidiya. *Wayward Lives, Beautiful Experiments: Intimate Histories of Social Upheaval.* New York: Norton, 2019.

Hasson, Nir. "The Finest Photographs of Early 20th Century Palestine, Shuttered in Controversy." *Haaretz*, Feb. 5, 2012. http://www.haaretz.com/print-edition/features/the-finest-photographs-of-early-20th-century-palestine-shuttered-in-controversy-1.411086. Last accessed Feb. 2, 2020.

Kelly, Matthew Kraig. "The Revolt of 1936: A Revision." *Journal of Palestine Studies* VLIV, no. 2 (2015): 28–42.

Khalidi, Walid. *Before Their Diaspora: A Photographic History of the Palestinians 1876–1948.* Washington D.C.: Institute for Palestine Studies, 1984.

Lacan, Jacques. *The Seminar Book I: Freud's Papers on Technique 1953–54*. Translated by John Forrester. New York: Norton, 1988.

Lacan, Jacques. *The Seminar. Book III. The Psychoses, 1955–56*. Translated by Russell Grigg. New York: Norton, 1993.

Marx, Karl. "Introduction to a Critique of Political Economy." In *The German Ideology*. Amherst, NY: Prometheus, 1988.

McKittrick, Katherine. "Mathematics Black Life." *The Black Scholar* 44, no. 2 (2014): 16–28.

Mirzoeff, Nicholas. *The Right to Look: A Counterhistory of Visuality*. Durham, NC: Duke University Press, 2011.

Kahvedjian, Kevork. *Jerusalem Through My Father's Eyes*. Jerusalem: Elia Photo Service, 1998.

Pappé, Ilan. *The Ethnic Cleansing of Palestine*. London and New York: Oneworld, 2006.

Peteet, Julie. *Gender in Crisis: Women and the Palestinian Resistance Movement*. New York: Columbia University Press, 1991.

Phillips, Melanie. "Faking a Killing." Standpoint, June 27, 2008. Found at https://standpointmag.co.uk/faking-a-killing-july/?page=0%2C0%2C0%2C0%2C0%2C0%2C0%2C0%2C0%2C0%2C0%2C2.

Qassim, Samih. "Kafr Qassim." (Poem in Arabic).

Quijano, Aníbal. "Coloniality and Modernity/Rationality." *Cultural Studies* 21, nos. 2–3 (2007): 168–178.

Shaheen, Naseeb. *A Pictorial History of Ramallah*. Beirut: Arab Institute for Research and Publishing, 1992.

Sheehi, Stephen. "The Nahda After-Image, or All Photography Expresses Social Relations." *Third Text* 26, no. 4 (July 2012): 401–414.

Sheehi, Stephen. *Arab Imago: A Social History of Portrait Photography, 1860–1910*. Princeton: University of Princeton Press, 2016.

Swedenburg, Ted. *Memories of Revolt: The 1936–1939 Rebellion and the Palestinian National Past*. Fayetteville: University of Arkansas, 2003.

Williams, Allen. "Dom Photographs in the Collection of Elia Kahvedjian." in *Kuri: Journal of the Dom Research Center* 1, no. 10 (2004). Found at http://www.domresearchcenter.com/journal/110/elia110.html. Last accessed Feb. 2, 2020.

CHAPTER 11

Urban Encounters: Imaging the City in Mandate Palestine

Nadi Abusaada

In the first half of the twentieth century, Palestine witnessed significant transformations in its urban built environment. These changes, while originating in the late Ottoman era, intensified under the British Mandate with the introduction of new inter-urban infrastructures and regional and urban planning policies that controlled urban expansion and the construction of new urban and rural settlements.[1] The new urban planning development procedures, however, were not merely a technical exercise – they supplemented British imperial aspirations and their endorsement of Jewish settlement in Palestine. In the interwar period, urban affairs turned into a primary field of political confrontation and contestation between the local Arab population, Zionist settlers and the British administration.

This period of urban change in Palestine paralleled the rise of photographic production as a principal method for documenting and representing the built environment. Until the late nineteenth century, the dominant depictions of Palestine's urban and rural landscapes were the works of Orientalists and Biblical scholars interested in excavating and documenting sites of holy relevance for European audiences. By the start of the Mandate period, photography had already become a common practice by foreign groups and locals alike. Arabs, Zionists, the British administration, and other interest groups (e.g. foreign missionaries) all grew increasingly aware of the power of photographic representations of the urban built environment, albeit utilising this power to serve ideologically distinctive, even oppositional, visions and projects.[2]

This chapter examines the historical intersection between photographic practice and urban change in the colonial context of interwar Palestine. More specifically, it aims to trace the different ways in which photographs were

---

1 J. Fruchtman, "Statutory Planning as a Form of Social Control: The Evolution of Town Planning Law in Mandatory Palestine and Israel 1917–1980's" (PhD diss., University of London, 1986), http://discovery.ucl.ac.uk/1317972/.

2 See in this volume chapters by Karène Sanchez Summerer and Norig Neveu, Sary Zananiri, and Yazan Kopty.

utilised to represent the cities of Palestine, mainly from British and Arab perspectives.[3] With this in mind, the following sections will shed light on a variety of photographic perspectives in representing Palestine's urban built environment in the interwar era. To highlight the links between these different perspectives and the varying visions among and between British and Arab actors in Palestine, however, the chapter focuses not on the original photographs or photographers themselves, but on the deliberate reproduction of photographs and photographic collections by groups or individuals interested in expressing a particular vision, colonial or otherwise, of the urban built environment.

To this end, the following sections will shed light on three interrelated attitudes of photographic representation of Palestine's urban fabrics in the interwar period. First, the city as a target for military operations, focusing on the advent of aerial photography in the Great War, its development in the Mandate period, and its relationship to British imperial visions in Palestine. Second, the utilisation of *vues d'ensemble* ('holistic views') of urban fabrics in the documentation and intervention in urban analysis and planning, through the use of both aerial photographic and ground panoramas of urban spaces. Countering these two attitudes, which were mainly a product of foreign and imperial activities, the third section addresses the rising interest among Palestine's local Arab population in the photographic imaging of their cities as a reflection of their new societal ideals of progress, modernity and development, particularly in Arabic-language press. These three distinctive yet interrelated attitudes towards urban photography offer an understanding of photography not only as an end in itself, but as a means to an end, linked to colonial and native desires not only to represent but also reshape urban spaces.

The materials in which these three different approaches to representing the urban built environment appear have been collected from a wide range of sources. The archival sources include the Bavarian State Archives, the Australian War Museum, the National Library of Israel, and the Qatar Digital Library. In addition, a collection of original publications including books, reports and magazines from the 1920s–30s in English, Arabic and German are also consulted and examined. Hence, if the focus in this article is mostly on the immediate after-lives of photographs – that is, on the ways original

---

3 While it is realised that the Zionists, too, had a vested interest in the photographic representation of the urban built environment and urban development in Palestine during this period, a thorough analysis of Zionist imaging of the cities is beyond the scope of this study. Nonetheless, given that many aspects of British and Arab representations of cities in Palestine were ultimately shaped or influenced by their interactions with the Zionist movement, some elements of such encounters are addressed.

photographs were re-produced in different formats within a few years of their production – then the stories of how these different reproductions ended up where they did adds additional layers and raise further questions regarding the complex and multifaceted nature of these photographs' afterlives.

1   Aerial Imagery and Military Strategy

In 1915, following Ottoman-German advancement into the British-controlled Sinai Peninsula and their attempt to invade the Suez Canal, several battles were fought in southern Palestine. As the war commenced, and as German-Ottoman armies retreated, these battles shifted north until British armies gained full control of Palestine. The visually abundant nature of these battles was unlike anything the country had witnessed in its long history of foreign invasions. This was not only because of the nature of the Great War as an event covered by media outlets globally, but also in the then-new advancements in photography and aerial warfare technology – producing the first ever aerial photographs of landscapes. In the Great War, the ability to see cities from above became intractably tied to gaining military advantage over enemy troops. In their confrontations, both German and British armies used airplanes to drop bombs on enemy territory. They also utilised aeroplanes for aerial reconnaissance and the production of war maps.

By the time British troops reached northern Palestine, British-Australian and Bavarian squadrons had captured several thousand aerial photographs covering wide expanses of Palestine as well as Egypt, Lebanon, and Jordan (Fig. 11.1). These photographs were used to detect the abilities of enemy troops and predict their movements, and both the British and the Germans devised military handbooks to assist in their analysis. Comparing British and German handbooks on the tactical use of photographs from the war, Benjamin Kedar points to the higher level of sophistication presented by the Germans. Kedar notes that whereas the British booklets only present a 'series of rudimentarily interpreted photographs', the German booklets include a 'table of the various types of British tents, the purposes they serve, their surface in square meters, and the number of men they can accommodate' in addition to methodically grouped photographs that provide clues to the size of the enemy in question.[4]

---

4 Benjamin Z. Kedar, *The Changing Land: Between the Jordan and the Sea: Aerial Photographs from 1917 to the Present* (Detroit: Wayne State University Press, 1999), 28.

The culmination of these photographic advancements with the war effort produced an entirely new understanding not only of warfare strategies but also of landscapes. In the Bavarian and Australian aerial photographs alike, the urban landscape below was abstracted into a series of quantifiable features that marked the extent to which the territory depicted in the photograph poses a threat. On many of the aerial photographs that survive in the Bavarian State Archives and the Australian War Memorial, hand-drawn lines around targeted areas appear, marking the locations of enemy targets. These targets were often troop camps, located outside the towns, but in close proximity to them to ensure their connection to the main transport infrastructures and access to essential utilities (particularly water and health facilities). In most cases, the defeat of these suburban camps entailed the capture of the towns that they encircled. Overall, it can be said that although the cities' surroundings were clear military targets for the Germans and the British during the war, their inner built fabrics remained, for the most part, relatively unharmed by the war effort.

While for the Germans, the Great War marked the end of their imperial interests and aerial navigations in the 'East', this was far from being the case for the British. After the war, the British devised new strategies of 'air control' over its new mandated territories, based on their desire to safeguard their imperial interests and contain attempts of rebellion. Among the earliest applications of this new scheme of 'air control' by the British Royal Air Force (RAF) was used in 1919 in Iraq in an effort to tame the Iraqi revolt against British colonial rule. In this new scheme, Priya Satia explains, 'the RAF collapsed the mission of regenerating Babylonia into the more urgent task of patrolling the country from a network of bases and coordinating information from agents on the ground to bombard subversive villages and tribes'.[5] Although airpower was also used elsewhere at the time, Satia shows that 'it was in Iraq that the British would rigorously practice, if never perfect, the technology of bombardment as a permanent method of colonial administration and surveillance and there that they would fully theorise the value of airpower as an independent arm of the military'.[6]

In Palestine, the most systematic use of airpower by the British took place nearly two decades later, in the context of the Arab-led Great Revolt against the British administration. The revolt, which was mainly directed against the British administration, demanded Arab independence, an end to the British

5   Priya Satia, *Spies in Arabia: The Great War and the Cultural Foundations of Britain's Covert Empire in the Middle East* (Oxford: Oxford University Press, 2008), 240.
6   Ibid., 240.

FIGURE 11.1   *Map of Bavarian aerial photographs in Palestine during the Great War, 1916–18.*
Map by author
DATA SOURCES: BAVARIAN STATE ARCHIVES, GOOGLE EARTH

endorsement of a 'Jewish National Home' in Palestine, and to cease its facilita-
tion of Zionist immigration and land settlement. As Jacob Norris illustrates, the
revolt initially manifested as an elitist and urban-led campaign of civil disobe-
dience and later developed into a far more violent and peasant-led resistance
movement.[7] While the eventual decline of the revolt in 1939 has often been
attributed to internal weaknesses and divisions among the Arab population,
Norris aptly shows that British counterinsurgency played a considerable role
in the revolt's demise.[8] Nonetheless, unlike in 1919 Iraq, British counterinsurgency activity in 1936 Palestine took place in the context of an established civil
administration and policy and, as a result, had to balance between its civil and
military forces. Hence, while it departed from the 'air control' schemes developed in Iraq, it still utilised what the British termed a strategy of 'combined

---

7   Jacob Norris, 'Repression and Rebellion: Britain's Response to the Arab Revolt in Palestine of
    1936–39', *The Journal of Imperial and Commonwealth History* 36, no. 1 (2008): 25–45; Weldon
    Matthews, *Confronting an Empire, Constructing a Nation: Arab Nationalists and Popular
    Politics in Mandate Palestine* (London: I.B.Tauris, 2006).
8   Ibid., 27.

action' based on full cooperation between ground and air forces to overcome the restrictions of British civil policy, particularly on the 'employment of land forces on offensive duties'.[9]

In 1938, the British published a report titled 'Military Lessons of the Arab Rebellion in Palestine 1936' which, as its title suggests, was based on their various operations during the period of the revolt. The sections in the report include a short history of the rebellion, conditions affecting operations, commanders and staffs, intelligence, intercommunications, administration, transport, weapons and equipment, the employment of the various arms, the employment of aircraft, defensive action, protection of communications and offensive action. The report also includes several photographs of the different military operations, assessments, and documentation of the different vehicles and equipment used in the duration of the revolt.[10] But the most striking among these are the series of aerial photographs of the Palestinian port city of Jaffa, in which one of the most destructive operations during the revolt was carried out: the demolition of a significant proportion of the Old City.

Between 30th May and 30th June 1936, the British undertook a series of operations that radically altered the future of the revolt and of the city of Jaffa. They realised the significance of conducting these operations in Jaffa, as one of the most principal centres for Arab economic and political urban life in Palestine. For them, however, it was Jaffa's Old City in particular that posed the most serious threat to their ability to maintain control over the city and tame Arab rebellious activity, despite the fact that by the 1930s it was merely a quarter within the much larger municipal area of Jaffa. 'The Old City of Jaffa', the 1938 British report states, 'had long been a hotbed of lawlessness and revolt, and such had usually set the example for rebellious activities all over the country'.[11] The concentration of British counterinsurgency on the Old City, and its distinction from the so-called New City, was not incidental. It was based on a culmination of British negative assumptions and attitudes regarding both the Old City's population, constituting one of the poorest quarters of the city, and its urban layout and built fabric.

---

9   'Military Lessons of the Arab Rebellion in Palestine 1936', 1938, IOR/L/MIL/17/16/16, British Library: India Office Records and Private Papers; For more on the British strategy of "combined action" in Palestine during the Great Revolt, see Nadi Abusaada, "Combined Action: Aerial Imagery and the Urban Landscape in Interwar Palestine," *Jerusalem Quarterly* 81 (2020): 20–36.

10   For more on the report, see Abusaada, 'Combined Action: Aerial Imagery and the Urban Landscape in Interwar Palestine, 1918–40'.

11   'Military Lessons of the Arab Rebellion in Palestine 1936,' 156.

The 1938 report explicitly links the targeting of the Old City to the socio-economic status of its inhabitants, which it describes as 'the toughest of all Arab elements, consisting mostly of boatmen of Greek descent who earned their living handling lighters in the Port of Jaffa, a difficult and dangerous occupation'.[12] It was this population in particular that suffered from the increased rivalry between Jaffa and its nearby new Jewish settlement of Tel Aviv. After the start of the British Mandate, Tel Aviv benefited immensely from the relaxed British policies towards Jewish immigration and development – all at the expense of Jaffa. In the early 1930s, schemes were made public for the construction of a new port in Tel Aviv, just north of Jaffa's historic Arab port.[13] Hence, while the report describes the Old City's inhabitants' 'natural dislike for authority,' it also admits the role of the 'shadow of a harbourage scheme for Tel Aviv, which appeared likely to strike directly at the livelihood of the Jaffa boatmen' in instigating their rebellion against the British administration.[14]

The targeting of the Old City was influenced not only by British attitudes towards the Old City's inhabitants but also towards its architecture. Unlike the broad avenues, detached buildings, open public squares and grid-like layout that characterised Jaffa's modern neighbourhoods, or the New City, the Old City was ordered according to a considerably different spatial logic. As with many historic cities of the Eastern Mediterranean whose main fabrics were built before the nineteenth century, the Old City of Jaffa is more densely built, and its roads are not straight and often end in cul-de-sacs. For the British, the fabric of the Old City provided an 'ample opportunity'[15] for its inhabitants' ability to conduct rebellion activities:

> Built upon a low hill flanked on one side by the sea, it completely dominated the Port and such buildings as the police station and barracks and the District Commissioner's offices, which lay in the New City. Moreover its houses formed a veritable rabbit warren through which dark and narrow streets turned and twisted into a maze in which the level of one street would often be the roof of the houses in the one below and where few passages were so wide that they could not be spanned by the reach of a man's arms. It represented in fact an exceedingly complicated trench

12   Ibid., 156.

13   Ibid.; for more on the historical relationship between the two cities of Jaffa and Tel Aviv, see Mark LeVine, *Overthrowing Geography: Jaffa, Tel Aviv, and the Struggle for Palestine, 1880–1948* (Berkeley: University of California Press, 2005); Sharon Rotbard, *White City, Black City: Architecture and War in Tel Aviv and Jaffa* (London: Pluto Press, 2015).

14   'Military Lessons of the Arab Rebellion in Palestine 1936,' 156.

15   Ibid., 157.

system with vertical slides some thirty to forty feet high, which could readily be converted into a regular citadel.[16]

While aspects of this description are specific to Jaffa's urban fabric, particularly the proximity of the Old City to the port and its topographical advantage over British administrative buildings in the New City, the negative attitude towards the Old City's 'dark and narrow streets' and 'maze'-like layout are not uncommon to British discourses surrounding poor urban quarters in the 1930s, an era that witnessed an upsurge in 'urban renewal' projects and 'slum clearances' in England.[17] In fact, before the start of the operation, British aeroplanes dropped down leaflets that described the demolitions as being 'for the improvement of the Old City'[18] echoing these new discourses. Needless to say, however, the nature and motivations of the operations at Jaffa, carried by a military force and intended to serve imperial aspirations, were markedly distinct from slum clearances in England that were carried on the basis of Housing and Town Planning acts, despite their similar outcomes.

The British divided their operations in Jaffa into four different phases: first, a retaliatory offensive attack against houses from which fire had been directed; second, the clearing of the approaches and cleaning up of the town at the edge of the Old City; third, the driving of a road through the Old City from East to West by means of demolition; and fourth, the driving of a similar road to run North and South in a crescent shape.[19] Significantly, these operations relied heavily on a series of aerial photographs taken by a Royal Air Force Squadron. These photographs, included in the British report on the operation, were used to study the Old City of Jaffa from above – and to identify the exact areas where the demolition activities in the operation's third and fourth phases were to take place (Fig. 11.2). Points labelled 'A', 'B', 'C' and 'D' were marked on the aerial photographs, and lines were drawn connecting them indicating the buildings to be demolished. Additional aerial photographs were taken following the operation, showing the newly-opened arteries or, as the British called them, 'good wide roads' that aggressively ran through the heart of the Old City.[20] It was this operation, the British write in their report, that 'mark[ed] the end of organised resistance in the towns' during the period of the revolt, before the main rebel activities were transferred to the hills and the countryside.[21]

16   Ibid., 157.
17   Arthur Peter Becker, "Housing in England and Wales during the Business Depression of the 1930's," *The Economic History Review* 3, no. 3 (1951): 321–41.
18   'Military Lessons of the Arab Rebellion in Palestine 1936,' 158.
19   'Military Lessons of the Arab Rebellion in Palestine 1936,' 157–8.
20   Ibid., 159.
21   Ibid., 159.

FIGURE 11.2   'Jaffa Old City – The dotted line A-B marks the approximate line of the first Demolitions'
SOURCE: 'MILITARY LESSONS OF THE ARAB REBELLION IN PALESTINE,' 1936, 1938 IOR/L/MIL/17/16/16, BRITISH LIBRARY: INDIA OFFICE RECORDS AND PRIVATE PAPERS

Looking at the 1936 aerial photographs of Jaffa against British aerial photographs from the Great War reveals the shifting official British attitude towards the cities of Palestine, from one that deliberately avoided urban destruction to the taking of drastic measures against an urban population and their city. Aerial photography, a practice that paralleled the developments in warfare technologies during the Great War, has enabled a different view of cities that changed the relationship between photography and the city. Seeing the city from above, while not sufficient for targeting cities, has played a considerable role in enabling such targeting where the necessary power for it became available. Hovering over territories and capturing them from above enabled the representation of places that are inaccessible at ground-level. Clearly, aerial power was not limited to photography (e.g. direct bombardment), and photography that enabled the targeting of cities was not limited to aerial photography (e.g. ground photographic surveillance). Nonetheless, it was the culmination of aerial power and photography that produced the most effective results in targeting urban spaces. With these representations, operations on the ground became more informed, and hence more prone to success – qualities that proved especially useful for the Germans and the British in the context of the Great War and the British taming of the Great Revolt in Palestine.

2   Holistic Views and Colonial Planning

The militaristic targeting of urban spaces during the Great War and in the interwar period presented what is arguably the most direct, and violently destructive, form of imperial and colonial confrontation with Palestine's urban landscape in the interwar period. Nonetheless, it was not the only, or even most significant, shift in representations of and interventions in Palestine's urban landscape that paralleled interwar photographic developments. In this period, photography, and especially views from above that provided a *vue d'ensemble* – a comprehensive picture of the landscape – proved to be an instrumental tool for the development of what Jeanne Haffner identifies as a new 'science of social space'[22] which, though critical for militaristic and warfare operations, was also crucial for the work of professionals interested in the scientific study and intervention in the urban landscape, including archaeologists, planners, engineers and architects. These 'scientific' approaches to photography and the urban landscape were particularly significant in the context of Palestine, whose urban landscape had been primarily approached by European Orientalists in the nineteenth century as the Biblical Holy Land.[23]

    In Palestine, aerial photography proved instrumental not only for the emergence of new methods of urban representation, but also interpretation, that departed from typical Biblical frameworks. The first extensive publication to scientifically interpret the aerial photographs and the *vue d'ensemble* of Palestine's urban landscape for non-militaristic purposes after the Great War was Gustaf Dalman's 1925 book, *Hundert deutsche Fliegerbilder aus Palästina*.[24] Dalman, a German Lutheran theologian and archaeologist, had a long

---

22   Jeanne Haffner, *The View from Above: The Science of Social Space* (Cambridge: MIT Press, 2013).

23   See in this volume chapters by Yazan Kopty, Sary Zananiri, and Karène Sanchez Summerer and Norig Neveu; Beshara Doumani, "Rediscovering Ottoman Palestine: Writing Palestinians into History," *Journal of Palestine Studies* 21, no. 2 (1 January 1992): 5–28.

24   Archaeological efforts were a key element of Ottoman-German interest during the war. Under the instructions of the German archaeologist Theodor Wiegand (1864–1936), who served as a captain of the Ottoman-German militia artillery in the Asia Corps, Bavarian aeroplanes captured photographs of some of the main archaeological sites in the region. In 1918, based on a direct order from Djemal Pasha, Wiegand published *Alte Denkmäler aus Syrien, Palästina und Westarabien*, a bilingual Ottoman-Turkish and German book. The book included two sections: an introduction by Djemal Pasha in which he states some administrative measures he took to improve the preservation of historical monuments and to 'protect them' from the Allies, and a commentary essay by Wiegand, based on a series of one hundred illustrations (mainly photographs) of major archaeological sites and textual descriptions. See Theodor Wiegand and Ahmed Djemal Pascha, *Alte*

experience working in Palestine before the war where he worked as the first director of the Jerusalem-based German Protestant Institute for the Study of Archaeology in the Holy Land (DIEAHL), founded in 1900.[25] During his time in Palestine, Dalman led several excavations at archaeological sites around the country, took hundreds photographs and glass slides, and published numerous academic writings including the annual volumes of DIEAHL's Palestine Yearbook.

In the book, Dalman explicitly expresses his criticism of mainstream productions and photobooks of Biblical sites in Palestine produced by other Orientalists. Crucially, Dalman celebrates the role of nineteenth century photographic imagery of Palestine including, for example, the work of the Beirut-based Bonfils photographic studio, in replacing the 'fantasy images' and 'romantic depictions' of Biblical sites and landscapes.[26] For Dalman, these early photographs hold a 'special value' because they depict cities and their surroundings before they became 'heavily disfigured by the effects of Europeanization'.[27] Describing urban change in Nazareth, he writes, 'today's Nazareth is almost in the style of an Italian town, entirely unlike the image of Nazareth around 1870, which is in two large photographs before me, and so uncharacteristic that I found it difficult to recognise the details, though I visited Nazareth twice in 1899'.[28]

Despite his appreciation for these early photographs, Dalman does not shy away from expressing his reservations about the works of professional photographers in Palestine. He is critical of the tendency in photographic publications to exclude descriptions of what is being represented, the direction in which the photograph is taken or the exact time of recording the landscape.[29] In addition, he also problematises the one-sidedness of their attitudes toward holy places and historical sites and the lack of reliable, unbiased, information about their general situation or the nature of the land with which their history is connected.[30] 'The professional photographers in Palestine,' Dalman argues, 'are too dependent on what geographically and historically uninformed

Denkmäler aus Syrien, Palästina und Westarabien: 100 Tafeln mit beschreibendem Text (Berlin: G. Reimer, 1918).

25 "Foundation and First Aims (1900–1914)," *German Protestant Institute of Archeology* (blog), 20 July 2019, https://www.deiahl.de/ueber-das-dei/geschichte/1900-1914/.

26 Gustaf Dalman, *Hundert Deutsche Fliegerbilder Aus Palästina* (Gütersloh: Bertelsmann, 1925), 3.

27 Ibid., 3.

28 Ibid., 3.

29 Ibid., 3.

30 Ibid., 3.

tourists want to buy as souvenirs', thereby producing piecemeal images of 'antiquities' without sufficiently addressing the history and geography of the represented landscape.[31]

Dalman compiles a series of one hundred aerial photographs of Palestine's landscape, which to him presented an opportunity 'not only to see landscapes from above but to understand them'.[32] For each photograph, Dalman added a textual description of what is being represented, along with brief geographical and historical information on each specific site and its surroundings. These texts are not simply complementary, rather, they set the specific frame in which the spectator would gaze towards the photographs and interpret them. Dalman's descriptions are mainly spatial: he outlined, for each photograph, geographical features (topography and land and water features), the main neighbourhoods shown, the main public buildings and architectural monuments (hospitals, cemeteries, holy places, etc.) and the main routes leading in and out of urban centres (Fig. 11.3). It situated the depicted area within its wider regional context, including both the cities and the routes to their hinterlands or nearby suburbs, including the German Colonies in Jerusalem and Haifa. The fact that his main emphasis was on the *vue d'ensemble* of the geography and topography of the urban landscape, rather than isolated historical notes on these monuments, distinguished his book from the typical Biblical frameworks in which Palestine and its landscape had been understood throughout the nineteenth century.

As Dalman was preparing his study of Palestine's landscape in Germany, in Palestine, the British were devising new planning frameworks and policies for their intervention in urban built fabrics. The British concentrated their new planning policies on the city of Jerusalem, the religious and political capital of Mandate Palestine. In 1917, Colonel Ronald Storrs was appointed as the first military governor of Jerusalem. Storrs was heavily invested in the historical preservation of Jerusalem's built fabric.[33] Already in the first weeks of the military occupation, he announced a public notice intended to maintain the city's status quo in terms of construction activity. This was clear in the public notice he announced in the first weeks of the occupation:

> No Person shall demolish, erect, alter, or repair the structure of any building in the city of Jerusalem or its environs within a radius of 2,500 metres

31   Ibid., 3.
32   Ibid., 4.
33   Sir Ronald Storrs, *Orientations* (London: I. Nicholson & Watson, 1939).

FIGURE 11.3   Example of two pages from Gustaf Dalman's 1925 book, including descriptive texts for two
aerial photographs of Jerusalem
SOURCE: GUSTAF DALMAN, *HUNDERT DEUTSCHE FLIEGERBILDER AUS PALÄSTINA*
(GÜTERSLOH: BERTELSMANN, 1925), 12–13

from the Damascus Gate (Bab al Amud) until he has obtained a written
permit from the Military Governor.[34]

The notice was only intended as a temporary measure until matters of town
planning and building policies in Jerusalem were sorted. In 1918, Storrs
established the Pro-Jerusalem Society (1918–1926) which was aimed at: 'the
preservation and advancement of the interests of Jerusalem, its district and
inhabitants' and avoiding potential conflict between the different ethnic
groups in Jerusalem.[35] Storrs also appointed Charles Ashbee, a British architect

---

34   Charles Robert Ashbee, ed., *Jerusalem, 1918–1920: Being the Records of the Pro-Jerusalem
Council During the Period of the British Military Administration* (London: J. Murray, for the
Council of the Pro-Jerusalem Society, 1921), v.
35   Ibid., vii.

and planner, as the society's Civic Advisor and Secretary. These two decisions, it would later turn out, were incredibly significant for the future development of the city and would have a lasting effect on its inhabitants in the decades that followed.

At the time of his appointment, Ashbee, a friend and disciple of William Morris, was already known for his skill and enthusiasm for the Arts and Crafts movement of the late nineteenth and early twentieth centuries. In Britain, he was also a member of the Society for the Protection of Ancient Buildings and the National Trust. Though his stay in Jerusalem for a few years was short compared to the three decades of British rule over Palestine, his visions for the future of the city and its inhabitants, inspired by the Arts and Crafts movement, albeit accommodated for the context of Palestine, remain highly relevant for understanding the terms in which the British approached the city and its physical fabric in the years of military occupation and in the early stages of the civil administration.[36]

Crucially, Ashbee paid considerable attention to photographic materials and utilised them extensively in documenting, studying, and planning urban developments in the city of Jerusalem. This is evident in his Palestine notebook and two published reports he edited of the work of the Pro-Jerusalem Society, documenting their work in Jerusalem during the initial period of British military occupation (1918–20) and the first two years of the Mandate (1920–22).[37] The two reports include long sections on urban planning activities written by Ashbee, in addition to a number of short essays written by other European practitioners and scholars of archaeology and architecture in Palestine. In the sections written by Ashbee, he included several sub-sections reporting on the works undertaken under his supervisions reflecting, for the most part, his assessment of these works and visions for the future of the city. These were accompanied by sketches he drew and photographs that were mostly captured by American Colony photographers.

A key aspect of Ashbee's vision for Jerusalem is his clear distinction between the 'Old City' and the 'New City'. Ashbee's attitude towards the Old City, however, was not like the British attitude towards Jaffa in the 1930s. It rather stemmed, for the most part, from his architectural and archaeological

---

36   Wendy Pullan and Lefkos Kyriacou, "The Work of Charles Ashbee: Ideological Urban Visions with Everyday City Spaces," *Jerusalem Quarterly* 39 (2009): 51–61.

37   Charles Robert Ashbee, *A Palestine Notebook, 1918–1923* [1st ed.] (New York: Garden City, 1923); Ashbee, *Jerusalem, 1918–1920*; Charles Robert Ashbee, ed., *Jerusalem, 1920–1922: Being the Records of the Pro-Jerusalem Council During the First Two Years of the Civil Administration* (London: J. Murray, for the Council of the Pro-Jerusalem Society, 1924).

interest in the city's historic centre and his desire to preserve it from potential destruction: 'the disaster of the Great War has forced upon all men and women the necessity of preserving all that is possible of the beauty and the purpose, in actual form, of the civilisations that have passed before.' To him, however, this was not a 'mere matter of archaeology or the protection of ancient buildings'. As an active member of the Arts and Crafts movement, he also believed in preserving urban ideals from the 'blind mechanical order' which, to him, threatened the destruction of everything associated with 'beauty', that is, the 'landscape, the unities of streets and sites, the embodied vision of men that set the great whole together, [and] the sense of colour which in any Oriental city is still a living sense'.[38]

What is noteworthy about Ashbee's work in Jerusalem is not only what he envisioned for the city, but also the tools he used to articulate his visions. Photography was arguably one of the most important tools for him. Unlike Dalman, Ashbee's *vue d'ensemble* of Jerusalem's relied not on aerial photographs, but ground panoramic photographs taken from elevated positions by his staff and by American Colony photographers. For Ashbee, these panoramas were an essential medium to establish a visual hierarchy of what ought to be seen and what was deemed a visual nuisance. Since Ashbee treated the Old City as a 'unity in itself' that had to be protected from the encroachments of the New City, many of his plans were concentrated on the contact zone between the Old and New quarters.[39] In addition to his suggestions for the creation of a green buffer belt around the Old City's historical walls, Ashbee paid considerable attention to the opening-up of the panoramic views towards the Old City when it is approached from the New City. Two of his photograph-sketch compositions published in the 1921 report of the Pro-Jerusalem Society illustrate the primacy of the visual relationship between the Old City and the New City in his urban visions.

The first composition depicts a view of Jerusalem approached from south-west, on the Jaffa road (Fig. 11.4). The panoramic photograph depicts the view in its present state, overlooking the citadel, the Ottoman clocktower, the Old City – all at a higher elevation than the valley from which the photograph is captured. Some buildings also appear outside of the Old City, blocking parts of the view of the historic walls. Next to the photograph, Ashbee includes a photo caption: 'the Jaffa Gate reconstruction as at present, looking towards the city', omitting the Ottoman clocktower, which Ashbee had been mobilising for its destruction. Below the photograph, he sketched his own vision of the

---

38   Ashbee, *Jerusalem, 1918–1920*, 4.
39   Ashbee, *Jerusalem, 1920–1922*, 1.

panorama captioned: 'as suggested when the unsightly obstruction that hides
the walls are cleaned away'. In the sketch, the 'obstructive' buildings of the New
City do not appear, and the citadel and the city's historic walls appear enlarged
and more visible.

The second composition similarly depicts the approaches to the Old City
overlooking the road to Bethlehem, but in the opposite direction (Fig. 11.5). The
photograph, captured from an elevated viewpoint outside the historical walls,
shows Jaffa gate, the citadel, an informal Arab market, and Bethlehem in the distance. Ashbee notes: 'the Jaffa gate reconstruction at present, looking towards
Bethlehem'. Below, Ashbee adds his own diagram of the view of the road he had
in mind. He explains: 'the same, as suggested after the removal of the market to
the other side of the road' reflecting, not only the desire for their destruction, as
the case with the first composition, but also their relocation into a more formal
market arrangement. In the report, Ashbee even includes several architectural
schemes for new formal markets both in the Old and New cities to replace such
informal arrangements with formal market schemes with 'definite boundaries'
to conceal them away from the approaches to the Old and New cities.[40]

In a sense, Ashbee's vision for the city of Jerusalem, despite its more critical
stance regarding architecture and its basis on rigourous study, did not radically
depart from its representation by European visitors in the late nineteenth century as an 'open-air biblical museum.'[41] Like these visitors, who would often
climb the Mount of Olives to admire the panoramic view over the 'city of Jesus',
Ashbee's plans and sketches for Jerusalem reflect more interest in distant views
of the city than in the conditions of its local inhabitants. The two panoramic
photographs captured from the perspective of an outsider entering the city
attest to this. As with Dalman's 'scientific' analysis of aerial photographs, this
physical distance raises an important question regarding the manifestations
of relations of power in representations of the urban landscape. Both Ashbee
and Dalman dismiss the role or fate of the local inhabitants in their representations of the urban landscape. While in Dalman's distant photographs the Arab
population makes no appearance and their architectural contribution is not
mentioned, in Ashbee's compositions, they are either depicted as ghostly silhouette figures in the landscape, or as a population whose building activity
poses an obstruction to romanticised and sanitised colonial visions of the
Holy City.

---

40   Ibid., 26.
41   Vincent Lemire, *Jerusalem 1900: The Holy City in the Age of Possibilities* (Chicago: University
      of Chicago Press, 2017), 55.

FIGURE 11.4   Above: 'The Jaffa Gate reconstruction as at present, looking towards the city.'
Below: 'The same, as suggested when the unsightly obstruction that hides the
walls are cleaned away'
SOURCE: CHARLES ROBERT ASHBEE, ED., *JERUSALEM, 1918–1920: BEING
THE RECORDS OF THE PRO-JERUSALEM COUNCIL DURING THE PERIOD OF
THE BRITISH MILITARY ADMINISTRATION* (LONDON: J. MURRAY, FOR THE
COUNCIL OF THE PRO-JERUSALEM SOCIETY, 1921)

3   The City in Print and Arab Self-Image

Photographs of urban spaces and landscapes, particularly distant aerial and
panoramic views, proved instrumental for reifying imperial and colonial representations of the urban landscape and the carrying out of colonial urban
counterinsurgency activities and planning projects. It would be false, however,
to assume that photography and photographic representations of urban landscapes in interwar Palestine were a product of and served colonial interests
alone. Palestine's native Arab population, particularly urbanites, also utilised
the power of photographic imagery in this period to articulate their own conceptions and visions for Arab nationhood, modernity and progress in the
interwar period. These new national conceptions and visions were undoubtedly shaped by the native populations' desire to respond to colonialism and

The Jaffa Gate reconstruction as at present, looking towards Bethlehem.   No. 42.

The same, as suggested after the removal of the Market to the other side of the road.   No. 43.

FIGURE 11.5   Above: 'The Jaffa gate reconstruction at present, looking towards Bethlehem.'
Below: 'The same, as suggested after the removal of the market to the other
side of the road'
SOURCE: CHARLES ROBERT ASHBEE, ED., *JERUSALEM, 1918–1920: BEING
THE RECORDS OF THE PRO-JERUSALEM COUNCIL DURING THE PERIOD OF
THE BRITISH MILITARY ADMINISTRATION* (LONDON: J. MURRAY, FOR THE
COUNCIL OF THE PRO-JERUSALEM SOCIETY, 1921)

colonial imagery. However, they were also the product of internal social and
class shifts and ruptures among urban populations, particularly the rise of a
new urban middle class of *effendiyya* with new forms of social and cultural
values, systems of identification and forms of expression.[42]

Most works that address the rise of 'vernacular' photographic imagery in late
nineteenth and early twentieth century Palestine focus on family portraits.[43]
This is not surprising given that, with only a few exceptions like the works
of Khalīl Raʿad and Ḥannā Ṣāfiyya,[44] Arab photographers in Palestine and
the region were much less interested in the photography of cities and urban

---

42   On the expressions of these socioeconomic shifts in the realm of portrait photography,
see Stephen Sheehi, *The Arab Imago: A Social History of Portrait Photography, 1860–1910*
(Princeton: Princeton University Press, 2016), xxiv.
43   Issam Nassar, "Familial Snapshots: Representing Palestine in the Work of the First Local
Photographers," *History & Memory* 18, no. 2 (2006): 139–155.
44   See the chapters of Rona Sela and Issam Nassar in this volume.

landscapes than they were in the production of studio portraits and the photography of weddings and social events.[45] Nonetheless, in the 1930s and 40s, an era marked by an increased confrontation with the Zionists and the British, and a growing interest by the local Arab population in taking part in urban affairs and projects, the reproduction of photographic materials that depict urban events and built forms played an instrumental role in Arab expressions for their desire for the building of their national consciousness and institutions, and countering their depiction as 'unprogressive' and 'backward' in British and Zionist imagery of Palestine.[46] Hence, from the 1930s onwards, numerous Arab publications surfaced that included photographs of urban events and spaces as a form of documentation and evidence of both colonial repression of urban populations and progressive Arab-led urban-based national activities and projects, targeted at audiences both within and beyond Palestine.

Among the Arab-led urban activities that received extensive coverage across Arab print media in Palestine were the organisation and inauguration of the 1933 and 1934 National Arab Exhibitions in Jerusalem. Held at a critical period between the 1929 Buraq Revolt and the 1936 Great Revolt, the two exhibitions 'were intended to demonstrate that Arab countries were witnessing remarkable innovations in the industrial and agricultural sectors despite, and not because of, European colonisation'.[47] The British administration, which had previously partnered with the Zionists on several exhibitions in Palestine and abroad, refused to endorse the exhibition and even placed several hurdles in the way of its execution.[48] Hence, the exhibitions were entirely financed, organised and executed by Palestine's new group of Arab urban middle class elites who were leading Palestine's Arab national and economic *Nahda* ('renaissance').[49]

With the two exhibitions, the organisers intended to boost economic development, with political end goals, at both the national and urban levels. On the one hand, the exhibitions were executed with the aim of forging new economic bonds between the Arab countries that had been fragmented and disconnected in the Great War. At the same time, the organisers were aware of

45   Issam Nassar, "A Jerusalem Photographer: The Life and Work of Hanna Safieh," *Jerusalem Quarterly* 7 (2000): 26.

46   Mark LeVine, "The Discourses of Development in Mandate Palestine," *Arab Studies Quarterly* (1995): 95–124.

47   Nadi Abusaada, "Self-Portrait of a Nation: The Arab Exhibition in Mandate Jerusalem, 1931–1934," *Jerusalem Quarterly* 77 (2019): 122.

48   There were many hurdles. Besides refusing some of the plans for the exhibition by the Town Planning Commission, the British administration also rejected the allocation of municipal funds for the exhibitions. Ibid., 128.

49   Ibid., 128.; Sherene Seikaly, *Men of Capital: Scarcity and Economy in Mandate Palestine* (Stanford: Stanford University Press, 2015).

the specific threats taking place in Palestine, and the significance of organising
an event of this sort in one of the country's main urban centres. The relationship between the exhibitions and the city was a key issue since the former's
earliest articulations. While the initial intent was to host the exhibition in Jaffa,
in close proximity to the Zionist Levant Fair in Tel Aviv, after several debates
and conflicts, the final decision was made to host the exhibitions at the Palace
Hotel in Jerusalem, a building owned and run by the Supreme Muslim Council
(SMC) – the primary representative body for Palestine's Arab population at the
time.[50] Taking place only a few years after the Buraq revolt, and in the context
of the turbulences of 1933, hosting the Arab exhibition in Jerusalem was a clear
statement regarding the Arab claim over the city and its public sphere.

A photograph of the opening of the second exhibition in 1934 from the
private collection of Sa'id Ḥusaynī illustrates the urban nature of the event
(Fig. 11.6). In the photograph, a large crowd of men appear to have gathered
outside the Palace Hotel building, the venue where the two exhibitions were
held, to celebrate the second exhibition's inauguration. The building is decorated with flags and two banners that read 'the second Arab exhibition' and
'loving the nation is an act of faith'. A vertical distance appears between the
crowds outside the gate and the fewer individuals who occupied the building's front balcony. Numerous Arabic newspaper articles covered details of the
opening ceremony, which included a speech by 'Ajāj Nuwayhiḍ, a member of
the exhibition's board of directors, on the board's behalf. In his speech, fully
transcribed by the Jerusalemite al-'Arab newspaper, Nuwayhid emphasised
the 'Arab-ness' of the city and the event, thanked its supporters, welcomed
its visitors from across the country, and explained the motivations behind the
exhibition as 'developing Arab capital, rejuvenating national projects, supporting Arab labourers by strengthening Arab factories, supporting artists and
innovators to make use of their talents, and consolidating economic bonds
between Arab sectors to achieve Arab economic independence'.[51]

The numerous Arabic newspaper articles that covered the opening of
the first and second exhibitions included multiple photographs, predominantly focused on the Palace Hotel's exterior and interior spaces. Built by the
Supreme Muslim Council and registered as a Waqf property, the Palace Hotel
was distinguished in its architectural style and location. It was designed by two
well-known Turkish architects, Ahmet Kemaleddin and his disciple Mehmed
Nihad, who had initially arrived in Jerusalem to lead the renovations in Haram

---

50   Abusaada, "Self-Portrait of a Nation: The Arab Exhibition in Mandate Jerusalem, 1931–
      1934," 128–129.
51   al-'Arab, 'khitab al-iftitah', 14 April 1934.

FIGURE 11.6   'A black-and-white photograph of a crowd gathered in front of al-Awqaf, Ma'man Allah St during the opening of the Second Arab Industrial Exhibition, in 1934, in Palace Hotel, in response to the Zionist Exhibition which had opened in Tel Aviv'

SOURCE: SAID AL-HUSSEINI COLLECTION, PALESTINIAN MUSEUM DIGITAL ARCHIVE. IMAGE COURTESY OF THE PALESTINIAN MUSEUM

al-Sharif.[52] It was the largest and most grandiose Arab building in Palestine constructed in the era of the British Mandate. The hotel's location on Mamilla Street in what Charles Ashbee has defined as the New City outside the historical walls of Jerusalem, in the vicinity of new Jewish neighbourhoods and colonial construction projects, was a clear statement about the Arab claim over the New City and participation in Jerusalem's extra-muros modern developments and tourism industry. The building was also of regional significance. In 1931, the Islamic Congress bringing leaders from all over the Muslim world was held at the Palace Hotel. With this in mind, it is not surprising that the hotel figured extensively in the exhibitions' photographic and textual representations, both in the Arabic press and in the official manuals prepared for the two exhibitions, and was described as an emblem for Arab national progress and cultural renaissance.[53]

---

52   Yıldırım Yavuz, "The Influence of Late Ottoman Architecture in the Arab Provinces: The Case of the Palace Hotel in Jerusalem," *Proceedings of the International Congress of Turkish Arts* 1 (2003): 1–22.

53   On 15th July 1933, an article appeared in al-Arab that included a series of three photographs of the Palace Hotel at the time of the first exhibition, with the following accompanying captions: 'the view of the Waqf Hotel, where the exhibition is held. The building is

The press coverage and photographic representations of the Arab exhibitions in the early 1930s were mainly directed towards an Arabic readership within Palestine. Nonetheless, this audience was not the only target that Arab urbanites wanted to reach in this period. The British support for the Zionist movement was a growing concern among Arab intellectuals and politicians, both those who resided in Palestine and abroad. By the 1930s and 40s, Palestinians had realised the extent of Zionist propaganda outside of Palestine. Its representations at multiple World Fairs around the world at that time was one of many indicators of the power of the Biblical image of Palestine that they had presented to the world, as a deserted land that required Zionist colonial settlement and modernisation. Hence, by the mid 1930s and early 40s, there was an increased desire by key Arab figures to counter the image of British Mandatory rule and Zionist settler colonialism as 'civilised' and 'modern' regimes not only in Palestine, but also abroad, particularly in Europe and the United States.

In October 1933, only three months after the inauguration of the first Arab exhibition in Jerusalem, major Arab demonstrations took place in Jerusalem and Jaffa, initiated by the Arab Executive Committee's call for a national strike to protest British policy regarding Zionist settlement in Palestine. By November, the demonstrations escalated and spread to other principal urban centres including Haifa and Nablus and were met by extreme use of force by the British Police Force in Palestine. Like the Arab exhibitions, the events received considerable attention in local Arabic newspapers, detailing both protest activities and British acts of repression. Unlike the coverage for the two Arab exhibitions, however, reporting on the 1933 demonstrations was predominantly textual, and lacked photographic materials. Realising this gap, by the end of 1933, Theodore Sarrouf, an Arab nationalist and the founder of the Press and Publication Office in Jaffa, one of the first Arab advertising agencies of its kind in the country, began collecting photographs of the October-November demonstrations with the purpose of their publication.

On 12th January 1934, Sarrouf published a 43-page photographic album of the 1933 demonstrations.[54] The album's pages included tens of photographs

---

constructed in the glamorous Arab-style, consists of four stories, and it costed no less than 70,000 Palestinian pounds and rented annually for about 8,000 pounds'; 'a view of the large lobby on the ground floor before the exhibition was held'; and 'upon entering the building, the visitor is faced with a spectacular elevated dome, scraping the clouds, and this is its photograph.' 'al ma'rad al-'arabi al-awwal ('the first Arab exhibition')', al-Arab, 15 July 1933: 21–30, 22, 26.

54   Theodore Sarrouf, *Photographs of the Demonstrations Which Took Place in Palestine 1933* (Jaffa: Press and Publication Office, 1934).

of demonstrations (including women's demonstrations), police repression, funerals, relief work and portraits of detainees and families of martyrs in the principal Arab cities of Jerusalem, Jaffa, Haifa and Nablus, separated by pages of private advertisement similar to those published in local newspapers. For each photograph, Sarrouf included a caption describing the event photographed and its date and location. Significantly, Sarrouf decided to write these captions in both Arabic and English. In a short preface titled 'Explanation of the Publisher,' he elucidates the motivation behind his collection:

> While contributing news material to certain papers about the recent disturbances and demonstrations which resulted in considerable loss of life in most towns of Palestine, I realised how anxious the reading public was to get hold of as many pictures as possible so that it may possess a pictorial souvenir of these important events. Losing neither time nor opportunity, I set myself earnestly in collecting almost every picture taken by local and foreign photographers both professional and amateur of the demonstrations [...] My sole aim in furnishing the English reading people with such a collection, is the hope that they will form to themselves a clear and correct impression of the demonstrations held by the suppressed Arabs as a cry for justice in Palestine, this unfortunate part of the Arab World.[55]

Hence, although Sarrouf describes the photographs as 'pictorial souvenirs,' he is aware of the importance of photography not only as a documentary tool of Arab dissatisfaction and British police repression, but also as a powerful universal language in which he is able to communicate the political injustices taking place in Palestine to a global audience. With this photographic collection, Sarrouf writes in the Arabic version of the preface, he intended to 'provide Eastern and Western audiences with a living memory of what happened in this holy place at the height of the age of civilisation'.[56]

In the photographs Sarrouf included, an important aspect of the demonstrations in the major Arab cities is brought to light, namely the effort by Arab protestors in occupying the central public spaces in the cities, particularly those surrounded by buildings of British official institutions, and their obstruction from reaching their destinations by British police forces. In Jaffa, the main confrontations took place in the city's main public square adjacent to the Mahmudiyyah Mosque, the Ottoman clocktower and the government

55   Ibid.
56   Ibid.

ABUSAADA

headquarters. In one of the photographs Sarrouf includes, he shows that the police used barbed wires on the main intersections to block demonstrations from reaching the main square which he refers to as 'Martyrs' Square' in reference to the Arab victims of police repression (Fig. 11.7). Sarrouf's photographs depict similar confrontations between Arab demonstrators and British police in Jerusalem, including the police attack on the protestors at the New Gate, at the boundary of the Old and New cities, and against an Arab women's demonstration (Fig. 11.8). Unlike the perceptions of Jaffa and Jerusalem in RAF aerial imagery and Ashbee's panoramic photographs, the cities in these photographs appear not as distant and sanitised objects, but as animated sites of direct confrontation between natives and colonial forces.

Until the mid 1940s, Arab efforts to counter British and Zionist colonial imagery of Palestine remained uninstitutionalised and were primarily based on individual efforts like Sarrouf's. This gap was filled in 1944, when the Institute of Arab American Affairs (IAAA) was established in New York, aiming to represent 'thousands of loyal American citizens of Arabic-speaking stock' and 'promote understanding and encourage friendly relations between the United States and the Arabic-speaking peoples'.[57] The institute also had a clear anti-Zionist political stance towards the question of Palestine, which was articulated in a manifesto it published in 1945, and submitted to the delegates of the United Nations Conference on International Organization, opposing the establishment of a Jewish state in Palestine. That same year, Khalīl Totah, a renowned Palestinian educator, had been appointed as the institute's executive director, replacing Phillip Hitti who had served an interim period while he was on temporary leave from Princeton University. 'Though forced to disband in 1950 due to a lack of funds', Denise Laszewski Jenison explains, 'the institute was quite active during its tenure, publishing pamphlets and newsletters, sending members to give speeches and testify in various hearings about the Palestine question, and writing to politicians at all levels in an effort to draw attention of the Arab side of the story'.[58]

In 1946, the IAAA published a report on 'Arab Progress in Palestine'.[59] The report, authored by Totah, intended to offer an otherwise dismissed

---

57   'Manifesto of the Institute of Arab American Affairs on Palestine' (New York: Institute of Arab American Affairs, 1945).

58   Denise Laszewski Jenison, '"American Citizens of Arabic-Speaking Stock": The Institute of Arab American Affairs and Questions of Identity in the Debate over Palestine,' in *New Horizons of Muslim Diaspora in North America and Europe*, ed. Moha Ennaji (New York: Palgrave Macmillan US, 2016), 36.

59   Khalil Totah, "Arab Progress in Palestine" (New York: Institute of Arab American Affairs, 1946).

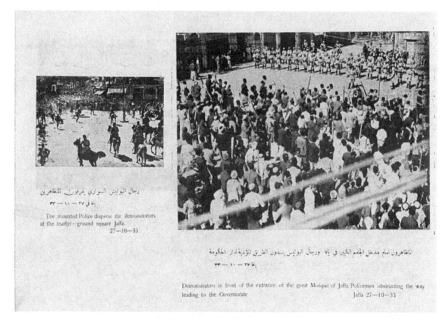

FIGURE 11.7   A page including photographs in Jaffa from Theodore Sarrouf's album.
The captions read: 'The mounted Police disperse the demonstrators at the
martyr-ground square Jaffa'; and 'Demonstrators in front of the entrance
of the great Mosque of Jaffa, Policemen obstructing the way leading to the
Governorate'
SOURCE: THEODORE SARROUF, PHOTOGRAPHS OF THE DEMONSTRATIONS
WHICH TOOK PLACE IN PALESTINE 1933 (JAFFA: PRESS AND PUBLICATION
OFFICE, 1934)

perspective on Palestine to the American public. It is divided into sections on
economic progress, weaving and textiles, the building trade, cement, insurance, airways, motor transport, shipbuilding, cigarette factories, the Summer
Resort Company, cinemas, salt, mother-of-pearl, olive wood, banking, the
Arab National Bank, chambers of commerce, telephones and education. What
these all have in common is that they are all led by Arab actors. Names of Arab
corporations, organisations and individuals proliferate throughout the entire
report, painting an impression of the nature of 'Arab progress' in Palestine.
This impression, however, is not only textual but visual. The report includes
six enlarged photographs depicting Arab economic, industrial and cultural
advancements in Palestine. Of these, five are located in main urban centres
and depict urban-based activities.

Two of the photographs depict features of progress in Jaffa. The first photograph is of al-Hamrā' cinema and the second is of a machine shop. The
report stresses the Arab identity of these two establishments. The caption of

FIGURE 11.8   A page including photographs in Jerusalem from Theodore Sarrouf's
album. The captions read: 'Constables & Police Officers are attacking the
demonstrators at the New Gate & striking them with their batons. Some
are thrown as illustrated'; and 'the mounted Police are rushing upon the
demonstrating ladies'
SOURCE: THEODORE SARROUF, PHOTOGRAPHS OF THE DEMONSTRATIONS
WHICH TOOK PLACE IN PALESTINE 1933 (JAFFA: PRESS AND PUBLICATION
OFFICE, 1934)

al-Hamrā's photograph reads: 'an Arab cinema in Jaffa designed by an Arab
architect and built by an Arab company'.[60] The caption of the workshop's
photograph similarly reads: 'an Arab machine shop'.[61] Two other photographs
present urban street views of Palestine's Arab cities (Fig. 11.9–10). The first photograph captioned 'modern Arab houses in Jerusalem' depicts Bauhaus-style
private dwellings in one of Jerusalem's Arab neighbourhoods – a rather unique
image of Arab Jerusalem which is often represented through religious architecture or symbolism attached to the Dome of the Rock and the Church of
the Holy Sepulchre. The second photograph is captioned 'municipal park at
Gaza. Gaza is a purely Arab town' – displaying a long promenade lined by palm
trees, ordered green spaces, and fountains.[62] Together, these images present

---

60   Ibid.
61   Ibid.
62   Ibid.

FIGURES 11.9 AND 11.10   Two pages from 'Arab Progress in Palestine' report by Khalil Totah

SOURCE: TOTAH, "ARAB PROGRESS IN PALESTINE," 1946

Palestine as it had never been known to a Western, not to mention American, audience before. That is, not only as the 'land of promise' but as a 'land of progress' where 'progress' is not only defined by the actions of the British and the Zionists but also by the country's native Arab population.[63]

4 Conclusion

In examining a range of photographic representations of the urban built environment in Mandate Palestine, it is evident that these representations varied considerably based not only on who produced them, but also how and for whom they were produced. Considering these factors brings to light a series of three photographic approaches to the photographic representation of the cities of Palestine: the city as target, the city as a *vue d'ensemble* and the city as self-image. With each of these approaches, a different attitude towards the cities and their inhabitants is expressed. The first, usually based on distant representations of the urban landscape, is mostly concerned with its domination. The second, meanwhile, sees the city through a romantic lens, and is equally concerned with the preservation of a certain idea of the city as with the destruction of this idea's outcasts. The third, on the other hand, is an image of the modern city where its representation is equated with an entire social formation and cultural identity.

These different attitudes appeared, for the most part, not only in the photographs themselves and the intentions of the photographers but in the ways in which the photographs have been re-packaged to satisfy different, even oppositional, visions and representations of urban space and its inhabitants. For instance, Dalman's reproduction of Bavarian aerial photographs with the intention of the scientific study of the history and geography of Palestine's landscape departed significantly from the initial intentions of the Bavarian air squadrons who took these aerial photographs as part of their military reconnaissance against British troops. Other aspects regarding the specifics of reproduction, including the medium (e.g. magazine, newspaper, report, sketch book), their accompanying text (e.g. captions, essays, titles) and its language and audience also played an important role in serving the reproducers' ideological urban visions. These aspects in particular distinguished in Arab photographic reproductions from their colonial counterparts. Whereas the

---

63   On the shifting conception of Palestine from 'land of promise' a 'land of progress' in the late nineteenth and early twentieth centuries, see Jacob Norris, *Land of Progress: Palestine in the Age of Colonial Development, 1905–1948* (Oxford: Oxford University Press, 2013).

latter were usually published in the form of private and inaccessible reports, with the exception of Dalman, the former were intentionally reproduced in Arabic and English public media to ensure their mass dissemination locally and globally.

The categorical separation of three above-mentioned representational approaches to urban space, however, must not lead to the assumption that these approaches were always mutually exclusive. In fact, there are many cases where the opposite is true, that is, where one of these approaches towards the city has directly or indirectly triggered, reinforced or enabled the other. For example, despite the differences in the motifs of Ashbee's 1920s panoramas of the Old City of Jerusalem, in which he envisioned 'improvement plans' for the city, and the 1936 British aerial photographs of the Old City Jaffa before destroying large parts of it also in the name of 'improvement plans', and the different attitudes of each of these representations towards the city, their connection cannot be dismissed. That is, the colonial objectification and destruction of the native urban built environment. It can even be argued that it is the same distorted Orientalist representations of Arab cities, which Ashbee accepted and contributed to, which informed the British administration's attitude towards the Old City of Jaffa as a disorderly 'old labyrinth of alleys'[64] that posed a threat to colonial domination. In a similar fashion, while the Arab photographic representations of the city as sites of Arab-led progress should not be reduced to reactions to colonial representations, it is beyond doubt that the two oppositional Arab national and colonial representational attitudes played key roles in each other's formation.

Bibliography

Abusaada, Nadi. 'Combined Action: Aerial Imagery and the Urban Landscape in Interwar Palestine, 1918–40'. *Jerusalem Quarterly* 81 (2020): 20–36.

Abusaada, Nadi. 'Self-Portrait of a Nation: The Arab Exhibition in Mandate Jerusalem, 1931–1934'. *Jerusalem Quarterly* 77 (2019): 122–35.

'al ma'rad al-'arabi al-awwal ('the first Arab exhibition')'. *al-Arab*. 15 July 1933.

al-'Arab. 'khitab al-iftitah'. 14 April 1934.

Ashbee, Charles Robert. *A Palestine Notebook, 1918–1923*. [1st ed.]. New York: Garden City, 1923.

---

64   'Military Lessons of the Arab Rebellion in Palestine 1936,' 159.

Ashbee, Charles Robert, ed. *Jerusalem, 1918–1920: Being the Records of the Pro-Jerusalem Council During the Period of the British Military Administration*. London: J. Murray, for the Council of the Pro-Jerusalem Society, 1921.

Ashbee, Charles Robert, ed. *Jerusalem, 1920–1922: Being the Records of the Pro-Jerusalem Council During the First Two Years of the Civil Administration*. London: J. Murray, for the Council of the Pro-Jerusalem Society, 1924.

Becker, Arthur Peter. 'Housing in England and Wales during the Business Depression of the 1930's'. *The Economic History Review* 3, no. 3 (1951): 321–41.

Dalman, Gustaf. *Hundert Deutsche Fliegerbilder Aus Palästina*. Bertelsmann, 1925.

Doumani, Beshara. 'Rediscovering Ottoman Palestine: Writing Palestinians into History'. *Journal of Palestine Studies* 21, no. 2 (1992): 5–28.

Fruchtman, J. 'Statutory Planning as a Form of Social Control: The Evolution of Town Planning Law in Mandatory Palestine and Israel 1917–1980's'. Doctoral, University of London, 1986. http://discovery.ucl.ac.uk/1317972/.

German Protestant Institute of Archeology. 'Foundation and First Aims (1900–1914)', 20 July 2019. https://www.deiahl.de/ueber-das-dei/geschichte/1900-1914/.

Haffner, Jeanne. *The View from Above: The Science of Social Space*. MIT Press, 2013.

Jenison, Denise Laszewski. '"American Citizens of Arabic-Speaking Stock": The Institute of Arab American Affairs and Questions of Identity in the Debate over Palestine'. In *New Horizons of Muslim Diaspora in North America and Europe*, edited by Moha Ennaji, 35–51. New York: Palgrave Macmillan US, 2016.

Kedar, Benjamin Z. *The Changing Land: Between the Jordan and the Sea: Aerial Photographs from 1917 to the Present*. Wayne State University Press, 1999.

Lemire, Vincent. *Jerusalem 1900: The Holy City in the Age of Possibilities*. Chicago: University of Chicago Press, 2017.

LeVine, Mark. *Overthrowing Geography: Jaffa, Tel Aviv, and the Struggle for Palestine, 1880–1948*. University of California Press, 2005.

LeVine, Mark. 'The Discourses of Development in Mandate Palestine'. *Arab Studies Quarterly*, 1995, 95–124.

'Manifesto of the Institute of Arab American Affairs on Palestine'. New York: Institute of Arab American Affairs, 1945.

Matthews, Weldon. *Confronting an Empire, Constructing a Nation: Arab Nationalists and Popular Politics in Mandate Palestine*. London: I.B.Tauris, 2006.

'Military Lessons of the Arab Rebellion in Palestine 1936', 1938. IOR/L/MIL/17/16/16. British Library: India Office Records and Private Papers.

Nassar, Issam. 'A Jerusalem Photographer: The Life and Work of Hanna Safieh'. *Jerusalem Quarterly* 7 (2000): 24–28.

Nassar, Issam. 'Familial Snapshots: Representing Palestine in the Work of the First Local Photographers'. *History & Memory* 18, no. 2 (2006): 139–155.

Norris, Jacob. *Land of Progress: Palestine in the Age of Colonial Development, 1905–1948.* OUP Oxford, 2013.

Norris, Jacob. 'Repression and Rebellion: Britain's Response to the Arab Revolt in Palestine of 1936–39'. *The Journal of Imperial and Commonwealth History* 36, no. 1 (2008): 25–45.

Pullan, Wendy, and Lefkos Kyriacou. 'The Work of Charles Ashbee: Ideological Urban Visions with Everyday City Spaces'. *Jerusalem Quarterly* 39 (2009): 51–61.

Rotbard, Sharon. *White City, Black City: Architecture and War in Tel Aviv and Jaffa.* London: Pluto Press, 2015.

Sarrouf, Theodore. *Photographs of the Demonstrations Which Took Place in Palestine 1933.* Jaffa: Press and Publication Office, 1934.

Satia, Priya. *Spies in Arabia: The Great War and the Cultural Foundations of Britain's Covert Empire in the Middle East.* Oxford: Oxford University Press, 2008.

Seikaly, Sherene. *Men of Capital: Scarcity and Economy in Mandate Palestine.* Paolo Alto CA: Stanford University Press, 2015.

Sheehi, Stephen Paul. *The Arab Imago: A Social History of Portrait Photography, 1860–1910.* Princeton: Princeton University Press, 2016.

Storrs, Sir Ronald. *Orientations.* I. Nicholson & Watson, 1939.

Totah, Khalil. 'Arab Progress in Palestine'. New York: Institute of Arab American Affairs, 1946.

Wiegand, Theodor, and Ahmed Djemal Pascha. *Alte Denkmäler aus Syrien, Palästina und Westarabien: 100 Tafeln mit beschreibendem Text.* G. Reimer, 1918.

Yavuz, Yıldırım. 'The Influence of Late Ottoman Architecture in the Arab Provinces: The Case of the Palace Hotel in Jerusalem'. *Proceedings of the International Congress of Turkish Arts* 1 (2003): 1–22.

CHAPTER 12

Epilogue

Özge Calafato and Aude Aylin de Tapia

From heated debates on access and transparency of archives to large-scale digitisation projects, the field of photography witnesses an opportune moment with a wealth of new material being made publicly available. Interdisciplinarity opens up the field, shifting the focus towards the study of photographs as objects of cultural analysis, beyond their use as mere illustrations. Recent historiography looks at photographs as new primary sources, rather than accompaniments to written sources. In the past two decades, the field has seen a rise in scholarly work that deals with materiality of photographs, practices of photographic production, and circulation. Particularly vernacular photography has emerged as a key area of focus that offers new and much more nuanced readings on socio-economic, cultural and political histories.

In this opportune moment for the study of photographs, *Imaging and Imagining Palestine: Photography, Modernity and the Biblical Lens, 1918–1948* offers a great invitation to rethink the British Mandate period through the works of professional and amateur photographers from different classes and communities. Exploring the works of those who photographed Palestine, the way they understood and imagined it back then, this volume is a much-needed exercise to trace the visual history before 1948, and examine the making of Mandatory Palestine within the framework of biblification that reproduced Palestine as 'a familiar site of European consciousness', and Orientalism that imagined Palestine as the exotic other.[1] In its three sections, this volume focused on specific photographic archives in and outside Palestine, the perspective of individual photographers, as well as conceptual and methodological approaches to the study of photography.

Palestine in the British Mandate period, much like the Middle East, witnessed a major shift in political and social mobilities following the collapse of the perennial Ottoman rule. This shift, leading up to the *Nakba* and the foundation of the State of Israel, laid the foundation for a renewed identity for Palestinian photography outside the centre-periphery dynamics of the Ottoman Empire. At the same time, the Mandate-era Palestinian photography

---

1 Issam Nassar, "'Biblification' in the Service of Colonialism: Jerusalem in Nineteenth-century Photography," *Third Text* 20, no. 374 (2006): 317–326.

was marked by increasing social, political and religious tensions due to the ownership of heritage, modernity and economic renaissance.

Having inherited the modernist agenda of the Ottoman elites, the British Mandate era corresponds to a period where, with the introduction of new technologies, studio photography rapidly spread while snapshot photography increasingly entered upper and middle class households across the region. Studio and itinerant photographers remained instrumental in the growth of vernacular portraiture from the 1910s to the late 1940s. Commercial photographers continued to be involved in the production of biblified material, catering to the needs of the market in Palestine and abroad, from local inhabitants and Western travellers in the Holy Land to 'armchair tourists' at home in the West. As Nassar points out, the photographic production of Biblical scenes was not limited to the nineteenth-century but persisted throughout the Mandate period as a tradition that many Western and indigenous photographers continued to follow. Accordingly, this volume has examined the role of the market of photography and the various taxonomies it catered to within the context of Mandatory Palestine. It explored the work of Palestine's indigenous Arab and Armenian photographers as well as the affinities between British colonial photography and Zionism while probing the class connotations of photographic representations and the role of Christianity in the production and dissemination of photography of the era.

For many decades, the process of interpreting Palestine and Palestinians in photography among Western networks focused on the use of Biblical themes to domesticate what was seen as a 'foreign' world. The familiarity of the Biblical as a textual narrative and as a familiar imaging trope served to bridge the gap between the Western consumer and the otherness of the 'Orient' through the construction of a Western Biblical imaginary as Zananiri has shown in his study of the Frank Scholten Collection. Ironically, biblified imaging was in fact enabled by modernity, while actively excluding and erasing Palestinian modernity. Aiming to reverse this omission and help decolonise photography, this volume has proposed the concept of 'speaking back' or 'writing back' in order to indigenise narratives and counter the marginalisation of Palestinians. Looking at the archives like the National Geographic Society archive (Kopty) and the Dominican photographic-library of Jerusalem (Sanchez Summerer and Neveu), the work of studio photographers such as Khalil Raad and Elia Kahvedjian (Sela and Sheehi respectively), as well as the collection of the Dutch traveller Frank Scholten (Zananiri), we have been urged to question the ways in which photographic production can propose readings that challenge Orientalist narratives surrounding the biblification of Palestine and holiness of the 'Holy Land', and more specifically of Jerusalem. In this, Kopty's *Imagining the Holy* offers a fascinating example of producing new indigenous knowledge and narrative. By connecting thousands of images of historic Palestine from the National Geographic Society archive with Palestinian community elders and scholars, Kopty explores as to how memory can be activated as a form of resistance. These images and their original captions give new insights into the processes of image production, selection and circulation, and provide a candid view of how photographers and editors participated in and reinforced the power-relations between the colonised and colonisers.

The study of photographs from the archives of missionaries, such as the photographs from the American Colony's Christian Herald Orphanage and the Swedish School in Jerusalem, analysed by Jacobson and Okkenhaug respectively, gives us a better understanding of how photographs were produced, and circulated and consumed among humanitarian and other networks in Palestine and abroad, and the colonial tensions that resulted from such photographic interactions. Throughout the volume, a number of case studies have thus examined the ways in which institutions like the National Geographic Society (Kopty) and the American Colony (Lev, Okkenhaug, Jacobson) adopted underlying colonial narratives of bringing modernity and humanitarianism to Palestine and Palestinians through Western intervention.

In the first half of the twentieth century, Palestine witnessed remarkable transformations in its urban built environment, exacerbated under the British Mandate with the introduction of new urban infrastructures and statutory planning policies that controlled urban expansion and the construction of new settlements. Illustrating the idea of the *Biblical Moderne*, Abusaada has shown that the shift in the photographic representation of Palestine from a 'land of promise' to a 'land of progress' is discernible in the utilisation of photography by colonial architects and planners. Through photographic representations, urban environments were produced and repackaged to create a vision of Palestine according to distinct political agendas. An indigenous-produced vision was developed during this process as part of such tensions, which tasked itself with promoting the Arab-led nature of the remaking of modern urban spaces, concerned with offsetting and diffusing the discourses of Zionism and British colonialism. In this context, Abusaada has brought up the question as to what extent the cities captured in photographs are colonial cities and to what extent they are Arab, problematising the categories of 'colonial' and 'Oriental' themselves when examining photographic reproductions.

As Zananiri has pointed out, the formative period witnessed the setting up of a plethora of ethno-confessional taxonomies with different political inclinations and interests. 'Arab' and 'Jew', a by-product of a modern colonial terminology, as Zananiri, Abusaada, and Kopty have analysed, served to wash

away the complexities within indigenous communities and further oriental-
ise the existing social fabric. This volume is thus concerned with addressing
the cultural porosity across indigenous, transnational and transcolonial categorisations in British Mandate Palestine when exploring the narratives of
conformity and strategies of resistance among a great diversity of ethnic, religious and cultural taxonomies that came to reside in Palestine. Simultaneously,
it also examines possible internalisations of the Western colonial discourse by
Palestinian actors as we delve deeper into the entanglements and permeabili-
ties across the different communities.

The concern to promote indigenous-led urban progress is closely linked
to the formation and propagation of the Palestinian middle-class identity in
the 1920s and 1930s, whose visual representations were marginalised by the
dominant Zionist, British and more generally Western narratives. The relationship between biblification and modernity is implicitly vested in transnational
questions of class. Photography itself largely remained an activity of middle
and upper-middle classes in the 1920s and 1930s. In this context, Nassar has
asserted that family albums offer a wealth of material in terms of looking at
classed and gendered selves within Palestinian communities. Family albums
function as affective tools through which to build a family's narrative as much
as they serve as an attempt to affirm a normality for a Europeanised bourgeois life. Family albums provide intimate stories from within, challenging the
ways in which Palestinians were imaged and imagined by colonisers, Zionists,
Western travellers and journalists over decades. Similarly, Lev, Jacobson and
Okkenhaug have shown that albums and travel books produced for commercial or institutional use offer more carefully constructed narratives than an
individual photograph might be able to offer. Whose stories are told in albums?
Who produced them and for whom? How have photo albums survived? Do
albums transmit a coherent and distinct narrative or do we need to intellec-
tualise the production of the album to construct a narrative? As we attempt
to find answers to some of these questions, the album presents itself as an
archive, a source giving meaning to the photographs it integrates. As Nassar
has highlighted, for the collectors of photographs and albums today, the act of
collecting becomes an act of reclaiming and re-narrating Palestinian history
and collective memory post-1948, which represents a great juncture in the historical narrative of the Palestinians.

This volume has demonstrated that negotiations of colonial tensions
between different groups among the Palestinians and the British, and the resistance to the Mandate and the Zionist agenda, can be observed not only in the
photographic representations (Abusaada, Nassar, Zananiri, Sheehi, Sanchez
Summerer and Neveu), but also in business practices of photographers and

photo studios as well as the local and foreign consumers they catered to (Sela, Kopty, Lev, Jacobson), bringing up once again the notions of locality, indigeneity and agency. How do we position an American Colony photographer like Whiting, who, at 14, became a member of the American Colony Photo Department and soon started to lead archaeological expeditions through Palestine? How do we negotiate Larsson's documentation on the pupils of the Swedish School as Head of the American Colony photo department? How do we interpret the agency of Khalīl Raʿad whose work was intertwined with the colonial regime of knowledge and biblified cultural material? The issue of agency urges us to explore the dynamics of the market, and its intended and unintended audiences.

The issue of textuality through the captions on photographs, as Kopty, Sanchez Summerer and Neveu, Nassar and Abusaada have questioned, has emerged as another central theme across the chapters in this volume. Recent historiography has looked at photographs as new sources, as alternatives to written sources, giving historians new objects and new ways to do research without necessarily using writings. In this regard, captions on photographs provide multiple layers of metadata for the study of photographs. What do captions tell us about the production and circulation of images? Several chapters have explored what text does to, for and against a photograph, as well as how the process of selecting and captioning images transforms and restricts their meaning. Several authors in this book have investigated how we can work with textuality to unpack the ideological mechanisms in which captions were generated, revised, rewritten and disseminated, and the ways in which to gauge the audience the captions were intended for. Similarly, scholars like Nassar have asked how captions on family photographs and albums, meant to be shared primarily among familiar networks, can help decolonise photography. This volume has thus examined the ways in which to disentangle the politics behind the production of photographic captions in archives, create tools for the indigenisation of photography and provide new voices for those in photographs.

Tackling all of these issues, *Imaging and Imagining Palestine: Photography, Modernity and the Biblical Lens 1918–1948*, encourages us to rethink photography of and by the Palestinians in a cross-regional approach integrated into the social and political histories of the broader region. In this, vernacular photography emerges as a key area to explore in imagining Palestine in personalised and intimate ways. Family albums need a particular attention, as this volume has revealed, where a sense of intimacy takes the centre stage. The dynamics between photography and gender have also been touched upon across chapters through various case studies and microhistories from Scholten's sexuality and its effect on his photography (Zananiri) to the politics of photographing the sisters in the collection of the French Biblical and Archaeological School in Jerusalem (Sanchez Summerer and Neveu).

Looking at an intricate network of producers and consumers of photography, the volume offers a comprehensive overview of photography of the Mandate period, placed within a broader transnational narrative that highlights the complexities of Palestine's social fabric at the time. In the past two decades, the rapid growth of institutionalised collections and digital resources accessible to researchers and general public has broadened the study of Palestinian photography in unprecedented ways. These resources proffer a much broader perspective on the social histories of the region, encompassing multi-layered stories of the diverse communities that came to reside in Palestine. Among the new exciting initiatives, the Armenian Museum, designed by Raymond Kevorkian and Claude Mutafian, will showcase the Armenian presence in the 'Holy Land' from antiquity to the present day, displaying a large variety of Armenian objects from fifth- and sixth-century mosaics to medieval manuscripts. Instrumental in the growth of indigenous photography of Palestine, the works of Armenian photographers are expected to take the centre stage in the museum. The photography section will draw on three major collections, namely the Armenian Patriarchate of Jerusalem collection (Fig. 12.1 & 12.2), the Armenian General Benevolent Union (AGBU) collection hosted at the headquarters of the Union in Heliopolis, Cairo, and the AGBU Nubar Library collection in Paris (Fig. 12.3). Due to open in 2021, the Armenian museum will not only examine the role of Armenians in the history of Palestine and the broader region but also the significance and function of photography in shaping, assembling and evincing the collective memory of a nation.[2]

Photographic collections, series and albums as 'objects' offer different tools for studying photographs, with the multiple layers of curation that they go through at different times periods. Despite the recent growth in available digital resources, the question of access to archives remains a key issue that needs to be addressed immediately by scholars and policy-makers alike. In the case of Palestine, the situation includes a political difficulty, due to the fact that a great number of materials are in Israeli archives that Palestinians have no access to. A starting point for addressing this issue could be a comprehensive mapping project of Palestinian archives and collections, along with the details of access with regard to each archive, not only within the Eastern Mediterranean region but more globally to include collections like the Scholten Collection at Netherlands Institute for the Near East (NINO), the Swedish Jerusalem Society

---

2 Email interview with Raymond Kevorkian by Karène Sanchez Summerer, October 2020.

FIGURE 12.1   *Ceremony to lay the foundation stone of the Calouste Gulbenkian Library, Jerusalem,* 1930.
IMAGE COURTESY OF THE ARMENIAN PATRIARCHATE OF
JERUSALEM COLLECTION

FIGURE 12.2   *Untitled,* 1920s. Members of the Jerusalem community, with in the centre a secular priest, probably not belonging to the congregation of St James, who is also a refugee in the neighbourhood, 1920s
IMAGE COURTESY OF THE ARMENIAN PATRIARCHATE OF
JERUSALEM COLLECTION

FIGURE 12.3   *Departure of the children to Jerusalem*
IMAGE COURTESY OF THE AGBU NUBAR LIBRARY

collection at the Uppsala University Library, the G. Eric and Edith Matson Photograph Collection at the Library of Congress as well as the collections at the Harvard Museum of the Ancient Near East (HMANE) and the Palestine Exploration Fund (PEF). Decolonising photography is only possible through the decolonisation of archives, making them available with consistent access and transparency to all researchers, including Palestinians.

We hope that *Imaging and Imagining Palestine* will pave the way for further works, books and exhibitions, focusing on photography and photographic archives with regard to the histories of Palestine as well as the broader region.

Abstracts

Chapter 2. 'Little Orphans of Jerusalem': The American Colony's Christian Herald Orphanage in Photographs and Negatives

Abstract

The American Colony Christian Herald Orphanage was established following World War I, as part of the American Colony's aid Association. Hosting around 36 girls, Christians and Muslims, between the ages 3 and 15, the Orphanage served as a home for girls whose families were harshly affected from the war crisis. Some lost both parents, some lost their fathers with their mother not being able to support them, and some were sent to Jerusalem by relatives from Syria and Transjordan in order to rescue them from 'going to the wrong'.

This chapter recovers the social history of this institution by using three main sources. The first is the Photographic Album of the Orphanage, consisting of 36 captioned prints from the Orphanage life and 46 portraits of girls. The second source is the original negatives of the photographs, kept at the American Colony Archive in Jerusalem. The third source is the Record List of all girls who received support from the Orphanage. Each entry includes a newspaper clipping briefly introducing the girl, together with handwritten records about the money donated to the Orphanage for supporting this girl.

The paper will embark on two main missions. The first is to study the institute's short history, as part of the 'politics of relief' held by the American Colony. Unlike other institutions of the Colony, the Orphanage was introduced to its Christian donors as 'an opportunity to get in personal touch with a Jerusalem child and influence her entire life'. The second would be to use the photography history that the Album offers us and compare the photographs in it to the original negatives, in order to investigate the ways the girls were displayed for different audiences and purposes.

Chapter 3. Swedish Imaginings, Investments and Local Photography in Jerusalem, 1925–1939

Abstract

This chapter focuses on photographs of the Swedish School in Jerusalem in the interwar period. The photographs were taken by photographers from the American

Colony in Jerusalem and the Swedish headmistress Signe Ekblad and were intended for a Swedish audience of potential donors. This chapter argues that the photographs, together with printed reports dealing with the Swedish humanitarian efforts in Palestine, visualised the imagined need for a Swedish presence in 'The Holy Land', but even more so the tangible results the Swedish engagement had in the country. Moreover, the article shows that while the photographs are visual documents of religious longing, they do not tend to dwell on ahistorical Biblical motifs. Instead, they reflect the thriving, intense process of modernity taking place in Palestine at the time, a process the Swedes wanted to take part in as a way of manifesting their claim to a national presence in the Holy Land. In addition, the photographs visualise the extent to which the Swedish enterprise was Palestinian; the staff was mainly Arab and the school was part of a local Jerusalemite neighbourhood. Even so, the people in charge were always Swedish. This uneven relationship can be depicted in the photographs, verifying the colonial aspect of the Swedish humanitarian enterprise in Mandatory Palestine.

Chapter 4. The Dominicans' Photographic Collection in Jerusalem: Beyond a Catholic Perception of the Holy Land?

Abstract

The photographic collection of the French biblical and archaeological school in Jerusalem is constituted of more than 25,000 glass plates, photographs and slides of Palestine from the last quarter of the nineteenth century onwards, reflecting the Catholic institutions presence in the region but also diverse realities of the social history of Palestine.

The history of this collection is intimately linked to that of the *Ecole biblique*, founded in 1890 in Jerusalem and whose programme of studies included annual trips to research the lands of the Bible, especially Jerusalem and Palestine. With the help of the Assumptionists, the Dominicans of the *Ecole biblique* learned photography in order to reproduce archaeological sites, sites connected with Christian and Moslem holy places, the history of their own religious house as well as scenes of everyday life and portraits. These photographs were taken as much like the rubbings, the drawings and the sketches used during lectures or published in the *Revue biblique*. The period of the British Mandate includes more photographs about everyday life scenes than archaeological sites; they reveal a proximity of the photographers with the local Arab population. The collection is also constituted by digitised photographs of the other Catholic institutions in Palestine (Latin Patriarchate of Jerusalem, Assumptionists, White Fathers, Salesians, Rosary Sisters, Sisters of Sion, St Joseph Sisters).

The chapter analyses the photographer's points of view on Palestine and its society, bringing to light not only the exchanges between these various actors but also the gendered dimension of their activity. Who photographed the sisters and how? Is Arabisation of the clergy noticeable from the photographers' point of view? How did photographs present their actions of collecting Orientalist knowledge, theatre and music, education and medicine developing in these Catholic institutions? These collections will thus be decoded as 'action-sources' bearers of a discourse on the history of Palestine at the beginning of the twentieth century, in order to understand the social imprint they intended to represent.

Chapter 5. Bearers of Memory: Photo Albums as Sources of Historical Study in Palestine

Abstract

This chapter focuses on three personal and family albums. With the destruction of Palestinian society Palestinians were left with mostly memories of their lives before they became refugees. In the chapter, I argue that photographic albums constitute personal archives that narrates history from a familial perspective as well as preserves visual evidence of a life lost. The chapter examines three albums whose owners lived in western suburbs of Jerusalem. The albums are those of musician Wāṣif Jawhariyyah, Julia Lucy and George Mushabek. The first, Jawharriyeh's, is a collection of seven albums that are divided chronologically, starting from the late Ottoman period and ending shortly before the events of 1948. The second, Luci's, could be described as a typical family album that document her family's life from the 1920s through the late 1940s. The third, Mushabek's, is an album that is devoted to the journey he took, with his four friends in 1936, to the Berlin Olympic.

From today's standpoint, the discussed albums put together can be described as records documenting the liminal period separating between Ottoman rule in Palestine and the creation of the State of Israel. In this sense, they function as an infusion of memories from a period that predates their owners' departure from Jerusalem in 1948.

The albums constitute three different types of compilation not merely due to the differences in ways of collecting, but also in the very fact that they were put together by very different kinds of individuals with different intentions. A person who saw himself as the storyteller of Jerusalem and its historian, produced the first collection of albums over a longer period of time. A playful young athlete documenting a short period of time and a specific event created the second single album of Mushabek. The third, crafted by an upper-class woman, was clearly intended to narrate – whether intentionally or not – the highlights in her life and that of her family. I examine the albums as narrative, because the albums come to us from Palestinians who became refugees they represent us with a narrative that is mired with nostalgia and future meanings that were not intended when the albums were created.

Chapter 6. Resilient Resistance: Colonial Biblical, Archaeological and Ethnographical Imaginaries in the Work of Chalil Raad (Khalīl Raʿd), 1891–1948

Abstract

Chalil (Khalil) Raad (Raʾd) was born in Lebanon (1869) and is considered the first Arab photographer to operate in Palestine in the years 1891–1948. He moved to Jerusalem as a child and learned the art of photography from the local Armenian photographer, Garabed Krikorian and in Basel.

The core of Raad's work was dedicated to describing the life of the Palestinian community – its urban, cultural, economic and political richness. While he documented the Near East and the local communities of the region, he gave the Palestinians a presence and visibility rarely seen in foreign photographs of Palestine in the late nineteenth century or in Jewish Zionist photographs of the early twentieth century, which concealed and excluded them in a tendentious manner.

The essay will show how Raad's work was affected by the colonial regime of knowledge in two levels. The first, the way the local inhabitants responded to and experienced the prevailing western viewpoint forced on the region, and the complexity and duality of the relationship that was born in the wake of the colonial situation. The second, Raad's studio was destroyed in the 1948 war, and parts of it (prints) were looted by Israeli soldiers and passers-by. I will show how the construction of a decolonial array may assist in bypassing the complexity of the repressive colonial relationship.

Chapter 7. Open Roads: John D. Whiting, *Diary in Photos*, 1934–1939

Abstract

The photographic album series 'Diary in Photos' was created by the American Colony in Jerusalem member John D. Whiting (1882–1951). It is a poetic, personal visual account of life in Palestine and the Levant during the 1930s. The series consists of five volumes comprising some 900 photographs featuring Whiting's travels as a personal tour-guide in Syria, Lebanon, Jordan, Turkey, Palestine and Sinai, between 1934 and 1939. Like written diaries, and life itself, where public and private space are intertwined, Whiting's visual diaries present in a refined manner the major historical events, people and sites, from wedding ceremonies of princes to a turtle laying her eggs to Zionist demonstrations against the White Paper. The diaries constitute an unusual panorama of life in the Levant seen from a traveller's perspective during the second decade of the British Mandate in Palestine.

At the young age of 14, Whiting became a member of the American Colony Photo-Dept. and by 21 was leading archaeological expeditions through Palestine whose landscapes and history he had mastered. From 1913 to 1939, Whiting published several articles in the National Geographic magazine, illustrated with American Colony Photo-Dept. photographs, in which he linked the local cultures he explored with the biblical ethos of the Holy Land. Whiting was also a collector, antiques dealer and curator of archaeological collections for museums in Europe and America. He was the US deputy consul in Palestine from 1908 to 1915.

Whiting's photographic diaries were created in parallel to the escalating political situation in Palestine. A few of the notables he guided across the Levant were British diplomats and Palestinian dignitaries, but the space he created around them engendered unusual human encounters with local cultures and guests, and manifested only indirectly the British influence on Palestine. Traveling with his camera, Whiting reframed the wealth of unfamiliar alternative histories of the Levant, rarely seen after 1948.

Chapter 8. Documenting the Social: Frank Scholten Taxonomising Identity in British Mandate Palestine

Abstract

In 1920 Dutchman and photographer Frank Scholten left the Netherlands amidst legal troubles. He arrived in Palestine in 1921, spending two years there during a period of great flux with the establishment of the British Mandate after the collapse of the Ottoman Empire. A Catholic convert and homosexual, Scholten shows us a vision of Palestine that differs greatly from other visiting European photographers. His photographs depict a multi-communal world in the throes of transition in which he clearly moved through multiple cultural spheres.

Working with this understudied archive, this chapter considers the complicated taxonomies that Scholten employed in photographic approach to Palestine. It postulates that his Dutch background – and the consequent context of pillarisation – as well as the informal scholarly networks within which Scholten moved, informed this sensitivity to ethnographic taxonomy, which is rare among visiting photographers.

Scholten imaged people in the context of their daily lives, both at work and leisure, rather than in studio settings making his work particularly valuable in reassessing social histories of the British Mandate. His corpus gives us a vision of another world which undermines and problematises the dominant taxonomies that were cemented during the British Mandate period and continue to inform the ongoing paradigms of the region to this day.

Chapter 9. Edward Keith-Roach's Favourite Things: Indigenising National Geographic's Images of Mandatory Palestine

Abstract

Over the past 110 years, *National Geographic Magazine*'s coverage of Palestine has spanned more than 80 published features illustrated by over 2,300 photographs. In October 1918, in a feature titled 'An Old Jewel in the Proper Setting: An Eyewitness's Account of the Reconquest of the Holy Land by Twentieth Century Crusaders', the magazine welcomed the beginning of British rule over Palestine and marked the beginnings of three decades of positive coverage that presented Palestine as a territory in the midst of exciting change. Coverage during the Mandate period often presented narratives that ran alongside and overlapped with British colonial and Zionist representations; in some cases, they were indistinguishable, as was the case with two features written by a high-ranking member of the British colonial administration, Major Edward Keith-Roach.

For every image published in the magazine from the Mandate period, dozens of others that were taken, commissioned or collected remained unpublished and are kept in the editorial archive of the National Geographic Society. These images and their original captions give new insights into the processes of image production, selection, and circulation, and offer a candid view of how photographers and editors participated in and reinforced the power-relations between the colonised and colonisers. This chapter begins by examining National Geographic's coverage of Palestine leading up to and during the Mandate period, focusing specifically on how the images of Palestine and Palestinians were used to justify and promote British colonialism. The second part of the chapter, introduces *Imagining the Holy* as a project that aims to indigenise these same photographs and transform them into sites of gathering, remembering and collective storytelling for Palestinians at home and across the diaspora.

Chapter 10. Decolonising the Photography of Palestine: Searching for a Method in a Plate of Hummus

Abstract

It is well known that Palestine and the 'Holy Land' played a central role in the early history of photography through the Mandate period. While the role of photography in Orientalism is known, this chapter seeks to explore an alternative method of decolonising the photography of Palestine. I argue that Orientalist photography is a form theft of the visual index of photography. This chapter concentrates on two photographs, 'Eating Hummus', 1935 by Elia Kahvedjian and 'Turkish Official Taunting Armenians with Bread', also known as 'Famished Armenian Children', 1915. Kahvedjian worked with the British Army and Air Force, developing and printing their pictures. 'Famished Armenian Children' is, however, not of starving and taunted Armenians but a staged French image used for funding raising to alleviate the Great Famine in Lebanon. Rather than being identified as a scholarly error or a misidentified image, the photograph was deemed a 'forgery' by Genocide-deniers.

In discussing these photographs, I seek out a methodology of decolonising photography, which avoids considering representation and their images as 'false' or 'true'. Rather, I argue the historical contexts of images are predicated on a colonial 'sensibility', to borrow from Rancière. In turn, through a small number of examples, I hope to begin to explore a new method that connects a reclaimed visual archive with the reclamation of historical narrative itself for the Palestinian inhabitants who populate these images.

Chapter 11. Urban Encounters: Imaging the City in Mandate Palestine

Abstract

This chapter examines the historical intersection between photographic practice and urban change in the colonial context of interwar Palestine. More specifically, it aims to trace the different ways in which photographs were utilised to represent the cities of Palestine, by German, British and native Arab actors. It demonstrates that these photographic representations did not merely provide new portrayals of cities and landscapes, but that they were also key instruments for shaping and framing their material transformations.

The chapter is divided into three thematic sections addressing interrelated modes of photographic representation of Palestine's urban landscape. The first section sheds light on the manifestations of the rise of aerial photography, and the narrow modes of sight they engender, on German and British depictions of Palestine's landscapes in the Great War and on British military operations during the 1936–39 Great Arab Revolt in Palestine. The second section moves beyond militaristic operations to address how 'holistic views' of urban landscapes, in the form of aerial photography and ground panoramas, influenced a new genre for the 'scientific' study of urban environments and proved to be instrumental for British colonial urban planning schemes in Jerusalem. Moving away from foreign and colonial actors, the third section presents an overview of the utilisation of Arab Palestinians of urban photography, focusing on its uses in Arabic and English prints, as a means to advance a self-image of Arab 'modernity' and 'progress' that are possible despite, not because of, colonial presence in Palestine.

To chart these three entangled trajectories of urban photography in interwar Palestine, the chapter consults a wide range of visual and textual archival sources. The archival sources include the Bavarian State Archives, the Australian War Museum, the National Library of Israel, and the Qatar Digital Library. In addition, a collection of original publications including books, reports, and magazines from the 1920s–30s in English, Arabic and German are also examined and cross-studied. Together, these usages display a different narrative of photography, not merely as a documentation of urban reality but as essential planforms for intervening in the city and for recrafting its image.

Index

Page references marked in **bold type** indicate a more in-depth treatment of the subject.